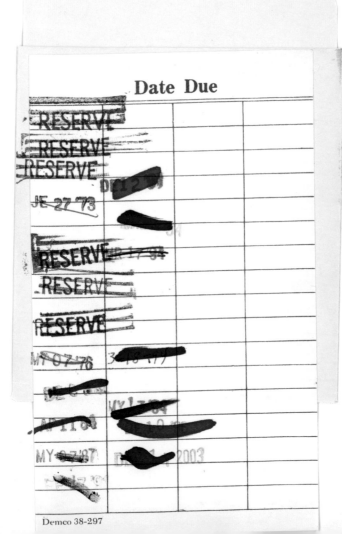

Date Due

RESERVE		
RESERVE		
RESERVE		
JE 27 73		
RESERVE		
RESERVE		
RESERVE		
MY 07 76		
MY 07 87	DE 1 2003	

FROM RACE RIOT TO SIT-IN

A Book from the
Institute for Policy Studies

Books by Arthur I. Waskow

THE LIMITS OF DEFENSE

AMERICA IN HIDING (*with Stanley L. Newman*)

THE WORRIED MAN'S GUIDE TO WORLD PEACE

THE DEBATE OVER THERMONUCLEAR STRATEGY (*editor*)

FROM RACE RIOT TO SIT-IN, 1919 AND THE 1960S

From Race Riot
to Sit-In,
1919 and the 1960s

A STUDY IN THE CONNECTIONS BETWEEN

CONFLICT AND VIOLENCE

BY

Arthur I. Waskow

GARDEN CITY, NEW YORK

Doubleday & Company, Inc.

1966

Library of Congress Catalog Card Number 66–11737
Copyright © 1966 by Doubleday & Company, Inc.
All rights reserved
Printed in the United States of America
First edition

In Memory Of

HOWARD K. BEALE

free scholar and free citizen

112-5

CONTENTS

Preface

This study of the two great crises of racial conflict that the United States experienced in 1919 and the early 1960s is the product of three separate periods in my own life. The study was begun in Madison, Wisconsin, when it was aimed at exploring the great rash of race riots that appeared across the United States in 1919. My chief interests then were the ways in which Americans had thought about and dealt with private violence on a large scale and the ways in which they had thought about and dealt with relations between Negroes and whites. The study was continued in Washington, D.C., after a gap of several years during which I had turned from the study of mob violence on a limited scale in the past to the study of the prospect of international violence on an unimaginable scale in the future. It was completed after I had turned my attention once more to racial conflict and had begun to take not only a scholar's interest but also a citizen's part in the great conflict of the 1960s over the achievement of racial equality in America.

That first gap of several years changed my understanding of what this study should be trying to do. The longer I studied thermonuclear strategies for World Wars III and IV, the more convinced I became that in international conflict we were beginning to witness the elimination of political significance from war, and that therefore we might bring about the elimination of war as a means of carrying on political conflicts. I therefore grew more interested in the historical study of the ways in which violence has over a period of time been replaced by other means for the pursuit of conflicting political ends. Racial conflict in the United States is an example of one arena in which a major effort has been made to replace violence by other means of carrying on conflict, and the effort has partially succeeded. Between the race riots of 1919 and the sit-ins, freedom rides, and rent strikes of the early 1960s there intervened major changes in the processes by which racial conflict was carried on, but no diminution of the conflict.

When I was ready to return to the study of racial conflict and violence, I came therefore with some new interests. I continued to be interested in the 1919 riots as a critical incident in the process of change in American race relations and American treatment of private violence. But now I was also interested in them as examples of group violence brought under control by the society in which and the governments under which they occurred, and as examples of inter-group conflict pursued through violence that might profitably be compared with the sit-ins as examples of similar conflict pursued without violence. I had come to believe that the historical study of past techniques of controlling violence and managing conflict was a study of crucial importance to the future of mankind.

Just at this point in my own development, the direct-action movement of Negroes for racial integration reached its point of no return at Birmingham in May 1963. I found myself not only curious about the ways in which the new conflicts were being pursued and sometimes resolved without violence, but more and more committed to joining as a citizen in the effort to achieve racial equality. During 1963 and 1964 I joined in a few of the nonviolent encounters and had a chance to meet some of the new nonviolent leaders of the civil rights movement. I count myself lucky both as a scholar and as a citizen to have had the chance to be a participant-observer in those events; I believe that my understanding of the problem of conflict and violence was considerably deepened by even this peripheral involvement, just as my involvement was itself shaped in part by what I had already learned about 1919.

From this account one fact should be clear: I consider myself a firm supporter of the movement toward racial equality and of that movement's use of the approach that in this study I call "creative disorder." It is through the support of these ends and means that I see the best hope of both avoiding racial bloodshed and establishing racial justice in America. These are my values. I have consciously and carefully tried to keep them from blinding me to any of the historical facts, either those of 1919 or those of the 1960s. I have especially tried not to impose either my own values or others' present standards of belief and action on Americans who lived in 1919. But readers should understand that there can be (and should be) no such thing as "value-free" or "neutral" history. The problems historians choose to study are determined in part by the social values they hold when they begin. If they are serious about their historianship, they will probably learn from their study enough to change their values somewhat—as I learned from my initial work on 1919 enough to make my response to 1963 different from what it might otherwise have been. The relationship between historical scholarship and social values is no one-way street. The best any historian can do is to know and let his readers know what his own values were and are, and then to let the reader judge.

* * *

In undertaking this examination of racial conflict with and without violence, I begin with an overview of the relations between governmental and private use of violence in the United States of 1919. Then I examine the seven important race riots of 1919, from the Charleston affair of May to the Arkansas explosion of October. In my study of the three major riots—Washington, Chicago, and Arkansas—I examine in considerable detail the way in which the riot was fought and quelled, the response of the locality and the nation, and the ways in which attempts were made over the next few years to cope with the conflicts that had been exposed and the threat of future violence. In one case—the Chicago riot—I look carefully at an early attempt to study the riot in detail and to recommend new policies for preventing riots. In thus making what may at first glance look like a detour from the main road of my study, I hope to suggest ways in which my own work might profit from some of the successes and some of the failures of previous efforts to study the policy issues raised by racial conflict. Then, back on the main road, I look at the reaction of the country to having lived through this experience, and the discordant demands for racial equality, racial hierarchy, racial accommodation, law and order, or creative disorder that came from different persons, groups, and institutions. I examine with special care the different roles played by, and urged upon, the police in responding to the 1919 riots.

Then I turn to the more recent past. Again I examine the over-all relationship between the public and the private use of violence in the United States, this time for the 1960s. I compare the racial crisis of 1919 with the racial crisis of 1960–1964, with special attention to the emergence in the 1960s of "creative disorder" as a way of carrying on racial conflict, and to changes in the roles of

American police and political authorities in general in dealing with racial conflict. Finally, I try to draw from the study some generalizations about the control of conflict, and especially some understanding of the ways in which conflict could be carried on so that the parties do not resort to violence.

In approaching the problem in this fashion, I have tried to ignore the artificial separation of "history" and "sociology" into distinct departments of knowledge. I have used the historian's typical sources to build as complete a story as I could of what were clearly "unique" events in the past; but then, as a sociologist might, I have tried to develop from these unique events a model of the way in which conflict does or does not explode into outright violence. I have used the shift from 1919 to the 1960s in part as a chronological development and in part as providing two separate situations for comparative analysis. I continue to think of myself as a historian, but this is not an orthodox history. I hope it may suggest some directions in which historical scholarship might move.

The major sources for this work were a number of manuscript collections of organizations and individuals active in one way or another in coping with the 1919 riots, and the public record and my own observations and interviews for the period of racial conflict in 1960–1964. The three most important collections I used were those of the National Association for the Advancement of Colored People, the Chicago Commission on Race Relations, and the National Archives. Of these, only the Chicago Commission collection was available to scholars on wholly satisfactory terms. The NAACP files were well-preserved, but accessible only with difficulty in a New York warehouse. I am grateful to Roy Wilkins of the NAACP for permission to use these files. I am deeply thankful also for a long succession of NAACP staff personnel who by preserving letters, press clippings, internal memoranda, and other material in categories by subject and date have kept in existence a most important archive of the history of race relations in the United States. But I fervently hope that steps will be taken to make this remarkable archive more easily accessible to scholars.

The National Archives were especially important to me for the records of Army and Justice Department intervention in the various 1919 riots. But for some reason the Army still has under seal all records of its activities in the Washington riot—though records from the Arkansas and Omaha riots are open. In order to apply for permission to use the closed files, it would have been necessary to agree in advance that not only all notes taken but the entire manuscript of this study would be submitted to the Department of the Army "for security review." In the belief that such a requirement raised problems of scholarly and academic freedom, I chose not to request permission. The Department of Justice papers, which included a few letters concerning the work of the Federal Bureau of Investigation, would probably have been a great deal more useful if all FBI reports about the riots had been available. These, however, "can only be furnished to authorized law enforcement agencies or other governmental agencies which are specifically permitted to receive this information under our laws." (J. Edgar Hoover to Arthur Waskow, October 28, 1960.) Scholars might well consider taking action to get materials earlier than a given date open to the public in the case of the FBI as well as the army records.

One important point should be noted about the private records of some of the leaders and organizations on various sides of racial conflict in 1919. Except for the national office of the NAACP, American Negroes of the 1919 period evidently tended not to preserve papers that would now be of great historical interest. No indication could be found in Chicago that a single Negro member of the Commission on Race Relations had preserved his papers, even the publisher of the *Chicago Defender*. The records of the research staff of the Chicago Commission (as distinct from the official records of the Commission itself) were turned over to the Chicago Urban League, where they perished in an office fire. Papers of the Chicago Branch of the NAACP were kept for decades but destroyed in 1959 only days before I requested permission to examine them. The relevant records of the National Urban League were destroyed when the League moved its offices. Among organized white opponents of racial equality, too, the tendency was evidently not to preserve records. Thus the old Hyde Park Property Owners Association in Chicago has left no papers I could find. Even the official papers of the governors, attorney-generals, and relevant commissions of Arkansas in the 1919 period were ill-preserved, so that practically no manuscripts concerning the Arkansas race riots seem to exist in the state archives and only a few elsewhere in the state.

If there is any lesson to be learned from this series of frustrations, it is that all the state governments and private organizations involved on all sides of the civil rights struggle of the 1960s should make every effort—despite their understandable preoccupation with their current problems—to keep their records safe so that historians half a century hence will have the data they will badly need. And scholars, libraries, and universities should now be making every effort to keep such records safe.

*   *   *

The beginnings of my work on the 1919 race riots owed much to my studies under several professors at the University of Wisconsin. First among these was the late

Howard K. Beale. From him I learned not only American history and the historian's craft, but what few historians could have taught so well: the burning desire to be a free scholar and a free citizen at the same time, to make the study of past issues illuminate present ones without letting devotion to present political solutions distort perceptions of the past.

To the extent that I have been able to use effectively the sociologist's angle of vision along with the historian's, I owe thanks to Hans H. Gerth. His trenchant comments on the nature of the state and of violence helped stir me to examine the riot as a social phenomenon.

In first planning my research and working through my material, I was greatly helped by the criticisms and comments of Merle Curti. His readiness to see sociological concepts and approaches used in the study of history, together with his insistence that they be used well, was a guide and challenge to me.

Since my training at the University of Wisconsin, the development of my ideas on the general problem of conflict and violence and the specific problem of racial violence and nonviolence owes much to the free and vigorous discussions carried on by the Institute for Policy Studies on the specific problem of racial conflict and on the more general problems of social change and the relation of the scholar to politics and policy. From my individual colleagues at the Institute—especially Marcus G. Raskin, Richard J. Barnet, David T. Bazelon, Paul Goodman, Christopher Jencks, Milton Kotler, Donald N. Michael, and Paul Timothy Gorman—I have learned a great deal. From our joint efforts to create and sustain a new method in the study of society I have learned much more.

The searching questions and criticisms of a number of my friends have helped to improve this study, or parts of it. I must warmly thank several scholars—especially A. Gerd Korman of Cornell University, Fredric Solomon of Howard University, and Ernest Isaacs of the University of Maryland; several lawyers concerned with civil rights —especially Hal Witt, William Higgs, and Stanley L. Newman; and several activist students—especially Frank Smith, Jr., and Charles Sherrod of the Student Nonviolent Coordinating Committee and Todd Gitlin, Kenneth Mc-Eldowney, and Carol McEldowney of Students for a Democratic Society.

In my work on this and other problems in the study of conflict, I have had superlative research, secretarial, and administrative assistance from Jacqueline Lushin, Janet Irons, Laura McConnell, Carol McEldowney, Patricia Gaddy, Stella Stewart, Barbara Turner, Sandra London, Joan Heifetz, Evelyn Edson, and Jeanette Gaskins.

At many stages of my research and writing, my mother and father, Hannah and Henry Waskow, helped with the work in ways that were crucial to its completion. And above all, I was helped to cope with the successive crises and problems that I faced in carrying out this study by the steadfast, warm encouragement and the scholarly criticism of my wife Irene. She alone read and assessed every word of every successive proposal for and draft of this study, she alone understood every choice I faced and helped me to think through every decision I made on the sources, direction, and focus of my work.

What all these people have taught me has benefited this study enormously; its remaining defects are of course my own.

A.I.W.

Institute for Policy Studies
Washington, D.C.
January 1965

POSTSCRIPT

Almost nine months after I finished reworking the manuscript of this book for the last time and writing the preface above, I am reading the printer's proofs in the afterglare of the Los Angeles race riot of August 12–16, 1965. That riot is a confirmation in blood of the warning I had written in Chapter XVI, that "Negro leaders in the North seem to have had difficulty in inventing new forms of disorder ['creative disorder' without violence] that would appeal to one specific and extremely important group: adolescent youths and young men without jobs or education. . . . In the absence of new inventions in creative disorder that appeal to young men in the North, therefore, riots there may become more likely." In the light of Los Angeles, perhaps I will be pardoned if I urge readers to examine closely the theory of riots and their avoidance that is developed in this book and the proposals for action that grow out of the theory, especially those suggested in Chapter XVI.

A.I.W.
August 27, 1965

FROM RACE RIOT TO SIT-IN

CHAPTER I

Public and Private Violence: 1919

When John dos Passos sought a date upon which to center *U.S.A.*, his trilogy about intense social conflict and a crisis in American values, he chose 1919.[1] The choice was no mistake. In the development of American attitudes toward the public and private use of violence in dealing with intense social conflicts, 1919 was a critical year. It was particularly critical as the year in which Americans began to cope with racial upheavals of a new kind.

In the wake of the greatest war that had ever scourged the West, upheavals were perhaps to be expected. As Hannah Arendt has written, "The magnitude of the violence let loose in the First World War might indeed have been enough to cause revolutions in its aftermath even without any revolutionary tradition and even if no revolution had ever occurred before."[2] Although in the United States there was no single revolutionary attack upon the basic structure of society or the state, there were a number of intense clashes of power between various social groups. Some of these conflicts exploded into outright violence, in the form of head-on local riots; others remained non-violent but nonetheless intense confrontations.

The authorities whose job it was to cope with such clashes of power were deeply ambivalent. The choices before them, real though never faced in such terms, were these: Should they support one side in these conflicts between different economic and racial groups? Should they stand aside and allow the conflicts to be resolved according to the relative strength of the parties? When actual violence broke out in these conflicts, ought they to play a role that would be different from the role they should play so long as the conflicts were being fought out by non-violent means?

The proper role of the state in dealing with internal conflict and violence was not, in 1919, an issue to be faced by American political authorities alone, but by the authorities of other nations as well. Max Weber was treating it as a general problem of the postwar world rather than as a special problem of the American state, when he remarked in 1918: "Today the relation between the state and violence is an especially intimate one." He explained that "a state is a human community that (successfully) claims the *monopoly of the legitimate use of physical force* within a given territory."[3] By Weber's definition, it should be noted, the police forces of a state are using violence—legitimate violence—whenever they use physical force to arrest private citizens. Violence, in other words, is not synonymous with brutality; legitimate violence, as expressed in an arrest by authority of the state, may be used brutally or courteously. The state may also use violence either neutrally as between different social groups, or with a bias against one or another social group. To be an act of "state," the violence must simply be carried out by the one institution that within a given territory is agreed to be the only legitimate user of violence.

Weber evidently thought his definition of "the state" would have almost universal applicability. But in suggesting that the relation between the state and violence had become especially intimate after World War I, Weber was himself suggesting that his definition might arise out of particular historical circumstances. Indeed, if one examines his definition it seems much more easily applicable to the European states he knew at first hand than to the American situation. For what most people tended to think was "the state" in America, had by no means always enforced a monopoly of the legitimate use of violence—or, if we accept Weber's definition, the United States was one human community that had never been or claimed to be a "state."

The failure to establish an American "state" with a monopoly of legitimate violence can be seen at two levels of American society. At one level, there had been a long-standing reluctance to proscribe private violence. That reluctance was expressed early in American history by assertions of "the right of revolution" in a number of state constitutions and by the Second Amendment to the Federal Constitution, which specified "the right of the people to keep and bear arms." The political logic of the Second Amendment was followed through most of American history by treating religious riots,[4] vigilante hangings,[5] labor dynamitings, private businessmen's armies,[6] and southern lynching parties[7] all as half-accepted aspects of American life. Not only the right to keep and bear arms, but the right to use them was accorded private citizens carrying on their political quarrels. As for larger aggregations of citizens, it was not until after the Civil War that Americans agreed that the various component states of the Union could not legitimately make war on each other; and even then, long after the Civil War, industrial empires and labor unions made war on each other, often with impunity. Thus, until the First World War the United States still seemed to be following the logic of the Second Amendment, denying to any institution the monopoly of legitimate violence that would have made it what Weber could recognize as a "state."

On a second level as well, the United States avoided

centralization of the public use of violence in the European mode to which Weber was accustomed. Through most of American history, the "European" way of institutionalizing public violence in a large standing army had been most deeply feared. The tradition of the Farewell Address, in which Washington had warned that "overgrown military establishments" were "inauspicious to liberty,"[8] had been not merely applauded in rhetoric but obeyed in action. The standing army had been kept small, and only during the overwhelming crisis of the Civil War had a mass army been created, then to be soon disbanded.

The First World War, however, again called into question the relationship of the United States, state, and local governments to the use of violence by private persons or institutions. The use of conscription and the creation of a mass army for the first time since the Civil War had emphasized for the United States, as the war itself had done in other countries, what Weber called the "intimate relation" between the state and violence. This relation was intensified by the fears of revolution that haunted many Americans from 1917 on, stimulating them to demand controls over private groups that might advocate or use violence.

By 1919, then, American society was again facing a series of major issues concerning the public and private use of violence, although these issues were only half articulated. Should the old pattern of semi-acquiescence in private violence be allowed to continue, or should European norms of "the state" with a monopoly of legitimate violence be applied in America? Should the political authorities go even further than controlling private violence, and intervene in intense conflicts even when the parties in conflict did not resort to violence?

* * *

These questions most frequently arose in connection with the intense labor disputes of 1919 and the upsurge in labor radicalism. What Selig Perlman and Philip Taft called the period of "post-war militancy"[9] among laboring men forced many localities, states, and the federal government to reassess their role as monopolists of legitimate violence.

In February, the city of Seattle experienced a general strike. The striking workers, by Mayor Ole Hanson's own account, never offered to use violence against business, non-striking workmen, or the government. But, the mayor warned, "Revolution . . . doesn't need violence." He pointed to the unions' announcement that *Labor will preserve order* as an indication of the revolutionary intent of the strikers to take over the government, and he threatened to shoot the first man who tried to do so.[10]

In line with these pronouncements, Hanson met the strike with preparations to use state-legitimated violence. He spent $50,000 on the hiring of special police.[11] He arranged for United States soldiers to aid police in keeping order and to guard a newspaper that published despite the strike. Finally, he threatened to impose martial law to end the strike unless it were called off voluntarily.[12]

After the Seattle workers had returned to their jobs, the state's power to use legitimate violence was directed against "radicals," even though they had not taken any part in calling or running the strike. Members of the Industrial Workers of the World (IWW) were arrested, the Socialist Party's offices were raided and its candidate for City Council arrested, and a labor-owned printing plant was closed down by the police.[13] Thus the Seattle affair indicated the readiness of at least some local officials to have "the state" use its own physical force against even the specter, let alone the actuality, of the use of private violence by organized labor.

This motif of state action to suppress radicalism can be followed through the year. Aliens who were members of the IWW in Seattle were hurriedly deported from the state, and many of them from the country, by the federal government.[14] The Immigration Bureau and the Department of Justice joined hands to hunt down radicals, both aliens and American citizens, and to deport or jail them. In November, some 300 members of the Union of Russian Workers were arrested on suspicion of anarchism and sedition; and the technique of mass raiding reached its climax just after New Year's Day, when thousands of presumed radicals were arrested and held incommunicado by order of Attorney-General A. Mitchell Palmer.[15] These attacks on radical persons and organizations were justified by the fear that such groups were contemplating private revolutionary violence, so that public use of violence was necessary to assert the state's monopoly of legitimate force.

On the local level, the fear of private violence from radical labor organizations sometimes led the state to co-opt, in effect, some private groups as arms of the state itself in the permissible use of violence. Thus in Centralia, Washington, on November 11, 1919, an IWW union hall was attacked by ex-soldiers parading in commemoration of Armistice Day. "Wobblies" barricaded within opened fire on the attackers, killed four of them, and wounded four. It was the Wobblies who were jailed, and that night the police allowed one of them to be taken from his jail cell and lynched. Seven others were convicted of second-degree murder.[16] In effect, the ex-soldiers had been treated by the officials of Centralia as if they were still in the armed forces, with the authority to use violence against private groups that might be contemplating the use of violence. Thus the men who had defended the IWW hall against attack had been treated as if they had killed policemen or soldiers while resisting arrest.

What many governmental officials thought an even more direct challenge to the state's monopoly of police power than the Seattle general strike or the theories of radicals came in 1919, when efforts were made to unionize local police forces. In thirty-seven different cities across the country, attempts to form police unions troubled city governments, whose officials claimed to fear that a police union might turn the symbols of legitimate violence to the use of particular private interests. An effort to unionize the police of Washington, D.C., brought opposition from the President and the Secretary of War, who together with local officials prepared to use the Army to replace the police if necessary, and ordered policemen to quit the union.[17] In Boston, the police union's leaders were suspended from the force and the policemen went on strike September 9. Street rowdyism and mob attacks on property followed, and were stopped only when state troops took over the police powers. All strikers were dismissed, and Calvin Coolidge, then the governor of Massachusetts, made clear that private interference with the public police powers would not be tolerated.[18] President Woodrow Wilson added his belief that "any association of the police force . . . such as will endanger the public peace" should not be permitted.[19] Thus the new American emphasis upon state control of the use of violence was strengthened.

In two other instances, state police power was used to suppress labor union activity that was thought to threaten the social order, even though the unions did not use violence. These occasions were the great strikes in steel, which began September 23, 1919, and in coal, which began November 1.

In the steel strike, Pennsylvania state troopers dispersed groups of strikers from the streets and forbade the holding of union meetings. The fear that the strike leaders were revolutionists was used in justifying attempts to suppress the strike.[20] When violence did break out between steel-union men and strikebreakers in Gary, Indiana, the state's National Guard was dispatched to keep order and then was followed by federal troops when the strikers held a parade against the militia's orders. The federal troops imposed martial law and limited picketing.[21]

The coal miners were faced with a federal court order to halt their strike, an order based on the war powers of the federal government and on the President's warning that a strike would interfere with American aid to the Allied Powers during the continued legal state of war.[22] Federal troops moved into the coal fields in Utah, Washington, New Mexico, Oklahoma, and Pennsylvania in accordance with the federal government's attempts to end the strike.[23] In Kansas, the governor first recruited strikebreakers and then gave them military protection to reopen the mines.[24]

In almost all of these cases, as in most of those in which force was used against radicals, the state's legitimate violence was being used or threatened not against the actual outbreak of private violence but against the possibility that some private group might begin to use violence. In the postwar atmosphere of 1919, under the pressures of fear of radical social upheaval and in the consciousness that it actually possessed enough armed forces to effect its will, the federal government acted not only to monopolize violence but to use its monopoly to take one side in conflicts that had not yet become violent.

* * *

Although the threat of attacks on the social order by labor organizations frightened officials most, less actual violence occurred during 1919 in connection with struggles between labor and capital than in connection with conflicts between Negroes and whites.

In many parts of the United States, the semi-private use of violence by whites to control Negroes had long been permitted by the state in the form of lynchings which, though formally illegal, were rarely punished.[25] In addition, there occurred on several occasions what Gunnar Myrdal has called a "terrorization or massacre."[26] Such events were "mass lynchings," analogous to the Eastern European "pogrom," in which a large number of whites attacked a large number of Negroes and the state did little or nothing to interfere.

Myrdal has distinguished such a pogrom against Negroes from a true riot, which he said was "not a one-way punishment but a two-way battle." In a riot, he explains,[27]

The Negroes may be hopelessly outnumbered and beaten, but they fight back. There is danger to the white man participating in the riot as there usually is not when he engages in other forms of violence against Negroes.

This distinction between a "pogrom" and a "riot" is not intended to suggest that all occasions on which racial mob violence occurs can be easily assigned to one or the other category. The two words, rather, express "ideal types" which are useful in discussing phenomena that in reality exist on a continuum, not in two neat packages.

The kind of continuum involved in the one-sidedness or two-sidedness of mass racial violence can be seen by looking at several instances. One almost pure example of a "pogrom" was the New York "draft riots" of 1863, in which hundreds of Negroes were killed and many of their homes and businesses burned by Irish-Americans who were enraged at being conscripted to fight in a war to free Negroes while the Negroes stayed at home.[28] An example of a mostly one-sided affray in which a few Negroes did fight back was the Atlanta eruption of 1906. Ten Negroes were killed, but so were two whites. The general impact of the riot was more one-sided than these figures would indicate, however, since many Negroes had their houses looted and burned, and many of them afterward sold their property and left the city.[29]

In all American history, perhaps the event that most nearly approximated the "ideal type" of a riot was the Chicago riot of 1919, in which twenty-three Negroes and fifteen whites were killed, and many observers noted the wholehearted commitment of the Negro community to "fighting back" when attacked. Other racial confrontations that occurred in 1919 were not quite so clearly "riots" as the Chicago affair, but many of them were far closer to the "riot" end of the continuum than previous racial violence in the United States had been.

This group of riots was, however, only one index to an atmosphere that permeated the Negro community in America after the First World War. Indeed, the propensity of Negroes in 1919 to challenge the assumption of their own subordination startled America and constitutes one major reason to study the explosion of race riots that characterized 1919. For the 1919 riots gave birth to "the new Negro"—the first generation of Negroes to win that appellation—and signaled the first new departure since Emancipation in the history of Negroes' efforts to end their subordination.

The 1919 race riots merit study not only for their importance as a turning point in race relations, but also because they confronted the holders of office with the necessity of dealing with actual private violence on a large scale. The complex arrangement of local, state, and federal responsibilities for police action to control public and private violence, an arrangement that had emerged from the Civil War and the industrial upheavals of the 1890s, stood in the balance. For not since the Civil War had the federal government had at its disposal as large an army as it did during and just after the First World War, and perhaps not since the Civil War itself had it been confronted with the occurrence of mass violence of such great size in so many places across the country. In 1919 the new American "state" that had emerged from the First World War was forced to decide whether to enforce its monopoly of violence or instead to allow private violence full sway. Although federal officials were not conscious of making a momentous choice of the future role of "state" power in America and did not theorize about their choice, their actions did in fact embody a decision.

CHAPTER II

The Premonitory Riots

What an official of the National Association for the Advancement of Colored People (NAACP) called the "Red Summer" of 1919[1] began early and ended late. Estimates of the number of "race riots" have run as high as twenty-five;[2] and any such count would have to include an affray in Berkeley, Georgia, on February 28 and another in Bogalusa, Louisiana, on November 23.[3] But not all these twenty-five can qualify as riots—some were expanded lynchings, others brief clashes of sullen crowds which quickly dispersed—and many made little impact (except a cumulative one) on the national mind.[4] But even by reducing the number of "riots" to the seven that seem most important because they evoked a national response, the "Red Summer" must be reckoned to have lasted from May 10, when Charleston, South Carolina, had its riot, to September 30, when Phillips County, Arkansas, had its. Between these dates came major explosions in Longview, Texas; Washington, D.C.; Chicago; Knoxville; and Omaha.

The first two riots, in Charleston and Longview, had a greater impact upon the NAACP's professional staff of experts on racial conflict than they did upon the nation at large. They served as advance warnings of the racial tensions that had built up in the wake of the war and that exploded in full fury in the later riots.

Charleston in 1919 was a city of more than 100,000 people, about 60 per cent of them Negro. But the riot that began May 10 did not pit local whites and Negroes against each other. Instead the chief opponents were local Negroes and white sailors from a nearby naval training base.

The outbreak began in the evening of May 10 with a street altercation between a Negro and two sailors on Saturday night liberty. The Negro was shot and killed, and a series of fights broke out between other sailors and Negroes, with clubs and guns being used on both sides. Charleston police arrested the sailors who had fired first and attempted to clear the streets. But as the sporadic fighting spread, hundreds of sailors joined in a march toward the Negro district of Charleston. They captured, beat, and shot several Negroes along their route, looted shooting galleries for rifles and ammunition, and attacked stores owned by Negroes.[5]

When the city police realized they had lost control of the situation, they called for help from the Navy. At midnight Marines arrived to act as patrolmen and were armed with riot guns to hold back the mob if necessary. Fixed bayonets, however, proved sufficient to stop the sailors' march. The Marines ordered all sailors back to the Navy Yard, and trucks, streetcars, and taxicabs were used to send them back. Negroes began sniping at these returning sailors, and the police and Marines ordered all Negroes off the streets. By 1:30 A.M. all pedestrians in Charleston were being stopped and searched for concealed weapons, and the violence had been checked. Two Negroes had been killed and seventeen wounded; seven sailors and one white policeman had been wounded.[6]

To prevent a recurrence of the riot on Sunday, naval authorities canceled all liberties. Only a few incidents occurred, the most serious when some Negroes in an automobile exchanged shots with a group of Marines on patrol. The mayor of Charleston warned that if any additional trouble occurred he would invoke martial law. He also urged that the Navy recompense the Negro owner of the one shop that had been badly damaged, because "the negroes of Charleston must be protected."* A coroner's jury assembled several days later placed all blame for the riot on attacks from the sailors, exonerating the Negroes who acted in self-defense.[7]

The city of Charleston thus demonstrated throughout its system of police, law enforcement, and government, and from the very beginning of the riot, a degree of neutrality between the races that was unique in the seven major riots of 1919. It was probably because of this quick action to control the aggressors and protect the victims that the riot was brought to an end so quickly. Had the local police sided with the whites (as they did at first in most of the seven jurisdictions), it is likely that the sailors would have been able to beat and kill many more Negroes than they did. It is also likely that the Negroes would have felt it much more necessary to use violence in their own self-defense had swift action not been taken by the state arm of legitimate violence to defend them. In short, a higher casualty list on both sides was probably averted by the efforts of the police to halt the use of violence by either side and to disarm everyone of either race.

The Charleston authorities were probably left more free to be neutral by the fact that the whites on one side of the riot were not their own constituents, but outsiders. The mayor, the newspapers, and white Charlestonians

* Wherever in quotations the word "negro" has appeared in lower case, it has been left in lower case; the author himself capitalizes it. Whenever someone in 1919 capitalized "Negro," he can be assumed to have been strongly committed to racial equality, but the reverse was not so: some equalitarians had not yet accepted the convention that the word should be capitalized.

were quick to emphasize that there had been relatively
little friction between the races in the city itself, and that
practically no white civilians had joined the mob.[8] The
local authorities were probably also unwilling to use the
police solely against Negroes because the Negroes were a
majority of the city's population and might have been
uncontrollable if they had been goaded into attacking the
police.

The NAACP's national headquarters was brought into
the Charleston riot by the efforts of its branch there to
see that the Navy took steps to punish the guilty men
and prevent a recurrence of the riot.[9] The branch sent a
series of resolutions to Secretary of the Navy Josephus
Daniels,[10] and the national staff of the NAACP added
its inquiries.[11] The Navy Department reported that a
board of investigation was already inquiring into the
Charleston riot.[12]

This board found a number of sailors responsible for
the riot, and six men were ordered held for general court-
martial, charged with "conduct to the prejudice of good
order and discipline" and "manslaughter." They were
convicted.[13]

The national staff of the NAACP also urged its members in Charleston to have the city's congressman present
a bill that would direct the Navy to reimburse Negroes
for property damage.[14] Requests by several Negroes for
compensation from the Navy for personal injuries suffered during the riot were refused on the grounds that
an Act of Congress would be necessary.[15] No further effort to obtain relief seems to have been made.

A British subject, a Negro West Indian, was more successful in recovering partial damages for the theft of his
money when he was beaten during the Charleston riot.[16]
The British Embassy pressed his claim upon the State
Department,[17] which asked the Navy Department to re-

view the case.[18] The Navy replied that it could out of
contingent funds pay for property lost, but not for the
loss of time or the personal injuries suffered by the West
Indian, unless special legislation were passed.[19] The
State Department politely wrote back that it would "be
glad to learn whether the Navy Department is disposed
to take steps with a view to obtaining special legislation."[20] The Navy did finally recommend such legislation,[21] but shortly afterward the West Indian closed the
matter by accepting repayment of his lost $25.00 in full
discharge of his claim.[22] With this settlement, the few
ripples of concern that were created by the Charleston
riot died out.

* * *

The next riot to disturb the NAACP was an outbreak
in Longview, Texas, that was more deeply rooted in local
racial conflicts. Longview was an East Texas town of
about 5000 population, around 30 per cent Negro, that
was closely tied to the cotton-planting economy of the
area. Racial discord had been aroused when a Dr. C. P.
Davis had organized a Negro Business Men's League to
get higher prices for Negro cotton growers by sending the
cotton direct to buyers at Galveston, thus eliminating the
profit generally taken by local white middlemen. Davis
also organized co-operative stores which gave Negroes
the chance to buy merchandise more cheaply than local
white dealers would supply it.[23]

While these arrangements were increasing racial tensions in Longview, white annoyance with the *Chicago
Defender* began to grow. The *Defender* had made a
habit of urging Negroes to move north, and many Southern whites had objected to the upsetting effect such ex-
hortations had had on the supply of cheap and docile
Negro labor.[24] In Longview, the economic pressure from

the Negro Business Men's League had seemed to whites to be connected to the *Defender's* incitements.[25]

Then the *Defender* overstepped the bounds of etiquette set by southern whites. The July 4 issue carried a story on a lynching several months before in a town near Longview. The Negro who had been lynched was accused of raping a young white woman. The *Defender* now claimed that the woman had been in love with the Negro and had been prostrated by his lynching.[26]

This story infuriated Longview's whites. In the belief that it had been written by a Negro schoolteacher named Samuel L. Jones (who was also a leader in the Business Men's League and like Davis an "independent type"), a group of whites on July 11 sought Jones out, beat him with iron rods and gun butts, and ordered him to leave Longview. The police did not interfere.[27]

Several hours after the beating, an even larger group of whites marched into the Negro section of Longview "to look up the professor and see what condition he was in." They were met by gunfire from houses nearby, and four of them were wounded, one seriously. They retreated, roused reinforcements, returned to the Negro area, and on finding it deserted set fire to Jones's house, a number of Negro shops and other houses, and Davis's office, which was used as a lodge hall by the Negro Business Men's League.[28]

At this point, the police intervened by arresting six members of the Business Men's League for rioting. Posses were sent out to scour the countryside for Jones and Davis, who had disappeared.[29] The mayor of Longview called upon the governor to send Texas Rangers or national guardsmen to keep the peace. Several hundred guardsmen were sent.[30]

Before they could arrive, the local police re-emphasized their partiality. The sheriff ordered all undistributed copies of the *Defender* destroyed and its future circulation halted.[31] The police also tried to arrest Jones's father-in-law and were able to do so only after he fired upon them.[32] When the militia took command, on the afternoon of July 12, order was enforced for the first time upon whites and Negroes impartially. All citizens were ordered to turn in their firearms, a 10 P.M. curfew was imposed on all townspeople, and both whites and Negroes obeyed these orders.[33] Under this neutral enforcement of the law, Longview quieted down.[34]

Once order had been restored, the leading bankers, merchants, lawyers, and farmers of Longview issued a statement condemning with equal fervor Jones for circulating the *Defender* and the white mob for burning Negro houses. As the statement put it, "We will not permit the negroes of this community and country to in any way interfere with our social affairs, or to write or circulate articles about the white people"; but at the same time, "we do not believe in applying the torch, even to the homes of negroes."[35] Clearly this statement was not so much a "neutral" act as one endorsing the notion of white supremacy but warning that mob rule was no way to uphold it.

The leaders of Longview at the same time, however, resigned control over events to the outside militia and announced that they approved "in advance . . . any steps that they might take."[36] Under this sweeping mandate, the militia acted with considerably more neutrality than the local leadership had been willing to adopt. The guardsmen and the Texas Rangers arrested twenty-three white men, charging all of them with arson and seventeen of them with assault with intent to commit murder. All were released on bail. Twenty Negroes who had been arrested were removed to Austin, presumably to keep them safe from possible mob violence.[37]

Ten days later, when the danger of violence had died down, the Austin and San Antonio branches of the NAACP arranged conferences with the Assistant Adjutant General of Texas to urge that these men be released. The NAACP conferees explained that they were "respectable law abiding citizens and property owners," and obtained a promise that the situation would be reviewed. Most of the men had no charges placed against them.[38]

Two days later, half of the imprisoned Negroes were allowed to return to Longview, make bond, and go free. By this time—July 27—Longview was back to normal, with no friction apparent between the races. It was reported that "no resentment" was shown at the release of the Negroes, and "their return was considered entirely proper by white people."[39] On August 13, the remaining men were freed on condition that they not return to Longview. This second group included the men who had actually fired on the white mob, and presumably it was thought that their return might still make trouble.[40]

The state authorities had evidently decided that although formal charges against Negroes who were acting in self-defense could not be supported, it would be embarrassing to the whites of Longview if these men who had helped defend the "arrogant impudent" Jones were to be free again in Longview. The degree of neutrality of the state authorities as against the local police can be measured thus: where the local police had wholly failed to protect the Negro community against attack, the state militia had acted to punish white marauders and had extended what was in part a hesitant, paternalistic protection and in part a punishment to the Negroes. The local forces had acted as if the guilty were innocent and the innocent guilty; the state forces, as if both the innocent and guilty were to be treated alike. The importance of the more nearly neutral police can be seen from the way in which the private violence stopped only when the state militia entered Longview.

The Texas branches of the NAACP did alert their national office to the facts of the riot[41] and kept headquarters abreast of their own efforts to get the Negro prisoners released.[42] The national office attempted to encourage such activities.[43] But when the full fury of the midsummer series of race riots broke, the national office turned its attention to problems more pressing, more widely publicized, and far more bloody.

CHAPTER III

The Washington Riot

The first of the 1919 riots to attract great national attention occurred in Washington, D.C., where a summer of increasing tension between Negroes and whites culminated in an explosion in mid-July.

Relations between the races in the capital had been affected by the accession of the southern-oriented Wilson administration and by the World War. Beginning in 1913, Negroes in the federal service had been segregated at work by their new southern supervisors, where they had never been segregated before; and there had been stirrings of anger among Washington's Negroes over the suddenly more "southern" outlook of their lives.[1]

Then, with the coming of the war, job prospects changed again. As Emmett Scott, secretary-treasurer of Howard University, described the situation, the war boom in federal employment in Washington gave additional jobs to whites, some of whom left private jobs which Negroes then took over. Negroes were both angered by civil-service discrimination against them and rewarded with a sudden surge in income and self-respect in private employment, where some skilled laborers among them made more money than the white civil servants. Some whites in their turn resented this sudden twist of events.[2] Scott's analysis was confirmed by Louis Brownlow, a commissioner of the District of Columbia, who felt that jealousy among whites at the relatively greater prosperity of Negroes since the war had stirred bitterness between the races.[3]

The fact that Washington's population had been swelled during the war by a major influx of southern whites and a moderate influx of southern Negroes, the one group still intending to "teach any fresh 'nigger' his place" and the other determined to be free or to win revenge, exacerbated the racial tensions within the city.[4] The Negroes' sense of independence was strengthened by their service in France during the war, frequently under officers who had been trained in the Reserve Officers Training Corps (ROTC) at Washington's Howard University.[5]

The existing conflicts were brought to a boil by opportunistic journalism. The *Washington Post*, then published by Ned McLean, was bitterly antagonistic to the District of Columbia government and especially to the top command of the police force. McLean especially objected to tough police enforcement of Prohibition. He began hounding the police through his newspaper, and in the summer of 1919 began to criticize them for not controlling a "crime wave" of assaults and robberies. The *Post* kept the idea of a "crime wave" alive by sensationalizing the usual summer crime statistics and playing up ordinary cases of assault. Prominent among these were alleged instances of attempts by Negroes to rape white women.[6]

On July 9, the Washington branch of the NAACP sent a letter to all four daily newspapers in the city, "calling their attention to the fact that they were sowing the seeds of a race riot by their inflammatory headlines." According to the branch, only one newspaper answered—the *Star* —and that acknowledged the justice of the complaint.[7] The next day, however, the *Times* printed a news story emphasizing the NAACP's interest in bringing to justice all Negroes accused of crime, and leaving out its criticism of the tendency of the press to identify particular Negro criminals with the entire Negro population.[8]

The tension continued to increase. Suspects were arrested in some of the attempted rape cases and then released to the accompaniment of more attacks on police "laxity" by the *Post*.[9] On Saturday, July 19, the *Post* featured another case of alleged assault with the headline, "NEGROES ATTACK GIRL . . . WHITE MEN VAINLY PURSUE." The body of the story described an "attack" in which two Negroes jostled a secretary on her way home, tried to seize her umbrella, and "frightened at her resistance to their insulting actions," fled. The paper also reported that the chief of police, Major Raymond W. Pullman, had ordered all young men "found in isolated or suspicious parts of the city after nightfall" held for questioning.[10]

The incident reported by the *Post* on Saturday morning bore deadly fruit on Saturday night. The girl "attacked" was the wife of a man in the naval aviation department. Two hundred sailors and marines decided to avenge the slight to his and their honor by lynching two Negroes who had been suspected of the attack but released by the police. The sailors began a march into southwest Washington, stopping every Negro they met and beating several, both men and women. Civilians began to join the march, and when one Negro and his wife fled to their home the mob followed and attempted to break in through hastily set up barricades.[11]

At that point, both District and military police responded to a riot call and dispersed the mob. Ten arrests were made: two of white navy men, and eight of Negroes who were "held for investigation." When three more Negroes were later stopped on the street by District police patrolling the area, one of them fired at the police-

men and wounded one of them. This last event was the
first use of violence by Negroes on Saturday night, although the eight-to-two arrest rate might be imagined to
have indicated a higher rate of lawbreaking by Negroes.[12] It is hard to avoid concluding that the unneutral
behavior of the police had much to do with the Negro
attack on them and with the later increase in violence
from both Negroes and whites.

On Sunday morning, the Washington branch of the
NAACP asked Josephus Daniels, the Secretary of the
Navy, to restrain the sailors and marines who had led
the attack. They warned of a more serious clash if no
action were taken.[13] But none was taken. Indeed,
Daniels' later diary notes on the riot suggest that he
blamed most of it on the Negroes and was not greatly
interested in protecting them.*

On Sunday night the situation exploded. Shortly before
10 P.M., a policeman arrested a young Negro on a minor
charge at a heavily trafficked corner on Pennsylvania
Avenue, halfway between the Capitol and the White
House. While the policeman waited for the patrol wagon,
"hundreds of men in khaki and blue and many negroes"
crowded around. The Negro under arrest was snatched
away from the police by several white men and beaten
over the head. The police recovered him and dispersed
the crowd, but arrested no whites. Down the street, a
few minutes later, another fight broke out between white
servicemen and Negro civilians. This time three Negroes
were badly injured.[15]

From then on, the violence multiplied. Soldiers and

* On Sunday night he wrote there had been a "Riot—race—following negro assaults on white women," and on Monday, out of all
the many cases of racial violence going in both directions, selected
to note in his diary only that "carriage full of negroes drove by
Naval Hospital and wantonly fired into party of convalescent sailors
and marines."[14]

sailors marched up Pennsylvania Avenue, chasing and beating Negroes, yanking them off streetcars, and growing ever more belligerent. The police, few in number and aided only by a handful of soldiers detailed as a provost guard, scarcely interfered, except to arrest about fifteen men, white and Negro, on charges of disorderly conduct. Most Negroes fled, but some fought back. At midnight, the soldiers and sailors had to return to their barracks. But after 1 A.M., even more violent struggles broke out at several corners in the downtown area, with white as well as Negro civilians involved in these clashes.[16]

In reporting the riot on Monday morning, the *Washington Post* gave it the leading place and large black headlines. The paper added a crucial paragraph:[17]

It was learned that a mobilization of every available service man stationed in or near Washington or on leave here has been ordered for tomorrow evening near the Knights of Columbus hut on Pennsylvania Avenue between Seventh and Eighth Streets. The hour of assembly is 9 o'clock and the purpose is a "clean up" that will cause the events of the last two evenings to pale into insignificance.

No explanation was made of where the "orders" came from, and the publication of this notice brought the strongest condemnation of the *Post* from the Negro community and the District officials.[18]

During the day on Monday, a flurry of meetings were held and statements issued on the violence of Sunday night. The George Washington Post of the American Legion condemned the participation of servicemen or ex-servicemen in the nightly race riots.[19] The NAACP asked the Secretary of War to investigate and punish the guilty soldiers. It also sent a committee to the District commissioners and the Chief of Police to ask for more effective action by the police to protect Negroes. Herbert J. Seligmann of the NAACP's national office in New York arrived in Washington to get firsthand information on the riot.[20] Pastors of Negro churches, meeting under the sponsorship of the National Race Congress, condemned the police force for taking "no precaution that a competent and efficient police department would have employed," and demanded that the War and Navy departments cancel the leaves of all servicemen in the Washington area.[21]

In Congress, members of the Senate and House committees on the District of Columbia expressed their hope that the riots would cease or be suppressed, but did not recommend any specific action. Congressmen not on these committees were more specific. A Florida congressman demanded a congressional investigation of the failure of the police to apprehend Negro assailants of white women, arguing that this failure had caused the riot. A New York congressman demanded that the Army, Navy, and Marine Corps prevent their men from joining the riots, and received assurances from three high-ranking officers that servicemen would be prevented from participating in any renewal of the riots Monday night. Two other members of the House demanded that the President declare martial law.[22]

District Commissioner Brownlow met with Secretary of War Newton D. Baker and Army Chief of Staff Peyton March in order to plan for the use of troops to quell the rioting. Brownlow told the press that co-operation between the District police and the Army was certain to end the trouble. He said preparations had been made to bring troops in from army camps in the District and even from Camp Meade, Maryland, if necessary to police the District. Brownlow also urged Washingtonians to stay out of the downtown area Monday night. No general cancellation of servicemen's leaves was announced, but base commanders were told to detain in barracks all men "without a good excuse for leave."[23]

While this flurry of conferences and statements continued, the first riot cases were being disposed of in police court. Four Negroes who had been arrested Sunday night on charges of disorderly conduct and unlawful assembly were set free. A white sailor was found guilty of disorderly conduct in organizing the original mob march on Saturday night, and was turned over to the Navy for punishment.

During Monday afternoon, Negroes who were alarmed by the *Post's* "mobilization notice" began to arm themselves. Guns were bought in Washington and Baltimore. "Alley Negroes," some of them soldiers from the Negro regiment recruited in Washington, took out the rifles they had used in France.[24] One story that persisted for decades had it that officers at the Howard University ROTC prepared to give arms and ammunition to the Negro population if it should become necessary.[25] During the day came the first evidence of the new determination of Negroes to "fight back" and even to attack. One mob of twenty-five or thirty boarded a streetcar and beat the motorman and conductors. Others fired from a speeding automobile on sailors in the Naval Hospital grounds. Still others set out in a gang for the Navy Yard, presumably to be on hand when employees finished work; but these were dispersed by the police before they could reach the Yard.[26]

But Monday afternoon was only a faint prelude. That night, despite the precautions and the public statements, the riot was renewed, in a form far worse than before. Four men were killed outright, eleven others mortally or seriously wounded. Of these fifteen, six were white policemen, one a white Marine, three white civilians, and five Negro civilians. Dozens of others sustained injuries that were less serious but required hospitalization. Three hundred men were arrested for riotous behavior or for carrying concealed weapons.[27]

The force that had been set up to cope with the riots was made up of 700 Washington police and 400 soldiers, sailors, and Marines organized as an emergency provost guard. Few servicemen took part in the Monday night disturbances. But a surging mob of 1000 white civilians made repeated attempts to break through a cavalry cordon in order to attack the Negro residential areas, once almost doing so after massing at the Treasury and marching past the White House. But several cavalry charges broke up these attempts. Whenever the mob found Negroes in the downtown area, the Negroes were savagely beaten. Police were able only to keep the mob moving, not to disperse it. Some Negroes caught in this melee responded to attack by firing pistols at the mob.[28]

Meanwhile, in the Negro areas Negroes were beating white men, and were firing upon passing streetcars and automobiles from houses along the way. Eight or ten automobiles were manned by armed Negroes and were used as armored cavalry in lightning attacks on white residential districts, randomly firing at houses and people. Other automobiles were used by whites in the same fashion, and at least one running dogfight was reported between Negroes and whites in two such cars. Several policemen were wounded or killed while trying to arrest armed Negroes or to raid houses that had been used as sniper centers.[29]

On Tuesday, a startled press was calling for "uncompromising measures," for more military patrols, even for martial law.[30] The District Commissioners rejected suggestions that President Wilson be asked to declare martial law, and instead worked out plans for much more forceful military support of the civil government.[31] President Wilson called in Secretary of War Baker, who then arranged with General March, Secretary of the Navy Daniels, and the Washington police chief to order into the District additional troops from Camp Meade, marines from Quantico, and sailors from two ships lying in the Potomac. In command of these augmented military forces was placed Major General William G. Haan, who ordered troops into every section of the city.[32]

Early in the evening, Baker and Brownlow conferred on the troop dispositions. Haan, accompanied by Police Chief Pullman, drove through the city to inspect the troops. Haan announced publicly that he was satisfied that the situation was well in hand, with one third of his force on actual patrol and two thirds in reserve with speedy transport available to be hurried to any danger point.[33] But privately he talked with military men in New York about the possibility that troops might have to be sent from there.[34] In effect, these arrangements all but supplanted local police, who had become suspect to the Negro community, by the more nearly neutral federal troops.

General Haan also exerted himself to control the city's newspapers, on the theory that much of the riot was "merely a newspaper war." He later wrote a brother officer, "When I got them [the newspapers] to agree to say approximately what I wanted them to say, which was the truth, then soon everything was over."[35]

While these military preparations were being made, the Negro community took steps both to protect its members and to reduce the chance of violence. The NAACP's local legal committee arranged to defend many Negroes who had been arrested for carrying weapons, protesting against the arrests of many such men "while the white men from whom they were attempting to protect themselves were not molested." Another NAACP committee visited Brownlow to report that Negro prisoners after being arrested "were often beaten up and abused by the police officers." They asked to be deputized to visit various precinct stations to see that Negro prisoners were treated well, but Brownlow spoke with the police authorities and later said full provision had been made through regular channels for correct treatment of prisoners.[36] Other Negro leaders visited Capitol Hill to ask for a congressional investigation of what they thought was police antagonism to Negroes, exemplified by the failure of the police to hire a single Negro patrolman in four years.[37] Police captains in the heavily Negro precincts met with local Negro leaders and arranged for the early closing of moving-picture theaters, near-beer saloons, and poolrooms in the Negro areas. Leading Negro ministers urged their congregations to keep off the streets.

Minor efforts to prevent another outbreak were made within the federal bureaucracy. The Commerce Department urged all its employees to keep off the street at night and to discuss the subject of race relations "temperately."[38] In the Division of Negro Economics in the Labor Department, the assistant director was asked to get in touch with leading Negro ministers in Washington and try to arrange a meeting with white clergymen that might produce a joint statement to calm the public. The Assistant Secretary of Labor advised against letting even the slightest "tinge" of official sanction be lent to any activity involving the race riot; but he suggested that names of ministers who might be interested could be given as "a personal matter" to an outsider who could then make the contacts himself.[39]

All these efforts at peace-making and order-keeping finally bore fruit on Tuesday night, July 22. Two thousand federal troops, the admonitions for self-control, and

an intermittent driving rain together succeeded in preventing crowds from gathering. Only two important
incidents marred the night. One Negro tried to escape
arrest and was shot, but not seriously hurt, by a Marine
on patrol. Two white men on guard duty as officers of
the Home Defense League (a police reserve created
during the war) were shot, and one of them was killed,
when they attempted to halt a Negro for questioning.
But aside from these events, a night of rumors and alarms
held little violence. "Several times," according to one
newspaper, "the cavalry galloped through the streets to
answer calls for assistance and found on their arrival that
they were not needed." Toward morning, as it became
clear that there would be little trouble, and as the wet
streets made more and more difficulty for the cavalry
detachment, it was withdrawn and put on reserve. At
dawn the infantry and naval patrols were withdrawn.[40]

The relaxation allowed Secretary Baker to write the
President on Wednesday that the situation was finally in
hand. Baker explained that the one death had grown
"out of no controversy or excitement but . . . an unprovoked and impulsive act, perhaps the act of a man of
unstable mind, deranged by excitement growing out of
the general situation." He reported that the attitude of
the Negroes, particularly their leaders, had been helpful.
As for Wednesday evening, Baker said he had instructed
Haan to keep his troops on duty at points from which
they could quickly meet any emergency.[41]

The rest was anticlimax. Several members of the
NAACP staff visited Senator Arthur Capper, a Kansas
Republican, Wednesday and won his support for a congressional investigation of race riots and lynching.[42] On
Thursday, a coroner's jury held one Negro for murder of
a white Marine, although the Negro claimed he had
drawn his pistol in self-defense against a mob and had

hit the Marine accidentally.[43] But by Thursday it was clear that the riot was over, and attention turned to the prevention of future riots.

In considering the future, both General Haan and Police Chief Pullman emphasized the need for troops to police the capital in order to prevent or cope with a recurrence of any sort of mob violence. As the authorities pointed out, "disturbances in national capitals abroad and the general feeling of unrest throughout the world, coupled with the fact that the United States has assumed the position of the leading democratic nation, all demand that no small causes be allowed to throw the city into a state of lawlessness."[44] In line with this strong-police approach to the prevention of violence, Police Chief Pullman and Commissioner Brownlow asked Congress to increase the number and the pay of policemen.[45]

Negroes reacted somewhat differently. One pamphlet issued soon after the riots crowed about the "heroic resistance" of the young Negroes who "defied the point of bayonets, the sting of blackjacks and the hail of bullets in defending themselves." This pamphlet insisted that only the abolition of the "Mobocratic Lyncherized system . . . of Jim Crow" would ultimately satisfy Washington's Negroes.[46] Even the far more cautious and conservative statement issued by Emmett Scott of Howard University and Judge Robert Terrell of the Municipal Court placed the blame for the riots on the white mob and called Negro retaliation deplorable but natural. Scott and Terrell specified that interracial co-operation to prevent riots must be based on mutual sharing of the rewards of American life, rather than on Negro subordination.[47]

A middle position of Negro indignation, somewhere between the Scott-Terrell caution and the pamphleteer's anger, was taken by the NAACP. The national office wrote Attorney-General A. Mitchell Palmer to ask whether he intended to proceed against the *Washington Post* for inciting to riot by printing its "mobilization notice." (The answer was no.)[48]

Similarly moderate criticism came from a Washington Negro minister, who asked Palmer to intervene in behalf of Negroes accused of carrying concealed weapons who were being charged "unreasonable" bonds and jailed for "extreme" periods. Palmer did write the district attorney for Washington, who said he would make sure that no such discrimination took place.[49] Requests of the same type that discrimination against Negroes be avoided in the post-riot trials came from Congressman Isaac Siegel, a New York Republican, who reported that a number of letters from both whites and Negroes had called the matter to his attention. Siegel received assurances of fair treatment.[50]

But the courts continued to hand down sentences that seemed severe to the Negro community, and in September a group of Negro ministers gathered what were reported to be 30,000 signatures on a petition for presidential clemency. The leader of the drive said he would present the petition to the President, on Wilson's return from his nationwide tour for the League of Nations.[51] But that tour ended in Wilson's physical breakdown, and nothing more was heard of the bid for executive clemency.

✿   ✿   ✿

As was to be expected, the four days of rioting in the national capital stirred thought and feeling all across the United States. Much of it focused on the problems of official and private violence, but some dealt with the issues of racial equality and subordination that were basically in conflict.

One of the widespread reactions outside Washington,

as it had been a strong reaction inside Washington, was to demand tougher policing of the city. Criticism of Congress for not providing enough money to attract enough able men to the police force was the response of several newspapers as far away as Rochester and Minneapolis,[52] and of United States senators from California and Kansas.[53] "A larger, better drilled and more ably commanded police organization" in Washington was called for by the *New York Herald*.[54] The *Utica Press* translated Washington's troubles into a demand that Utica enact a law preventing the promiscuous sale of firearms.[55] And the *New York Globe* summed up the entire approach embodied in demands for a larger police force when it said: "There is nothing to be done but to quiet the rioters by force. We make no pretense nowadays of settling the race question; we simply keep it in abeyance."[56]

This emphasis upon the need for a *strong* police was countered by many Negroes and some whites with demands for a *neutral* police. W.E.B. Du Bois, editor of *The Crisis,* insisted that Washington policemen were notoriously anti-Negro, and had intervened to stop the riots only when whites began to get the worst of the battles.[57] The *Amsterdam News* cited the rejection of Negro candidates for the Washington police force and the failure to use existing Negro patrolmen in the riot when "their moral influence would have been valuable" as evidence of the "antipathy of Washington police toward negroes."[58] What the partiality of the Washington police had meant to Negroes and would continue to mean in the future was spelled out by the *New York Commoner:*[59]

As the police have failed to protect the Negroes of the capital there is but one course open. Let every Negro arm himself and swear to die fighting in defense of his home, his rights and his person. In every place where the law will not protect their lives, Negroes should buy and hoard arms.

This analysis of the Washington riots as an index of the Negroes' readiness to fight back on their own when the police would not protect them was echoed by James Weldon Johnson of the NAACP staff. He said that if Washington had had officers with "the courage to enforce the law against the white man as well as against the colored," the Washington riot would have ended the Saturday it began, and Negroes would not have gone on the offensive Monday.[60] White newspapers like the *New York Call* and *New York Globe* agreed that where Negroes felt unprotected by the law, they were now prepared to protect themselves.[61]

Judgments differed when the press tried to evaluate this new readiness to fight back. Some papers, like the *Commoner*, applauded the new atmosphere. The *Pittsburgh Courier* said proudly that Negroes had learned "a bullet in Washington has no more terrors than . . . in the Argonne."[62] Others, especially white newspapers, saw it as an inevitable but not especially laudable response of self-defense.[63] But some white editors warned that "any Negro in his senses ought to know that violence is the last thing in the world that can help his cause." The *New York Globe* and the *New York World* argued that every appeal that Negroes made should be to the law, to its impartiality if possible, but always to the law. "Oppressed as they are, they cannot free themselves by force," the *Globe* insisted.[64]

The alternative to self-defense was transformation of the police power into a neutral force. To some people, the Washington riot seemed a demonstration of the need for the federal government to provide that neutral police force. Specifically, it was argued that federal anti-lynching legislation would force local and state police to defend Negroes against white lynch mobs. The distinction between the partiality of the Washington police and the relative impartiality of the federal troops once they intervened as an official unit was not lost on observers. Thus, showing his respect for federal impartiality, a Negro who had in 1916 led a delegation from the African Methodist Episcopal Church to see the President now wrote him a long, impassioned letter begging for a law to make lynching a federal crime.[65] The *New York Post* and the *Survey* similarly argued for a neutral federal intervention to end lynching, in order to prevent "a terrible race war."[66]

There were, of course, some commentators who saw the problem as much deeper than the provision of a more powerful or more neutral police force, and who believed more basic change was necessary. But there were disagreements on the direction that basic change should take.

To some, a letup in racial violence was hard to imagine short of the attainment of racial equality. Thus a writer in *The American Teacher* called for an end to the segregation that had kept not only Washington's schoolchildren but her whole society cut into two warring parts.[67] Several French newspapers and a New York magazine espoused racial equality as the goal but warned that its achievement would probably require successive race riots to urge the process on, for the "antipathy of whites towards blacks grows stronger in direct ratio to the amount of progress made by the Negro race."[68]

To a number of other editors, North and South, it seemed clear that Negro insubordination was the cause of the riots and that a return of order could only be accomplished if the Negro would go back to and stay in his place. The *New York Times*, for example, mourned the passing of that Washington in which "the negroes, before the great war, were well behaved, . . . even submissive."[69] The *Brooklyn Eagle* similarly headlined its report, "RACE WAR IN WASHINGTON SHOWS BLACK AND WHITE EQUALITY NOT PRACTICAL," and went on to blame the riot on the full employment, high wages, and increasing independence that Washington Negroes had won from the war.[70] Newspapers in Syracuse and Albany[71] were no more cautious in assuming Negro inferiority and the need to control Negroes who acted as if they were equal than were newspapers in Memphis and Nashville.[72] A more official southern view of the relative places of whites and Negroes in society was set forth by the Alabama legislature. By joint resolution, the legislature chided the white leadership of the North for trying to act by "purely idealistic and theoretical considerations," rather than in a "practical way." This theoretical spirit, the legislators said, had led to the kind of hatred between the races in the "disordered" North that did not exist in the South.[73]

Having aroused these thoughts across the nation, the Washington riot faded away. The talk of an investigation came to nothing, the *Washington Post's* attack on the District of Columbia administration and police chief had no lasting effect, and race relations in the capital underwent no overt change, either in the direction of equality or of subordination for Negroes. According to some who lived through the riots, there was a new self-respect among Negroes, a readiness to face white society as equals because Negroes had fought back when they were attacked.[74] The Washington riot demonstrated that neither the silent mass of "alley Negroes" nor the articulate leaders of the Negro community could be counted on to knuckle under, even in a largely southern city with a hostile police force and a press that had been harping on the unforgivable "Negro" crime.

CHAPTER IV

Chicago: Riot and Response

The nation had scarcely caught its breath from the shock of rioting in front of the White House when a new race riot began, considerably longer and bloodier than Washington's. At a bathing beach in Chicago, on Sunday July 27, an angry dispute erupted over the stoning of a Negro swimmer who had crossed an extralegal boundary into a "white" swimming area, and who drowned under the hail of stones. When a white policeman refused to arrest whites who were accused by Negro bystanders of having stoned the swimmer, and then arrested a Negro on a white's complaint of some minor offense, Negroes mobbed the white policeman. Reports of his behavior spread and aroused indignant Negro crowds. Gunfire broke out between Negroes and the police, and by nightfall white and Negro mobs were clashing in many sections of the city. Before the riot was over, one week later, fifteen whites and twenty-three Negroes had been killed.[1]

The bathing-beach incident brought to a boil conflict between Chicago's whites and Negroes that had been simmering for several years. Beginning in 1917, more than 50,000 Negroes had come to Chicago in two years' time, slightly more than doubling the city's Negro population in that short span. Most of the immigrants were Southerners and rural, unready to cope with life in a great metropolis.[2] Their coming strained to the bursting point the established area of Negro residence, bringing much more crowding within that area and stimulating attempts by more established Negroes to move into traditionally white areas. Some whites had resisted such changes in residence patterns in fear that the value of their own property would drop, and a series of bombing attacks had been made on Negroes who had moved outside the "Black Belt."[3] Reflecting residential shifts and the hostilities that had sprung up over them, there occurred a series of clashes over "possession" of public parks in different neighborhoods.[4]

The influx of Negroes made available to some large industrial firms, especially the meatpackers, a supply of labor that was more accustomed to low wages and less accustomed to union organization than many of the white laborers employed in such firms. Fear that Negroes would work for lower wages and anger at the occasional use of Negroes as strikebreakers, as well as non-economic interests such as unwillingness to share the camaraderie of work or union fellowship with Negroes, led some labor unions to oppose the entry of Negroes into the unions as members and into the factories or yards as workers on an equal footing. Thus hostility between white and Negro workers grew in the period during and after World War I, though it did not break out into violence comparable to the residential bombings or the park fracases.[5]

That hostility existed between the races in Chicago and might explode into violence was no secret. In March 1919, the City Club of Chicago, made up of intellectual and business leaders, heard Alexander L. Jackson, director of the Negro branch of the Chicago Young Men's Christian Association on Wabash Avenue, explain that the pressures of migration and housing, combined with a "new mind among colored soldiers," could lead to trouble. Jackson warned that the Negro soldiers were returning with "a consciousness of power hitherto unrealized" and a new "sense of manhood." In response to his talk, the philosopher-sociologist George Herbert Mead, who was president of the City Club, asked whether Chicago was "far-sighted enough to avoid a calamity."[6] Similarly, the Chicago Urban League, with the sociologist Robert E. Park at its head, warned the public that the World War had "disturbed the equilibrium of the races," and asked, "What is going to happen when the negro troops return from France?"[7]

The governor of Illinois, Frank O. Lowden, had reason to fear an outbreak of race violence in Chicago. In May 1917, the race riot in East St. Louis had forced Lowden to send the state militia to restore order after about fifty deaths, and he heard from some Chicagoans that Negroes, frightened by the East St. Louis affair, were collecting arms. In September 1917, Lowden even hastened to Chicago for fear that a riot would erupt when word got out of a racial outbreak in Omaha.[8] The mayor of Chicago was much less prepared for a race riot. He was William Hale Thompson, "Big Bill," who had been bitterly opposed as a "spoils politician" by the intellectual and social elite of Chicago. Thus Thompson had few if any connections with the Meads, Parks, or Addamses of the University of Chicago or the "socially conscious" men in the business and welfare communities who were worrying over race relations. Thompson had his own contacts in the Negro community, since the "Black Belt" was his area of strongest support in the city; but there is no evidence that the Negroes he appointed to high office warned him of racial tensions near the breaking point.[9]

When the tension did break in July 1919, there was symbolic significance in its breaking on the issues of racial boundary lines at a public beach and police protection for Negroes. The use of violence to keep Negroes out of "white" areas and the failure of the police to make arrests in the bombing cases had long angered the Negro community, and the insistence of Negroes on pressing into new territory had been angering whites. The events on the Lake Michigan shore on Sunday, July 27, simply focused within a few minutes all the outstanding grievances. As the City Club and the Urban League had warned, there was already a new postwar spirit of readiness among Negroes, especially returning soldiers, to defend themselves. National publicity for the Washington riot did its part. Instead of acquiescing in the "invisible line" drawn against them or in police indifference, Negroes fought back. On their side, angry whites took the behavior of the police as a certificate of permission for them to enforce their wishes by using violence.

After news of the lake-front affray spread, white and Negro gangs sprang into action. Among the whites, gangs were frequently formed from "athletic clubs" of late adolescents and young men that were connected with particular neighborhood politicians. Negro gangs were formed more spontaneously, perhaps because there were in 1919 few organized Negro clubs. The whites demonstrated their superior numbers and power on Sunday night by beating twenty-seven Negroes, stabbing seven, and shooting four, while Negroes were beating four whites, stabbing five, and shooting one. On Monday morning, July 28, the violence died down while Negroes and whites reported to work. But that afternoon, as workers started to return home, gangs of white adolescents and young men began to incite crowds at streetcar transfer points to drag Negroes off the streetcars and beat them. Four died. One white assailant was stabbed by a Negro he was trying to kill.

As reports of these attacks spread through the Negro district, bands of Negro boys and men set upon whites and stabbed or beat four of them to death. Negroes besieged a white apartment building in the "Black Belt" and attacked the police when they massed at the building. The police fired on the crowd and killed four Negroes.

During Monday evening, whites began to drive automobiles at high speed through Negro areas and to fire rifles and revolvers from them at random. Negroes replied by sniping from rooftops at all automobiles being driven through the streets.

The toll of injured Monday reached 229, about two-thirds Negro. Governor Lowden was alarmed enough at this news to order that the Illinois militia prepare for riot duty. Mayor Thompson, late Monday afternoon, asked that the militia be mobilized in a Chicago armory but refused to request that they actually intervene in the riot. He insisted that the police could handle the situation. Arrangements were made for deployment of the militia at any moment the mayor asked for them.[10]

A joint committee from the Union League Club and the Urban League urgently asked the chief of police to press his men to enforce the law against rioters without regard to race. They specifically asked that charges be preferred against the policeman who had refused to make the original arrest of the white man on the beach Sunday night. On the theory that knowledge of police neutrality would help calm the city, the committee asked for a public announcement of these measures. No action was taken by the police along these lines.[11]

On Tuesday, a streetcar strike forced workers to walk to their jobs, and Negroes found themselves especially vulnerable as they walked long distances through white areas to their jobs. Many of them decided to stay home thereafter. Negro homes were burned. A mob of white soldiers and sailors as well as civilians swept through the Loop of downtown Chicago, where they killed two Negroes. Because four fifths of Chicago's 3500 police had been concentrated in the "Black Belt" in order to control the Negroes, few were available in the Loop to protect Negroes from these marauders. Another Negro was killed in a mostly Italian community on the West Side. Several were killed after firing on policemen. Four whites were killed, some by marauding Negro youths and others by Negroes they had attacked. The toll of injured on Tuesday was shorter—only 139—but still so high that the mayor continued to be pressed to ask for the militia. He continued to refuse.

On Wednesday, the pace of the rioting slackened. Two Negroes and two whites were killed, and the injury list dropped to forty-two, evenly split between whites and Negroes. Part of the reduction occurred because rain kept many citizens off the streets Wednesday night.

During the day, a delegation of Negro leaders, including several strong political supporters of Mayor Thompson, told the mayor that the city police were failing to protect Negroes and that the militia must be called in. He finally did so at 10:30 P.M. on Wednesday, and 6000 state infantrymen took posts across the city.[12] They carefully co-operated with the Chicago police rather than replacing them, and were distributed according to police wishes.[13] Some of the white "athletic clubs" displayed particular hostility to the militia when it formed a line to defend the "Black Belt" from invasion, but otherwise the people of Chicago and the police force welcomed the soldiers.

The rain continued Thursday, July 31, and the temperature fell from the plateau of 90° F. and more, at which it had stood for a week. The militia stood guard at all known danger points, and did so impartially. Only one death occurred, that of a Negro at the hands of a mob of white stockyards workers. Only nineteen injuries were reported.

By Friday, the riot was clearly under excellent control. Only one injury was reported. At 3:35 Saturday morning, fires were set in the Lithuanian neighborhood near the stockyards, and forty-nine houses were burned; but the responsibility for the arson was never fixed either on individuals or on any racial group. From then on till the next Saturday, August 9, rarely was more than one "riot" injury reported each day. On August 5, a young white man was killed by a militiaman and another wounded when they failed to "move on" as quickly as the militiaman would have liked.

On August 8, with the city back to normal, the militia was withdrawn.*

After the burst of violence had been brought under control, a number of agencies and individuals in Chicago began to try to cope with the aftermath of violence. Procedures for punishing the rioters began to operate, as well as some less coherent processes for dealing with the long-range causes and effects of the riots.

A number of different agencies had some responsibility for coping with the immediate questions of apprehending and punishing the guilty. At the request of Major

* One source for an understanding of the impact of the riot on the Negro community, a source not exploited in *The Negro in Chicago*, is a collection of posters, notices, and throwaways in the files of the NAACP. These are of sufficient interest that they are reproduced verbatim in Appendix B. Particular attention should be paid to the way in which particular individuals (especially politicians) and organizations tried to turn the fears engendered by the riot to their own advantage; to the emphasis by several would-be leaders on their alleged acceptability in high places among the whites; to the deep economic problems, including sheer hunger, in which a few days absence from work plunged many Negroes; to the preoccupation with assuring Negroes of their jobs; and to the evident necessity of reiterated warnings to respect and obey police, repeated so often as to suggest the warnings were being ignored.

General Leonard Wood, who commanded the military district of which Chicago was a part, the Federal Bureau of Investigation looked into the fires that had swept the Lithuanian district; but none of its findings, if there were any, were made public.[14] The federal government made no other official entrance into the Chicago riots. Several different state and local agencies did, however, and occasionally wrangled over jurisdiction or findings.

One such wrangle was between a court-martial of the Illinois militia and a special Cook County coroner's jury. Both examined the case in which a militia private had killed a white man who had refused to "move along" quickly enough. The coroner's jury bound the soldier over to the grand jury on a charge of manslaughter; but the court-martial, composed of officers of the militia, acquitted him. After a few demands by the coroner for a court decision on jurisdiction, the coroner's jury bowed to the advice of the state attorney-general that the military authorities were paramount, since they had decided the soldier's acts occurred in pursuance of duty.[15]

The grand jury, working in conjunction with the state's attorney, began to return indictments in various riot cases as soon as the fighting died down. The state's attorney was Maclay Hoyne, a bitter opponent of Mayor Thompson who had criticized Thompson's ties to Negro politicians and who owed his election to Cook County as a whole, where the Negro vote was less important than within the limits of Chicago itself.[16] Hoyne was strongly criticized by a number of law-enforcement officials when the first list of alleged rioters he gave the grand jury was wholly Negro: as one newspaper put it, "all the shades of black and chocolate and tan, but . . . no sign of white."[17] The grand jury itself rebuked him by adjourning in protest, and then the attorney-general of Illinois withdrew from prosecution of the cases. By August

15, the grand jury had indicted fifty Negroes and seventeen white men for various parts they played in the riots, although the fact that more Negroes than whites had been killed and injured would suggest that more whites had used violence.[18]

Mostly because of apprehension that the police, the state's attorney, the grand jury, and the trial courts might be biased against Negroes, a number of organizations like the NAACP arranged to defend Negroes accused of riot crimes. This effort began during the "quiet week" following the riot. Local and national representatives of the NAACP, the Negro YMCA, the Urban League, the Cook County Bar Association (a Negro group), and an emergency conference of ministers and social workers set up a Joint Emergency Committee under the chairmanship of sociologist and Urban League President Robert E. Park. The committee arranged for lawyers to be made available at every police station and court each morning, without charge, to defend any Negro brought in for arraignment. It also began to examine the possibility of setting up a defense for all indicted Negroes.[19]

An important role in forming and guiding the Joint Emergency Committee was taken by John R. Shillady and Walter F. White of the national staff of the NAACP, who had come to Chicago on urgent orders to protect the interests of Negroes during the riot.[20] The Chicago NAACP branch was in difficulties. A. Clement MacNeal, one of its leaders, had been arrested by police and charged with assault with intent to kill, because he was in a house from which shots had been fired at a white mob outside.[21] Another of its leaders, Charles A. Bentley, was extremely cautious and hesitated to take on any new functions for the association. Moreover, Shillady reported, the branch had little money and suffered from sharing an office with a Negro alderman "whose reputation . . . with the reputable white community" was not good.[22]

Under the circumstances, Shillady and White felt that the future of the NAACP in Chicago depended on bold action by the national staff in the absence of local initiative. They talked with white and Negro editors in town and met such leading civic workers as Park of the Urban League and Graham Taylor of the Chicago Commons, a settlement house, in an effort to improve the NAACP's reputation.[23] Mary White Ovington, chairman of the national NAACP, warned that "Robert Park . . . has never been aggressive . . . would dally and fail,"[24] was a "slow going conservative, the astute political kind,"[25] and that Graham Taylor had "proved a coward the one time he was put to the test."[26] She agreed, therefore, that the national NAACP should bring its own resources to bear on organizing publicity, legal talent, and political pressure in defense of Chicago's Negroes.[27]

The first major effort of the Joint Emergency Committee was an attempt to arrange for Negroes to collect for property damaged in the riots. The committee announced that under Illinois law, whenever "any building or other real or personal property . . . shall be destroyed in consequence of any mob or riot of twelve or more persons, the City shall be liable for three fourths of the damage sustained" if a claim were filed within thirty days. In a release to the Chicago Negro press, the committee urged that anyone who had suffered such losses should report them in writing to committee headquarters, where lawyers would be available at no charge to file claims with the city.[28] Several such cases were taken by Augustus L. Williams, a Negro attorney who was also the great-uncle of the Negro boy who had drowned in the incident that started the riot. Williams won several

cases, and then the city council voted thirty grants of
$4500 apiece to a number of Negro riot victims.[29]

The defense of Negroes accused of crime did not go so
smoothly. Organizational jealousies plagued the Emergency Committee. The conference of Negro ministers
and social workers that had sprung up during the riot
formed itself into the Chicago Peace and Protective Association. Between it and the NAACP there was recur-
rent conflict, since the Protective Association had "national ambitions" and the NAACP wanted to "spike" it in
order to gain for its own local branch the support of the
Negro ministers.[30] After a great deal of backing and fill-
ing, the Protective Association withdrew from the committee, which in October reconstituted itself as a Committee to Secure Equal Justice for Colored Riot
Defendants, dominated by the NAACP.[31]

Some debate over the merits of an effort to defend all
Negroes accused of rioting also delayed the taking of action. Former Judge Edward O. Brown, a white man of
high prestige in Chicago, doubted that the NAACP
should "get the reputation of defending or espousing the
cause . . . of all colored persons accused of crime."[32] The
Chicago branch debated the issue and finally drew up a
statement to be reviewed by the national office, with the
Chicago "conservatives"—especially Brown—"privileged
to resign . . . rather than commit themselves to a policy
that might place them in a bad light with their 'white'
confreres."[33] The national NAACP agreed to the statement, specifying that it was not condoning mob violence
but trying to safeguard the right of Negroes to fair trials.
In addition, the NAACP argued, the fact that defense
had been provided would prevent bitterness among Negroes in case of conviction and would warn would-be
white rioters that Negroes could not be victimized.[34] No

one resigned because of the statement, which was published nationally.

The NAACP did consider the somewhat more radical position of defending and supporting admitted rioters on the ground that "every act committed by colored men and women during the race disturbances, even though apparently an act of aggression, was directly or indirectly the result of intolerable conditions which were the fundamental cause of the riots . . . and that the responsibility for their acts rests with those who are responsible for such conditions."[35] The nationally famous lawyer Clarence Darrow wanted to take "the most flagrant cases" of rioting and try to make this sociological argument for "aggressive self-defense."[36] Darrow actually agreed at one point to defend Clement MacNeal, the Chicago NAACP leader who was accused of assault with intent to kill.[37] But partly because the NAACP was unwilling to support the radical position outlined by Darrow, partly because the prosecution's case against MacNeal collapsed, and probably also because the expense of retaining Darrow would have been too high, this whole notion was dropped. The charge against MacNeal was reduced and then he was discharged for lack of evidence.[38]

The original cost estimates ran to $50,000 for a full-scale defense of all accused Negroes, if the cases were prosecuted effectively and such an attorney as Darrow were retained. Four fifths of this sum was to come from outside Chicago and was to be raised by the national office of the NAACP.[39] These estimates were continuously reduced, however. The NAACP decided that it would raise $5000, to be matched dollar for dollar by Chicago sources.[40] By November, however, it was clear that some prosecution cases had evaporated as had MacNeal's, and by then also the NAACP had other riot problems on its hands that required money.[41] By January 1, only $1000 had been sent by the national office to Chicago, and the Chicago branch had raised $1500.[42] Another $1000 was paid by defendants. The total of attorneys' bills had come to $10,000; so the defense effort was $6500 in arrears.[43] The national office of the NAACP responded to an urgent appeal for help by sending $1500 at once and promising to match the Chicagoans in raising money to meet the remaining debts.[44]

Late in January, the Joint Committee to Secure Equal Justice for Colored Riot Defendants reported that of seventy-five Negroes accused, fifty-eight had been acquitted or had their cases discharged for lack of evidence, six had been convicted and sentenced, two had been convicted and were appealing, four had met hung juries and were awaiting retrial, and five were still to be tried.[45]

The NAACP also tried to press State's Attorney Hoyne to move for indictment of more white rioters. Walter White persuaded the Woman's City Club to "lobby" Hoyne, the state attorney-general, and the coroner's office to act against whites. White also collected affidavits alleging that a white policeman, John T. Cunningham, had driven down State Street firing a gun at passersby during the riot but had been returned to duty without punishment. He presented these to the foreman of the grand jury, to Hoyne, and ultimately to a Negro alderman. His perseverance finally resulted in Cunningham's suspension and trial, after the alderman had presented the evidence to Mayor Thompson.[46] Despite such pressures, the year's-end report of the Joint Committee noted that only seven whites had been listed for trial, of whom four had been convicted.[47] The only other important action taken against white rioters was the temporary closing by police of several "athletic clubs" that had supplied youthful cadres to the riot mobs.[48] By the time the various kinds of pressure for and against action had worked through the political system, not much action of any sort was being taken to punish rioters of either race.

In addition to functioning as agents of punishment and redress, the coroner's jury and grand jury tried to analyze the causes of the riot and recommend ways of preventing or controlling similar outbreaks. Both groups suggested that "voluntary segregation" would probably greatly reduce tension between the races. Both recommended strengthening the police force, and the coroner's jury particularly warned that the police had acted with favoritism toward whites during the riot and must act impartially to prevent future trouble. The grand jury emphasized the connections of the "athletic clubs," of "vice of all kinds" in the "Black Belt," and of criminal gangsterism with local political organizations, and urged that the connections be severed and the dangerous activities rooted out. The coroner's jury, on the other hand, doubted that "politics . . . or catering to the white or colored vote, had much of anything to do with the production of race rioting" or that the athletic clubs had been responsible for the riots.[49]

The major themes of these jury reports were paralleled in the reactions of other Chicagoans to the riot. The first response of editors looking about themselves in horror at a bloody city was that the police should have been stronger, should have acted sooner, and should have acted with more severity. The most violent presentation of this solution for rioting was the threat of the *Chicago Herald-Examiner* that race rioters should and would suffer the fate of the four men who "died at the rope's end for the Haymarket riot," and whose bones would "bleach only a few years longer than the bones of the rioters of 1919."[50] Other papers urged severe punishment in more moderate language and asked why the mayor and governor had waited three days to use troops to put down the

riots.[51] The first reaction against this viewpoint came a
month later, when the *Daily News* called the grand jury's
request for another 1000 police a "curious error." The
News argued that "a well-directed, efficient and honest"
police department would not need more men to deal
with riots, whereas "a demoralized, politics-ridden" force
would merely fatten on the spoils of another 1000 jobs.
The *News* urged that attention be paid not to "negative
measures alone" but to such positive work as better housing and recreation for Negroes, in order to prevent race
riots from starting.[52]

Similar emphasis on sharing the fruits of American society with Negroes came from other spokesmen of the
white community. A number of ministers referred to "our
debt of gratitude to the Colored man for the part he
played in the World War," to the necessity of basing race
relations on sympathy, to the elimination of such "sur-
vivals of savagery" as race hatred.[53] The Chicago Association of Congregational Churches announced its belief
that "the colonization and exploitation of negro labor,"
"failure to meet the housing needs of the negro," and "a
lack of fair play and justice by representatives of the
white race" needed to be corrected in order to prevent
future riots.[54] One of the white newspapers pointed out
that Negro hoodlums created by the demoralizing conditions "we" forced upon the Negro community had
joined with "our" white hoodlums to make the riot.[55]

One special case of the argument for according more
equal shares to the Negro was the argument for work-
ing-class solidarity of whites and Negroes. The Chicago
Federation of Labor newspaper claimed credit on behalf
of the stockyards union leaders for preventing violence
when Negroes returned to work after the riot.[56] Whether
or not the claim was correct, the fact that it was made
suggests an acceptance, at least in rhetoric, of the notion

of worker solidarity across color lines. Similarly, a stockyards labor leader explained that only the employers
could benefit from division between the races and the exclusion or abstention of Negroes from union membership.[57] It was argued that only "when the White man
and the Black man" grasped hands "in the fraternal grip
of industrial unionism" would race conflict come to an
end.[58]

On the other hand, the *Chicago Defender,* a nationally
known Negro paper, pointed out that white workers had
been the first and bitterest enemies of Negro workers who
were seeking jobs, and suggested that the race riots had
originated from this hostility.[59] The attorney-general of
Illinois echoed this view, and added that in return for
hostility from white workers "the negro . . . resents the
assumptions of superiority by [immigrant] white compet-
itors unable to speak the language of the land."[60] One
possible line of thought from these assumptions of hostility between white and Negro labor was followed by
the Wabash Avenue YMCA, the Negro center. Through
"efficiency" clubs set up presumably to teach vocational
skills to Negroes, the YMCA officials urged Negroes not
to go on strike at the stockyards, in order to preserve
their good relations with their allies the employers.[61]
This train of thought accepted the notion that the Negro's
share in society should be increased, but looked to business instead of labor for help and protection.

Out of the Chicago riot, as out of the one in Washington, there also came a demand for subordinating and controlling Negroes rather than aiding them to move toward
equality. Illinois' United States Senator Medill McCormick commented that southern Negroes in Chicago
thought that now they were North "they could sit in your
lap or do anything they pleased," and needed to be
taught their place.[62] To some Chicagoans, that place was

a segregated one. "Whites and blacks will not mix any more than fire and water," one editor wrote.[63] The *Tribune* was particularly emphatic about the need for segregation in housing and public accommodations.[64] Its wish was probably father to its report that Negro families were moving back into the "Black Belt," that Negro schoolchildren were preparing to abandon predominantly white schools, and that Negroes were traveling back to the South because of the riot.[65] Some city councilmen discussed allotting residential zones to Negroes by law,[66] and a number of white businessmen from the Real Estate Board and the Association of Commerce discussed the revitalization of the "Black Belt" with new—but racially segregated—housing.[67] Even Graham Taylor of the Chicago Commons settlement house, who would not have publicly endorsed segregation, wrote privately that he thought right after the riot was no time to start putting Negroes into new residential areas where they would encounter intense racial antagonism.[68]

Much the fiercest proponents of keeping Negroes out of "white" districts were the members of the Kenwood and Hyde Park Property Owners Association. The white homeowners and real estate dealers of this neighborhood near the University of Chicago had before the riot talked of "bombing out" Negroes who had bought property there.[69] The association did not change its views because of the riot. On August 5 it wrote the mayor that there had been "a movement by the vicious element of negro to harangue about constitutional rights" and that part of the program of this vicious element was "the promiscuous scattering of negroes throughout white residential sections." It particularly singled out a Negro banker living in a "white" block as "the type of man that brings discredit on the honest negroes" by taking the stand that "his means justify his living among the

whites." The association called for city-wide arrangements to make sure Negroes stayed out of white residential districts.[70] The association continued to press its
views through posters and mass meetings. Over and over
again it argued that the race riots would not have occurred if the association's program had been in effect. As
the autumn wore on without any withdrawal by Negroes
or imposition of segregation by the city, the tone of the
Property Owners' speeches got more and more violent.[71]
Rumors that it was actually sponsoring bomb attacks on
Negroes' houses led agents of the Department of Justice
to look into the association, but no action was taken.[72]

Regardless of the doubtful responsibility for these
bombings, there is no doubt that they resumed after the
race riot. From February to May, 1920, the frequency was
higher than before the riot.[73] For much of the spring,
such persons as Governor Lowden, the leaders of the Chicago Presbytery, and some Negro leaders feared that another riot was brewing.[74] Two outbreaks of racial conflict
in June and September, 1920, that might well have lit the
fuse for another great riot, were, however, controlled by
fair and effective police action within the first several
hours after the initial disturbance.[75]

But no measures were taken to deal with the underlying conflicts that had sparked the great riot of 1919. Neither changes in the direction of racial equality nor
changes in the direction of putting Negroes "in their
place" were undertaken in Chicago, any more than they
had been in Washington.[76]

Outside Chicago, the race riot of late July stirred great
concern. Journals like *The Survey,* the *New Republic,*
The Nation, and *Current Opinion* showed deep interest.[77] Rumors spread across the nation that hundreds of
deaths had occurred and had been hushed up.[78] News-
reel films of troops with bayonets charging rioters were

shown across the country.[79] Students from a number of colleges and universities asked for information so that they could write research papers.[80]

Proposals from the national press on how to deal with the riot did not always emphasize the same issues that Chicagoans had emphasized. Three Chicago themes that were picked up outside Chicago were those of putting Negroes "in their place," the economic roots of rioting, and the involvement of vice and "politics" in urban race relations. But others—especially the "fighting back" theme and the fear that Bolshevism was involved in the Chicago riot—were much stronger outside Chicago than in it.

Southerners argued that "this ugly business could not have occurred in the South" because the races would not have been "so close together."[81] Some southern planters thought the riot showed that Negroes were better off in subordinate status in the South, and sent agents to Chicago to recruit Negroes for the cotton plantations.[82] What one southern Negro editor thought of this approach was that "any Negro who in any way assists a family to return South to the land of lynching and burning is worse than a murderer." To clinch his point, he told a story:[83]

. . . The big white Southerner was present, before an assembly of more than one hundred Negro workmen. He described enthusiastically that on his plantation there are many logs that needed sawing up. Railroad transportation would be furnished and four dollars per day paid to the laborers. "How many of you wish to go?" he asked. There was painful silence. Finally, one brother spoke up and said, deliberately, "I tell you what you do, you send the logs up to Chicago and we'll saw 'em here."

The idea that competition for jobs had caused the Chicago explosion was set forth by the Inter-Church World Movement[84] and by the Associated Negro Press[85] as well as by several New York newspapers.[86] As in Chicago, there was disagreement between those who felt the Negroes should defend themselves in this competition by embracing the labor unions and those who favored their embracing the employers.

Attacks on the Republican Mayor Thompson of Chicago, partially cloaked by blaming "local politics" for the race riot, were the chief responses of two New York Democratic newspapers to the riot. The *Times* blamed Thompson for teaching Negroes disrespect for law, by taking the lid off the "Black Belt" and allowing "whites and blacks [to] intermingle in carousal at . . . all-night cabarets."[87] The *World* said that Thompson had been elected precisely to allow continuation of "the tragedy of Chicago, . . . that it is a lawless city with a lawless government."[88]

The realization that the Chicago riot demonstrated the readiness of Negroes to fight back was clearer outside Chicago than in it. "The Negro did not run in Chicago nor in Washington and in my judgment he is not going to run anywhere," the socialist writer and journalist Charles Edward Russell wrote; "he will stand and fight . . . would as lieve die as continue to live under . . . intolerable . . . injustice, and when any men reach that state of mind it is but wisdom to heed their protests."[89] The New York banker and leading Democrat George Foster Peabody also noted that Negroes were now conscious of their power and ready to use fear as a weapon, though he thought the new direction sad.[90] In the NAACP, Mary White Ovington reported that the fear of Negro self-defense was inspiring "concerted action . . . from Canada to the Gulf of Mexico . . . to refuse to sell arms to Negroes" but allow whites to buy arms. She called this "the most terrible situation the Negro has yet met," and supported the right of Negroes to fight back against white "injustice."[91]

Some Americans who noted the new tendency of Negroes to "fight back" thought it must have been inspired by some malign and alien influence. The *New York Times* remarked, "The outbreak of race riots in Chicago, following so closely on those reported from Washington, shows clearly enough that the thing is not sporadic [but has] . . . intelligent direction and management . . . [It seems probable] that the Bolshevist agitation has been extended among the Negroes."[92] Similarly, other newspapers warned of agitation by some Negroes in favor of buying arms and preparing to use violence in defense of their rights, and attributed such sentiments to propaganda from Bolsheviks and Wobblies.[93] All urged additional surveillance and if necessary action by the federal government, and one of the newspapers criticized the Chicago editors for their failure to take the possibility of Bolshevism seriously.[94]

One more consideration occurred to an East Coast newspaper that had not occurred to the inland Chicagoans as they considered their own riot: that the foreign policy of the United States would be injured until the nation could "live down the race riots of Washington and Chicago"—and it would "take a long time," the *New York Globe* warned. What worried the *Globe* was that the United States had been criticizing "with missionary zeal" those foreign countries in which revolution and internal disorder had been rife. Now Americans had their own bloodshed to plague them, and could scarcely call the kettle black—or red.[95]

The Chicago affair was the most "fully developed" riot of the 1919 series. It was the one in which the street violence was allowed to go on longest before outside troops were called in, and it was the one in which Negroes most fully demonstrated their intention to fight back, against white mobs or the white police. Perhaps because in the longer period of fighting Negroes were more able to make clear and to act out their distrust of the police, Chicago signaled to some of the nation the danger that a basic attack on authority, what they called "Bolshevism," might be involved in the rioting. To others, particularly those in Chicago who knew that Bolsheviks had not been propagandizing the "Black Belt" and that the "authority" being challenged was not an impartial one, the Chicago riot signaled the need for an impartial police.

Still others noted that this riot, far more clearly than those that had preceded it or all but one of those that followed, had deep roots in the social and economic structure of the city. These people responded to the riot in terms of dealing with such root causes of racial conflict. But to many it seemed far more important, at least as an immediate problem, to make sure that such large-scale violence should not recur. It was these people, focusing on the elimination of violence rather than on changes in race relations, who gave their attention to problems of strengthening or "impartializing" the police.

As for the actual "solution" of the Chicago riot, it is noteworthy that those in authority attempted to punish some of those thought responsible for the violence but scarcely succeeded in doing so, since almost all of the accused went free. Partial redress was given to some of the riot victims, in the form of damages paid to Negroes. But the chief accomplishment of the authorities was putting a halt to the riot itself. As we shall see in the next chapter, the authorities also attempted to examine what basic problems had given rise to the riot. They did not, however, attempt to deal with those problems.

CHAPTER V

Chicago: The Riot Studied

On the fourth day of the Chicago riot, while men were still dying in the streets and before the militia had gone on active duty, the governor of Illinois was asked to appoint a commission "to study troubles & formulate definite programme of race relations for state." That request came from a committee hastily assembled by the NAACP.[1] Two days later, a much more powerful group of Chicagoans asked Governor Frank Lowden to create "an emergency state committee to study the psychological, social, and economic causes underlying the present race riot and to make such recommendations as will tend to prevent a recurrence of such conditions in the future."[2] Out of these two appeals came the Chicago Commission on Race Relations.

The first call for a commission was suggested by Major Joel E. Spingarn, an NAACP director who had been visiting Chicago when the riot broke out. Spingarn wrote Mary White Ovington, the NAACP's national chairman, that the committee that waited upon Governor Frank Lowden included former judges Robert McMurdy and Edward Osgood Brown (a former president of the Chicago NAACP); judges Orrin Carter and Henry Horner; Dr. Charles E. Bentley, a Negro physician; Carl Sandburg, then a reporter on the *Chicago Daily News;* Robert S. Abbott, publisher of the leading Chicago Negro newspaper, the *Defender;* Father E. A. Kelly, a "Catholic priest in the black district"; Col. Franklin A. Denison, commander of a Negro regiment in the Illinois National Guard; Marcus A. Hirschl, secretary of the Chicago NAACP; and Clarence Darrow, the renowned lawyer. This group suggested to Governor Lowden a commission of five or eight members, and Lowden replied that he would consult with Francis W. Shepardson, the state Director of Registration and Education, a former professor of history at the University of Chicago and Lowden's house expert on race relations.[3]

Despite Governor Lowden's promise of July 30 to consult with Shepardson, he was probably more powerfully influenced by the second call for a commission. For the power behind this second appeal was much greater than could have been wielded by a committee including a Negro publisher, a minor Catholic priest, and a heterodox lawyer like Clarence Darrow. The second appeal was issued on August 1 by a meeting at the Union League Club in Chicago. Among the signers were Cyrus Hall McCormick, Mary McDowell, Graham Taylor, and Harriet Vittum—pillars of the community all; and among the organizations represented were the Armour and Swift meat-packing houses, the Chicago Association of Commerce, the Chicago Federation of Settlements, the City Club, the Joint Committee on Americanization, the Real Estate Board, and the Medical and Bar associations.[4] The meeting had been called by the Joint Commission on Americanization, "representing the twenty-two leading clubs in Chicago." It was chaired by Charles W. Folds, president of the Union League Club, and led by Taylor, who headed the Chicago Commons, one of the city's best-known settlement houses, and who wrote frequent columns for the *Chicago Daily News*.[5] Certainly the Chicago Commission on Race Relations itself later believed that this appeal from some of the most influential citizens of Chicago was what moved the governor to announce he would appoint a mixed commission.[6]

Governor Lowden turned the problem over to Francis Shepardson, his cabinet member for education, who had been involved before the riot in an attempt to create by legislative act an official state commission on race relations and who would have been chairman of that commission if the bill had passed.[7] Shepardson later reported that the governor had followed this bill carefully, had been disappointed in its failure, and was thus mentally prepared for the possibility of an inter-racial commission when the riots came. Lowden was especially anxious for the commission to start work quickly because of the rash of riots across the country. He hoped the Chicago Commission might act as a model for other American cities.[8]

Most of the job of choosing members for the commission was left to Shepardson. At once he began to receive unsolicited nominations from white real estate interests and from Negro small businessmen, minor politicians, and church and lodge leaders, but these he ignored.[9] Out of his own knowledge of Illinois affairs, he decided on white members of the commission. When it came to Negroes, however, he had to seek advice concerning suitable leaders of the Negro community. On this question Shepardson talked with Julius Rosenwald of Sears, Roebuck and Company, who had long been involved in philanthropy for Negroes in Chicago and throughout the nation. From this beginning Shepardson built a relationship with Rosenwald that drew heavily upon his help for the commission and that later provided Shepardson with a profession in race relations as director of the Julius Rosenwald Fund. At Rosenwald's suggestion, Shepardson called upon A. L. Jackson, executive secretary of the Wabash Avenue YMCA (the Negro branch, which had benefited heavily from Rosenwald's philanthropies). He also corresponded with several social workers and with Father E. A. Kelly of Saint Anne's Rectory, that "Catholic priest in the black district" who had seen the governor on July 30.[10]

There are only two surviving indications of the bases on which Shepardson made his judgments from the various recommendations he received. One is an explanation that despite the ability of T. Arnold Hill, executive secretary of the Chicago chapter of the Urban League, he could not be appointed because "leading colored citizens of Chicago feel quite strongly that in a Commission composed only of six negroes, there are others whose claims to consideration are superior to those of one who has been in Chicago only three or four years and who is not widely known among the negro citizens."[11] The other is a fragment of Shepardson's handwritten notes on two Negroes he did name to the commission: Adelbert H. Roberts whom he described to himself (or to the governor) as "member of the Illinois legislature and sponsor . . . for a bill proposing a commission to consider race relationships," and Dr. George Cleveland Hall, "a physician long identified with all movements looking toward the betterment of the conditions of the colored people."[12] These notations suggest (as does the actual list of appointments) that Shepardson was seeking persons prominent and powerful in the white and Negro communities who had also in some way concerned themselves with race relations, rather than scholars or professional experts in race relations. The image of a permanent race commission able to sway public opinion and adjust issues in conflict seems to have been as much in his mind as the image of a special commission to study the causes of a particular riot.

The final report of the commission identified those

members whom Governor Lowden appointed on August 20 as follows (the starred members being Negroes):[13]

* ROBERT S. ABBOTT, Editor.
  Born, Savannah, Georgia; graduate, Hampton Institute; graduate, Kent College of Law; owner and publisher, the *Chicago Defender*.

EDGAR ADDISON BANCROFT, Chairman, Lawyer.
  Born, Galesburg, Illinois; graduate, Knox College; graduate, Columbia Law School; ex-president, Chicago Bar Association, Illinois State Bar Association; trustee, Knox College, Carnegie Endowment for International Peace, and Tuskegee Institute; Senator of Phi Beta Kappa.

WILLIAM SCOTT BOND, Real Estate Dealer.
  Born, Chicago, Illinois; graduate, University of Chicago; graduate, Kent College of Law; member, real estate firm William A. Bond & Company; trustee, University of Chicago.

EDWARD OSGOOD BROWN, Lawyer.
  Born Salem, Massachusetts; graduate, Brown University; graduate, Harvard Law School; for ten years judge of the Illinois Appellate Court, First District; for some years president, Chicago Branch of National Association for the Advancement of Colored People.

* GEORGE CLEVELAND HALL, Physician and Surgeon.
  Born, Ypsilanti, Michigan; graduate, Lincoln University; graduate, Bennett Medical College; trustee, Provident Hospital; vice-president, Chicago Urban League; orator at dedication of Booker T. Washington memorial monument at Tuskegee, 1922.

* GEORGE H. JACKSON, Real Estate Dealer.
  Born in Canada; graduate, Cincinnati Law School; former member, Ohio Legislature; president, Pyramid Building and Loan Association.

HARRY EUGENE KELLY, Lawyer.
  Born, Des Moines, Iowa; graduate State University of Iowa; former member, Colorado Legislature; for some years United States district attorney for Colorado; for-

mer president, Denver Bar Association; attorney for Interstate Commerce Commission; regional counsel at Chicago for Director General of Railroads.

VICTOR F. LAWSON, Editor.

Born, Chicago, Illinois; graduate, Phillips Academy, Andover, Massachusetts; owner, editor, and publisher, *Chicago Daily News* since 1876; ex-president and now a director, Associated Press; founder, Daily News Fresh Air Fund and Daily News Free Lectures; called "father of postal savings bank in America."

* EDWARD H. MORRIS, Lawyer.

Born in Kentucky; for two terms representative in Illinois General Assembly; member of Illinois Constitutional Convention, 1920–21; for eleven years Grand Master of the Colored Odd Fellows of America.

* ADELBERT H. ROBERTS, Lawyer.

Born in Michigan; student, University of Michigan; graduate, Northwestern University Law School; for two terms representative in Illinois General Assembly.

JULIUS ROSENWALD, Merchant.

Born, Springfield, Illinois; president, Sears, Roebuck & Company; philanthropist, stimulated construction and contributed $325,000 toward total cost of Y.M.C.A. buildings for Negroes in thirteen cities; contributed over $1,000,000 toward rural schools for Negroes in fourteen southern states; trustee, Tuskegee Institute, University of Chicago, Rockefeller Foundation.

* LACEY KIRK WILLIAMS, Minister.

Born, Eufaula, Alabama; graduate, Arkansas Baptist College; pastor, Olivet Baptist Church, Chicago, since 1916 (largest Protestant Church in America); president, Illinois General Baptist State Convention; vice-president, Colored National Baptist Convention.

Shepardson himself was not initially named; but during a long illness of Bancroft, the designated chairman, Shepardson acted as chairman and was later formally added to the roster of members.[14] His was the energy that carried the commission through to the completion of its work. Of the other members, Shepardson leaned most heavily on Rosenwald with his great influence in the business and philanthropic worlds.

Once the members of the commission had been appointed, they had to face in several different ways the problem of building an identity for the commission. The two simplest possible roles were that of a political body which could mediate, manage, and "accommodate" new racial disputes as they arose; and that of a purely scholarly body which could study, analyze, and explain the one historical event of the 1919 Chicago riot. There was a third possibility, less obvious and more difficult: to unite the functions of scholarship and politics, by applying an analysis of past racial clashes like the Chicago riot to the control of continuing racial conflict. Governor Lowden evidently hoped that the Commission would take on the political role, for he wrote its members that his purpose was "to secure harmonious cooperation where there is friction, . . . [by getting] representatives of the interests affected together, to talk things over and settle mooted points in free and friendly discussion."[15] But the financial problems the commission faced and the decisions it made concerning staff led it in the direction of more scholarly concerns. Ultimately, the commission essayed the third role, that of the expert in policy who bases his recommendations for change in the future upon his scholarly analysis of the past.

The commission's status as a private rather than an official state agency helped to direct its energies away from politics toward scholarship and expertise. For the absence of state funds meant, first, that the finances of the commission were always so precarious and its life so clearly temporary that it had to focus upon studying an event in the past, upon a scholarly project whose end could be seen in advance, rather than upon the open-ended, continuing problem of assuaging future racial unrest. Moreover, since the commission's financial support came not from the public but from the voluntary contributions of the wealthiest citizens of Chicago, the commission was more dependent than it might otherwise have been on their basic outlook on racial policy. To operate as an effective political instrument, the commission would have had to be more closely attuned to demands of both the Negro community and those less well established whites who had been most hostile to Negroes. The Negroes had a voice on the commission, though a much weaker one than that of the wealthy whites who sponsored it; the less comfortable, more angry whites had not even a voice. Thus at least one of the "interests affected," in the governor's terms, was not even present "to talk things over and settle mooted points." They would probably have been present if the commission had been a public body; but without them the commission found study of the problem and recommendations of new policy an easier task than the actual politics of managing conflict.

Anxiety over its precarious finances plagued the commission throughout its life. The question arose almost at once when William C. Graves, Rosenwald's secretary and the man who was to be his alter ego in the actual workings of the commission, asked Shepardson "whether any of the Governor's emergency fund or any other state fund is available for expenses of this commission and if so in what maximum sum."[16] Shepardson explained that no state money was available, but that he had been told by the Chicagoans he had talked with "that there would be no difficulty in raising the necessary funds in Chicago."[17] Although Shepardson did not mention it at the time—at least on paper—he had also been told by the governor that if all else failed, Lowden himself would see that the commission had money for its work.[18] The commission was ultimately to find the governor's help necessary to speed up collection of funds from the upper class of Chicago.

Indeed, the commission tried to turn the governor's promise to some immediate use. In their first meeting, the members asked Lowden to appoint a fund-raising committee so that their own independence need not be compromised. When he refused, the commission had to turn to its own myriad acquaintanceships among wealthy Chicagoans. It asked the Chicago Association of Commerce, the Union League Club, and the City Club to co-operate as a finance committee for the commission.[19] And Shepardson got James B. Forgan of the First National Bank of Chicago to set up a fund-raising committee of prominent white citizens, after assuring Forgan that the entire commission approved of his choice to do the job.[20]

Not until months later was an attempt made to raise money from Chicago's Negro community, and then chiefly because trouble was at hand in meeting the budget. At that point, a Negro Finance Committee was set up with considerable direct help from Negro members of the commission's staff (despite the stated hopes of the commission that neither members nor staff would be compromised in this way). The 300 Negroes to whom an appeal was sent were asked to contribute enough so that Negroes would provide about one third of the commission's treasury—that is, approximately $8000. By November 23, total Negro contributions were $349.[21]

Estimates of the commission's needs fluctuated during its work. Its own budget committee reported on October 20, 1919, that $20,000 would be necessary. Shepardson himself thought one month later that $12,000 to

$14,000 would be enough. By March 1920, the commission thought that $30,000 would be necessary, and in November and December 1920 hiked its estimate first to $34,000 and then to $36,000.[22]

This succession of reassessments imposed a series of financial crises on the commission. At the very beginning of its work, before any contributions had been made, Julius Rosenwald lent it enough money to start, but that was repaid within a month.[23] In March 1920, Shepardson began to worry over the rate of contributions. He cautioned the staff that cutbacks in the proposed research might be necessary, nor was he wholly calmed by their proposal that the indicated shortage of $5000 might be raised from Negro contributors, from sale of the commission's furniture and typewriters, and by slight reductions in staff.[24] Through the spring and summer of 1920, the commission kept only one month ahead of its bills, and by late August its executive secretary was urging that Shepardson consider cashing in the governor's promise to make sure money was available.[25] In October, a loan from Rosenwald again met the payroll. Almost all pretense of non-involvement by staff and members of the commission in money-raising was dropped, as all hands turned to public speaking, and as possible contributors were invited to observe operations at commission headquarters.[26] Emergency conferences with the staff of the Association of Commerce indicated that banker Forgan's special finance committee had already milked that source dry. It was pointed out, however, that eight or ten individuals who had not responded to letters from the finance committee might be expected to give a total of about $8000 if they were more directly solicited. And Shepardson was specifically requested to ask the governor to appeal to the few wealthy men who might provide the needed cash.[27]

Before turning to this last resort, however, Shepardson
tried using Forgan's finance committee once more. The
Union League Club itself gave $1000. Edgar Bancroft,
the commission's chairman-designate, who had returned
in June after an illness but had not spent enough time in
the commission office to understand the staff's work and
had not taken over the real direction of the commission
from Shepardson, was brought into the financial campaign. Forgan, although he was not optimistic about the
prospects, asked for second contributions from those who
had already given.[28]

But this attempt by Shepardson and the commission
to make ends meet without the governor's help was a
failure. Not until after the staff had completed almost all
the work on the report and Lowden had left the gover-
norship did the commission meet its bills, and then only
with Lowden's help. In April 1921, a luncheon was arranged by Lowden for a number of wealthy Chicagoans
in order to raise the commission's remaining deficit.
Rosenwald withheld the announcement of his planned
second $1000 gift until the luncheon, and Lowden him-
self gave $1000. He later wrote sixteen Chicago business-
men to thank them for their gifts. So the Chicago Commission on Race Relations ended, as it had begun, in the
hands and with the support of the most substantial,
powerful, and honored men of the city.[29]

* * *

When in October 1919 the commission began its sub-
stantive work with the search for an executive secretary,
the members had not yet decided between being a
politics-oriented organization, resolving racial tensions, or
a research-oriented organization, studying only the past.
Nor had they begun to work out the role with which
they concluded: that of an organization oriented to the

study and invention, but not the implementation of new policy. Even before the commission met for the first time, Rosenwald—with Shepardson's blessing—had begun to canvas such leading white scholars as the sociologist Edward A. Ross of the University of Wisconsin and such leading Negro educators as Robert R. Moton of Tuskegee Institute for names of possible secretaries. The suggestions ranged from Robert E. Park, an eminent sociologist at the University of Chicago, to Will W. Alexander, then with the YMCA's War Work Council and later director of the Commission on Interracial Cooperation, to Mordecai Johnson, then a clergyman in Charleston, West Virginia, and later the president of Howard University, to Charles S. Johnson, director of research of the Chicago branch of the Urban League. Some of these men were scholars; some were interracial "accommodators" who could have directed the commission's work toward semi-private coping with racial conflict.[30]

A considerable discussion arose at once over whether the executive secretary should be white or Negro, or whether there should be two secretaries. The commission generally agreed that a Chicago man would be best for the job. Rosenwald, Hall, Jackson, and Shepardson were designated to seek out a secretary, and by October 20 had narrowed the field to seven men. One of these, Charles S. Johnson, a Negro, had already filed a proposed outline on how to go about studying the Chicago riot. He was a graduate student in social science at the University of Chicago, under Robert E. Park, as well as a researcher for the Urban League. Another, Graham Romeyn Taylor, a white man, was the son of the Graham Taylor who had helped initiate the commission. He had just returned from several years abroad, doing social service work in Russia and East Asia and acting as a special assistant to the American ambassador to Russia during and after the 1917 revolutions. He had written a book and a number of articles on urban problems, and was reported by an editor for whom he had written to have made an extraordinarily fair study of the great Calumet strike.[31]

Taylor and Johnson were approached by the commission—Taylor by Rosenwald's secretary, William Graves, and Johnson by the commission's senior Negro member, George Cleveland Hall. Both were interested. Still the commission was unsure how to equalize racial status in its staff. In November, five of the members "favored two secretaries with equal rank, and three, while recognizing the importance of having investigations made both by whites and colored people, favored but one secretary." One suggestion that won considerable approval was to have the chairman of an executive committee of the commission act as staff director over two equal secretaries; but no decision was made until both Taylor and Johnson had appeared before the commission. The latter was reported to have "made a favorable impression . . . in a brief talk in which he called attention to the available material for study already gathered by other agencies and to the machinery through which investigations might be made." The commission then decided to hire both men, Taylor as executive secretary at a salary of $5000 and Johnson as associate executive secretary at $3500.[32] The decision to hire two men whose chief work had been in research and writing rather than in actual politics or racial conciliation clearly bespoke the commission's choice of the role of policy expert rather than that of active politician.

A lingering unpleasantness over the staff problem— what Graves called "the clash of authority which threatened a few weeks ago"—was dissolved when Taylor and Johnson presented on December 11 a joint outline of the

way in which they proposed to study race relations in
Chicago as they bore upon the riot. Graves himself
thought the outline a "marvel," and Shepardson said it
was "the finest thing of the kind" he had ever seen.[33]
Most of this outline can be attributed to Johnson, who
according to Taylor's widow "set up the study" and was
the researcher of the two men. Taylor, she recalled, was
"skilled in writing but not in research." In addition to her
testimony, there is the evidence of the two outlines—one
formally submitted by Taylor and Johnson on December 12 and one sent by Johnson to Shepardson on October 5 as part of his application for a job with the commission. The two outlines show a close resemblance, and
the commission's final report is clearly the direct offspring
of the second outline, which is itself a direct offspring
of the first.[34]

From this point on, the efforts of the commission were
more and more directed at supporting, reviewing, and
supervising the research work of the staff, and at keeping
the commission's money in balance with its needs. With
the staff organized, the commission also began to meet
less often as a unit; from October 8 to December 18, 1919,
it met ten times, and only another eight times in all of
1920. The burden of research and writing was turned
over to the staff.[35]

To oversee this work, the commission divided into six
committees: on racial clashes, housing, industry, crime
and police, racial contact, and public opinion. Each committee kept in touch with the staff research going on in
its own area. Each of the six areas had been set forth in
the Taylor-Johnson outline and each developed into a
major section of the commission's final report. Two areas
that had been suggested in the original Johnson outline
were dropped in the second outline and in the final report: the politics of the Black Belt, and the extent and

causes of racial segregation (as distinguished from in-equality).[36]

In addition to the six sub-committees, the commission appointed an executive committee made up of Brown, Hall, Kelly, Morris, Rosenwald, and Shepardson *ex officio*.[37] This group—but chiefly Shepardson, and Graves acting for Rosenwald—effectively managed most of the over-all work for the rest of the commission's history.

Before we enter upon a discussion of the commission's research efforts, however, it should be noted that the role as racial adjuster and accommodator early envisioned for the commission was not wholly abandoned. On four occasions, the commission felt it necessary to concern itself with current racial unrest.

The first came in late October 1919, when the commission issued press releases to all the Chicago newspapers, white and Negro, saying that it had heard reports of "a continued state of unrest in neighborhoods where white and black people live," and urging calmness, patience, and tolerance.[38] In December, Shepardson told the commission he had had a reporter attend and take notes on the Kenwood and Hyde Park Property Owners Association meeting at which threats were made against Negroes who "invaded" those residential areas; and the commission staff expressed its concern with the meeting and the "inflammatory" newspaper of the association, but did not recommend any action.[39]

In February 1920, an increase in bombings of Negro property and in hostile statements by white real estate dealers prompted Governor Lowden to ask that Shepardson have the commission look into the problem. Shepardson agreed, writing the governor, "There seems to be no authority interested in the protection of Americans whose skins are black." Considering that he was writing the fountainhead of police authority in the state of Illinois, Shepardson's comment seems full of irony—probably unconscious. When Shepardson talked the problem over with the commission's executive committee, they voted to send committees to the mayor of Chicago and the state's attorney to see what they had done to investigate the bombings. These committees were to report back to the commission, but no record exists of their having done so.[40]

Shepardson himself, however, spoke publicly of existing troubles as evidence of an approaching volcanic eruption, which would occur unless terrorism and bomb-throwing ceased. Shepardson added, "The negro does not desire to scatter himself over the entire city . . . We have no intelligent segregation that will permit the negro to live among those of his own kind whom he prefers, but a segregation that throws all negroes into one vicious neighborhood."[41] Shepardson did not make clear that this acceptance of a racially segregated city (albeit "intelligently" segregated) was his own, not the commission's. He probably thereby contributed to the belief, later reported by Johnson to be held by many Negroes, that the commission would propose a scheme for compulsory segregation.[42] Shepardson's concern to keep the peace may thus have backfired and stirred new resentments in the city.

In June 1920, another flurry of concern by the commission over immediate problems was stirred by a clash in which two whites were killed by members of the Star Order of Ethiopia. These men had been publicly burning an American flag in order to demonstrate their loyalty to the King of Ethiopia. When several Negro and white passersby objected, the "Ethiopians" shot them. Shepardson, reading of this incident in the newspapers, hastened to ask Taylor to investigate it, although he said he gathered "this was a sporadic outbreak not blameable on

Chicago negroes at all but upon that special company of people." Taylor replied that he and Johnson (who had been very near the scene of the clash and was investigating it within twenty minutes) had found that all was now quiet on the South Side.[43]

Taylor did warn, however, that the *Chicago Tribune's* attempt to connect the Star Order of Ethiopia with the NAACP and W.E.B. Du Bois would anger the very Negro leaders who had condemned the "Ethiopians." Shepardson answered that he too was sorry to see the NAACP confused in the press with the "Ethiopians," adding that he found the writings of Du Bois impressive but disturbing. Then Shepardson wrote the governor that no further racial clashes were likely and added the somewhat puzzling comment that his "advices from Chicago" suggested that the affair might "be helpful rather than hurtful to the general cause for which we have been working."[44]

That the degree of involvement of the commission in easing current racial tensions was being reduced can be seen from the way in which it disengaged itself as a body from even those efforts that were undertaken. Thus, in October 1919, the full commission was publicly involved; in February 1920, only its chairman was speaking publicly; by June, the chairman and staff were acting in private. After June 1920, the commission did not again take action as a racial accommodator or adjuster and instead focused upon the role of investigator and researcher. An estimate of the relative importance of these roles to the commission can be made from its reaction to a suggestion that it ask newspapers to stop labeling criminals as Negroes. It was pointed out that such requests might give the impression of complaint or special pleading, and might thereby interfere with the readiness of newspaper editors to co-operate in the commission's research into public opinion. For this reason, the commission decided not to urge changes in newspaper habits until it had completed its study and was ready to adopt final recommendations.[45]

On two matters of investigation, the commission itself took a considerable hand. One of these was the question of radical and seditious incitement of Negroes as a factor in causing the riot.

The commission's attention was first drawn to the possible involvement of "bolshevists," "radicals," or the Industrial Workers of the World (IWW) by a syndicated column by David Lawrence in the *Chicago Daily News* of November 5, 1919. Lawrence reported that the United States Government had evidence of sedition among some Negro leaders, in the form of such attitudes as "an ill-governed reaction toward race rioting; . . . the threat of retaliatory measures in connection with lynching; . . . demand for social equality; . . . advocacy of the bolshevist or soviet doctrine." The *Daily News* also published on the same day a local story reporting the presence of an IWW organizer in Chicago and an increased amount of radical propaganda among Negroes but cautioned that there was no widespread interest in radicalism among Chicago Negroes. The *News* also quoted Dr. George Cleveland Hall, calling him "one of the leaders of the colored race in Chicago and a member of the state's Race Relationships Committee," to the effect that there was far more sedition in the southern whites' attack on the Negro than in the Negro's defense organizations.[46]

The day these stories appeared, Rosenwald had his secretary write David Lawrence to ask for references to the reports on which the story was based. Lawrence answered that he had been given access to an unpublished report and could not disclose who had given him the story; but he suggested that Francis Garvan, the Assis-

tant Attorney-General in whose jurisdiction fell the
Federal Bureau of Investigation, could help Rosenwald
out.[47]

Shepardson then took the matter up. On behalf of the
commission, he wrote Garvan to ask for any information
that could help determine whether the Chicago riot was
in any part due to radical propaganda among the Negroes. Shortly afterward, a lodge brother of Shepardson's,
who happened also to be an army intelligence agent,
wrote Shepardson of an army intelligence report on
"Radicalism and Race Riots" and explained how Shepardson could get a copy for the commission's use.[48]

Shepardson did so, and on December 4 read the
commission parts of "a confidential report from the Department Intelligence Office of the United States Army
located at Chicago." The report claimed that IWW propaganda among Negroes had a major role in inciting the
1919 riot. Some of the "facts" adduced, however, made
the commission dubious of the entire report. It listed the
National Urban League and the NAACP as organizations
engaged in spreading IWW propaganda, and commission members knew from their own memberships in these
organizations that they had no interest in the IWW's
program; indeed, much the reverse.[49]

The commission's minutes report its reactions this
way:

Some of the items were not considered significant because it
happened that members of the Commission had attended
some of the meetings referred to and were able to report
personally the entire absence of any of the features described
in the report. In other cases, members of the Commission had
knowledge of facts which seemed to cast doubt upon the
conclusion of the report, but it was felt that the Commission
should have the benefit of all information in the hands of
the government and it was voted that the officer in charge be

thanked for his courtesy in permitting the Commission to see the confidential material and be asked to furnish the Commission any material which might be helpful to it and its study.

A much more disapproving assessment was ultimately made in the commission's report, which remarked, "These reports were founded upon scarcely anything more than suspicion due to lack of information and acquaintance with the Negro group." That the commission felt strongly is made clear in Shepardson's letter thanking his friend in the intelligence service, for Shepardson mentioned a "lively discussion" and "sharp expression of dissent" from the army report.[50]

The other research problem in which the commission itself took a major hand grew out of difficulties made by the Pullman Company for staff researchers seeking data on the Negro's place in industry. When the staff and the commission members found they were unable to get the Pullman Company to co-operate (or even to be polite), Shepardson wrote the governor. The chief difficulty had been with the president of Pullman, John S. Runnells, both a personal and a business associate of the governor; so Shepardson asked the governor to drop a word that would secure the company's co-operation.[51]

Lowden was obviously reluctant to act. The original request came in June 1920. In August, Taylor reminded Shepardson of the problem and added that Pullman had not only refused to give any information to the research staff, but was also the only large industry that had refused to contribute any money. In December Shepardson reported that he had talked with Lowden again; but not till February 1921 did Lowden telegraph Runnells asking him to see Edgar Bancroft, the commission's chairman, in order to learn about its work. By that time the research work of the commission was complete.[52]

Aside from these two incidents, the commission allowed the staff to carry out the research work with considerable independence and to make its own arrangements with sources of information. The research job
began with the commission's approval of the Taylor-
Johnson outline in December, although the hiring of
more than a dozen full-time and half-time staff investigators took much of January and February.[53] The work
program outlined by Taylor and Johnson was to begin
with the study of a mass of data on hand, including all
the testimony on the riot given to the coroner's jury, six
studies of Negro housing in Chicago done by various
scholars or social agencies, the Urban League's collection
of 3000 letters of migrating southern Negroes, and a file
of white and Negro press clippings on the riots and on
racial matters in Chicago. From this material, the research work would move on to the collection of new
data from police court records, from interviews with
industrialists, teachers, and labor leaders, and from other
such sources of information.[54]

To gather this material, Johnson and Taylor hired
eighteen staff researchers, about equally divided between whites and Negroes and between half-time and
full-time workers. Most of them had been social workers
in such institutions as the Red Cross, the Urban League,
the Federal Children's Bureau, and the Juvenile Protective Association; three were, like Johnson himself, students of Robert E. Park at the University of Chicago.[55]
Seven other persons were hired later to compile the collected data and write drafts of sections of the commission's report. Of these, three had studied under Park.

Park had not only studied race relations and the process of acculturation in Negroes and immigrants but during 1917 and 1918 had been president of the Chicago
Urban League. Before the riot, he had predicted an ex-

acerbation of racial conflict resulting from the great Negro migration North and from the unsettling effects of the exposure of Negro troops to new ideas and conditions. Park had also espoused the Urban League's distinctive approach to Negro betterment through industrial employment and social welfare agencies. Park thus joined in himself the dominant orientations of the commission, both in its approach to racial policy and its research program.

He was able to impress these orientations on the work of the commission staff even more strongly than many of the commission members themselves could have. For he influenced the research process not only indirectly through what he had previously taught his students, but directly, through constant consultation during both the investigation and writing periods of the staff's work. An internal memorandum from Taylor and Johnson to the commission's executive committee noted that Park had "given seriously of his time," had "more familiarity than anyone else" except the commission and the staff with the data collected, and was prepared to help organize the report. In these ways, he colored the research work with his interests in great popular migrations, in the city as a confluence of various cultures, in the impact of urban industrialism on the rurally bred, and in the growth of popular stereotypes and their influence on public opinion.[56]

When the investigators started work, they organized their efforts around the six areas that Taylor and Johnson had spelled out: race clashes, housing, industry, crime and police, racial contacts, and public opinion. Some of their work was semi-formal observation of interracial behavior on streetcars, in factory areas, etc., and door-to-door interviews in white and Negro homes. But most of it centered around the distribution of formal questionnaires to various leadership groups in the schools, labor unions, social-service agencies, industries, and other segments of society, and in the organization of thirty conferences or informal hearings at which members of the staff and the relevant subcommittee of the commission interviewed community leaders.[57]

These conferences provided much of the richest and meatiest material in the commission's final report. A sampling of them will indicate the sorts of problems examined and sources used. One conference, on Negro housing in outlying areas, brought together members of the Chicago Planning Commission and the Park Board, the secretary of the Lower North Community Council, real estate men on the west side, and an official of the West Englewood Savings Bank. Another, on the Negro in industry, had in attendance the managers of industrial relations at International Harvester and Armour and Company, the superintendent of Argo Corn Products, a labor administrator at the Yellow Cab Company, and the industrial secretary of the Chicago Urban League. The investigation of public opinion brought editors and reporters from the white and Negro press, but separately —at the suggestion of Victor Lawson, commission member who was publisher of the *Chicago Daily News*.[58] Other conferences assembled similar community spokesmen and leaders to review the state of race relations in their own bailiwicks.

It would be enlightening to review the research methods used by the commission in these interviews and in its other work. But unfortunately, the data that were turned up by the commission's researchers—conference transcripts, door-to-door interviews, maps, questionnaires —were destroyed in a fire at the offices of the Chicago Urban League, where the research files were deposited after the commission had completed its work.[59] Aside

from the final report itself, only a few items remain—
some blank questionnaires, fragments of conference
transcripts, some reports in commission minutes of staff
activities.

Nevertheless, a review of these fragments sheds some
light on the commission's approach in the six different
sub-studies.

The first sub-study, "racial clashes," covered both the
Chicago riot and a number of smaller events, including
two other major Illinois riots, one at Springfield in 1908
and one at East St. Louis in 1917. Not much effort was
put into research on these older riots, because East St.
Louis had been carefully examined by a congressional
committee and Springfield seemed to Taylor not indica-
tive of the kind of racial conflict "in which economic,
industrial and housing factors, resulting from the migration, played an important part." Instead, Taylor thought,
the Springfield riot was "a sudden racial outbreak of
passion, following two terrible crimes," and therefore relatively unimportant.[60]

In the only other indication of the approach with
which the commission came to the "racial clashes" part
of its research, Shepardson expressed considerable interest in a conference to be held with some of the militia
who had helped quell the Chicago riot, because "quite a
number of them who were college boys . . . might be
able to say a few things worth knowing."[61] This statement of the superior value of elite perceptions and defi-
nitions of racial problems was unusual in its explicitness;
but the very structure of the conferences was a silent
endorsement of the value of testimony from a number of
different leadership groups rather than from randomly
selected residents of Chicago, or from a representative
sample of the entire population.

A partial attempt to redress the balance and reach out

to a broader population was made in the studies of Negro housing and employment. The "housing" sub-study
did examine census data and got out into the neighborhoods, in order to map out the boundaries of the Negro
population and to look at the sort of housing available to
Negroes. The study included two-hour interviews with
274 Negro families living in all sections of Chicago.[62]
But even this sub-study did not attempt to search out
the opinions or situations of ordinary whites living in or
near "negro neighborhoods," in any fashion similar to its
interviews of Negro families. And the housing study
turned to leadership groups like "real estate companies,
various organizations on the south side and key people"
to learn what the impact of the expiration of yearly
leases was on the Negro population.[63] It was of the home
builders and real estate managers, not of the white or
Negro residents, that the commission asked, "What accounts for the run-down appearance of many homes in
negro communities? . . . What types of the negro population are most in need of homes? . . . Do you know of
cases in which 'accommodation' that is, total or partial
absence of friction, has followed the moving of a negro
family into a white neighborhood? . . . Do you believe
that any agencies, real estate firms or Associations have
exploited or attempted to exploit negroes in search of
homes?"[64]

In the study of the Negro in industry, researchers conducted interviews with 865 Negro workers. Again, they
did not parallel these with a series of interviews of white
workers. And once again, the study placed great emphasis on several conferences with leaders of Chicago industry and labor unions.[65] In the industrial sub-study there
occurred the only case for which evidence has survived
of the commission's ordering the staff to drop a question
it had proposed to ask during its research. That was a

question to be asked of all industrial concerns in Chicago employing 500 persons or more: "Is your plant an open or closed shop?" The commission ordered this omitted, "it being felt that some managers might not wish, for various reasons, to answer this question, and that sufficient information for the purposes of the commission could be secured by subsequent intensive study of typical industries by the commission's investigators."[66]

For the sub-study of "crime and the police," the commission's staff contemplated administering to prisoners a questionnaire asking their life histories, the nature of the crimes for which they were convicted, former arrests, the treatment accorded them by officers of the law, etc.[67] But no report of results from this questionnaire is presented in the relevant pages of the commission's final report,[68] nor is it mentioned anywhere in the minutes of commission meetings. It seems, therefore, not to have been given; and almost all the information reported on Negro crime and the treatment of Negroes accused of crime is taken from conferences in which municipal judges, police officials, or social workers answered such questions as, "Is the hearing of colored cases as serious and dignified in manner as the hearing of white cases, or is it likely to be more on the comedy order . . . Please discuss the relative place of gangs or criminal bands in crimes committed by white and colored boys."[69]

The "racial contacts" sub-study is the only one in which even a fragment survives of the transcript of one of the investigatory conferences. This fragment is of particular interest because direct quotations from the commission members present are included. The conference was concerned with high schools, and three school principals were present in addition to both Taylor and Johnson, and commission members Williams, Brown,

Jackson, and Rosenwald. In this conference, one of the principals mentioned that he had abandoned the notion of a racially mixed glee club because white children would not take part. He had proposed setting up two racially separate glee clubs, and explained how shocked he was the next day to have "two or three hundred white and colored gathered in the assembly hall, with both aldermen, wanting to know why I wanted to start segregation. I did not intend to start segregation."

Three commission members reacted to this statement. Edward Osgood Brown, the white lawyer who had for years been president of the Chicago branch of the NAACP, asked the principal, "You could not understand this . . . protest of what seemed segregation? Is there not danger that the colored parents feared that their children were put into a musical society by themselves with the idea that they were not good enough to be put in the other class's?" Julius Rosenwald, expressing more readiness to accept segregation under some circumstances, commented, "With the [racially mixed] system that exists, might not those on both sides be losing? White children are losing the advantage they would get under this arrangement of segregation, and both might have it if they were willing to say we find this way is not possible, we will try another way." But Lacey K. Williams, the Negro Baptist minister, at once replied, "Voluntary grouping represents the white pupil's idea, not the negro's. Segregation is the white children's notion; voluntary on the part of the whites and forced on the colored"; and Brown spoke again to back him up. In the commission's final report, the principal's action was described; but there was no hint of a description of the commission's reaction.[70]

The sixth sub-study, that on "public opinion," engaged more of the staff's interest and energy than any of the others. It was the only one in which Taylor urged that every member of the commission attend each of several research conferences,[71] and it takes more space than that allotted to any other of the six areas in the commission's final report.[72] Once again, Park's interest may have been responsible, since the chief researchers in the "public opinion" sub-study were students in his class on "The Crowd and the Public," chosen by Taylor for that reason.[73]

Despite the staff's emphasis on public opinion, no more of the research materials have survived in this field than in the others. One item is a list of questions prepared for the conference of white newspapermen, such as, "Are negroes of reliability used as information checks on serious matters regarding negroes?" and "Are there issues, items, or incidents involving negroes which stimulate an unusual public interest measurable by an increased sale of papers?"[74] Another surviving item is a memorandum on reactions of white newspapermen to being invited to this conference, in which it was noted that the *Chicago Tribune's* editor "could only be described as churlish, if not insolent," though men from the other newspapers and the Associated Press were wholly co-operative.[75]

Although most of the task of gathering data in the six sub-studies had been completed by September 15, 1920, additional research conferences were held into December. In September the commission replaced many of its data-gathering staff with new personnel equipped to digest and write up the data. Indexes to the conference reports were prepared, the statistics were tabulated, and maps were drawn during October, November, and December. As a draft version of each sub-study was completed by the staff, it was brought before the relevant committee of the commission for discussion and revision and then before the full commission for its approval.[76]

But it was not until January 1921, that the commission, with a finished text of the report before it, could begin to consider what conclusions and recommendations it would draw from the study.[77] (The staff had presumably avoided thinking about recommendations at all, "believing that the work of investigation and collection of data should not be even unconsciously influenced by preconceived ideas of what ought to be done.")[78] The recommendations were drafted by Taylor, Johnson, and Shepardson, and were circulated for the commission's approval.[79]

The rest of 1921 was used in completing and polishing the report, in raising money to meet the commission's deficit, and in seeking a publisher for the full report. Commission chairman Bancroft talked with Macmillan and with Harper and Brothers, only to find that the length of the manuscript and its comparatively restricted appeal made it an unlikely commercial venture. One publisher asked for a $5000 subsidy and the other suggested "distilling" the report into a short book. Neither approach was practicable, and so the commission turned to the University of Chicago Press, which agreed to publish the full book of almost 700 pages in September 1922.[80]

Former Governor Lowden gave the proofs a final look in order to write a foreword to the volume, and had one suggestion to make. Whereas in the proofs the commission called the notion "that Negroes have inferior mentality" a "prevailing misconception," Lowden explained that he was "not persuaded that the commission acted upon sufficient evidence." He argued that the intelligence tests used in the Army during the war found Negroes mentally inferior, and expressed the belief that although recent Negro progress had been great, Negroes were still inferior to "the race which furnished . . . [the world] with Aristotle more than 2000 years ago."[81]

Although Lowden made clear that he was not insisting on any change, the passage first was revised slightly to read that the "prevailing misconceptions" were that Negroes are "capable of mental and moral development only to an inferior degree."[82] In the end it was removed from the report. Where the comment probably originally stood, there appears this paragraph:[83]

Much might be said of influences which have operated to counteract the opinion-making literature as to the utterly hopeless condition of Negroes. The object of this study, however, is not to attack these conclusions, but merely to cite them as indicating how certain attitudes detrimental to racial friendliness and understanding have had their rise.

One other last-minute hitch had to be resolved. Edward Morris, a Negro member of the commission, had refused to sign the preliminary report to the governor because the word "Negro" had been used instead of "colored person." In the final report he requested that his dissent be recorded, explaining that he disagreed with the summary and recommendations but not indicating any particular points of disagreement.[84] His dissent was recorded in the report, although Bancroft had hoped merely to omit his signature.[85]

These, then, were the final decisions of the Chicago Commission on Race Relations. In September 1922 the University of Chicago Press published *The Negro in Chicago: A Study of Race Relations and a Race Riot*. Copies of the book were distributed free to many influential Chicagoans, especially to those who had made financial contributions to the commission.[86] And so the work that had begun over three years before in the midst of the riot itself was completed in an atmosphere of scholarly calm. As the first call for the commission had asked, the racial troubles of Chicago had been studied; but had a "definite programme of race relations" been formulated?

*　*　*

Certainly a definite series of recommendations were made, but it is not at once clear whether these made up a program in the sense of a set of proposals that would actually change race relations in Chicago. It is necessary to examine closely these recommendations and the underlying logic and assumptions of the study, in order to come to some conclusions on whether or not a "definite programme" was formulated.

Without ever directly raising the issue of racial equality or inferiority, *The Negro in Chicago* makes clear in a number of places that it assumes the equality of Negroes and whites in their capabilities for life in an urban industrial society.

This assumption is made clear in the report's discussion of education, crime, employment, the press, and racial contacts. Thus in an examination of child retardation, it is noted that "of course. . . . comparisons of Negro with white children are hardly fair, since Negro children have not had the same opportunities as whites to make normal progress."[87] An important distinction is made between Negroes born and bred in the North and in the South, a distinction based on the lack of general education and of training for urban life that was said to be characteristic in the South.[88] Thus economic and social causes, rather than biologically racial causes, were assumed to account for the difficulty that comparatively high proportions of Negroes had in coping with formal education.

The report on crime carefully points out that statistics indicating higher Negro than white crime rates are misleading because of "the disposition, conscious or unconscious, to arrest Negroes more freely than whites, to book them on more serious charges, to convict them more readily, and to give them longer sentences."[89] For these reasons, the commission decided not to use crime figures "which carried . . . clear evidence of their own inaccuracy and misrepresentation," in order to avoid giving such figures currency.[90] Responsibility for the existence of many houses of prostitution in the Negro residential districts is laid to laxity in law enforcement, rather than to Negro complacency, and instances are cited in which respectable Negroes have requested the closing of such places, only to find the police turning a deaf ear.[91] The report also points out that crimes of Negroes may have a special origin in "the traditional ostracism, exploitation, and petty daily insults" that have "doubtless provoked . . . a pathological attitude toward society which sometimes expresses itself defensively in acts of violence."[92]

The study of Negroes in industry emphasized that a great proportion of establishments employing five or more Negroes reported that their work had proved satisfactory. Simultaneously, however, there was cited the warning that a direct comparison of Negro and white workers was unfair because the Negro "was still a newcomer in manufacturing and could not be expected to be as efficient, reliable, and regular as the white worker."[93] Lack of "hope on the job" was also cited by *The Negro in Chicago* as an explanation for the faster turnover of Negro labor.[94] And the doubts held by white labor-unionists of Negroes' capacity for loyalty to unionism were explained by the commission in terms of the Negroes' antagonism to racially exclusive unions and their loyalty to employers who have, "sometimes at considerable risk, . . . opened . . . new opportunities."[95] The commission also cited cases in which white unionists

who did have Negroes as co-members found them con-
scientious.[96] Again, in discussing contacts between the
races in public transportation the commission examined
claims that such contacts were made specially unpleasant by the dirt and unpleasant smell often attributed to
Negroes as Negroes. First the commission reported finding that the difficulty was actually due to the sorts of
work most Negroes did (for example, at the stockyards),
and in many cases to the lack of enough facilities for
cleaning up after such work. Then the report added
that white workers often had the same difficulty and
that complaints were made about them as well.[97] Indeed, this analysis is a paradigm of the way in which the
commission took up claims of Negro inferiority, reported that in actuality Negroes were not so inferior as
had been claimed, and argued further that what inferiority existed was caused by social and economic conditions, not by racial differences.

A second major assumption underlying *The Negro in
Chicago* was that there is no instinctual hostility between
whites and Negroes. The commission reported that friction existed in only a minority of shops between the races
in which both were hired,[98] in only a minority of
unions in which both were allowed equal membership
rights,[99] in very few penal and correctional institutions,[100] in a minority of schools,[101] and in only those
public parks where Negroes were newcomers, not in
those where Negroes had long been present.[102] The
commission suggested that the most important differences between those situations in which racial contacts
were hostile and those where they were friendly were
the attitude of authoritative figures in the particular
setting, and the length of time that the racial confrontation had been occurring. The commission referred repeatedly to the attitudes of principals as governing race

relations in the schools and those of employers as governing on the job.[103] In the field of housing, the commission
distinguished two large areas of Chicago in which Negroes lived: one, the "adjusted neighborhoods" in which
Negroes had been long established, represented a majority (but not an overwhelming one) of the residents,
and got along amicably with whites; and the other,
neighborhoods of sporadic or organized antagonism between the races, where few Negroes lived but the
whites feared an "invasion."[104]

The two assumptions—that neither biological inequality of the races nor instinctual hostility between the
races existed but rather social pressures and institutions
that could either reinforce or eliminate inequality and
hostility—run through and under the text of *The Negro
in Chicago*. For that reason it is especially interesting
that the one place in which one of these assumptions
would have been explicitly stated (or at least its opposite described as "mistaken") was changed in accord with
Governor Lowden's doubts. It is also interesting that the
two assumptions seem not to have been made by the
author of a two-page preface to the body of the report
entitled "The Problem."[105]

In that prefatory note, the race problem is said to be
based on "the instinct of each race to preserve its type."
Phrases like "our Negro problem" and "old prejudices
against the Negroes" are used in such a way as to give
the impression that whites are discussing among themselves a problem somehow tied to "those others," thus
creating an atmosphere quite different from that of the
body of the report. In the report itself, the writing is so
effectively detached that neither a Negro nor a white
seems to be writing (and in a sense this was the case,
since the writing was done by Negroes and whites in
close collaboration). Again, the prefatory note refers to

the need for "the Negro race" to "develop, as all races
have developed, from lower to higher planes of living."
No such acceptance of the notion that the Negro race is
on a lower plane of living is apparent in the report itself.
Training for Negroes in "industry, efficiency, and moral
character" is called the fundamental need in the prefatory note, although the report itself does not single out
either race in this way.

In short, the prefatory note called "The Problem" gives
the impression of having been written by a white man,
separately from the report, and of not having been reviewed by Negroes before printing. No signature is attached, and no records of the commission mention this
note. It may well have been written, along with Lowden's "Foreword" and an "Introduction" describing the
origin of the commission, for the published version of the
report—long after the commission had disbanded. Perhaps Shepardson or Bancroft was responsible for it. In
any case, its chief effect is to highlight by contrast the
presence in the report itself of the two assumptions of
equal racial capabilities and racial amity.

Several assumptions involving wise racial policy
(rather than the nature of human psychology or biology)
can be identified in *The Negro in Chicago*. The possible
values of a "pluralist" or "separatist" racial-cultural
structure for the United States are not seriously examined. The assumption of the commission seems to
have been that a constant evolution of America in the
direction of a "quasi-white" society, racially integrated
and possessed of white middle-class values, would be
best for whites, Negroes, and the nation.

This assumption can clearly be seen in the report's descriptions and recommendations. Both the political separatism that later came to be called Black Nationalism,

and the cultural separatism that later made up the Harlem Renaissance, are dismissed by the commission.

Marcus Garvey's version of Black Nationalism is described with considerable neutrality—in part, the report makes clear, because its slogan is really "Back to Africa," not, as rumors had said, "Down with the United States."[106] But the Star Order of Ethiopia, quite aside from the deaths caused by its members, is described in hostile terms.[107] And the commission explicitly recommended that Negroes discourage "propaganda and agitators seeking to inflame racial animosity,"[108] and warned Negroes "that thinking and talking too much in terms of . . . race pride . . . and race alone are calculated to promote separation of race interests and thereby to interfere with racial adjustment."[109] The creation by Negroes of separate labor unions (in trades where Negroes were admitted to unions on an equal footing with whites) was strongly condemned.[110]

The commission rejected not only Negro nationalism and separatism, but the notion that a separate contribution was possible from Negro culture to American culture. This second rejection is the more surprising in that Taylor had expressed warm approval of a book by the NAACP's Herbert Seligmann, *The Negro Faces America*, which had argued that Negro jazz, the Negro's capacity to play, sing, and dance "for the love of what he is doing and experiencing," had "introduced human values into American civilization of a sort in which it has been found peculiarly lacking."[111] No hint of this view of the Negro as teacher and vivifying force comes through in *The Negro in Chicago*. For example, the report applauds Negroes who respectably opposed the "black and tan" cabarets in which racially mixed couples enjoyed "coarse and vulgar dancing," and these troublesome contacts were contrasted with the beneficial effects of interracial contacts under the auspices of "institutions of learning" such as libraries and universities.[112] The latter contacts were clearly those in which Negroes did the learning of white art and music, rather than the reverse. Again, the report directly recommended "that Negroes completely abandon the practice of seeking petty advance payments on wages and the practice of laying off work without good cause."[113] Seligmann's line of argument, that just such "Negro" habits might teach white America how to enjoy itself, was not examined.

Just as the commission's crucial assumption concerning wise racial policy was that the goal should be an integrated quasi-white society, so the crucial assumption on wise economic policy was that the goal should be a more effectively rationalized private-enterprise society. The rationalization of practices on hiring and on admission to labor unions was understood to require that all qualified personnel be treated equally, regardless of race, so that an indigestible mass of irrationally excluded persons would not clog the efficient processes of economic enterprise. The commission recommended that employers hire, train, pay, and promote their workers on grounds of merit alone (but not that the state intervene to enforce this recommendation). The commission also urged that labor unions admit Negroes on an equal standing "whenever they apply . . . and possess the qualifications required of white workers." The commission carefully avoided taking sides on the question whether Negro workers should seek protection by joining unions or by "loyalty" to the employer. It urged only that Negroes who did want to join unions choose integrated unions where they were available, rather than establish separate ones.[114]

In its only reference to a model of the future economy other than rationalized private enterprise, the commis-

sion reported on the IWW's attempts to appeal to Negro workers. There was no direct criticism of the IWW's
argument for a joint effort by the working class of all
races to abolish the capitalist system. Indeed, the commission's report presented almost two full pages of direct
quotations from the IWW almost without comment.[115]
But the commission's own view was clearly that race relations could and should be transformed within the capitalist system. The report referred to A. Philip Randolph
and Chandler Owen's magazine, *The Messenger,* but
did not explain their argument that racial equality—even
equality with white workingmen—could be achieved
only under socialism, and that socialism could only be
achieved if racial equality also were. Again, this omission
is surprising in the light of Taylor's admiration for the
parts of Seligmann's book which described *The Messenger's* position.[116]

Any close examination of *The Negro in Chicago* must
confront the question of how the commission expected
its recommendations to come into force. To fill ade-
quately the role it had chosen to play of expert on policy
and policy change, the commission needed to explain
clearly what sort of power must be exerted in order to
bring about changes in policy on race relations.

But except for a few scattered hints, *The Negro in
Chicago* avoided the problem of power relations in the
city. The report did say that part of the Negroes' difficulty in securing decent housing stemmed from their
exclusion from most of the banking system that lent
money to build or buy housing.[117] The report also made
clear the one-sidedness of the police in protecting whites
and arresting Negroes during the riot, the unreadiness of
the police force to protect Negro homes from bombings,
and the refusal of the police to enforce laws against prostitution and gambling in the Negro residential areas.[118]

Again, the report pointed out that many of the violently anti-Negro teen-age "athletic clubs" had been founded by white politicians in order to reach young men before they had attained voting age.[119] Yet the commission did not examine in any systematic way the questions of why the police and politicians acted in these ways, or what ramifications grew out of the exclusion of Negroes from financial power. No study was made, in short, of the ways in which the pattern of race relations in Chicago fit into the political structure of the city, or the connections between the political system and various urban economic interests as they affected race relations. Johnson's first outlined suggestions for the study had proposed a section on just such questions, but by the time he had been hired and had worked out with Taylor the actual guide for the study, that section had been dropped.[120]

The omission of any section on politics and power probably contributed to the difficulty of finding in the commission's recommendations any clear indication of how they were to be put into effect. Many recommendations were made, for example, that the police act with far more energy and neutrality to protect Negroes, to eliminate vice in Negro districts, and to control the white adolescent "athletic clubs" that had proved a source of anti-Negro violence in sporadic race conflict and in the riot. No consideration was given, however, to the problem of what interests of their own the police would have to jettison, in order to act in these fashions. What might their own interests have been in protecting houses of prostitution? in looking the other way when white real estate dealers and property owners tried to force Negroes to move? in protecting and encouraging "athletic clubs" that were sponsored by particular white politicians? Simply because such questions were not asked, there is no way of telling what the commission thought would have to be done to get the police to act in accord with their recommendations.

From the absence of explicit discussion of levers of change, from the commission's emphasis on the importance of public opinion and the press as an instrument in forming public opinion, from the report's interest in the power of authoritative figures in particular institutions to affect race relations within those institutions, and from the way in which the commission distributed the report to "opinion leaders" in Chicago, it may be gathered that the commission expected its constituency of powerful and prestigious Chicagoans to act quietly to implement the recommendations. Such men could presumably reorient the newspapers, open the banks to Negro employment and order loans granted on Negro housing, insist that politicians allow the "athletic clubs" to be watched and order the police to protect Negroes and their property, and begin to hire and pay workers without regard to race. And presumably such men could do all this without making any public fuss.

This view of the commission's expectations would explain what is otherwise difficult to explain, the absence of any recommendations (other than "thrift" and "industry") to Negroes on how to *take* the progress that the commission was urging should be *given* them. Nor were there any suggestions to whites who wanted race relations altered but did not hold positions of power, on how to get neighborhood associations to change their attitudes or how to open labor unions to Negroes.

The question must then be raised, why did the commission expect its audience of the city's leaders to act in accord with its recommendations, when these would interfere with interests and attitudes long cherished? What new element in the situation was expected to stimulate leaders into changing their approach, in the absence of any pressure from below by Negroes or whites? Why should white bankers channel their loans to Negro home-builders, white newspapermen stop exaggerating Negro peculiarities and race conflict in order to build their circulation, white politicians transfer their protection from white to Negro interests? The only answer that can emerge from a study of *The Negro in Chicago* is: fear of future violence in the pattern of the 1919 race riot.

In other words, the commission was warning that more violence awaited Chicago unless many accommodations were made to Negro demands, many white myths about Negroes were exposed as untrue and eliminated from white minds, harmony between whites and Negroes was deliberately encouraged, and the city was set on the road toward being economically rationalized and racially integrated—a larger version of the best-organized, most "industrious" and "thrifty," and most highly respectable segments of white society. Frank Lowden, in his fore-word to the report, explicitly pointed to the commission's recommendations as a means to make impossible a repetition of "the appalling tragedy which brought disgrace to Chicago in July of 1919."[121] And in this direct statement Lowden was only summarizing the intentions of the commission, referred to in a number of places in the report.[122]

A review of the origins, the work, and the recommendations of the Chicago Commission on Race Relations must emphasize the following important points:

That the commission was mostly instigated by, half made up of, and heavily financed by the prominent and powerful men of Chicago's white community;

That its research was heavily, but not wholly, oriented to the examination of facts known to and opinions held by a number of different leadership groups in the city;

That the commission's image of a future Chicago was

one in which Negroes had joined—but not essentially changed—the existing white society, and had changed whichever of their own values and behavior were incompatible with that society;

That its view of the way in which this should be accomplished was that persons of power and prestige in the white community should influence that community to accept the entrance into it on an equal footing of Negroes who had learned how to behave in it;

That the commission expected the fear of future "disgraces to Chicago" like the riot of 1919 to move Chicago's leadership to implement the commission's recommendations, as a way of preventing future violence and thus of preventing the damage to its own interests and feelings that such violence would cause.

How can one measure the effects of the commission's work and recommendations? In part by looking at the verbal response of Chicago and the nation to the commission's efforts; in part by examining whether the recommendations were in fact adopted; and in part by assessing the impact of the commission's scholarship on later social science.

Many Negroes in Chicago made clear by word and deed that they were thoroughly suspicious of the commission's efforts. Although Walter White of the NAACP had responded favorably to the first announcement of the men who were to make up the commission,[123] one Negro newspaper, the *Broad Axe*, bitterly attacked the commission because one of its members, the white real estate dealer William Scott Bond, was listed as a member of the executive committee of the anti-Negro Kenwood and Hyde Park Property Owners Association.[124] Bond had already written to the association that his name had been used without his permission and demanded its removal from the list. At the request of the commission, Charles

S. Johnson called on the editor of the *Broad Axe* to explain the misuse of Bond's name.[125] Yet the commission
continued to be aware of the opposition of many Negroes.

The attempts of the commission to raise money from
the Negro community involved constant efforts to overcome suspicion. The Negro Finance Committee went out
of its way to explain that neither politics nor "preconceived opinions" had entered into the choice or the work
of the commission and that its staff was biracial.[126] Yet
still the belief persisted among some Negroes that the
commission was planning to propose a scheme for compulsory segregation,[127] and Hall and Johnson finally told
the commission that both "political struggles" among the
Negroes (probably involving opposition to Lowden) and
"misunderstanding of the function of the Commission"
had damaged the prestige of the commission.[128]

Outside Chicago as well, the commission found some
Negroes mistrustful. W.E.B. Du Bois, the editor of *The
Crisis,* major militant Negro magazine published by the
NAACP, denounced a questionnaire on racial matters
that the commission had asked him, among other Negro
leaders, to fill out. He called the questionnaire an insidi-
ous way of "pushing . . . a program of racial segregation."[129]

When the commission issued its report, responses were
generally favorable. The *Daily News* and the *Defender,*
as could have been expected from the involvement of
their publisher-editors in the commission, supported the
report vigorously. The *Chicago Post* echoed their approval, and the New York *Herald* and the *Times* placed
great value on the commission's findings and recommendations.[130]

From a southern white man, however, came strong
criticism of the report. Alexander Lawton, addressing the

alumni of the University of Georgia, praised such efforts at betterment of race relations as those of the Southern Commission on Interracial Cooperation. But he cited the commission's findings as evidence that "race instinct and race prejudice in Chicago are at least as strong in proportion to contact as in Georgia." On that basis he ridiculed almost all the commission's recommendations as attempts to suppress rather than recognize "race instinct"— attempts that would be "impracticable, visionary, and impossible."[131]

By the second standard for measuring the commission's work, the extent to which its recommendations were adopted, the commission would not fare well. By the report of the leading historians of black Chicago, no major break was made in the racial lines around skilled jobs, union membership, residential areas, or public myth-making until long after 1922.[132] Even the commission's one institutional recommendation—that a permanent commission like itself be created—was not accomplished till the 1940s, when the mayor of Chicago (in fear of another riot) appointed a Committee on Race Relations that included Charles S. Johnson as one member.[133] A white expert on Chicago race relations, a Negro journalist, two former members of the commission's research staff, and a Negro lawyer who had pressed some damage suits on behalf of Negroes hurt in the 1919 riot all agree that *The Negro in Chicago* had little effect on racial practices.[134]

The report did have more effect upon social science. The commission's account of the riot itself and its description of the Negro's status in Chicago have been taken as major sources by sociologists and historians.

Theoretical examinations of rioting have drawn heavily upon the commission's account of the ways in which late-adolescent gangs formed nuclei for mobs; unneutral acts of the police both instigated the riot and exacerbated it;

hot weather first assisted and then rainy weather discouraged and helped end the milling of crowds which turned into mobs; and the swift spread of fearful rumors fed the hatred that spawned violence.[135]

Similarly, the leading history of American Negroes cites *The Negro in Chicago* as a major source for understanding "the period of reaction."[136] Discussions of Chicago's juvenile gangs[137] and the Chicago Negro community[138] have drawn heavily upon the commission's report. Gunnar Myrdal's classic study of American racial patterns, *An American Dilemma*, cites *The Negro in Chicago* in discussing race riots, but does not use it for data on general Negro urbanization or Chicago in particular.[139]

The Negro in Chicago may thus be said to have exerted considerable influence among scholars as a study of the troubles that had brought on the 1919 riot and as a study of the riot itself. But in terms of its own choice of role, as the policy expert concerned with social change rather than as pure scholar concerned simply with social science, the commission accomplished little. Its unwillingness to give its recommendations a political cast and political relevance was probably the major factor in preventing its work from having a social effect. Its analysis stopped short of looking hard at the power structure of Chicago, by which change could be induced; and that was a crucial failing not only in the analysis but in any attempt to play a role in bringing change about.

CHAPTER VI

The Jailhouse Riots

In the two months after the Chicago riot, two medium-sized American cities suffered violence in which racial tensions played a major part and in which the precipitating event was an attack by white mobs on the city jail in order to capture and lynch a Negro prisoner.

As such beginnings might suggest, the Knoxville and Omaha riots were not of the same type as those that occurred in Washington and Chicago. Both of them began more as an insurrection by whites against the police authority of the state as symbolized in the jailhouse and then developed more as a white "pogrom" against Negroes than as a fully two-sided riot. In Knoxville, though not in Omaha, as the riot continued, some Negroes did try to "fight back." But even in Knoxville, Negroes were much less ready to fight back effectively than in Washington or Chicago. Despite the differences between these "jailhouse riots" and the earlier, larger-scale events, the national consciousness of the earlier events colored perceptions of the later ones, so that these too were seen as full-scale race riots.

Knoxville in 1919 was a commercial and light industrial center of some 77,000 people, of whom about one seventh were Negroes. Its political life was in turmoil as a result of a recent expansion of the city to take in some nearby suburbs. Political conflicts among the city authorities, the county authorities, and various disgruntled groups helped to make violence possible.[1]

The racial trouble in Knoxville began early August 30 with the arrest of a Negro, Maurice Mays, on charges of murdering a white woman. Mays denied any part in the crime and was taken by the sheriff to Chattanooga, for fear of mob violence. The fears materialized that evening. Despite public announcements that Mays had been taken elsewhere, and despite three inspections of the jail by three separate citizens committees to show that Mays was gone, a mob of whites stormed the jail. Several thousand men were in the crowd, of whom about a hundred actually entered the jail, smashing furniture, stealing equipment and money, and freeing most of the white prisoners, including some convicted murderers. Later testimony showed that many of the entrants were former convicts bent on plunder or on disgracing the sheriff, rather than on lynching Mays. But at the time, the crowd outside, the authorities, and Negroes interpreted events as racially motivated.[2]

After a number of deputy sheriffs, policemen, and militiamen were injured in defense of the jail, a company of the Tennessee National Guard was ordered to the jail. Stones, bricks, and bullets were added to the fray, until the jail itself and the grounds were cleared by the National Guard.[3] Then the mob turned to looting hardware stores and pawnshops of revolvers, rifles, and knives. Five truckfuls of men left for Chattanooga with the announced purpose of getting Mays.[4] Sporadic rioting began after midnight in Negro areas of the city, and reports spread that Negroes had fired upon and robbed some whites in these areas.[5]

The next morning, in response to these reports, a crowd of a hundred armed whites moved toward the Negro district but were met with gunfire from Negroes who had barricaded the way. Then twelve hundred National Guard troops were rushed to the scene and began to advance against the barricade. Reportedly the Negroes opened fire again, but the only white soldiers wounded were two accidentally shot by the troopers' own machine gun, which was firing at the Negroes. Both men died.[6]

The soldiers ordered all crowds to disperse and began searching all Negroes on the streets for arms. Two Negroes were shot and two bayoneted when, according to the Guardsmen, they resisted search. The Guard also mounted four machine guns at a commanding point in the heart of the Negro district, and forbade all traffic in the area.[7]

Some leaders of the Negro community of Knoxville, protesting bitterly at what they thought discriminatory treatment by the soldiers, asked the governor of Tennessee to withdraw the troops. Railroad agents reported that "many" Negroes had left the city. On Monday, September 1, the situation had quieted down so much that street searches were discontinued, the "barred area" in the Negro district abandoned, and a first contingent of Guardsmen sent home. Although all Labor Day celebrations had been canceled during the riot, the separate white and Negro celebrations that had originally been planned were permitted, and only a parade was prohibited. On Tuesday, the rest of the troops were relieved from duty and the authorities announced that no more trouble was expected.[8]

On Labor Day, the sheriff had begun arresting whites who had stormed the jail. By Wednesday he had fifty under arrest and had called a special session of the grand jury to take testimony on the riots. His life was threatened for making these arrests. Some whites expressed fear "as to how far the Grand Jury may go," since many prominent citizens were said to have been in the crowd outside the jail at various times.[9] No more arrests were made, but on September 9, the governor ordered out a machine-gun company of the Tennessee Guard to protect the jail, following threats that a mob would release the men under arrest for the first jail storming.[10]

No Negroes were arrested for any part in the two days of race rioting, despite the early claims that Negroes had fired on the National Guard. Maurice Mays, whose arrest had touched off the violence, was convicted of first-degree murder on October 4, and the trials of the men who had stormed the jail in search of him began shortly after.[11]

To the accompaniment of what the press reported as widespread surprise, all defendants on charges of storming the jail were acquitted, except five on whom the jury disagreed. The attorney-general who had tried the cases said that of the nineteen cases, he had had no doubts of conviction in eighteen. "The proof was so positive against the defendants," he said, "and with their admission of having been in the mob at the jail, that I didn't expect the jury to be out more than one hour until a verdict of guilty would be returned."[12] So incensed was he at what he evidently thought a deliberate refusal to do justice against lynchers that he announced that none of the men who had served on the jury would ever again serve on a jury in county criminal court, if he could help it. "I will always reserve a challenge for them in all cases tried by me," he said, "and after I am out of office I will use my influence with my successor to see that none of them is ever placed on another jury in criminal court."[13]

A similar estimate of the evidence, the cases, and the jury was made by the presiding judge. When court reconvened in November, he ordered that,[14]

Whereas, the verdict of the jury in said case was wholly unwarranted by the evidence,

The court is pleased to and doth order that none of said persons shall ever be allowed to sit as jurors in this court as long as this court is presided over by the present judge.

The sheriff concurred in deploring the acquittals and stressed his own pride in having protected Mays from the mob. From some of his comments and those of the attorney-general and the judge, it is clear that there was wide approval in the white community for the attempt to lynch Mays. From the Negro press came corresponding approval for the actions of county authorities in preventing the lynching.[15]

National reaction to the Knoxville riot focused on the failure of the police to cope with the mobs that stormed the jail and that resisted the militia. "Most of our municipalities," said the *New York World*, "appear to be organized solely for social service. In the presence of a mob their police officers are as helpless as their school-teachers or their hospital interns."[16] The *Scranton Times* and the *New York Evening Post* also argued that more, and more effective, police would stop race riots much more quickly.[17]

Few observers referred to deeper causes of the Knoxville disturbance. One mentioned vaguely that "broader tolerance" might prevent riots from beginning.[18] Only the *Knoxville Sentinel* intoned the usual southern argument that the riot had resulted from a dreadful overstepping of "the color line, [which] is a physical fact socially speaking that cannot be wiped out."[19] The *Daily News* of Greensboro, North Carolina, joined the *Sentinel* in attacking northern Negro "agitators" who were "preaching murder and arson," but it reported that southern Negroes, including those in Knoxville, had shown no sign of rebellion until the whites there had let their own "jumpy nerves" start the trouble.[20]

Two Negro papers noted the reports of partial resistance offered by the Knoxville Negroes to white attack, and praised it.[21]

*　*　*

In Omaha, the "riot" which began on September 28 did not give much opportunity to such newspapers for rejoicing over Negro readiness to "fight back." The violence had its roots in months of public denunciation of Negroes as criminals, by the Omaha press, the Chief of Police, and—not least—by parts of organized labor, which had considerable political strength in the city. Omaha was a meat-packing town of almost 200,000 people, 10,000 of them Negroes. White trade-union leaders were bitter about the recent use of Negroes to break strikes by meat packers and teamsters; and although the local NAACP had urged Negroes to support union labor, the workingmen's bitterness was often directed at the Negroes as well as at their employers.[22]

In April a meeting of 600 Negroes under NAACP sponsorship warned against the newspaper treatment of crime, "using in glaring and sensational headlines expressions of special reference to the race." The meeting censured the Chief of Police for saying, "If the better class Negroes did not get together and ferret out the criminals of the race there would be a repetition of the East St. Louis riots [of 1917]." Instead, the NAACP meeting suggested, if the Chief did "his whole and sworn duty" it would not be "any more necessary for Negroes to hunt down their criminals than . . . for white people to hunt down theirs."[23]

According to the local branch of the NAACP, the events of the riot summer of 1919 intensified the tension. The branch investigated a number of cases in which Negroes were accused of crime, and in several proved that at least the particular persons who were accused had not been involved.[24] The county attorney began to worry over the possible effects of "groundless stories" that numbers of Negroes accused of rape were being allowed to go free.[25] Then in late September came the last straw. A young white girl was raped, and she thought her assailant a Negro. Forty "undesirable" Negroes were forced to leave town by the police.[26] The NAACP's local president expressed the hope of the Negro community that the rapist would soon be brought to justice, whether he were a Negro or a dark-complexioned white, "perhaps a Mexican."[27] Mobs surrounded Negro suspects in the case, who then had to be rescued by police.[28]

Finally, on September 28, the police arrested a Negro, William Brown, and took him to the jail, which was on one floor of the county courthouse. Within hours, a mob had gathered at the courthouse to demand that Brown be turned over to them for lynching. The mayor of Omaha, Edward P. Smith, refused, and the mob captured the mayor and were on the verge of hanging him from a trolley pole when police officers cut the rope and rushed him to the hospital, badly injured.

The mob continued to demand Brown, and its numbers swelled into the thousands. The sheriff attempted to have fire hoses trained on them, but the hoses were cut and a hail of stones and bricks began to fly at the courthouse windows. Negroes who had been caught in the crowd, including a Negro policeman, were beaten. A gang of young men and adolescents swarmed into the building and began to shoot at the defending police, some of whom surrendered their clubs and guns peacefully when the mob demanded them.

By 7 P.M., the mob had started a fire on the first floor of the building. When the fire department attempted to stop the flames, its hoses were cut again. The fire advanced, until all of the one hundred prisoners in jail had to be sent to the roof. There, in fear of their own lives, several of the prisoners decided to throw Brown to the mob. When several of the mob pushed their way past the sheriff, who was still trying to persuade them to stop, the prisoners turned Brown over.

Once the mob had Brown, he was shot and hanged from a nearby lamp post, and then his body was burned and hung from a trolley pole at a major downtown intersection. Only then did the mob disperse so that firemen could check the flames and save the rest of the prisoners.[29]

Early in the evening the police had asked for help from the United States Army at Fort Crook and Fort Omaha, but the troops could not start out until too late to save Brown from the mob. Red tape in the offices of Nebraska's governor, who was out of the capital, and of the War Department, which was unprepared, slowed down the orders to send troops. Only after one of Nebraska's senators had called Secretary of War Newton D. Baker and Baker had called Fort Omaha directly did the troops march. The first detachments arrived at midnight.[30] By 2:04 A.M., 340 men were on duty. Though the situation was "more quiet," with the mob practically dispersed, further trouble was expected.[31]

More detailed orders went out the next morning through regular channels. Major General Leonard Wood, Commander of the Central Department of the Army, was ordered to send Omaha "one company at war strength completely equipped for riot and field duty and including extra ammunition and machine guns with rations for seven days."[32] He was authorized to order additional troops to Omaha if necessary.[33] Special trains from army camps in Iowa, Kansas, and South Dakota bore troops to Omaha.[34]

The soldiers stood guard on September 29. Machine guns were set up between the chief Negro residential area and the rest of the city, "to keep the negroes in and to keep the whites out." An army observation balloon floated above the city to watch for fires that authorities feared might be set by whites or Negroes.[35] Negro leaders reported to the city commissioners that their people were well armed and ready to fight in defense of their homes but would not attack whites.[36] The American Legion offered its help to the city fathers in keeping peace, although many recently returned soldiers in uniform had been in the mob that burned the courthouse.[37] According to one newspaper, Omaha businessmen had been dismayed by the mob attack, but "the ordinary clerk and the workingman" were not ashamed and were indeed rather proud of their work the night before.[38]

By evening, the tension was beginning to relax. At 6 P.M., the troop commander was still sufficiently worried to telegraph General Wood, "Persistent rumors indicate outbreak tonight."[39] Two hours later, he reported, "Everything still quiet probably due to heavy rain just now falling." Nothing had changed at 11:30 P.M.[40] The downpour of rain had indeed driven the city to cover, stopping even streetcars for half an hour and continuing steadily for so much of the night that no mob could get organized.[41]

The next morning, General Wood himself arrived in Omaha. He reported to Washington that he had begun making arrests of those implicated in lynching Brown and burning the courthouse, "no action to this end having been taken to date."[42] Wood took command of the city's police department, began to obtain all photographs of the rioters for use in prosecution, and announced that arrests would be made by the Army but trials would be held by the civil authorities. Machine guns were posted before the city hall, the courthouse, and other important buildings. Troops patrolled downtown streets and the Negro district. Street gatherings of more than two people were challenged by the troops, and Wood urged that all public meetings be prohibited. By nightfall on September 30, the *New York Times* estimated the white population to be neither glorying in their rebellion, as they had the day before, or ashamed of their acts. "Tonight they are in fear [of punishment]," the *Times* said.[43]

As the whites became chastened, Negroes lost some of their fear. On the day after the courthouse riot, many hundreds of Negroes had stayed home from work at the urging of the local NAACP. Railroad ticket sellers reported that about 2000 Negroes had left the city for Kansas City, St. Joseph, and St. Louis, Missouri. By September 30, however, Negroes were back at work under the Army's protection.[44]

Wood took control of a number of civil activities in Omaha. He organized the American Legion into a paramilitary police force for emergency use and began to train its men to replace his soldiers.[45] He also took partial control of the publication of news, urging the Omaha press not to print the story of another alleged rape of a white woman by a Negro. When out-of-town papers did print the story, Wood explained to their reporters that the victim had been "unable to say positively whether her assailant was a white man or a Negro." But in the prevailing tension, he did not want even that version of the story printed where Omaha could read it.[46] He even ordered a World Series scoreboard taken down from a major street intersection, because a crowd gathered to watch the scores posted.[47]

By October 2, fifty-nine men had been arrested for complicity in the original riot. The charges contemplated were arson, assault with intent to do great bodily injury, and murder. Rumors began to fly that some policemen were reluctant to name people who they knew had taken part in the riots, but the chief of police and the chief of detectives insisted that every effort was being made to apprehend all participants. Several of the known leaders of the mob, however, had disappeared from the city.[48]

As the roundups continued, Wood reported to Washington that the people of Omaha were "still nervous" but slowly quieting down. Because he felt the local police force was without adequate arms or equipment, he requested permission to sell the city a "limited number of revolvers shot guns machine guns etc . . . prior to withdrawal of last troops."[49] Washington replied that no legal authority existed for such a sale by the Army; so the city went to private markets for two machine guns, thirty riot guns, motorcycles, and a military instructor to rebuild the police department along semi-military lines.[50]

With the city effectively under control, Wood felt able to leave Omaha on October 5 for his command post in Chicago. The troops stayed in Omaha, however, on request of the acting mayor. Two fears governed his request: first, that the police were not yet organized to cope with threats of violence against the grand jury acting on the riot cases; secondly, that the Army would be needed to manage the crowds expected when the King and Queen of Belgium visited Omaha on October 21, as scheduled long before.[51]

On October 14, however, with the Belgian royal family safely rerouted, Wood wrote Governor Samuel F. McKelvie that he thought the federal troops no longer needed to be on active duty. He suggested that the mayor take over the city but the Army be held ready to respond promptly if necessary. The governor agreed, and Wood ordered the troops to withdraw, except for two companies of infantry that would stand prepared in the courthouse and would guard the American Legion's weapons there.[52] The field commander suggested one change: that one of the two companies be kept at the city firehouse so as to be nearer the Negro population. Wood agreed.[53]

Despite the withdrawal, the Army kept control of the prisoners accused of participating in the riot. The field commander noted on October 23 that there seemed to be "no legal way to hold these prisoners if the court . . . orders their release on a proper writ of habeas corpus." But he used semi-legal and extra-legal pressures to prevent their release. For example, despite his private understanding of the limits on military authority he acted as if there were no such limits, telling the sheriff that all the prisoners were being and would continue to be held by military authority regardless of civilian wishes. He then explained to his superiors, "As long as the military can block the courts in this way,"—that is, by misdirection without direct disobedience—"well and good."[54] Wood requested advice from Washington, however, and was told that habeas corpus from a state court could be politely declined and only from a federal court need habeas corpus be obeyed.[55]

This concern of the Army was connected with the bringing of indictments against the first ten alleged rioters and the withdrawal of charges from seven other youths who had been held for investigation. The first group of charges included counts of murdering Brown, arson, unlawful assembly, and carrying concealed weapons. Many of the prosecution witnesses listed were police officers.[56] A reporter for the *Omaha Bee*, who was charged with rioting, claimed he got the two witnesses who had testified against him before the grand jury to repudiate their testimony, and printed in the *Bee* a violent attack on the grand jury and the judges. His editor was fined for contempt of court for having published the attack instead of waiting for the alleged affidavits repudiating testimony to be produced in court.[57]

With the trials under way, the civil authority wholly restored, and racial conflict subdued, the Army completed its withdrawal in early November.[58] On November 19 the grand jury made its report, concentrating on such innocuous suggestions as relocation of the police headquarters, increases in the penalty for rape, and speedier trials.[59] The jury's foreman, however, said that one Omaha political faction had helped to foment the riot in order to discredit the police and benefit its own interests in prostitution and gambling unregulated by the police.[60]

From outside Omaha, responses to and judgments of the riot began as soon as news reached the country of the burned courthouse, the lynched Negro, and the battered mayor.

The NAACP's national headquarters in New York heard from its Omaha chapter early September 29.[61] At once the staff began to try stirring up public opinion. Senator Charles Curtis, who had put before the Senate a proposal to investigate riots and lynchings, was told that racial violence was "reaching a stage in which the vengeance of the mob is not directed solely against the Negro," so that federal investigation and legislation were all the more necessary.[62] An urgent letter to many NAACP supporters asked them to use the Omaha events to press support for the Curtis resolution.[63] The NAACP telegraphed the injured mayor its congratulations on his "courageous attempt to check mob violence" and reminded him of the Curtis resolution.[64]

In order to prepare press releases to answer news reports blaming the riot on twenty to forty attacks on women by colored men within a short time span in

Omaha, the national NAACP staff asked the Omaha branch to check these claims against police records and report the results as soon as possible. The national office also asked for a file of clippings covering "objectionable" newspaper stories over the past few months in Omaha.[65] In the meantime, it released to the national press the story of months of effort by its Omaha branch to stop the singling out of Negroes as criminals in flamboyant headlines.[66]

Once Omaha had been brought under control by the federal troops, the NAACP concentrated on publicizing the view of a civic leader in Omaha, H. J. Pinkett, that the riot had been caused by the attempts of the *Omaha Bee* and one political faction to discredit the city administration and police force. In order to accomplish this end, Pinkett claimed, the *Bee* sensationalized and headlined a series of unconfirmed reports of attacks by Negroes on white women, accusing the Omaha police department of criminal laxity in permitting this series of attacks to go unpunished. He further claimed that the mob that stormed the courthouse was chiefly incited by political enemies of the mayor who wanted to ruin his administration because of his opposition to liquor, prostitution, and gambling interests.[67] From the NAACP's standpoint, the importance of this version of events was in scotching the traditional justification of lynching as a punishment for rape; and the Pinkett memorandum, with its author's name removed because he feared reprisals, was strongly "pushed" by the NAACP's publicity men.[68]

The justification of lynching for rapists was an immediate response to the Omaha events, with some Southerners and many Omahans distinguishing the attack on the mayor from the lynching of Brown.[69] On the other hand, several northern and southern papers praised the mayor for his attempt to keep the mob from lynching Brown and urged that the law be upheld even in cases of rape.[70]

One of the stronger responses to the Omaha riot, both in Nebraska and outside, was that more police, better armed, were necessary in order to prevent or put down such riots. Governor McKelvie especially emphasized the need for strengthening of the state militia and creation of a state police force.[71] A newspaper in Lincoln, Nebraska, remarked that permits should be required to hold all public assemblies, so that police could supervise them and stop unauthorized meetings.[72] In Memphis, the news of Omaha brought a prohibition on sales of guns and tough police enforcement of laws regulating firearms.[73] Other newspapers thought federal punishment of lynching and the use of "the entire power of the Federal government" to uproot lynching the only effective answer.[74]

* * *

The two jailhouse riots had a number of peculiar features. Both were connected with local political factionalism and the control of underworld activities. Both originated in anger at a Negro accused of rape rather than in a multiplicity of racial conflicts over jobs, income, and housing. Both were stopped before the initial incident could turn into a full-scale violent confrontation between whites and Negroes, although in both, reports circulated that Negroes were ready for such a confrontation. Both were an odd combination of an insurrection against local authority and a "pogrom" against a few Negroes, rather than a true "riot" in which authority would have been ignored and two social groups would have fought squarely against each other.

Probably because of these peculiarities, both the Knoxville and Omaha riots brought forth the response of "more police" more often than the response of "better race relations." Even the NAACP responded to these affairs not in terms of the need for racial equality or civil rights but in terms of the need for more police power in the federal government to punish lynchings. The effectiveness of General Wood in using federal military power to bring white rioters to justice in Omaha could not help but be contrasted with the dénouement in Knoxville, where the would-be lynch mob went scot free.

But the importance of the Knoxville and Omaha riots in confirming national fears of impending "race war" should not be ignored. No one believed that either of the two lynch mobs would have gathered had the accused been white, or that white crimes could have been as easily manipulated as a local political issue as were the alleged crimes by Negroes. That racial tensions provided much of the fuel for these riots no one could deny; but from the peculiar circumstances of these riots came the belief that such tensions could be controlled and kept from violence by sheer police power.

CHAPTER VII

Arkansas: Riot and Response

On October 1, 1919, while federal troops were still guarding Omaha, reports of a Negro insurrection in rural Arkansas broke upon the nation. The town of Elaine was said to be "almost completely surrounded by blacks heavily armed," and southern white sheriffs and politicians called urgently for federal troops to stop the "uprising."[1] Over the next few months and years, a quite different picture began to emerge of what had happened in and near Elaine, and who had initiated the use of violence. What remained constant in the changing Arkansas story, however, was that Negro sharecroppers had determined, like their big-city brethren, to "fight back." And there was also no doubt that the events of October 1 had lit the fuse for a bloody week of racial conflict in Arkansas.

The violence had begun outside a Negro country church in Phillips County in east central Arkansas, just across the Mississippi River from the state of Mississippi. Within the church were meeting a number of sharecroppers who were dissatisfied with the prices they were receiving for cotton sold through the plantation owners and with the prices charged them for supplies bought from the owners. The Negroes had organized a "Progressive Farmers and Household Union of America," and were meeting to plan their campaign of action.[2]

Arkansas whites charged that this organization was planning an "uprising," and in a sense they were undoubtedly right—since a union of sharecroppers that gave

Negroes in rural Arkansas equal bargaining power with whites would have constituted a revolution of sorts, for Arkansas. But the weight of the evidence indicates that it was incorrect to charge that the union was a conspiracy for planning the mass murder of whites in the neighborhood.[3]

As early as 1916, federal investigators in Arkansas reported that "as a result both of the evils inherent in the tenant system and of the occasional oppression by landlords, a state of acute unrest is developing among the tenants and there are clear indications of the beginning cf organized resistance which may result in civil disturbances of a serious character."[4] By 1919, the "organized resistance" had come into existence, in the form of the Progressive Union.

This was a congeries of local groups of Negroes scattered in and around Phillips County. One of the Progressive Union's circulars used a confused combination of union-style rhetoric and biblical quotation, thus:

The time is at hand that all men, all nations and tongues must receive a just reward. This union wants to know why it is that the laborers cannot control their just earnings. . . . Remember the Holy Word, when the Almighty took John up on the mountain. . . . and John said, "I see all nations and tongues coming up before God." Now, we are a nation and a tongue. Why should we be cut off from fair play?

Its rallying song made neither a racial nor a class but an occupational appeal:

> *Your calling was the first on earth—*
> *Organize, oh organize!*
> *And ever since has proved its worth—*
> *Organize, oh organize!*
> *Then come ye farmers, good and true;*
> *The die is cast—it's up to you—*
> *Organize, oh organize!*

Its membership blanks presented an array of federal symbols and required applicants to promise to "defend this government and her constitution at all times."[5]

After a confused series of organizations, reorganizations, and incorporations, a Negro Arkansas farmer named Robert L. Hill emerged as leader of the Progressive Union. He was able to use the kinds of appeal described above—the most "inflammatory" that could be found and cited by a southern newspaper intensely hostile to the union—to encourage several hundred men who could afford a $1.50 initiation fee to join themselves into a loose organization of sharecroppers.

In September 1919, one local group of Progressive Union members asked a white Arkansas-born lawyer named U. S. Bratton to represent them in trying to get a fair settlement of what they owed to and were owed by the owner of their plantation. They had chosen Bratton because he had been an enemy of peonage and its perpetuation through the sharecrop system since 1897, when he had become Assistant United States Attorney. In that position he had pressed an investigation of peonage that resulted in assessment of heavy fines against some guilty planters. After Bratton returned to the private practice of law, Negroes came to him in Little Rock from distant parts of the state, since he was known not to be afraid to take their cases. In 1919, then, his services were requested by sixty-eight Negroes on a single plantation near Ratio in Phillips County. These were sharecroppers who were part of Hill's Progressive Union. On September 30, Bratton sent his son with Hill to talk with the farmers at Ratio and get the details of their complaints.[6]

Meanwhile, a local group of the union near Elaine, ten miles away, had heard that the Ratio group was calling Bratton in and decided to meet at a Hoop Spur church to discuss the possibility of retaining him for themselves

as well.[7] They may also, as a later investigatory committee of white Arkansans said, have discussed plans for
each member to "take a bale of cotton by . . . October 6
. . . to certain prominent land owners, plantation managers and merchants and demand a settlement."[8] The
meeting at Hoop Spur precipitated a bloody week in
Phillips County.

What happened at Hoop Spur? The story differed according to who told the tale. Even in 1919 it was difficult
for an independent investigator to establish the facts, as
one who tried—David Y. Thomas, a professor of history
and political science at the University of Arkansas—discovered.[9]

Whites in Phillips County reported that deputy sheriffs
traveling on a wholly different matter and totally ignorant
of the Progressive Union had stopped because of a punc-
tured tire near the Hoop Spur church at which the local
Progressive Union was meeting; that the deputy sheriffs
were fired upon by guards who feared discovery of the
union's plans to massacre whites; and that the meeting
broke up in a wild attack on the sheriffs' party and other
whites.[10]

Few facts could be found in 1919 by which outsiders
could refute this version. One such fact was that the
Arkansas Gazette and the *New York Times*, in stories
which otherwise accepted the "white" version, reported
that a committee of whites had been set up in Phillips
County two months before, to investigate rumors of a
Negro uprising.[11] So the disclaimers by local whites of
any foreknowledge of the union could be discounted.
David Thomas was skeptical enough about this "white"
version that when the *New York Times* printed both this
and an alternative version more sympathetic to the Negroes, he wrote the *Times* to correct some peripheral mis-
takes in the alternative version, without either denounc-

ing the pro-Negro version as a whole or endorsing the story told by Phillips County's whites. His silence provides the first evidence, negative evidence though it be, that an independent investigation had cast doubt on the "white" version.[12]

But it was only after Negroes had pieced the story together over a matter of months that they were able to supply a coherent alternative explanation and to refute, rather than simply deny, the white version of Hoop Spur. The main points of the "Negro" explanation were that there had been no plans to massacre whites; that information on the Progressive Union's plans to demand accurate accounts from the planters leaked out to the whites and alarmed them into using "every means they could apply" to force Negroes to leave the Union; that on September 30 a fusillade of shots from outside was fired into the Hoop Spur church before any attack had been made upon the whites; and that to destroy the evidence of this unprovoked assault the church was burned next day by a large number of armed white men.[13]

The Negro side of the story is very much strengthened in retrospect by affidavits made in 1921 by two white men, former residents of Helena who had moved to Memphis where they felt free to speak. Both of them were co-workers of the first man killed at Hoop Spur. They testified that when the report of the Hoop Spur shooting came around 2 A.M. on October 1, they had driven to the church and found it had been fired upon.[14] One of them, T. K. Jones, testified that he had talked the next day to a number of white planters who said the whites who had been shot at the church had gone there in order to break up the meeting. "One of these . . . white men," Jones continued, "said to the other that 'I told my negroes about two weeks ago that if they joined that blankety-blank union I would kill every one of them.' "[15]

The other man, H. F. Smiddy, said he had found a large amount of Progressive Union literature in the church, but nothing whatever in it to show a criminal or unlawful purpose. Smiddy also said he had talked with a Negro who had been riding with the white men who had been shot, and the Negro said they had fired upon the church first.[16]

When word got back to Elaine that the Negroes had turned dangerous, rumors of immediate attack flew among the whites. Women and children were put under special guard, and the American Legion was mobilized to patrol the streets and form posses. A large number of whites set out from the county seat, Helena, to scour the hinterland. Whites and Negroes exchanged fire, and although whites claimed the Negroes had been readied and armed, few whites and many Negroes were killed. Hundreds of Negroes were herded back into Helena, charged with murder or arrested as "material witnesses" or "for investigation."[17]

The posses reached Ratio on October 1 while Bratton's son, still ignorant of the whole affair, was discussing with each of about twenty-five Negroes in the Progressive Union the details of his claim upon his landlord, the size of his cotton crop, and the amount of the lawyer's fee to be charged. "While I was engaged in above manner," Bratton's son wrote him, "some of the Negroes announced that there came some men with guns."[18] He went ahead with his work, but some of the Negro women were "pitiful in their abject terror." The Negroes, Bratton explained, knew nothing of events at Hoop Spur and were wholly unprepared for what was shortly to happen to them. "They were simply," he explained, "like a drove of sheep, seeking protection from the thing which they felt

—from present as well as past experience—was about to consume their all."

The younger Bratton wrote that six or eight whites, heavily armed, had then arrested him and taken him to Elaine. He was still assuming that they were merely trying to get him out of the Ratio area, and had still heard nothing of the events at Hoop Spur. But in Elaine he was "met by the citizens en masse, who appeared in a very inflamed state and some of them appeared exceedingly anxious to deal out 'summary justice,' I suppose they termed it." They informed him that he was "the ring leader," and several who appeared to be leading citizens wanted to hang him to a telegraph pole forthwith. He was imprisoned in a brick store in Elaine, which had been chosen as the safest place for the citizens to make their "defense" from. With two Negroes from Ratio, he was chained in the back of the store. Shortly the report came that the Negroes were coming. "I was given a sack of flour and told by a deputy sheriff (and he was a real friend and worried to death for my life) to sit on it if the Negroes began shooting, as they might shoot me through the window," Bratton concluded.

This arrest, since Bratton was thought to be a white accomplice of the Negroes in insurrection, created another sensation. Rumors spread that "socialistic literature, including some written by Emma Goldman," had been found in Bratton's office.[19] By early October, however, the feeling against Bratton was said "to have somewhat diminished" and it was reported that "the papers found in his possession had no direct bearing on the action of the insurgent negroes, although they might have had some influence in that direction."[20] Word reached Governor Charles Brough that Bratton would soon be freed by the Phillips County authorities but that they might not give him "adequate protection from irresponsible persons whose minds have been inflamed against him." So Brough urgently telegraphed the local authorities to ask that Bratton be kept safe, and they promised to "make every effort to protect him."[21]

Meanwhile, the white posses had been keeping up their work. By October 4, according to various reports, five whites and somewhere between twenty-five and several hundred Negroes had been killed.* [22] Four Negro brothers who were medical men and who had achieved a reputation for not truckling to whites were arrested, and when one of them resisted and shot one of his captors, all four were killed.[24] It was reported in the same breath that Negro "desperadoes" had fled into the cane-brakes to resist, and that these "desperadoes" were found to be weaponless when captured.[25] A number of local leaders of the Progressive Union were captured, although Robert Hill's own whereabouts were still unknown.[26]

There can be no doubt that up to this point, the "legitimate violence" used by the state of Arkansas had been directed solely against one side in the racial conflict. Arkansas was, in fact, unique among the 1919 riots in that not a single white man was arrested, except one who was thought to be on the side of the Negroes. Thus the state and local authorities showed not even the degree of neutrality shown by the police of Charleston, Longview, and Washington.

While local whites were in this unneutral way pressing their efforts to smash the union and punish those who had "planned an insurrection," they were partly aided and

---

* George Washington Davis of Pine City, Arkansas, in 1920 told the NAACP that as acting grand secretary of the Negro Masonic Lodge there he had himself paid seventy-three death claims from families of lodge members killed during the riot. Walter White reported that it was simply impossible to tell how many Negroes were killed, but that fifty or sixty was a reasonable estimate.[23]

partly controlled by units of the United States Army. The Army's activities were somewhat more nearly neutral than those of the local posses, but by no stretch of the imagination can the Army be seen as an impartial keeper of the peace in Arkansas.

The Army's intervention was first requested by authorities in Elaine, who, at noon on October 1 wired Governor Charles Brough, "Having race riots here in Elaine and need some soldiers at once." Brough telephoned Secretary of War Newton D. Baker and received authority to call as many troops as necessary.[27] The War Department telegraphed "RUSH" to Camp Pike near Little Rock, Arkansas, that Baker had authorized the governor to call upon them, and ordered the camp to "render any assistance that may be needed with the troops under your command."[28] Meanwhile, messages from Helena asked the governor for "500 troops with machine guns." The request pointed out that "one hundred and seventy-five negro prisoners are expected to arrive at any moment among white men," and said that "presence of troops is earnestly desired on account of the moral effect." It is not clear from these remarks whether the local authorities hoped that the troops would help in tracking down Negro "insurgents," or would protect the prisoners from white lynch mobs, or both.[29]

At Camp Pike, the commanding general was not sure what his orders were; so the troops were prepared but their departure delayed. Twenty officers, four hundred men, medical detachments, and the machine gun battalion were ordered to be ready to move out at short notice.[30] But Arkansas Senator W. S. Kirby telegraphed the Army Chief of Staff that Camp Pike's commander was still refusing to furnish troops without orders from Washington; so Washington had to repeat its orders to Pike to act at once if the governor asked for help.[31] The mix-up worried the War Department so much that on October 3 all military departments in the continental United States were sent the following telegram:[32]

In case of riots, serious disorder or other emergency, requiring the employment of Federal troops . . . you are authorized to take necessary action in cases arising within your department, upon request of legislature, or proper executive when legislature is not in session, without reference to War Department . . . Governors have been advised to apply to you direct.

When the confusion had finally been cleared up, the Army entrained. It arrived in Elaine at 8:15 A.M. on October 2 to find the town in a great state of excitement, with hundreds of white men on the streets, all armed. Colonel Isaac C. Jenks, in command of the troops, ordered everyone in Elaine, white and Negro, disarmed—the first indication that he would be more nearly neutral than the local sheriff. He marched a battalion of men to a canebrake area north of town where heavy firing between whites and Negroes had been reported, lost one of his own men in an attack from this jungle, but found practically all the "colored outlaws" gone. Jenks also learned that practically all work in the fields had ceased, and that the inhabitants of both races were so panicky that women and children had been herded together for safety at a few strong points.[33]

Jenks specified four missions for his troops: guarding outlying areas against Negro attack; searching out Negro "ring leaders" and evidence of their activities; preventing lynchings of Negro prisoners and also of Bratton's son, the only white prisoner; and enabling both whites and Negroes to return to their work. These missions suggest a partly neutral frame of mind, but neither Jenks nor his men seem to have doubted the basic outline of the story with which they were met or to have questioned that their major task was to smash a threatened Negro insurrection. The independence of Jenks's own judgment must be questioned, in the light of his report to headquarters that Negroes in Elaine County were "generally very prosperous," since they could "all find work all the year round" and on the big cotton plantations made "anywhere from five hundred to two thousand dollars a year over and above all living expenses." He could have been told such tales only by the white planters and must not have tried to verify them.[34] As for the troops, they were reported by the *Arkansas Gazette* to be "anxious to get into battle with the blacks—not because they wanted to kill them but because they realized the negroes . . . should be stopped before women and children and more white men should be murdered."* [35]

The troops took several hundred Negroes into custody, examined them, and turned some over for trial while releasing others. Those who were released were given passes "to show that they were law-abiding and reliable."[36] The local white authorities enforced a rule that no Negro would be allowed "to appear upon the streets or work in the fields" without a pass, and the passes were issued only when the Negro's employer would vouch for him.[37] An NAACP investigator reported that this meant that Negroes who owned their own farms or Negroes who would not give their employer or plantation-owner "assurances" and "guarantees" as to work and wages were not released.[38]

The interrogation of prisoners was carried on in the

---

* The accuracy of this report of Army opinion from a newspaper already committed to the "white" view of events might be questioned, except that this news story was sent by Jenks to his superiors as an accurate report of his tour of duty in Elaine. So were other news clippings hereafter noted to be in War Department MSS.

county jail in Helena, under the joint authority of the military, the local officials, and a special Committee of Seven. This committee was formally appointed by Governor Brough, but in reality it had grown out of the earlier secret committee of Phillips County whites to investigate rumors of an uprising. There is no doubt that during these interrogations a number of prisoners confessed to having planned insurrection and murder. But there were serious doubts raised later as to whether these confessions were given voluntarily and were truthful, as the Committee of Seven claimed. The report of Colonel Jenks that during these interrogations the Negroes confessed plans for a massacre of whites is the nearest to independent testimony supporting the committee's claim that the confessions were truthful and voluntary. Yet it must be recalled that on other matters Jenks placidly accepted false information given him by the local whites. He appended no confessions to his report, and it is not clear from his report who actually carried on the questioning of the prisoners.[39] So it is impossible to accept even Jenks as a weighty witness for the "insurrection" theory, which leaned heavily on the confessions.

According to the chairman of the Committee of Seven, several leading Negroes in Helena had been invited to interview the prisoners and review their testimony; but all of them refused.[40] If the offer was in fact made, it may well have been rejected by the Negroes for fear that they would not be able to exercise any independent judgment or to announce a view different from that of the committee. Indeed, the man who said he had made the offer at once went on to say that one of the Negroes to whom he had offered this opportunity had since then "lost the confidence of the white people" because he had "not been square in his dealings" with them but instead had been "secretly urging the Negroes to resent present conditions . . . organized a 'Cook's Union' and told the Negro women to demand that their mistresses use the title of 'Miss' or 'Mrs.' in addressing them."[41] If such peccadilloes could forfeit the "confidence" of Phillips County whites, the historian may well wonder whether any Negro who reviewed the evidence would have been free to deny the "white" version of the "insurrection." Thus the purported offer to let Negroes sift the testimony of the convicted Negro prisoners cannot be taken as evidence, even negative evidence, for the impartiality of the committee's investigation and for the "insurrection" theory.

Moreover, there is some direct evidence concerning the committee's investigation. In a private letter to Mary White Ovington of the NAACP, in which it would have been absurd to overstate the case and mislead those who shared his views,* Bratton claimed to be able to "prove beyond question" that in these interrogations the Negroes "were placed in chairs wherein electricity was applied and they were shocked severely," were whipped, and were otherwise tortured until they confessed.[42] Afterward, several Negroes who had originally confessed reported to the courts of Arkansas and the United States that they had only done so because they had been tortured. For example, one of them testified:[43]

I was frequently whipped with great severity, and was also put into an electric chair and shocked . . . Once they took me upstairs, put a rope around my neck, having me blindfolded, pulled on the rope, and one of them said, "Don't knock the trick [sic] out yet, we can make him tell." . . . As they were taking me to the courtroom, they told me if I changed my testimony or did not testify as I had said, when

* The author has discovered no similar letters from supporters of the "white" version to persons who were fully in their confidence, and to whom they might have been expected to report events with utter freedom.

they took me back they would skin me alive. I testified as they had told me.

Finally, and probably conclusively, the two whites who in 1921 testified about the Hoop Spur incident also testified in full and elaborate detail that the confessions had been extorted. They described how they had with their own hands helped to torture Negroes who had denied all knowledge of an insurrection. Both Smiddy and Jones said not a single Negro prisoner had testified voluntarily to planning or knowing of plans for a massacre, and all had to be told between tortures what it was they must say.[44] Thus the weight of the evidence indicates that the original white version of events in Phillips County was false, and that the Negroes who joined the Progressive Union were not planning a massacre.

The Army's acceptance of the white version of incipient Negro insurrection led to one military sortie that itself created what seemed to be evidence confirming the Army's own original misconception. On orders from Washington, which had heard reports of danger elsewhere in Arkansas, Camp Pike sent an officer to inspect a Negro normal school at Pine Bluff. As suspected, quantities of rifles, automatic pistols, and ammunition were found in the possession of the Reserve Officers Training Corps at the school. Although the ROTC's possession of these arms was normal and legitimate, the army officer removed all bolts from the rifles and turned all ammunition over to the local sheriff, so that not even the slightest chance would remain that Negro insurgents could use the arms. The officer reported that he found no indication of incipient race riots in Pine Bluff, but some local uneasiness over this cache of arms in Negro hands. The uneasiness disappeared after he had acted.[45]

But elsewhere the discovery of ammunition at Pine Bluff was viewed as evidence of sinister preparations.

Authorities in Helena heard of the ammunition from the mayor of Pine Bluff, and at once jumped to the conclusion "that the contemplated uprising was of more than a local nature, possibly planned for the entire South."[46] And then, most ironic of all, the word that the "uprising" was to be more than local convinced the camp commander back at Camp Pike that "in view of the apparent extent of . . . [the Progressive Union] throughout the State . . . and the possibility of sympathetic or pre-arranged outbreaks elsewhere, I quietly strengthened the guard in Little Rock." He added that nothing had happened.[47] Since the whole Pine Bluff Affair had been conjured up out of his own acceptance of a false assumption, it is scarcely surprising that nothing did happen. But to the commander, this happy outcome indicated the success of his own policy.

By October 7, Colonel Jenks was satisfied that most of the ringleaders of the Negro "conspiracy" had been caught, that all prisoners were safe in the hands of the local authorities, and that workaday order had been restored. The county officials agreed, and circularized the area thus:[48]

TO THE NEGROES OF PHILLIPS COUNTY
Helena, Ark. October 7 1919.
The trouble at Hoops Spur and Elaine has been settled. Soldiers now here to preserve order will return to Little Rock within a short time.
No innocent negro has been arrested, and those of you who are at home and at work have no occasion to worry.
All you have to do is to remain at work just as if nothing had happened.
Phillips County has always been a peaceful law abiding community, and its normal conditions must be restored right away.
STOP TALKING! Stay at home—go to work—don't worry!

The next day, all but fifty of the troops returned to Camp

Pike, and prisoners, arms, and ammunition were turned over to local authorities. One week later, the final detachment withdrew.[49]

Their withdrawal left the local authorities with one embarrassing problem: the disposition of O. S. Bratton, the lawyer's son and assistant, who had been arrested while gathering information on the complaints of Negroes at Ratio. He had been held in the Helena jail, and on October 3 was protected by soldiers against a mob of 200 would-be lynchers. After the Army left he was told repeatedly by the sheriff "not to worry," that there was nothing against him but public opinion, and the authorities would keep him safe. After spending thirty days in jail with no charge placed against him, young Bratton was finally released through the back door, and with the connivance of the judge was helped to escape from Helena.[50] When a second son of Bratton's, Guy, went back to Helena to talk with the prosecuting attorney, he was told that the prosecutor "would have been run out of the county himself" had he not been prepared to press the cases against Bratton and the Negro insurrectionists. John E. Miller, the prosecutor, told Guy Bratton that strong pressure from the Committee of Seven and the mob had forced him to pretend to prosecute, but that he knew the charges were groundless and would pass the cases over to the next term of court and then drop them.[51] Guy Bratton's report did not make clear whether this attitude applied only to the Brattons (for not just one member but the whole family was being publicly attacked) or to the alleged Negro insurrectionists as well. But from the evidence of how the two sets of cases were treated, Miller was willing to abandon only the Bratton case. The case against them was allowed to lapse, and they were not only encouraged to leave Arkansas but forced to do so by economic pressures and threats of violence.[52] The Negroes, on the other hand, were tried and convicted.

The management of these cases, including the power to decide which to prosecute, was put in the hands of the Committee of Seven. This group included the sheriff, acting sheriff, and county judge of Phillips County, the mayor of Helena, and three prominent white businessmen. The chairman was E. M. Allen, a real estate dealer, president of the Helena Business Men's League, and treasurer of the Gerard B. Lambert Company.[53] The owner of this company was a St. Louis manufacturer who also owned a 21,000-acre cotton plantation near Elaine on which 750 Negroes were sharecroppers. He himself came to Arkansas and sat in on some of the sessions of the Committee of Seven.[54] It was the committee that conducted the investigation of the Elaine Affair and informed the press that the Progressive Union had planned an insurrection, they who dominated the grand jury that met to bring indictments against the Negroes, and they who were later accused of having permitted torture to be used to extract confessions.[55] The Seven made clear later that they had prevented sheer mob lynchings of the Negroes by promising the citizenry "that the law would be carried out" upon the prisoners.[56]

The courts fulfilled the committee's promise with vigor and dispatch. Of 143 men held by the Seven until October 28, 21 were discharged, and the rest were indicted in wholesale lots. The grand jury met only three days to hear testimony and in its peak performance, on October 30, indicted 73 Negroes. By November 3 these men were standing trial.[57]

Their attorneys were appointed by the court from the local bar, without any questioning of the Negroes as to whether they had their own counsel or what lawyers they might like to choose. None of the lawyers asked for a change of venue, though Helena's heat against the prisoners was high. None of the attorneys challenged the all-white juries, none asked for more time to prepare a defense (although they had not previously talked with most of the defendants), none challenged the use of confessions and evidence later claimed to have been obtained by torture.[58]

The first six men to face the jury produced no defense witnesses and did not take the stand themselves. They were convicted partly on the testimony of several other Negroes that the defendants had formed and commanded a "column" of Progressive Union members on October 1 to "help them people at Hoop Spur out," and that one of them had fired at a deputy sheriff. A member of the sheriff's posse testified to the deputy's death by gunfire, but not to the origin of the fire. The mayor of Elaine testified that "in statements made to himself and other white men" by Frank Hicks, one of the Progressive Union leaders, Hicks had told of killing the deputy. Hicks pleaded not guilty, but was not asked by his attorney to explain the discrepancy between his plea and the claimed confession.

He was convicted of first-degree murder after seven minutes of deliberation by the jury. The other five men were convicted of first-degree murder in aiding and abetting him, after eight minutes of deliberation by the jury. The convictions of all six took less than a full day at court, and the press announced that "the same steady grind will be continued until all the insurrection cases have been disposed of."[59]

Five more men were convicted of first-degree murder the next day, all of them within minutes after the jury left the courtroom. Then a series of charges of "night riding," second-degree murder, and other offenses were heard against the remaining Negroes. Thirty-seven in

one day were sentenced to prison for terms ranging from
five to twenty-one years. One acquittal was ordered by
the judge. On November 18, the last conviction of first-
degree murder was registered in the case of Ed Ware. He
took the stand and denied firing any shots at the Hoop
Spur church where he was charged with murder. He was
convicted by the jury in four minutes after a trial of two
hours and five minutes.[60]

All twelve men convicted of first-degree murder were
sentenced to death.[61]

Protests about these trials were heard almost at once,
but as far as Phillips County was concerned, the "insurrection" was over. The local legal and political authorities, the local businessmen and large planters, the state
incarnate in the governor, and even the United States
Army had combined to put down trouble. They had
turned a challenge to the power of white landholders
into an opportunity to show how effective sheer physical
force could be if it operated with legal sanction. For they
had rejected the lynch system and controlled the mob,
in order to show that the sheriff, the Army, and the courts
could do the job even better. As matters stood in November 1919, the whites of Arkansas had proved their case.
Suppression could work, even against Negroes who
wanted to "fight back," if suppression had the proper
aura of respectability and legality.

But even legal suppression could not restore to Arkansas the apathetic and the hopeless Negro that had been
its mudsill for a generation. In December, a "white moderate" recoiled with horror at the militance still expressed
by Negroes in the state. "I spoke at a negro conference
last Sunday night at Hot Springs," he reported. "The negro who spoke before me had much to say about freedom
and the crowd was deeply stirred. I spoke of duty and
Christian discipleship and got no response." He glumly

summed up, "Any negro today who wishes to stir his
people to uprising can easily do it."[62] The fighting-back
spirit had not died, although the fighting itself was over.

* * *

The Arkansas riot brought from Americans outside the
state a series of reactions that ran the gamut from alarm
at the nightmare of a black rebellion to anger at the reported system of Negro peonage.

The first responses were heavily influenced by the early
reports that plans for a Negro insurrection had been un-
covered. Many of them emphasized the belief that Negroes were a childlike people who had been cruelly
hoaxed by wily agitators. Thus a Mississippian who
came to examine the riot area told the press, "It is the
same old story of a bad leader exploiting and hoodwink-
ing the negro race for mercenary purposes."[63] A Louisiana paper reminded its readers of John Brown's attempt
at fomenting Negro insurrection and wondered whether
"racial prejudice" among Negroes explained their being
"misled by men from the North who get them into trouble."[64] But it was not only Southerners who took this
view. The *New York Sun* remarked that Negroes had until after the war "simply but soundly" resisted the efforts
of "Reds and enemy agents" to sap their loyalty, but that
since the war they had more often fallen prey to agitators. But, the *Sun* pointed out, the Arkansas incident
showed "the incapacity of the Southern rural negro for a
mass uprising on his own initiative."[65] By assuming the
passivity and incapacity of Negroes, these reports tended
to support the view that Negroes belonged in a subordinate place in society.

Another immediate reaction to the widespread reports
of insurrection was a demand for stronger police measures. "All persons who preach any sort of class strife in

this country are traitors [and] should be deprived of their power of evil," one editor wrote.[66] Another applauded the vigor with which the United States Army had intervened to check further riots in Elaine.[67] And as in the wake of the Washington riot, some citizens believed that the police power would be strengthened if the sale of firearms were prohibited.[68]

Those who did not accept the tale of insurrection in Arkansas reacted differently. Some of them asked for a congressional investigation to find out what had happened.[69] Others were aroused by news reports of the trials that Arkansas accorded the accused Negroes. These people concentrated on demanding fairer treatment for Negroes in the courts. One Negro editor asked the NAACP to intervene in the court cases but expressed doubt that its staff would dare brave the "jungles" of Arkansas.[70] A Baltimore paper commented, "If there is one infamy more damnable than another it is the infamy of the Elaine trials in excess of the infamy of the Elaine butchery of Negroes."[71] Mass meetings were held in New York and Philadelphia to protest the trials.[72] The Socialist Party of New York, a Massachusetts senator, a Negro insurance agent in Memphis, and an editor of *The Survey* typified those persons across the country who thought the Arkansas convictions unjust.[73] Indeed, concern over the trials seems to have been the most widespread response among articulate people who were involved in political thought and action.

The demand for fair trials for the accused Negroes was sometimes simply an insistence that the police power act impartially. From some quarters came demands not for impartiality but for efforts by the state to advance racial equality; thus several papers commented that Arkansas' remarks about the inability of Negroes to read or write indicated "some lack in the schools of that locality," a lack which Arkansas should quickly correct.[74] Several socialist newspapers demanded an end to the entire system of Negro peonage or semi-peonage that they saw exemplified in Phillips County.[75] Approval for the Progressive Union was voiced by several Northerners who felt that it represented "an encouraging awakening" by southern Negroes to "legitimate opportunity" and to the means of "defense of their rights by legal means."[76]

An even more radical position was taken by some Negro editors who supported the Arkansas Negroes who resorted to arms in self-defense. "Can anybody wonder," asked one editor, "that some Colored people, hiding for their lives in the woods, and not knowing the Governor of Arkansas from their other enemies, fired at him and his auto party when they passed along the road?"[77] Those who approved of Negroes' fighting back were especially critical of the actions of the Army in disarming Negroes.[78]

These reactions across the country indicated the direction in which further resolution of the Arkansas riot would come. For the concern with fair trials—far stronger than the reaction to local trials held after the other 1919 riots—indicated that legal challenges to the convictions of Negro "insurrectionists" would be forthcoming. Such challenges did indeed occur, and the aftermath of the Arkansas riot was a series of dramas played out in court.

CHAPTER VIII

Arkansas: The Riot Adjudicated

Negroes were still being hunted down in Arkansas and their plan for "insurrection" was still being told to horrified white readers all over America when the NAACP's headquarters in New York began to check on the situation with its own sources. The NAACP's investigation was ultimately to lead it to undertake a long struggle in the courts against the death sentences imposed on the "insurrectionists."

The NAACP's investigation began with letters to knowledgeable southern Negroes like Robert R. Church, Jr., of Memphis, a leading Republican politician. Questions about the four Negro brothers who were killed by a sheriff's posse, about the Progressive Farmers and Household Union, and about the Arkansas situation in general brought answers that convinced the NAACP an on-the-spot investigation would be worthwhile. Church wrote Walter F. White, assistant secretary of the NAACP, that the published reports of a barely averted massacre of whites "were too ridiculous to be given any thought," and he saw the Negroes' demand for legal help in settling their accounts as the precipitating factor in the trouble.[1]

With this report in mind, White determined to investigate the Phillips County bloodshed at first hand. Although a Negro by social definition, White was physically indistinguishable from any white man and so thought he might be able to nose out information that no recognizable Negro could in Arkansas. He realized, however, that there would be great danger if his identity were discovered, especially since he remembered the beating that had recently been given another NAACP staff worker on a similar mission in Texas.[2]

White left October 9, after arranging a "cover identity" as a white reporter by getting authorization from the *Chicago Daily News* to write an article on the events in Arkansas.[3] He had hoped to stop off in Washington to talk with officials of the Justice Department about reports of IWW involvement in the Arkansas riot, but postponed that meeting.[4] He did stop off in Memphis to be briefed by Church. There he worked out plans for his investigations in Phillips County and set a check going on the business connections of the Committee of Seven so as to assess "whether they are connected in the exploitation of Negro labor."[5]

White did not spend much time in Phillips County itself. He left Memphis on October 10 and on October 13 spent several hours in Little Rock with Governor Brough, who thought he was a white man and "one of the most brilliant reporters he had ever met." Brough gave White a letter of introduction to smooth his way in Phillips County. But after a short and useful stay there, spent interviewing whites, he learned that his true identity had been discovered and a lynching party was being planned. He left town in a hurry, just minutes ahead of the lynchers, and returned to New York October 17, greatly relieved at getting out safely from what he called "the most dangerous situation in which I have been."[6] He turned at once to writing his article for the *Chicago Daily News*.[7]

The report White issued, both to the *Daily News* and as an NAACP press release, claimed that the violence in Arkansas had been mostly white attacks upon Negroes rather than Negro attacks upon whites; that it was not clear whether the initial shootings at Hoop Spur had been started by whites or Negroes; and that at the root of the riots lay "systematic robbery of Negro tenant farmers and sharecroppers." Without quoting U. S. Bratton, whom he met in Little Rock, White drew upon his knowledge of particular Negro grievances to document his charge of "robbery."[8]

There was a wide response to this report by White contradicting the official and widely publicized report of a Negro insurrection. Many Negro newspapers carried a story from the Associated Negro Press to the effect that an anonymous NAACP correspondent in Arkansas who looked white had said that "there was no conspiracy or uprising of Negroes in Arkansas but rather a pogrom of sorts by whites against the Negroes."[9] Several southern papers attacked the NAACP's report, one of them calling the NAACP "an organization in New York that is doing much hurt and harm to the colored race."[10]

One long discussion of the events in Arkansas between E. M. Allen of the Committee of Seven in Helena and a Negro educator at Hampton Institute originated from the NAACP report. The Hampton teacher wrote Allen hinting that perhaps "some additional facts" might have come to light supporting Walter White's version of the Arkansas riots. Allen wrote back that he had read White's article but had been "unable to find that he ever came to Helena." He added that "the leading negroes here who have cooperated with us in this matter state that neither White nor any other representative of his Association has been in Helena since October first . . . [or] has ever been in Elaine." Allen denied that more than scattered cases of exploitation of Negroes had occurred in the South and insisted that freely given confessions showed an insurrection and massacre had been planned. He ended by saying that Dr. E. C. Morris, a leading Negro Baptist minister and president of the National Baptist Convention, would "verify everything I have said."[11]

Allen's letter was passed on to Robert R. Moton, the president of Tuskegee Institute, who wrote Morris and was told that Morris did not at all agree with Allen's view of the riot. "I cannot see how . . . [Allen] could have known the facts about the Elaine matter when he was fully eighteen miles from the scene of the riot," Morris wrote, and concluded: "I have never believed that the Negroes at Elaine had planned to murder the white planters and take their lands."[12]

Meanwhile, Walter White heard about the correspondence with Allen. White told the Hampton teacher who had started the quest for information that Bratton's story of conditions in rural Arkansas supported White's argument. But it could not be released for fear of endangering Bratton's life. Anyway, White wrote, "you are familiar with the South and you no doubt know of the vicious exploitation which exists and which the Arkansas authorities are attempting to cover up . . . I feel it is not necessary to convince you any further." White also directly accused some of the Committee of Seven of denying the NAACP reports because as plantation owners they directly profited "from the policy of obscurantism."[13]

In addition to seeking a public audience for his findings in Arkansas, White let the Department of Justice know what he had learned and what Bratton knew of the situation.[14] He also appealed quietly to several members of Congress to ask for a committee investigation of the riots.[15] The NAACP arranged for Bratton, a former Assistant United States Attorney, to come north in order to meet with government officials, both executive and congressional, to present his information and press his views. The Justice Department then telegraphed its agents at Little Rock to investigate the trouble at Helena "with particular reference to the case of the son of Mr. Bratton and the exploitation of Negroes." On Capitol Hill, Senator Charles Curtis responded to Bratton's story by asking that he dictate a full account and have eight copies made for circulation in Congress.[16]

The NAACP continued to try to find out what had happened and was happening in Arkansas. Its chairman, Mary White Ovington, wrote a lady recommended to her by a member of the Intercollegiate Socialist Society to try to learn whether the Progressive Union was an organization for united economic action by the sharecroppers, or a grandiose scheme by which Robert Hill expected to bilk sharecroppers of their cash. No reply survives.[17] White tried through intermediaries and without mentioning names to reach Hill, who had gone into hiding, but was unable to get him to come to New York.[18] White also asked Scipio A. Jones, an Arkansas Negro lawyer who was to become a constant associate of the NAACP in pressing the Elaine cases, for information to be used in publicity on the riot.[19] Herbert Seligmann, another member of the NAACP staff, asked Dr. E. C. Morris for his view of what had occurred.[20] Still another staff man asked for information from a Negro who like Morris was *persona grata* with Arkansas whites, President Joseph A. Booker of Arkansas Baptist College. Booker wrote that there was no doubt that the convicted Negroes had been given false trials on forced testimony.[21] But most of the NAACP's information on Arkansas continued to come through Bratton,[22] until April 1920, when a Tuskegee sociologist-historian, Monroe Work, sent a report that independently confirmed Bratton's and White's views of this situation.[23]

As news came in from Arkansas about the swift trials of

the Negroes charged with murder and insurrection, the NAACP stepped up its attempt to get a congressional investigation. Identical letters to George Wickersham, Charles Evans Hughes, William Howard Taft, Elihu Root, and Will Hays called on them, each as "a leader of American opinion . . . and a leader in the Republican party to which Negroes of America still look for protection of their fundamental rights," to speak for an investigation.[24] Wickersham wrote Senators Frank P. Kellogg and James W. Wadsworth that if the NAACP's facts were right "common humanity" demanded an investigation.[25]

The NAACP also issued a public appeal for Congress to look into the Phillips County trials,[26] and then wrote an open letter to President Wilson asking that he press an investigation through the executive branch.[27] An Assistant Attorney-General replied that the Federal Bureau of Investigation (FBI) was looking into the problem.[28] But privately the NAACP staff believed that because of "numerous difficulties in Washington with an adverse Administration"[29] and because concern over "the League of Nations and Peace Treaty" made it "almost impossible to get any action on any other matter,"[30] it was unlikely that any official investigation would be made. In the sense in which they meant it—a public inquiry to get all the facts before the American people—they were right, though the FBI did watch over the Arkansas cases for years.[31]

Cursory studies of the Arkansas riot were made by Congress. In January 1920, a brief hearing was held by the Judiciary Committee of the House of Representatives on a bill by Congressman Leonidas Dyer, a Missouri Republican, to make lynching a federal crime; and in that hearing some testimony was given about the Arkansas affair.[32] Shortly afterward, the Senate Judiciary

Committee met and heard testimony from Bratton.[33] But no extended study was made of the sort that had been done after the East St. Louis race riot of 1917.

Efforts by the NAACP to arouse public concern over the trials in Arkansas continued. W.E.B. Du Bois, editor of the Association's magazine, *The Crisis*, indignantly answered an article in the *New York World* that repeated the version of events put forward by the Committee of Seven.[34] White sent an article on the riot and the trials to the *New Republic*, where it was rejected, and to *The Nation*, where it was printed and won praise from the renowned critic, author, and editor H. L. Mencken.[35] Copies of the article were distributed to 5000 of the NAACP's mailing list, in order to arouse interest in freeing the convicted Negroes.[36]

The chief work of the NAACP, in the Elaine affair, however, was not public propaganda about Arkansas but a four-year campaign in the courts to protect the Negroes who had been accused of insurrection. That campaign included both the NAACP's efforts to save Robert Hill from being tried in Arkansas, and efforts to reverse the convictions of these Negroes who had already been tried.

The NAACP's work to protect Hill began in January 1920, when he was discovered hiding in Topeka, Kansas, and Arkansas requested his extradition. The national office of the NAACP telegraphed Governor Henry Allen of Kansas asking him to deny extradition until an attorney could be retained and a hearing held.[37] At the same time, the Association staff asked Hugh Fisher, the county attorney of Topeka, to act as Hill's counsel. His name had been suggested by United States Senator Arthur Capper of Kansas, a member of the NAACP's board of directors.[38] Fisher took the case without compensation and arranged for three Negro lawyers in Topeka to work on the case under his direction. What he and the NAACP set out to do was to prove that Hill was not guilty of the crimes alleged against him but could not receive a fair trial in Arkansas, and hence should not be returned there.[39]

Hill had two sets of charges to meet. One set was being pressed by the state of Arkansas, and alleged that by advising and planning a massacre of white planters he was an accessory before the fact in the murders for which twelve Negroes had already been sentenced to death. The second set was a federal charge, brought by the United States Attorney in Arkansas, of impersonating a federal officer in order to recruit Negro sharecroppers into the Progressive Union. Fisher managed to have the state charges taken up first, since it would be easier initially to persuade Governor Allen that Hill could not get a fair trial in the Arkansas state courts than it would be to persuade the Federal District Court in Kansas that Hill could not get a fair trial in the Federal District Court for Arkansas. If the governor refused extradition, his decision might weigh on Hill's side when the federal judge in Kansas considered whether to remand Hill for trial in Arkansas.[40]

Thus Fisher concentrated on convincing Governor Allen. He asked the NAACP for statistics showing "the large acreage owned by the few [in Arkansas] and upon which the colored man must toil at the mercy of these land speculators." Fisher knew that Allen was very much interested in a program to assist farm tenants to own their own land.[41] Fisher also arranged for U. S. Bratton to talk privately with the governor, to explain how a southern white man saw the situation in Arkansas.[42] James Weldon Johnson of the NAACP staff conferred with the governor, too, and reported he was convinced of the existence of peonage in Arkansas and of the difficulty in getting a fair trial there, but had still not been able to clear up the intentions of the Progressive Union.[43] The NAACP went to work at once to get copies of the union's literature for the governor.[44]

The only setback in the NAACP's campaign to convince the governor to refuse Hill's extradition was suffered when three Arkansas Negroes added their names to a request that Hill be returned for trial. The three were members of a biracial Commission on Race Relations that the governor of Arkansas had appointed in November 1919, with himself as chairman. They were Joseph A. Booker, the president of Arkansas Baptist College; Bishop J. M. Conner of the African Methodist Episcopal Church; and James M. Cox, president of Philander Smith College.* [45]

Their request for Hill's extradition greatly distressed the NAACP, which wrote to ask why they had signed it. Two of them wrote back to explain that Arkansas' Governor Brough, the state attorney-general, and "other prominent white citizens" had promised Hill would have a fair trial. A fair trial, they explained, would prove to the world that the Progressive Union had planned no massacre and that the previous trials in Phillips County had been false and forced. "We all further believe," Cox wrote, "that Hill's trial will do more than anything else to show the innocence of the other men." And Booker added, "We must play checkers fast, if we would save their lives." In desperation Cox concluded with "a plea for the sanity of the five hundred thousand Negroes of the state; for if we believed, as some other Negroes be-

---

* The commission itself had met only once or twice, had urged that every avenue be opened for review of the Phillips County convictions by the Supreme Court of Arkansas but that northern Negroes and their sympathizers stay out of the affair, and had then dropped out of sight.[46]

lieve, that Arkansas is a regular hell and that nowhere
in the state can the Negro get justice in the courts, we
would be the biggest fools possible to remain here."[47]

The NAACP staff replied sympathetically and carefully that Negroes in the North and South lived under
different conditions and no doubt must act differently.[48]
For its part, the NAACP moved quickly to counter any
effect the request for extradition might have had on
Governor Allen. The national headquarters asked every
branch in the country to write Allen that Hill should not
be extradited, and that Arkansas Negroes who thought
he should be were probably subject to local pressures.[49]

Whether such letters helped influence Allen or not, on
March 23, 1920, the governor announced that he would
not accede to Arkansas' request for Hill. He gave no
reasons for refusing, but Fisher told the NAACP that in
the hearing before the governor, Arkansas' attorney-general had become so rattled under Fisher's questioning
that he had "helped prove our case of feeling and prejudice in Arkansas."[50]

The battle shifted at once to the federal courts where
Hill was under indictment for impersonating a federal
officer.[51] What the NAACP most feared was that if Hill
were returned to Arkansas for federal trial he could be
arrested on the state charges, and convicted in state
court, even if he were found not guilty on the federal
charge.[52] For that reason, when the federal judge ordered Hill's removal to Arkansas he added the condition
that if Hill were acquitted in federal court he must be
returned at once to Kansas. Indeed, the judge demanded
that the federal judge in the district of Arkansas approve
this arrangement beforehand.[53]

Fisher and the NAACP considered appealing this removal order on the grounds that the judge should have
gone further, examined the sufficiency of the evidence,

and quashed the indictment against Hill for lack of sufficient evidence. But the judge threatened to drop his condition protecting Hill if an appeal were pressed; so Fisher reluctantly agreed to accept the arrangement as originally proposed.[54]

Before Hill could be sent back to Arkansas, however, the Justice Department in Washington reconsidered its case for prosecuting him. Attorney-General A. Mitchell Palmer let the defense know that evidence of irresistible prejudice in Arkansas would bring some reassessment of the case. If proof were given that U. S. Bratton had been forced to leave Arkansas because of his attempts to practice law on behalf of Negroes, the case against Hill would be dropped.[55] The NAACP asked Bratton for his testimony.[56] He replied from his new home in Detroit that his clients in Arkansas had been intimidated and he himself had been threatened with death.[57] Affidavits were also collected from lawyers who had heard Arkansas' attorney-general admit that Bratton's son had nearly been lynched and had been jailed for thirty days without being charged with any crime.[58]

The NAACP's chief staff official, Walter White, took these affidavits and other material about Arkansas to Washington, in the hope of persuading the Justice Department to drop the charges against Hill. White met first with Senator Arthur Capper of Kansas and got a letter of introduction and approval from him. Then White persuaded some high officials in the Justice Department that the case against Hill was at best flimsy. They demanded from the United States Attorney at Little Rock all evidence against Hill, to be forwarded to Washington for review. If this review should show the evidence to be as weak as the NAACP believed, the case would be dropped.[59]

It took another five months for the Justice Department

to change its mind and act upon the change, but that is what it ultimately did. In November 1920, the Attorney-General ordered the case against Hill dismissed, and he was freed from all charges—at least as long as he stayed in Kansas, since its governor had refused to extradite him on the state of Arkansas' charges. For fear that another governor might act differently, the NAACP dropped plans to have Hill tour the North as a speaker and money-raiser.[60]

Thus the NAACP brought the Hill case to a conclusion that was relatively early and easy, compared to the more troublesome cases of Negroes already convicted by the state of Arkansas. The result achieved with Hill demonstrated that it was possible for an organization of determined whites and Negroes to bring to bear the money, brains, and political influence necessary to redress the one-sided police enforcement of Arkansas. By its actions in the Hill case the federal government demonstrated that although its first responses through the Army and its prosecuting attorney in Little Rock had supported Arkansas' position, its second and third thoughts constrained it to a degree of impartiality unknown to the local authorities.

In its efforts to defend the Negroes already imprisoned or sentenced to death in Arkansas, the NAACP had a much more difficult problem. To begin with, the Association found that the use of its name would be a major liability in Arkansas, and decided to keep its role in the cases carefully hidden for fear that Arkansas whites would react with fury to its name.[61]

In mid-November of 1919, the NAACP took its first steps to arrange new counsel for the twelve men who were scheduled to die December 27 and January 2.[62] On Bratton's advice, they made contact with George W. Murphy, a white man, a Democrat, and a former attorney-general of Arkansas who was said to be both highly honored in the state and "very liberal on the Negro question."[63] Simultaneously, the Association tried to reduce its commitment to the defense of Negroes charged with crime in the Chicago riot, explaining to its representative there that Arkansas was a more serious and potentially far more expensive situation.[64] On November 24, the NAACP Board approved an agreement with Murphy's law firm, Murphy and McHaney, to pay $1000 at once and another $2000 later for the services of the firm and any lawyers it wished to associate with it in appealing the cases of the convicted Negroes "up to but not including the Supreme Court of the United States."[65]

The need to keep the NAACP's involvement quiet and Murphy's insistence on dealing only with Arkansans caused many of the arrangements with Murphy to be made through Bratton. This proliferation of secondhand agents and semi-secret contacts, together with the creation in Arkansas of a local fund-raising group, created a good deal of confusion, jealousy, and suspicion between different groups over who should get credit for raising money and who would get the money to spend.[66]

The NAACP began to raise funds for the Murphy defense on November 26, asking that its branches send ten to twenty-five dollars apiece, to be raised quietly from friends or voted from the branch treasuries rather than gathered in a general appeal.[67] The national office made its own quiet appeals to such sources of money as the New York Foundation and wealthy individuals who could hold "parlor meetings."[68]

In Arkansas, Murphy took on a Negro lawyer, Scipio A. Jones, to help him in the case. Governor Charles Brough's biracial Commission on Race Relations urged new trials for the Elaine rioters.[69] In early January, its Negro members decided to form a local fund-raising group to support the defense of the Elaine defendants.[70] This group claimed to have retained Scipio Jones as counsel for the convicted Negroes, and to have arranged for Jones to bring Murphy into the case.[71] It was the conflicting claims of this group and the NAACP that made difficulties through much of the court fight.

Because of the confusion and suspicion that began to grow, the NAACP took steps to watch over the lawyers it was secretly paying. Evidently two bits of information from Arkansas shocked the staff. One was a warning from Bratton that Scipio Jones and his partner Thomas Price had no idea that the NAACP was paying Murphy's fee. Bratton added that he had "talked with a number of leading Colored People" in Arkansas and found them, "the ministers in particular . . . not much in sympathy" with the NAACP, because the governor and other eminent southern whites were hostile to the Association. The second piece of information was a letter from Price himself, asking the NAACP to help the legal defense with the definite implication that it was not already doing so.[72]

The staff wrote Robert Church of Memphis, who had earlier acted as White's first informant on events in Arkansas, to ask him to keep an eye on Murphy and to let Jones and Price know orally what the NAACP had done. As James Weldon Johnson explained,[73]

We do not want Mr. Price to "gum up" the case. We do not know how good a lawyer he is. But if Colonel Murphy wishes Price or any other lawyer to associate with him in the case, that is all right with us. You can see there is a possibility of some colored lawyer's going off on a tangent to raise money and, of course, to figure in the cases, thereby messing up the whole matter. We want to avoid that just now.

We do not want any publicity in the Arkansas matter till we are out of the woods. If we save these men, we will flood the country with publicity on what we have done, but publicity now will not help us and will only hurt them.

In the spring of 1920, the NAACP's doubts increased as the secrecy imposed on the defense arrangements continued, and as the Citizens Defense Fund created by the Arkansas Negroes issued statements claiming all credit for the continuing defense.[74] Thus a set of expense accounts filed with the NAACP by some Negro lawyers was almost repudiated on the ground that no work had been done until it was discovered that "most of the work was really done by white men who would not permit their names to be used and the names of Negroes were substituted."[75]

The defense was thrown into further difficulties by the death of Murphy in October 1920. Several Negroes in Arkansas, together with Bratton, felt that Murphy's partners were too interested in moving ahead in the white community to press an unpopular case vigorously. But a change of attorneys would have cost the NAACP a new fee beyond the one it had already committed itself to pay the firm of Murphy and McHaney. So no change of firm was made, and from then on Scipio Jones took a more clearly leading role in the defense.[76]

Other flare-ups in the NAACP's relations with the Citizens Defense Fund came in March and September, 1921. In March, another public accounting by the Fund that slighted NAACP involvement finally stirred the NAACP into making its own role in the Arkansas cases public.[77] In September, the law firm asked for more money.[78] Despite all these clashes, however, the legal cases themselves suffered little apparent damage.

The legal fight in Arkansas had begun almost as soon as the swift series of trials in Helena had ended. At the request of his Commission on Race Relations, in late November of 1919, Governor Brough made it clear that he would if necessary stay the executions to allow appeals to be heard.[79]

On December 20, Murphy and Jones filed a motion with Phillips County Circuit Court for new trials for the men sentenced to die. The motion argued that the mob atmosphere dominated the entire trial; that no effective legal counsel was available to the accused; that their grand and petit juries were wholly made up of white men, by designed and deliberate exclusion of Negroes; that they were tortured to give false confessions; and that they were not informed of the charges against them in proper time. The motion for a new trial was denied on December 21, and the planned executions were automatically halted by filing of an appeal to Arkansas' Supreme Court.[80]

The appeal was argued in March, on the grounds listed in the motion for a new trial and on one other: that six of the twelve men had been incorrectly found "guilty as charged" by the jury instead of "guilty of murder in the first degree as charged."[81] It was this argument that on March 29 won reversal of these six convictions by the Arkansas Supreme Court, which ordered new trials for the group of six men that included the defendant Ed Ware.[82] But in examining the other six cases, the state Supreme Court said that the issue of an all-white jury had been raised too late in the proceedings to be cause for reversal, that the record showed a hasty trial but not one lacking in the formal guarantees of fairness, and that it would not look beyond the record. So the group of six headed by Frank Moore had their convictions upheld.[83]

From this point on the fates of the two sets of Arkansas defendants, six to each set, branched off. Both won their liberty in 1923, but by different routes.

Murphy was convinced that ultimately for the Moore group, and probably for all twelve men, he would have to resort to habeas corpus proceedings in federal court. But he wanted to hold habeas corpus for a last defense, and first to try applying for a writ of certiorari to the United States Supreme Court. This writ would have meant a review of the state court's findings as to the constitutionality of the conviction. But the request for certiorari was a form of appeal in which the Supreme Court could simply refuse to hear the merits argued, for reasons of convenience, time, or negative judgment of probable outcome.[84] The Moore cases were appealed in this fashion to the United States Supreme Court, but in October 1920 the Court refused certiorari and left these men open to possible execution.[85]

Meanwhile, the six Ware cases had gone back to Phillips County for retrial. Murphy "was taken violently ill, very near dying," just as these cases came to trial; and was unable to manage cross-examinations of white witnesses. He had thought he could show that "when that negro society was organized, the planters, of whom the sheriff was one, determined to break it up, to prevent meetings by terrorizing members, by shooting into their meetings, and organized, for that purpose, a meeting or committee rather, which they called a committee of safety or defense, which, immediately after the trouble, they converted into what they called a committee of investigation." Then, Murphy continued, the white planters "incarcerated all the negro men of the order, except the few unprincipled ones they could get to testify for them . . . and by torturing them, the negroes, forced them to confess guilt and falsely testify against others." But Murphy's illness prevented him from bringing out what he felt were the facts, and all he was able to accomplish was establishing at the right point in the pro-

ceedings the racial discrimination involved in selection
of the jury.[86]

On this ground of discrimination in choosing the jury,
a new appeal went to the state Supreme Court in November 1920.[87] In early November, therefore, six cases
had moved toward the execution of the death sentence
originally set, and six were in doubt. A movement was
launched to ask the governor to commute the death sentences, and a counter-movement tried to persuade him
not to budge.[88] The chief argument put forward on behalf of mercy was that the "mastermind" of the Elaine
"insurrection," Robert Hill, had escaped all punishment,
and that men who were merely his dupes should not be
executed.[89] The chief argument for carrying out the
death sentences, as the Committee of Seven explained,
was that Phillips County had refrained from lynching
only because the people were promised that "the law
would be carried out." Thus clemency would break the
promise and encourage lawlessness in the future.[90]

Governor Brough responded by adopting the position
of the Committee of Seven. He proclaimed that he would
allow the death sentences to be executed to fulfill the
promise made to Phillips County, in the absence of any
reason to believe the Negroes less guilty than they were
adjudged. Brough went on to say that the "misrepresentation" by the northern press of facts connected with the
Elaine "insurrection" would not deter him. And he made
a special point of "the fact that every business, civic, and
other organization in the [Phillips County] community"
had opposed clemency.[91]

Scipio Jones accused the governor of issuing his statement in order to influence the Arkansas Supreme Court
to deny the appeals before it.[92] In any case, the court
was not so influenced. On December 6, it reversed the
six Ware cases on the ground that "the discrimination of

the jury commissioners against the colored race in the
selection of the petit jury . . . rendered the selection illegal to the applicants." Thus the Ware cases were again
remanded for retrial.[93] This reversal was the first rebuke
by any court to the one-sidedness with which the Phillips
County police system had operated. It meant that in at
least one area of procedure—the selection of a jury—the
police system would have to act impartially if its decisions were to be considered legitimate.

This reversal of six convictions stymied for the moment the governor's plans to let the execution of the
other six men go forward. One white Arkansas newspaper reported that the governor would probably delay
until the six Ware cases were finally decided.[94] A delay
was granted; but in the spring of 1921, a new governor,
Thomas McRae, allowed the date of execution to be set
again for June 10.[95]

After the date was set by McRae, the NAACP took
silent part in a campaign begun by a white southern
professor to save the six men in the Moore group. The
Association was asked in May to help Robert Kerlin of
the Department of English at Virginia Military Institute
prepare an open letter to the governor of Arkansas.[96]
White sent Kerlin the brief that had been filed in Arkansas' Supreme Court, suggested several minor changes
in the draft of the letter that Kerlin had sent him, and
pointed out the crucial newspapers and press associations to which the letter should be sent.[97] On May 25,
Kerlin issued his plea to McRae to save the men scheduled to die on June 10. He argued that the Progressive
Union had been shown to be peaceable and aimed at
legal and economic pressures, not at insurrection; he
cited the testimony of several Negroes that they had
been tortured into confessing; and he called upon Mc-
Rae to heed "the still small voice . . . that bids you stand

for the eternal right . . . a vindicator of human dignity," rather than "the voice of the tempter of all men to . . . [submit] to the ill-guided multitude." And he urged that the churches of Arkansas prevent the commission of "a crime like that of Calvary . . . in a land where the Bible is an open and revered book, and the people are of the stock that has led the world in civilization."[98]

The letter caused a storm both in Arkansas and at Kerlin's college. The circuit judge and the prosecuting attorney of Phillips County both wrote angry letters to the governor denouncing Kerlin. The prosecutor said that the affidavits on torture that Kerlin cited "were written by some subtle hand with an end in view of creating public sentiment," rather than by the Negroes who signed and swore to them.[99]

Letters from Arkansas to the Superintendent of the Virginia Military Institute denounced Kerlin, and the Superintendent presented these letters to the Board of Visitors. Kerlin asked for and received from the NAACP additional material out of Arkansas to support his argument, but the Visitors dismissed him from the institute.[100]

Governor McRae refused to commute or delay the scheduled executions of the six men in the Moore group. But on June 8, 1921, two days before they were scheduled to take place, a petition for habeas corpus was presented to the Chancery Court of a county in Arkansas. The chancellor issued the writ and enjoined the state from executing the prisoners; he was held to be without jurisdiction by the Arkansas Supreme Court; and in September a similar petition for habeas corpus was presented to Federal District Court in Arkansas.[101]

That petition argued that the trials at which the six men had been convicted and sentenced to die were really a "prearranged scheme" to carry out a "mob verdict, dictated by a mob spirit," and that the men had therefore been denied both the equal protection of the laws and due process of law. The petition also argued that so helpless and without counsel were the defendants that they had been unable to assert their objections at the proper time, so that no adequate record could have been made on which normal methods of appeal could stand; and so an application for habeas corpus was the only means of protection available to them. Affidavits from the defendants themselves, from some Negroes who testified against them and were then let off with jail sentences on their pleas of guilty to second-degree murder, and from some white men who admitted having taken part in extorting the confessions, were introduced in support of the petition.[102]

Arkansas entered a demurrer, essentially arguing that even if the facts alleged were thought to be true, no action could be taken by the federal courts through use of habeas corpus. The state relied heavily on the Supreme Court decision in Frank vs. Mangum, in which the Court refused to issue habeas corpus in the Georgia trial of Leo Frank for murder. The Court had then held that Georgia provided sufficient safeguards against the alleged corruption of a trial by mob spirit that habeas corpus could not be used as a substitute for normal means of appeal.

The district court upheld this argument, agreed to Arkansas' demurrer, and dismissed the petition for habeas corpus. It was at that point, on October 24, 1921, that the six convicted men in the Moore group appealed to the Supreme Court to reverse the dismissal.[103]

The NAACP took steps at once to secure Moorfield Storey, a former president of the American Bar Association and the current president of the NAACP itself, to plead the case before the Supreme Court. Storey had already said he was unable to undertake the arduous and

tiring detail work that would go into preparation of the
entire brief, but he agreed to argue the case if the details
were undertaken by other men. In late 1921, the Association thought no one but Bratton capable of doing
this work. A year later, however, the NAACP's confidence in the legal abilities of Scipio Jones had grown to
the point where it was ready to have him prepare the
case if Storey could present it, and Jones himself was
strongly urging that Storey's appearance would be useful.[104]

The case was scheduled for hearing by the Supreme
Court in January 1923, and several months before that
Storey began to look over the record in the lower courts.
He shocked the NAACP staff no little by writing them
that he was "very much afraid that under the decision
of the Supreme Court in the case of Frank . . . we shall
not be able to win the case," but, he added, he was going
to try.[105] Then, a few days later, he calmed the Association headquarters down a bit by writing, "It is rather my
habit when I enlist in a case to grow more and more
confident that my cause is just, and that process is going
on in the Arkansas case. The Supreme Court in the Frank
case made it clear that a case can be presented on which
habeas corpus will issue, and I cannot help thinking that
if that is so, it would be impossible to find a stronger case
than the one which we have."[106]

As he began to think more about strategy for the appeal hearing, Storey suggested that it might impress the
Court if Bratton, a southern white man who knew conditions in Arkansas firsthand, helped to present the brief.
Scipio Jones was dubious, for fear that Bratton's name
would inflame public opinion in Arkansas and destroy
the last chance of executive clemency in case the petition for habeas corpus should fail. But he agreed on the

basis that Bratton should appear but his name not be used on the brief.[107]

The case was heard on January 9, 1923. The NAACP made careful arrangements for releasing Storey's arguments to the press in Washington, in the hope that the court case might serve as a public indictment of southern justice and as additional ammunition in the fight for federal anti-lynching legislation.[108]

The Storey brief distinguished the present case, Moore vs. Dempsey, from the Frank case on the ground that the courts of Arkansas had not provided an effective remedy of the sort the Supreme Court had found Georgia's courts offered in the Frank case. Instead, Storey argued, the Arkansas Supreme Court had treated the facts alleged about the trial as mere incidents, insufficient even if true to reverse the conviction. This, Storey said, differed from the situation in the Frank case, where the Georgia Supreme Court had affirmatively found the trial not so dominated by mob spirit as to be void. He bore heavily on the various affidavits claiming that torture was used to extort confessions.[109] Bratton, in his portion of the time set aside for oral argument, tried to "get a mental picture in the minds of the Court as to the exact conditions in Arkansas. I told the Court that conditions had grown up there that were worse than before the Civil War."[110]

Most of the Justices responded favorably to the NAACP's presentation. Oliver Wendell Holmes and William Howard Taft were particularly warm, according to Bratton and Herbert Seligmann of the NAACP's staff. Holmes emphasized his belief that if the trial had been a "mere sham," the Court could not possibly find itself powerless to intervene. He appeared to be directly answering Justice James C. McReynolds, who seemed least favorable to the NAACP argument and most dubious

that the Court could intervene whatever the facts. Mc-
Reynolds seemed most sympathetic to the Arkansas attorney-general's argument that habeas corpus could not
meet the questions at stake.[111]

After the case was heard, the NAACP settled back
for a nervous waiting period until the decision could be
handed down. Scipio Jones began to worry that the six
other prisoners sentenced to death, whose convictions
had been twice reversed by the Arkansas Supreme Court
and who were still waiting for retrial in the Helena jail,
might be lynched if the federal courts gave hope to the
six men in their jurisdiction.[112] Some comic relief was
injected into the waiting period when Phillips County
and the state of Arkansas started to wrangle over who
should pay the three years' board bill of the prisoners,
amounting to $7000.[113] For the men themselves, of
course, the long imprisonment was no joke. One of them,
Ed Ware, wrote Jones that "we is Suffering so much Here
on this Hard concreet floor, and We is kep so confine and
is fed so Bad untill we are Just about Woe out . . . if
there is any Way that you can give me Some Relief now
is the time."[114]

Neither Jones nor the NAACP could provide any immediate relief to the condemned men. But the first major
victory in their struggle against electrocution came just
one week later. The Supreme Court reversed the Federal District Court and ordered a hearing held on the
merits of their petition for habeas corpus.[115]

The decision in Moore *et al. vs.* Dempsey was written
by Holmes, with only McReynolds and George Suther-
land dissenting. Holmes pointed out that the Frank decision had recognized that some cases might arise in
which "the State, supplying no corrective process, . . .
deprives the accused of his life or liberty without due
process of law," and might be restrained by the use of

habeas corpus. This, Holmes said, was one such case. "If the case is that the whole proceeding is a mask—that counsel, jury and judge were swept to the fatal end by an irresistible wave of public passion, and that the State Courts failed to correct the wrong, neither perfection in the machinery for correction or the possibility that the trial court and counsel saw no other way of avoiding an immediate outbreak of the mob can prevent this Court from securing to the petitioners their constitutional rights." Habeas corpus was a legitimate means of securing such rights, Holmes said: "It does not seem to us sufficient to allow a Judge of the United States to escape the duty of examining the facts for himself when if true as alleged they make the trial absolutely void."[116]

McReynolds, dissenting, argued that "if every man convicted of crime in a state court may thereafter resort to the Federal court . . . and thereby obtain as of right further review, another way has been added to a list already unfortunately long to prevent prompt punishment." He cited the decision in the Frank case that habeas corpus should not be used to correct mere errors in point of law, however serious. He pointed out that the Negro appellants had "not been rushed towards the death chair; on the contrary there has been long delay and some impatience over the result is not unnatural." McReynolds concluded thus:[117]

Under the disclosed circumstances I cannot agree that the solemn adjudications by courts of a great State, which this Court has refused to review, can be successfully impeached by the mere *ex parte* affidavits made upon information and belief of ignorant convicts joined by two white men—confessedly atrocious criminals. The fact that petitioners are poor and ignorant and black naturally arouses sympathy; but that does not release us from enforcing principles which are essential to the orderly operation of our federal system.

The Moore decision brought varied responses across the country, as could have been expected. The *Arkansas Gazette* thought it "terrifying to contemplate the consequences."[118] The *Toledo Times,* on the other hand, approved the decision as putting the "strong arm of Uncle Sam . . . between colored citizens . . . and prejudiced courts."[119] The *St. Louis Post-Dispatch* expressed satisfaction at the prospect of a new hearing, on the ground that "The Arkansas formula in such cases seems to consist in hanging the negroes who escape the bullets."[120] A number of Negro newspapers hailed the NAACP for having won the victory and having thus proved the usefulness of "continued united racial effort."[121] The *Bulletin* of the American Civil Liberties Union called the case an important precedent in widening the scope of federal jurisdiction by allowing the use of habeas corpus to review state trials which were due process of law in form only.[122] In effect, the Supreme Court decision warned that new techniques would be used to prevent a state from manipulating its police powers against one of the parties in a racial conflict. The torture of prisoners to win confessions could not be defended as a legitimate use of the state's monopoly of violence.

But the NAACP could not simply rejoice. The staff began to plan for the next step: a hearing in Federal District Court on the merits of the NAACP's allegations that the original trials were a nullity.[123] It was not clear that the state of Arkansas would insist on the hearing, and Bratton's guess was that the state would "not want the real facts developed any more fully than they can avoid" and hence would drop the prosecution. But in case the state refused to drop the matter, the NAACP needed to be fully prepared for a court hearing. "If that bunch of murderers attempt to go in to try out the case," Bratton said, "then I want to see to it that all the facts possible are brought out . . . [and] a record made that will absolutely put all decent people of the South to shame and force them to rise up against such conditions."[124]

The first hint of the state's attitude came in a letter from the former prosecuting attorney in Phillips County, John E. Miller, to Scipio Jones. Miller said the letter was "strictly confidential," and reported that he had talked with his successor as prosecuting attorney about disposing of the Elaine cases. His successor would agree to "a plea of guilty of second degree murder, and a sentence of five years," to be counted retroactively so that the men could soon go free. But Miller said that careful negotiations with Phillips County authorities would be necessary.[125]

Jones raised the question with NAACP headquarters: Would such a compromise be acceptable?[126] The problem caused a stir in the New York office. The national board discussed it and referred it to Storey,[127] who leaned toward accepting such an arrangement. Storey pointed out that a refusal to accept the compromise would leave the imprisoned Negroes in jeopardy of their lives, whereas a compromise would probably give them no longer imprisonment than continuing the struggle in court. Storey was especially fearful that it would be "very difficult to prove the allegations in our petition, for the white witnesses who testified would hesitate very much to come and testify in person before the District Court, since they might well be lynched themselves." Storey felt that there would be no real surrender of moral victory involved in pleading guilty to second-degree murder, since the country would recognize the realities, the Negroes would be vindicated in the public mind, and Arkansas would be chastened.[128]

The NAACP agreed to this train of thought and told Jones to accept a compromise if it could be worked out.[129] But working it out was not easy. Who would undertake negotiations with the Arkansas authorities?

After a month of doubt and discussion, Storey reported that a leading Arkansas lawyer had told him that he had rendered Arkansas a great service by pleading the cause of the Elaine Negroes in the Supreme Court. Storey suggested that this lawyer, George B. Rose, might be able to work out a way of closing the cases.[130] Jones and the NAACP headquarters staff leaped at this suggestion, and asked Storey to write.[131]

What Storey asked Rose to do was to help the authorities of Arkansas let the Negroes go. "I think the men where the verdict has been set aside ought to be discharged, and . . . the proceedings against the men who stand under sentence . . . be dropped, and they also set free," Storey said. He asked Rose to discuss the matter with Jones and with the state officials who were concerned.[132]

Meanwhile, legal steps had been taken in the case of the Ware group of six men whose convictions had twice been reversed. They had been granted change of venue to another county, but since December 1920 their cases had been allowed to hang fire. In April 1923, Jones moved to discharge them under Arkansas law, because two terms of court had been allowed to pass without their cases having been brought to trial.[133] In June, the Supreme Court of Arkansas ordered them freed over various state objections.[134] In a staggering anticlimax, mere failure of the state to continue prosecuting gave six of the Elaine Negroes the first total victory won by any of the defendants since 1919. They were actually released almost as ingloriously. When the word of the Arkansas Supreme Court order reached the judge of Lee County, he ordered the sheriff to transfer the men to the state penitentiary in Little Rock. The sheriff took them to the gate, was refused entry by a puzzled warden, and "shook hands with the night watchman and a newspaper man and rounding up his deputies, entered their taxicab and rolled off the hill, leaving the Negroes looking after him in surprise."[135] At first they could not believe what had happened and looked fearfully at a row of armed penitentiary guards high on the wall above them, who they feared might shoot them down if they tried to leave. The Negroes inched away, looking back over their shoulders until they were certain no one would shoot. Then they broke into tears and songs and prayers. They were free.[136]

Inglorious or not, the release caused a minor explosion of joy and wrath. The NAACP telegraphed eleven Negro newspapers and the Associated Negro Press, "After nearly four years of fighting and cost of more than fourteen thousand dollars this marks beginning of end of greatest case of its kind in history of America."[137] Bratton warmly congratulated the New York office of what in his excitement he called "the National Association for the Uplift of the Colored People."[138] Several Arkansas white papers, however, angrily condemned the whole affair as a breakdown of law and justice. One paper named and attacked the NAACP, which "with its strong membership among the ignorant and prejudiced peoples about Boston and the east" was able to raise a "massive fund" to stymie justice. The six men released were called "fat and sleek," not interested in cotton patches after four years of being served their meals. Vague threats against them if they did not "get out of Arkansas at once" were heard.[139]

In the aftermath of this stir, Storey's lawyer friend George Rose took up the task that Storey had asked him to consider. He wrote John Miller, the former Phillips County prosecutor, to suggest that a new approach to the cases be considered, in view of the release of six of the accused; the impossibility of prosecuting Robert Hill, who had headed any conspiracy there had been; the simplicity and lack of malice of the Negro farmers who were still under sentence of death; and the widespread conviction throughout the North that the prosecutions were unjustified. Rose suggested that it might be wise to accept a plea of guilty of homicide and a retroactive three- or four-year sentence. Thus the law would be vindicated, the men would be freed, the good name of Arkansas upheld, and "it would do something to stop the emigration of negroes to the north, which is proving so disastrous to many of our Southern planters."[140] Miller replied that although the prosecutions were entirely justified and the Negroes certainly guilty, he would if he were still prosecuting attorney look favorably on Rose's solution. He added that he was informed that there would be no further prosecution in the Elaine cases.[141] The new prosecuting attorney wrote Rose along the same lines.[142]

The crucial element in this meeting of minds was the common belief of Rose and Miller that the outside world was too powerful a force for Arkansas to resist forever. Miller came to this belief out of sheer weariness from repeated defeats in the courts; Rose, from his respect for an outside lawyer of high prestige like Storey and from his belief that Arkansas needed to meet outside competition for Negro labor by treating its own Negroes better.

Once the basic agreement had been reached, Scipio Jones began to circulate a petition for a pardon for the six prisoners.[143] In Phillips County, members of the Committee of Seven and other prominent citizens petitioned the governor to commute their sentences to twelve years in the penitentiary.[144] Jones explained to the NAACP in New York that with a twelve-year sentence, Arkansas' parole law would free the men almost at once, since they would have spent one third of their sentence in prison.[145] Jones also told the NAACP that it would take a $1000 fee to persuade a key lawyer in Phillips County to present the petition for commutation, and without waiting for any decision from the NAACP accepted the law-yer's offer.[146] While the NAACP staff dithered over where the $1000 might come from, the governor of Arkansas commuted to twelve years the sentences of the six remaining men under sentence of death.[147] The NAACP claimed credit for the compromise, and on November 16, with the release of the men impending, publicly proclaimed the end of the four years of struggle in Arkansas, with vindication for the Negroes of Elaine.[148]

Thus the adjudication of the Arkansas riots drew to a close. The Arkansas "white" solution, which had seemed so efficacious in November 1919, had been nullified. Now it had been made impossible to use the formal apparatus of the law to accomplish the ends that mob violence would have accomplished. The facts that outside Arkansas there were Negroes who were organized and determined to "fight back" by legal means against legal attack and whites to help them do so and that outside Arkansas there were also courts unwilling to allow the use of the legal system as a mask for suppression stymied the Arkansas solution.

But these facts could only stymie the Arkansas solution, not reverse it: that is, there was no way for the NAACP or the Supreme Court to force the punishment of the whites who had actually been the aggressors in 1919. The outside world could forbid Arkansas to use its police powers openly and nakedly on behalf of one race against the other, but it could not force Arkansas to use its police powers neutrally.

The state was left precariously balanced between several choices of action, if racial conflicts were to erupt in the future. One choice might be for the state in effect to grant "permission" to white mobs to use private violence to keep Negroes under control. That choice would have the inherent dangers of possible Negro resistance and a breakdown in law and order. Another choice might be to use the legitimate violence of the police force in a neutral way. For example, non-violent means of carrying on racial conflict (such as formation of a Negro share-croppers' union) might be permitted, so long as neither whites nor Negroes used private violence. That choice might require Arkansas to embark on new adventures in partial accommodation to Negro discontent.

That the direction of Arkansas' evolution would be accommodation rather than naked mob violence was indicated, but not assured, by the attempts at compromise made by John Miller and George Rose, based on their belief that the world outside Arkansas was too powerful an opponent and too attractive a lure to resist.

Symbolically, though not in enforceable law, the result in Arkansas was a victory for the notion of a neutral police power. Neither the private use of violence nor the biased use of quasi-legitimate official violence was to be condoned. Arkansas Negroes had never been able to use violence effectively; they were too weak. The white mob had been tricked, controlled, and rewarded by the state of Arkansas itself so that it would not use violence, for fear that its doing so might upset the foundations of order and respectability. The state of Arkansas had used violence on behalf of the whites, but was reprimanded for doing so by the federal courts. The result was that the state had prohibited private violence, and the federal government had prohibited the one-sided use of public violence. If both parties adhered to their positions, the upshot would be that the only legitimate form of violence would be that used by the state, impartially, to prevent or punish private violence used by conflicting groups. But it should be clear that this was only the symbolic result of the Arkansas riot cases. It was not at all certain that both the federal and state authorities would in fact continue to insist upon their positions.

CHAPTER IX

Responding to Violence

The riots of 1919 shocked and troubled many Americans. Most of them did not accept large-scale violence in their cities and countryside as a reasonable way of working out the conflicts involved. Instead they thought of the use of physical force and violence as a prerogative of the state alone, were pleased when the police or Army put down the riots, and saw large-scale violence by mobs of private persons as a disgrace and a disaster to be prevented from happening again. How to prevent it, of course, divided Americans from each other.

The obvious division was between those who believed it necessary to wipe out racial inequalities in order to prevent racial conflicts; and those who believed it necessary to create a racial hierarchy, in which conflict would end because each race would know and accept its place. Both these responses have in common that they think it necessary to *settle the conflict* in order to end the violence engendered by the conflict. There were, however, three other responses that did not focus on the ambitious end of settling all racial conflicts. Instead, one of these approaches focused on the "accommodation" of society to particular pressures and conflicts of the moment, so that the level of tension would be reduced even though a permanent settlement could not be reached. The other two approaches focused on simply *enforcing rules against the use of violence*, rather than on changing the basic constitution of society (so far as race was concerned).

One of them emphasized the need for "law and order"; the other hinted at the possibility of carrying on racial conflict by means of what might be called "creative disorder." Although the relative weights of each of these five responses within the American public cannot be measured from the public record, something of the intellectual contours of each of the responses can be seen if the record is examined.

＊　＊　＊

The Demand for Racial Equality

Those who looked toward the establishment of eventual racial equality were not necessarily convinced that violence could be avoided in the process of achieving their goal. Many of them, for example, applauded the newly demonstrated readiness of Negroes to fight back against white attack. The battle cry of these believers in fighting for equality was penned in July 1919 by Claude McKay:[1]

> *If we must die, let it not be like hogs*
>   *Hunted and penned in an inglorious spot,*
> *While round us bark the mad and hungry dogs,*
>   *Making their mock at our accursed lot.*
> *If we must die, let it not be like hogs*
>   *So that our precious blood may not be shed*
> *In vain; then even the monsters we defy*
>   *Shall be constrained to honor us, though dead!*
>
> *Oh, kinsman! We must meet the common foe;*
>   *Though far outnumbered, let us still be brave,*
> *And for their thousand blows deal one deathblow!*
>   *What though before us lies the open grave?*
> *Like men we'll face the murderous, cowardly pack,*
>   *Pressed to the wall, dying, but—fighting back!*

One Negro organization phrased the argument for fighting back even more succinctly: "A Winchester speaks louder than words and only bad shots fail of attention."[2] And several Negroes cited the white American ethos as their justification: "You tell us that the man who will not protect himself is no man. We are putting your teaching into practice."[3] Sometimes pride in the effectiveness of Negro fighting men was the leitmotiv of comment.[4] At its bluntest, this theme was put by W.E.B. Du Bois, editor of *The Crisis* and a crucial figure in the founding of the NAACP: "When the mob moves, we propose to meet it with bricks and clubs and guns."[5]

That this argument for fighting back cut beneath the thin layer of Negro intellectuals is indicated not only by the actual behavior of Negro mobs and individuals in the riots themselves, but also by reports of widespread arming of Negroes in southern cities[6] and by the appearance of thousands of New York Negroes to cheer speakers at several mass meetings when they argued for fighting back.[7] Among the speakers were Monroe Trotter, editor of the *Boston Guardian* and proponent of a Negro presence at the Versailles Peace Conference, who warned that "unless the white American behaves he will find that in teaching our boys to fight for him he was starting something that he will not be able to stop." Others urged Negroes not to demand but to take their rights, to duplicate the "constructive work" of Washington Negro rioters if it became necessary.[8]

Frequently, though not always, calls for "fighting back" were careful to say that one-sided police action in favor of whites was the critical factor justifying the use of violence in self-defense.[9] No explicit demand survives for the use of violence as an aggressive technique, and careful distinctions between aggressive and defensive violence were made by a number of Negroes. Thus, when the *New York World* asked a number of Negro Methodist bishops to condemn the use of violence, many of the bishops answered that self-restraint and patience should be practiced but that if white assailants would not desist, Negroes should use arms if necessary to protect themselves and their homes.[10]

Among those equalitarians who did not counsel that Negroes fight back against white attack—who skirted the issue or thought "fighting back" unwise or unjust—the solution was generally thought to lie in a gift of equality by the white community. "This is a problem for the [white] majority to solve. . . . We cannot have one law for the white man and another law for the black man," one New York newspaper said.[11] John Haynes Holmes, a leading Unitarian minister, warned that there would be "no settlement of the negro question short of equality and brotherhood."[12] The National Urban League argued that "only by improving the housing, health, and recreation opportunities of the Negro at the same time that we demand of him the contribution of his hands and brain in industry can we look for fundamental improvement in race relations"—a plea that looked toward equality without specifying it, but that did specify the grant of new privileges by the dominant white community.[13]

The epitome of this argument for presenting equality as a gift from whites was the call of a Chicago newspaper: "Let *us* recognize *them* as fellow citizens . . . let *us* treat *them* as men and women entitled to share fully and equally the boasted opportunity of America."* [14] The tone of that approach can be contrasted with the tone of another statement, which emphasized Negroes' readiness to take equality as a right: "It is a new Negro that we have with us now, and may we not hope also that we have new white men?"[15] Here "we" means not whites

* Italics added.

but all Americans, since it is used neutrally as between
Negroes and whites; and the emphasis is primarily on the
"new Negro" who is demanding equality, only secondar-
ily on the "new white men" who can accept it.

The argument for an economic base for racial equality
was bolstered by the partially economic origins of some
of the riots. Both capitalists and socialists attempted to
benefit from events. The *Independent* suggested that a
crucial mistake in freeing the Negro had been the failure
to give him his own land and tools, so that he could establish a smallholder's economic independence from the
white community.[16] The *New York Call* urged that only
in a socialist labor movement could the Negroes "find
comrades who understand, comrades who share his long-
ing for the equality of opportunity, the leisure, education and happiness that can only be realized when workers of both races are members of a free world that knows
no race, color or class distinctions."[17] A dream less utopian, but similar in its assumption that racial equality
could be grounded only in broad social change, came
from Walter Lippmann:[18]

The race problem as we know it is really a by-product of our
planless, disordered, bedraggled, drifting democracy. Until
we have learned to house everybody, employ everybody at
decent wages in a self-respecting status, guarantee his civil
liberties, and bring education and play to him, the bulk of
our talk about "the race problem" will remain a sinister my-
thology. In a dirty civilization the relation between black men
and white will be a dirty one. In a clean civilization the two
races can conduct their business together cleanly, and not until then.

The "black nationalist" argument for racial equality
through separation may have been strengthened by the
1919 race riots. At least the leading black nationalist,
Marcus Garvey, thought that race riots worked to his ad-

vantage "by teaching the Negro that he must build a civilization of his own or forever remain the white man's
victim."[19] And in the immediate aftermath of the Washington riot, Garvey pointed to the appropriateness of
naming his Harlem headquarters "Liberty Hall."[20] On
the other hand, Garvey was not able to capitalize on the
Chicago riot to increase his following there in 1919; indeed, he was ignominiously run out of town by Robert S.
Abbott of the *Defender.** [21]

By far the most active of the organizations urging racial equality was the National Association for the Advancement of Colored People. Both its internal structure
and its external policy were interracial and integrationist, rather than all-Negro and separationist like Garvey's
Universal Negro Improvement Association. The NAACP
took a great deal of action in connection with most of the
1919 riots, trying to turn each riot to the advantage of
the campaign for equality.

As reports of each of the riots reached New York, the
NAACP tried to discover what had actually happened.
Its local branches and members in Charleston and Omaha
kept national headquarters informed of what was happening in those two riots.[23] The national staff depended
chiefly on newspaper accounts of the Longview and
Knoxville riots.[24] For Washington, Chicago, and Arkansas, members of the staff actually traveled to the riot area
and added their own reports to those of local NAACP
members. Confidential letters from aggrieved and frightened southern Negroes and from white community leaders who could not afford to have their sympathy with the

---

* Although *The Negro in Chicago* refers to and describes the Gar-
veyite movement, neither it nor any other surviving data give the
slightest indication of any involvement by Garvey's movement
either in the Chicago riot itself or in any of the attempts to cope
with the results of the riot.[22]

NAACP known, added to the Association's files on the riots.[25]

Once it was engaged in pinning down the facts about a riot, the NAACP began to work out ways of advancing the goal of equality. Publicity was sought for the special restraints and disadvantages under which Negroes had lived in the riot area. Through press releases to white and Negro newspapers,[26] special contacts with such journalists as Gilbert Seldes at *Collier's* and Edward L. Bernays of the new public relations industry,[27] and interviews with reporters,[28] the NAACP tried to get the press to cover news that would back up arguments for racial equality. The staff also wrote prolifically for journals like the *New Republic, Current Opinion, The American City,* the *Literary Digest, The Nation, The Survey,* the *Socialist Review,* the *Manchester Guardian,* and the *Chicago Daily News.*[29] The staff also wrote letters to the editors of various newspapers and magazines, criticizing or approving articles that had appeared.[30] One staff member, Herbert J. Seligmann, developed several of the articles he had written into a book, *The Negro Faces America,* that was published in 1920 by Harper and Brothers. It used the race riots as a base on which to discuss "the South's color psychosis," the Negro as "the scapegoat of city politics," the Negro's role in industry, and the rebellious "new Negro."[31]

The second major activity of the NAACP was the legal defense of Negroes it believed had been wrongly accused or might be unfairly tried. The NAACP took cases stemming from the Chicago and Arkansas riots, not only in the hope of protecting the particular Negroes on trial and of rebuking the local authorities, but also with the intention of turning the cases themselves into a public indictment of the racial practices that had led to the riots.

A third effort of the NAACP was directed at congres-

sional investigation of the race riots and passage of a
federal law to punish lynching and rioting. This effort
aimed not at the uprooting of racial inequalities which
was the NAACP's ultimate aim but rather at the elimination of violence as a means of enforcing those inequalities. The anti-violence campaign drew not only the support of those who wanted racial equality established,
but also the support of those who simply wanted bloodshed to be halted. It may therefore be discussed more
effectively as part of the demand for an end to violence
rather than as part of the demand for racial equality.

❖   ❖   ❖

The Demand for Racial Hierarchy

In the opposite direction from the demand for racial
equality, there came from many Americans a demand
for racial hierarchy that would eliminate the conflicts that
led to race riots. In 1919 no one was talking about "black
supremacy"; the demand for hierarchy was a demand for
the subordination of Negroes so that they no longer could
challenge white prerogatives.

In its most extreme form, the demand for subordination of Negroes argued that police action during and after the riots should have been directed wholly against
Negroes. Thus the *Memphis Press* condemned the Washington police for "sissyism" caused by "the influence of
aliens and of New England negro elements," resulting
in failure "to round up all negroes and disarm them, as
would have been done in any southern city or most any
other place."[32] The Savannah police department asked
all hardware stores and pawnshops not to sell firearms
to Negroes, but did not suggest prohibiting sales to
whites.[33] Similarly, Austin police confiscated all mem-

bership lists, by-laws, and correspondence of the Austin
branch of the NAACP and forced all meetings of the
branch to be called off.[34] Senator John Sharp Williams
of Mississippi applauded the Omaha lynching on the
ground that "race is greater than law . . . and protection of women transcends all law, human and divine."[35]

Most of those who believed in subordination of Negroes
were not, however, prepared to argue for their utter suppression by "legal" and illegal violence. The ideology of
racial hierarchy was built on an assumption of the biological, cultural, and political inferiority of Negroes and
on the belief that only evil for both races could come of
any attempt for whites to treat Negroes, or for Negroes
to act as anything but inferiors. Thus one southern paper
warned, "The downfall of the Confederacy never meant
the surrender of the land to the negro; . . . this is . . .
a white man's country . . . and shall be as long as the
people rule."[36] The Negro's alleged desire to undermine
the superior white race by polluting its women with "the
damned touch of the black"[37] was frequently referred
to.[38]

A number of observers thought that one reason for the
1919 race riots had been a general stirring up of the "inferior" race through its experiences during and as a result
of the war. Direct references were made to the freedom that France offered to Negroes who had never before seen a nearly color-blind society. Sometimes this result of the Army's expedition overseas was specifically
connected with the availability of white Frenchwomen to
American Negro soldiers, and from this came the fright-
ening thought that Negroes might now expect American
white women to cross racial barriers too.[39] Other commentators argued that the unsettling effects of war-in-
duced northern migration, or of mere membership in the
Army, with its more nearly equalitarian atmosphere, had

encouraged Negroes to strike out against the prewar racial hierarchy.[40]

Others contended that trickery and incitement by unscrupulous whites had stirred calm, "solid" Negroes into activities that would upset traditional patterns. The Arkansas riot especially encouraged suspicions that "unfortunate, ignorant negroes" had been misled by "vicious outside influences."[41]

What happened when Negroes who had been either dislocated by the war or incited by outsiders refused to stay "in their place"? Then, the hierarchists claimed, all social moorings were cast off: Negroes insisted on sitting next to white women on streetcars, they carried revolvers, they committed armed robberies, they dressed better than their white betters, they demanded boodle from the city political machines, they turned "cocky," they refused to work because they were "all . . . so well-to-do," they used their money for silk and diamonds and automobiles so as to "offer entertainment to white women."[42] "An increasing insolent pugnaciousness" colored the behavior of young Negroes so that they went "on the lookout for affronts," as one paper described it.[43] Or, as another reported, the young displayed "a new sense of manhood and self-respect" that was equally threatening to the hierarchical racial order.[44] Confronted with this upsetting development, Northerners and Southerners alike looked back with nostalgia to the South in which, according to some Southerners, the Negro could still find his comfortable place.[45]

To some who believed in racial hierarchy as a way of preventing racial violence, the form of that hierarchy might be one of segregation without obvious subordination. Thus the chairman of the Tennessee Law and Order League (an anti-lynching society) argued that "the more the negro can keep to himself, the more rapid and real

will be the development of the race. . . . Social inter-
mingling is no more helpful to them than to us."[46] Just
as a Salt Lake City newspaper found the riots evidence
for the wisdom of segregating Negroes and excluding
Japanese,[47] a southern newspaper presented the diagno-
sis that "the races should not have been so close together."[48]

Joining with and supporting the ideology of racial hierarchy was the ideology of anti-Bolshevism. Through
1918 and early 1919, much of the nation had taken part
in a surge of nativist, "100 per cent American" opposition
to radical ideas and organizations. Fears that alien and
subversive ideas were penetrating and endangering
American society as they seemed to be doing in Russia,
Germany, and Mexico aroused urgent demands for new
legislative and administrative action to control radical
dissent. Americans understood that some radical theory
endorsed the use of violence in some situations, that revolutionaries had used violence to overthrow some governments, and that occasional bombings had been ascribed
to American radicals. They were thus mentally prepared
to ascribe both naked violence and demands for changes
in American society to the influence and incitement of
radicals and aliens.[49]

In this atmosphere, it was relatively easy for some who
were shocked by the 1919 race riots to believe that radicals had incited them. No one suggested, however, that
radicals had incited white men in these riots. To those
who thought they had evidence of radical influence, it
seemed clear that radical incitement had encouraged Negroes to take up arms. This belief often went together
with a pastoral vision of contented Negroes who were
tricked into bloody revolt by unscrupulous agitators.
Sometimes, however, particular Negroes—especially
"Harvard-educated" ones—were singled out as equally

culpable with the alien Bolsheviks. In either case, Negroes were seen—like the broad mass of immigrants
against whom nativist legislation was enacted—as fertile
ground for un-American agitation. The anti-Bolshevik
campaign clearly suggested that Negro demands for
equality were radical and subversive, and that the Negro's place was in subordination to the dominant native
white Americans.

The *New York Times* indicated the direction of hierarchist thought when it warned that the Chicago and
Washington riots were too well-timed and well-fought to
have been spontaneous, but might well have been incited
by "Bolshevist agitation . . . among the negroes." The
Times reminded its readers that "we know that in the
early days of the war there was a pro-German and paci-
fist propaganda among the negroes, which may well have
turned into a Bolshevist or at least Socialist propaganda
since."[50] From Boston came a more specific denunciation of an unnamed "new Negro" publication, in which
"the sinister influence of the I.W.W. and of bolshevism"
were "clearly evident."[51]

The pastoral view of the Negro race was set forth by
a Baltimore newspaper. It acknowledged that Negroes
were "poor material for the vicious agitator" since they
were "naturally peaceful, kindly, good-natured and
loyal." But "on the other hand," it warned, "the ignorance
and poverty of many may become fuel for the incendi-
ary."[52] That the idyllic Southland might be turned into
"a little Russia" by IWW agitators among the Negroes
was suggested by an official of the National Security
League, which was conducting "an educational campaign
. . . aimed at counter-acting efforts to inflame the
blacks."[53] The partly contrary image of Negroes as somehow alien, despite their long sojourn in America, was
made explicit by the *Brooklyn Eagle*. It attacked the Chi-

cago press for lacking "the courage to say one word that might be remotely construed as censuring the negroes," and said such editorials "read as if they had been written by the type of parlor Bolsheviki who always have a kind word and a protecting hand for the foreigner against the native American."[54] A resolution of these conflicting images of the alien and dangerous Negro and the kindly but susceptible Negro was attempted by the *New York Times*. It warned against a small class of dangerous radical revolutionary Negroes (the "aliens") who were inflaming "the less informed class of negroes," the "element . . . in this country . . . [most] susceptible to organized propaganda of this kind."[55]

Some newspapers noted specific objections to this view of Bolshevik incitement. "Whenever there is trouble of any sort in America there are voices shouting 'Bolshevism,'" one editor protested. He added that no incitement was necessary to get Negroes to use the same weapons in self-defense that whites used against them.[56] Another newspaper suggested that blaming the riots on Bolshevik or IWW agitators was "too easy an explanation," since conflict and antagonism ran too deep in the relations between the races.[57] When the *New York World* wrote a number of Negro bishops, asking them to warn their people against "Bolshevism and violence which are being both openly and privately circulated," the bishops denounced Bolshevism but made clear that self-defense was not Bolshevism and could not be forbidden.[58] Even a southern newspaper suggested that equalitarian war experiences, rather than Bolshevik plots, had disturbed the nation's racial equilibrium.[59] And Herbert Seligmann of the NAACP sardonically suggested that the real revolutionaries were those journalists who bannered exaggerated crime stories "featuring the word Negro in huge headlines."[60]

In the wake of the Arkansas riot, charges of Bolshevik involvement in racial violence grew stronger.[61] Congressman James F. Byrnes of South Carolina charged that radicals had incited Negroes to riot. The Department of Justice was asked to investigate "negro plots" and to apply the Espionage Act "to certain New York and Chicago publications that arouse race hatred by cartoons and editorial attacks on white people."[62] The department had indeed already begun to investigate Negro radicalism as part of its more general inquiries into radical agitation. On August 1, 1919, the General Investigation Division was formed within the Federal Bureau of Investigation, and its chief—J. Edgar Hoover—began the work that led to preparation of a major report on Negro radicals.[63]

Newton D. Baker, the Secretary of War, added to the fear of Bolshevik penetration among Negroes when he lumped the race riots and mob disorder with industrial controversies as instances of violence partially caused by "so-called Bolsheviks and radicals . . . urging . . . social revolution."[64] The fear was intensified when a leak from the Justice Department to David Lawrence, a widely syndicated newspaper columnist, allowed Lawrence to quote extensively from the forthcoming report on Negro radicalism.[65] At once newspapers began to ask that the full report be made public, and a United States congressman asked the Department for it. He was told that it was on the verge of completion and would soon be officially sent to Congress.[66]

So that the Justice Department could reply to this request from Capitol Hill, the General Investigation Division had been asked to report on its activities. J. Edgar Hoover had told his superiors that agents in Arkansas had been instructed to prepare a special report on the riot there, but were waiting until the trials of Negroes charged with insurrection had been completed. Hoover also reported that he was himself "preparing . . . a complete report upon negro agitation in the United States" and would soon be submitting it through Assistant Attorney-General Francis Garvan to Congress.* [67]

In mid-November, the report on Negro radicalism was officially submitted by Attorney-General A. Mitchell Palmer to the Senate Committee on Judiciary as part of a 187-page report on radicalism, sedition, and anarchy in general. Hoover's report on Negro radicalism took up 27 pages of the full report. Although Hoover submitted it, in this final form it was adopted and presented as an official report of the Department and the Attorney-General.[69] On the basis of its findings, Palmer told the Senate in the main body of the report:[70]

Practically all of the radical organizations in this country have looked upon the Negroes as particularly fertile ground for the spreading of their doctrines. These radical organizations have endeavored to enlist Negroes on their side, and in many respects have been successful.

The Hoover report did not claim that the race riots had been directly instigated by Bolsheviks, but did report that Negro radicals had availed themselves of the riots "as causes for the utterance of inflammatory sentiment—utterances which in some cases have reached the limit of open defiance and a counsel of retaliation." He accused the Negro radicals of a constantly increasing "insubordination," and asserted that there could "no longer be any question of a well-concerted movement among a certain class of Negro leaders of thought and action to constitute

* From internal evidence in the final version of the report, it seems possible that Hoover worked from a draft prepared by an agent in New York, since New York is referred to as "this city" and other places as "out-of-town." The only identifiable author is Hoover himself, on the basis of the memo cited above; and the report on Negro radicalism will be referred to as the "Hoover report."[68]

themselves a determined and persistent source of a radical opposition to the Government, and to the established rule of law and order."[71] What this description might mean is suggested by Palmer's call for legislation defining a new crime, "promoting sedition," to consist of "writing, printing, or circulating of any . . . argument, or teaching, which advises, advocates, teaches or justifies any act . . . to cause the change, overthrow, or destruction of the Government or of any of the laws or authority thereof, or to cause the overthrow or destruction of all forms of law or organized government." The proposed legislation would have prescribed a prison term up to ten years or a fine up to $10,000, for "promoting sedition."[72] Hoover's description of certain Negro editorials and poems as "radical opposition to the Government, and to the established rule of law" might thus have meant that they would be considered criminal under the law proposed by Palmer.

Hoover's report noted as major points in the attitude of Negro leaders their "ill-governed reaction toward race rioting"; their "threat of retaliatory measures in connection with lynching"; their "demand for social equality"; their "identification of the Negro with such radical organizations as the I.W.W. and an outspoken advocacy of the Bolsheviki or Soviet doctrines"; and their "political stand . . . toward the present Federal administration, the South in general, and incidentally, toward the peace treaty and the league of nations." Beneath these salient characteristics, Hoover said there lay an "increasingly emphasized feeling of a race consciousness . . . openly, defiantly assertive of its own equality and even superiority."[73] And all this added up to what Hoover called "a radical opposition to the Government and to the established rule of law."

The report went on to note that the most radical journals were edited by men of education, "in at least one instance, men holding degrees conferred by Harvard University." It also pointed out that several of the magazines were expensively printed "on coated paper throughout." Thus, Hoover suggested, the Negro radicals could not be dismissed as poverty-stricken illiterates.[74]

Hoover acknowledged that there was a range of opinion within the Negro press. But the "number of restrained and conservative publications" was "relatively negligible," he said, "and even some of these . . . have indulged in most intemperate utterance." "It would be unfair not to state," he added, "that certain papers—I can think of no magazine—maintain an attitude of well-balanced sanity." As for the more radical publications, Hoover found them full of "defiance and insolently race-centered condemnation of the white race." He thought "the Negro" was "seeing red."[75]

The assumptions on which this description is based seem to include the belief that a challenge to white supremacy was not only "insolent" but a "radical opposition to the Government." For this reason, the Hoover report most clearly joins the ideologies of anti-Bolshevism and racial hierarchy, in that it regards an end of the Negro's subordination as equivalent to an attack on law, order, and Americanism—and believes both wholly illegitimate. In assessing the importance of the report it should be remembered that it not only reflected J. Edgar Hoover's own views in his official capacity, but may have governed the behavior of the General Investigation Division in this period when it had considerable power over political ideas, and certainly was adopted by the Attorney-General of the United States as his official view.

A review of Hoover's citation of evidence for his findings of radicalism indicate that the "fighting back" motif is frequently mentioned, including frequent references to Claude McKay's poem, *If We Must Die*.[76] "Inflammatory" attacks on lynching, in graphically descriptive news stories and poems, were listed as "particularly radical."[77] The espousal in some publications of "social equality, with all that is implied by that term," was specifically pointed out.[78] One article in the *Cleveland Gazette* was called "vicious" because it said:[79]

. . . the average white southerner . . . is a beast of the lowest prey . . . Colored men . . . should be careful and whenever in their innocence a Southern white brute attacks him, or attempts to arrest him on trumped-up crimes, kill him on the spot.

"The most able and the most dangerous" of all the Negro publications was, according to Hoover, the *Messenger*, edited by A. Philip Randolph and Chandler Owen. The *Messenger* was explicitly and avowedly socialist, and Hoover called it "the exponent of open defiance and sedition" for hymning the march of the soviet system across Europe and into South America. Hoover found especially significant the *Messenger's* praise for the National Civil Liberties Bureau and Roger N. Baldwin, its director, who was in jail for refusing to report for military service. Almost half the report on Negro radicalism was taken up by reprints of poems, articles, and editorials from the *Messenger*.[80]

With these views of the Justice Department before it, Congress proceeded to a debate over bills to deal with sedition. Hearings before the House Judiciary Committee on *Sedition, Syndicalism, Sabotage, and Anarchy* brought statements from Congressman Byrnes about the efforts of the IWW, through the *Messenger*, to get Negroes to join. Byrnes described the process this way:[81]

The I.W.W. . . . hold out the hope of tying up the railroads if they can get the negro firemen to join. They state they could then tie up the railroads, which they say is necessary to a successful revolution, because then they could stop the transportation of troops necessary to quell the riots and the revolution.

The *Messenger* would be outlawed under his proposed anti-sedition law, Byrnes explains, "because it aims at revolution." He cited a *Messenger* editorial that praised the Russian, German, Austrian, Hungarian, and Bulgarian revolutions, endorsed the "titanic strikes" in Great Britain, France, Italy, the United States, and Japan, and exalted "the new crowd negro" in these terms:[82]

The Washington, Chicago, Longview, Knoxville, Elaine, and Omaha riots are bright spots in the new negro's attitude toward American lawlessness and anarchy. They represent the new negro upholding the dignity of the law against both the white hoodlums and the Government, the latter of whom should have seen that law was upheld.

The Justice Department continued to act on the belief that Negro unrest was closely connected with "seditious" propaganda. In January, when a Senate Judiciary subcommittee met to consider resolutions proposing a full-scale investigation of race riots and lynching, Senator Charles Curtis reported that the Justice Department was continuing to pursue the issue of radical involvement in the race riots. As evidence of such involvement, the department identified one article "intended to arouse negroes" as having been written by an IWW official and printed at the expense of a man in Mexico City "who . . . was believed to be a German agent."[83] Attorney-General Palmer himself testified before the House Judiciary Committee in February that "thousands and thousands" of cases existed in which "appeals to racial hatred" had gone out from radical groups to Negroes, especially in the South but "all over the United States" as well. He cited a circular of the American Anarchist Federated

Commune Soviets, in which the Negroes were called upon to ignore the American Federation of Labor which had "boycotted" and "sneered at" them and instead to join the radical movement: "If battles must be fought, if riots must take place, if blood must be shed, in order to destroy the present slavery, then let us in our united strength start the real war—the social revolution."[84]

Simultaneously, Moorfield Storey, the eminent lawyer who headed the NAACP, wrote Palmer that he had heard that "some officers" of the Justice Department were connecting the NAACP and the Urban League with radical propaganda. Storey explained that there was "no justification for the suggestion that we are undertaking to do anything inconsistent with absolute loyalty to the government of the United States." He asked Palmer to "instruct . . . subordinates to be careful in making injurious accusations which rest merely upon vague suspicion."[85] Palmer's answer read, "The contents of your communication have been noted and will receive careful attention."* [86]

As late as 1921, the General Intelligence Division of the FBI was still following the aftermath of the Arkansas riots. A report on the request for discharge of the convicted Negroes and on reactions to Robert Kerlin's open letter of protest was filed by an agent at Little Rock. He added:[88]

---

* The NAACP was being kept under surveillance. As late as 1921, J. Edgar Hoover was informed by the State Department, "for any action that you may wish to take," that the NAACP had sent a leaflet on the burning at the stake of an American Negro to Latin American editors with the request that they "comment on the phases of American civilization which this publication reveals." The General Investigation Division checked off the names of the NAACP's officers as listed on the enclosed letter, as if their names had perhaps been noted.[87]

Information received by Agent through confidential sources indicate that the negro ministers of this place have in the past attempted to arouse feeling among the negroes by preaching social equality and advising the negroes of their equal rights, and if unable to obtain them through peaceable means, then resort to violence. It is a known fact that the majority of the negroes are well armed with high powered guns and ammunition.

Many who believed in racial equality rejected the notion that radicals or Bolsheviks had had any serious influence upon Negroes who were demanding equality. Thus a Washington high school teacher wrote Palmer, after requesting and reading the Justice Department's report on radicalism among Negroes, that he and his friends "were amused at your prolonged wail against the manly element of Negroes," those who boldly demanded equality. He told the Attorney General, "It is not an investigation that your department should recommend, but a system of justice which will square with Woodrow Wilson's rhetoric." And he warned that the government could only "check the spread of Bolshevism with democracy."[89] The Arkansas white lawyer U. S. Bratton, in addition to the NAACP's James Weldon Johnson, and the Washington lawyer Archibald H. Grimké, told the Senate Judiciary Committee that not radical agitators, but the conditions under which Negroes lived had made them determined to seek changes in their lot and to protect themselves against attack.[90] Howard University's Dean Kelly Miller took the same view.[91] The NAACP also testified against certain proposed legislation on sedition, for fear that under some provisions "the mere printing of facts and data about lynchings," or the printing of "just and legitimate protests" might become illegal.[92]

To many of those who saw the vision of a past and future America where the races had been and would be hierarchically ordered, it seemed wholly credible that the upsets of 1919 could be traced to alien schemes for disrupting that vision, and they tended to believe that suppression of the alien or alienated agitators would restore the hierarchy they envisioned. To supporters of racial equality, on the other hand, the only hope for an end to violence seemed to be the elimination of the special privileges and special disabilities that had been at issue in the riots. Both these groups saw the riots as one battle in an over-all struggle for the American way—to restore it, or to make it real for the first time.

* * *

The Demand for Racial Accommodation

Many other Americans despaired of ending racial conflict if the solution depended on deciding between equal status and subordination as the place of Negroes in American life. Instead, they focused on reaching some short-run settlements of the immediate issues in conflict. They talked of an "accommodation" to conflicting pressures, in order to take the heat off the racial mobs that were clashing in city and countryside.

One of the major spokesmen for "accommodation" was Robert Russa Moton, the successor of Booker T. Washington as head of Tuskegee Institute and as proponent of the go-slow approach. Moton, toward the end of the long, violent summer of 1919, said it was difficult to understand why the riots had erupted. "I never knew a time when the white people . . . were more anxious than at present to be absolutely fair and just to the Negro," he explained. He emphasized the value of working with "the leading white people" to smooth over the bitterness and suspicion that had erupted, and with the calmer heads among the Negro leadership to control the "intense feeling" that had sprung up "with little reason" among their people.[93]

From the white side, Senator Medill McCormick of Illinois demanded that "the two races . . . candidly take steps to accommodate their differences and their interests." He called for "successful, law abiding colored people, to join with white citizens immediately concerned in the problems of negro employment and residence" to "unite upon a policy."[94] The *New York Times* called for a new generation of moderate leaders like Booker T. Washington to forestall the "heavy attack of radicals and militants" by moving toward conciliation with the whites and accommodation of specific conflicts. The *Times* also called upon white leaders to help moderate Negroes against the militants, by moving toward "a fair and harmonious adjustment."[95] Similarly, the *Philadelphia Inquirer* called for "self-restraint on both sides," since "the causes at the bottom of these riots cannot be removed in a day or a generation; perhaps . . . never."[96]

To most of those who urged "accommodation," the way to bring it about seemed quiet negotiation between "calm" and "moderate" white and Negro leaders. Even before most of the riots, George Haynes, director of the Division of Negro Economics in the Department of Labor, had urged privately that riots be forestalled in areas of tension by calling together committees of whites and Negroes to work out the issues in controversy.[97] By October, Haynes was being quoted in the *New York Times* in favor of local and national biracial committees, to be called together by officials at every level of government in order "to map out some plans . . . that will gain the support of law-abiding citizens of both races."[98] Glenn Frank, associate editor of the *Century*, similarly called for "joint councils of blacks and whites" in which

Negro leaders like Washington rather than "the fire-brand type" could negotiate over interracial problems.[99]

Spurred on by the 1919 riots, white and Negro leaders did try to institutionalize the approach of "accommodation" and "negotiation" that these men had proposed. On July 24, a meeting of what became the Commission on Interracial Cooperation discussed the Washington riot and agreed there was an urgent need to cope with Negro restlessness and prevent more violence.[100] For its first two years, the commission was haunted by the memory of the 1919 riots and felt its chief task was the prevention of racial violence.[101] As described by Thomas Jesse Jones of the Phelps-Stokes Fund, which was helping finance the Interracial Commission, the commission had during 1919 emphasized the formation of local committees. In the South, each local group had two sections, white and Negro, which met separately. "The negroes," Jones reported, "draw up a prospectus of what they think they should have in the way of aid and recognition from the whites. The white committee then meets, considers the complaints and suggestions of the negroes, and devises means for bettering their condition."[102]

Although Jones expressed some hope of forming such committees in the North, the commission never became an important factor in northern cities.[103] The approach of "accommodation" was more applicable where Negro leadership was small, tightly bound together, and compelled by local racial patterns to eschew the drive for equality.

✽ ✽ ✽

The Demand for "Law and Order"

Some Americans reacted to the race riots not in terms of dealing with the racial conflicts that had provoked the riots but in terms of ending the violence itself. Of these people, many feared violence not only because they were horrified at brutality and death, or because they feared the weaker party would be crushed in any violent confrontation even if it had justice on its side, but especially because the riots basically undermined the authority of the state and might encourage radicalism at home and abroad. Such people saw the task of preventing violence as bound up with the restoration of "law and order."

In line with these reasons for re-establishing law and order, there was introduced into discussion of the 1919 riots a theme that grew in importance during the twentieth century: that racial strife at home would cloud the American image overseas and interfere with the fulfillment of American foreign policy. This foreign-policy emphasis was closely connected with the call from President Wilson and other political leaders for American involvement overseas in order to restore order and protect democracy. Thus George Haynes of the Division of Negro Economics pointed out that "as one of the great world powers, we are already face to face with . . . the darker peoples of Asia, Africa, Central and South America," and would have to answer to them for "the treatment of the darker peoples within our borders."[104] Direct embarrassment over the riots was expressed by an editor who noted, "When such things are done . . . by the Japanese in Korea, the Senate cries out upon it. When such wholesale race prejudice . . . is witnessed in Ireland, or in Mexico, Congress passes indignant resolutions. . . . The world will little heed nor long remember . . . [American] professions of love of justice and humanity . . . until the United States aligns itself with the reign of law [not violence]."[105]

Critics of the American "mission" overseas pointed to the race riots as one reason to abandon it. Thus a *Chicago Tribune* cartoon showed a missionary Uncle Sam lecturing to Turkey, Germany, and Italy while behind his back a number of rowdy boys carrying bombs, clubs, guns, and ropes cavorted in Chicago, Omaha, and Washington. These boys, the caption explained, were "The Missionary's Sons."[106] As another paper wryly remarked, a Republican leader in the House of Representatives was calling for intervention to re-establish order in Mexico precisely at the moment that American soldiers and sailors in uniform were attacking Negroes on the streets of Washington.[107] Whether these observers supported the American "mission" or not, it was clear they wanted law and order upheld.

The most important measure recommended by those who wanted law and order re-established was that the police power be strengthened until it could suppress riots. This demand for a stronger police was based on two social-psychological assumptions. Each was put succinctly by an eastern newspaper reacting to one of the race riots. One asserted, "There will always be a certain quota of persons who are kept within the pale only by force . . . by the sight of bayonets flashing in the street, and machine guns posted on the corner."[108] The other decided, "There is nothing to be done but to quiet the rioters by force. We make no pretense nowadays of settling the race question; we simply keep it in abeyance."[109]

Most editors who called for a stronger police thought

in terms of sheer force: "the stiffest . . . possible dose of police," as one put it.[110] More policemen,[111] more "vigor" and "severity" or "sterner measures,"[112] the recruitment of better men with higher pay,[113] and the improvement of the police high command,[114] were the measures urged by those who concentrated on strengthening of the local police.

Another major reaction was a demand for increasing the relative power of the police by decreasing that of private persons. Thus after the Omaha riot the police of Memphis ordered all guns seized that were being held for sale by pawnshops, sporting goods stores, and hardware stores.[115] A Utica newspaper had the same response to the Washington riot, as did the *Washington Post* itself.[116]

The training of local police to make them more expert in dealing with rioters, rather than simply more overwhelming in power, was urged by some observers. The *New York Times* suggested that part of the problem in Washington had been the lack of training for riot duty, and compared the trained New York police, who had accepted the metropolitan necessity of coping with rioters, with the out-of-date "peaceful small town" training of the Washington police.[117] An anonymous army lieutenant wrote to the *Times* that tear gas and sneezing gas, newly developed for use in the World War, should be turned to use in riot control. "Either kind of gas," he wrote, "would at once divert the attention of the mob, rendering the majority incapacitated for further violence, and the police, provided with goggles alone could easily round up the leaders."[118] Training in riot duty was also urged by an official War Department manual, prepared as a result of the race riots and other civil disturbances in 1919. The manual, for use by the National Guard, drew upon the race riots in Omaha and Chicago for examples of the sorts of problems to be met on riot duty. It explained that the sharp, precise use of the minimal amount of force necessary to deter rioters early in their congregation would be more effective and more merciful than waiting too long and then suppressing a full-blown mob. The author pointed out that such tactics were quite different from those useful in battle array, and would therefore require training specifically directed at riot duty.[119] Another manual on riot duty did not draw upon specific events of the 1919 riots, but the preface—dated August 1—specified "these times of riot and tumult" as the reason for writing it at all. It also prescribed training in the special means of handling riot duty as against regular warfare.[120]

Another approach to increasing the power of the police was the use of "outside" troops. Thus the *New York Post* urged the creation of a "mobile, well-trained State Constabulary" which could have acted quickly and powerfully to end the local violence.[121] To the federal government, the riots seemed reason to be better prepared in the future to send Federal troops as quickly as possible. Thus Secretary of War Baker directed all continental army commanders to intervene to end local disorder on direct request of state officials. It was hoped in this way to end the delay involved in referring requests to Washington.[122] "The timid may take heart," Baker announced, because "an army of tried soldiers, of true Americans, . . . will . . . suppress riots and disorder in any part of the country." He continued:[123]

They are not partisans in any dispute except one, and that is the dispute between those who want order and those who try to create disorder in America . . . They are on the side of order.

*   *   *

The Hint of "Creative Disorder" and a Neutral Police

Not all those Americans who focused upon the prevention of racial violence (rather than upon the settlement of racial conflict) saw the restoration of "law and order" as the best way of preventing violence. Some seemed instead to have a hazy notion that there might be forms of "creative disorder" that would not bring about violence. There were also some who believed that the police might be better able to prevent violence if they were more nearly neutral between the parties in conflict than if they tried to amass overwhelming power of their own. If these two approaches had been acted upon, a situation might have emerged in which a moderately powerful police force stood guard against violence, but permitted a considerable amount of disorder so long as it did not turn into violence.

Certainly there was in 1919 no well-worked-out theory of creative disorder without violence and a neutral police force against violence; that was to come almost half a century later. But the beginnings of the idea can be seen in an unofficial suggestion from James Weldon Johnson, Field Secretary for the NAACP. Before a New York audience meeting to protest the events in Elaine, Arkansas, Johnson suggested that "the negroes in a city like Jacksonville, Florida, could send a committee representing 10,000 negroes to the city government and tell them that if they did not receive protection they would not cook or work in any way." "Such a course," Johnson emphasized, "would be a method more effective than the shotgun."[124] Here can be seen the bare hints of the approach to "nonviolence as a tactic" that flowered in the 1960s, and here also can be seen the notion that the police must protect Negroes from violence if violence were to be avoided. If the police acted neutrally as between the races, protecting impartially anyone who suffered violence and acting impartially against anyone who used violence, perhaps both races could invent other ways of carrying on their conflict. Such techniques might be disorderly but need not be violent.

The notion of police neutrality must be carefully distinguished from that of strengthened police power. Indeed, one Negro leader believed that the one would make the other unnecessary. The director of the National Urban League, Eugene Kinckle Jones, argued that a neutral police force would make it unnecessary to use the "rule of the bayonet and the machine gun," which he called "oppression," in order to keep racial peace. Jones believed that if the Chicago or Washington police had acted fairly toward Negroes from the beginning, the initial incidents of violence would never have mushroomed into a riot. The "oppressive" machine-gun tactics, with their "attendant train of evils and bitterness and suspicion," would have been unnecessary.[125] W.E.B. Du Bois, editor of *The Crisis,* directly criticized the behavior of local police, arguing that their inaction against white hoodlums in effect gave "permission" to the whites to use more violence against Negroes.[126] The other side of the coin was emphasized by George E. Haynes, who suggested that police partiality made Negroes feel they must defend themselves.[127] Others did not bother to spell out which side they expected to use violence if the police took sides but agreed with the necessity of neutrality.[128]

The chief attempt to institutionalize the principle of police neutrality was oriented to federal action against lynching. What supporters of such action like the NAACP hoped was that federal pressures against lynching could force local officials to act more effectively to protect Negroes against white attack.

The campaign for some sort of federal action began in September 1919, when the NAACP focused on demands for a congressional investigation of race riots and lynching. Senator Charles Curtis of Kansas introduced a resolution to authorize such an investigation, and the NAACP used national concern aroused by the Omaha and Arkansas riots to support the Curtis resolution.[129] Petitions from across the country poured into various members of the Senate Judiciary Committee, which took first crack at the resolution for an investigation.[130] Among those who wrote Senator Knute Nelson, chairman of the committee, were the governor of Georgia, the editor of the *San Francisco Bulletin*, and a bishop of the Episcopal Church.[131] Former President William Howard Taft and Republican leader George W. Wickersham wrote senators at the NAACP's request.[132]

Questions of jurisdiction over the "local issue" of lynchings worried the Senate Judiciary Committee. It requested data from the Department of State on "our dual form of government and the limitations of the federal government in respect to breaches of the peace and their consequences in the several States."[133] When hearings on the resolution were about to be held, Curtis warned the NAACP to be ready to deal with the question of federal jurisdiction over lynching and riots, more than with the facts of violence.[134] Moorfield Storey, the lawyer president of the NAACP, wrote that he could find no doubt that Congress had the power to investigate violence that might interfere with interstate commerce or with the right to vote, and therefore to investigate lynching—even if Congress then found it had no authority to outlaw the crime.[135] But the committee concentrated on the problem of jurisdiction to punish rioters and lynchers and in the absence of any proposition for a federal law that most of its members found convincing as to constitutionality,[136] failed to take any action at all on the resolution to investigate the riots themselves.[137]

In the House of Representatives, discussion of Federal intervention into racial violence took a different tack. Congressman Dyer introduced not only an investigatory resolution like Curtis' but a bill directly intended to prevent lynching. The latter bill would have found that a successful lynching meant that the State had failed to provide equal protection of the laws, and on that basis would have fined the county in which the lynching occurred $5000 to $10,000 in damages for the family of the victim.[138] Dyer asked the NAACP both to stir up sentiment across the country in favor of the bill, and to testify on its behalf.[139] The NAACP did both,[140] and was responsible for the presence of most of the witnesses who testified before the committee.[141] Such witnesses as Archibald Grimké, Arthur Spingarn, and James Weldon Johnson, in addition to the congressional proponents of the legislation, pointed to the 1919 riots as demonstrating the need for the law.* [142]

The committee majority reported the bill favorably on May 20, with no dissent recorded.[144] But a week later Representatives Hatton Sumners of Texas and Thaddeus Caraway of Arkansas explained indignantly that they had left the room before the bill was taken up and had not been informed it was scheduled. They demanded and received leave to file a minority report.[145] The majority

---

* Although the published record indicates that none of the witnesses dwelt upon the "fighting back" theme as a reason for preventing violence, the committee clerk described the testimony as follows: "All of these speakers . . . cited instances of outrages on the colored race, making threats to the effect that if legislation was not forthcoming to relieve the present situation the colored people would be compelled to take the matter into their own hands."[143]

recounted the stories of Washington, Chicago, Omaha, and Arkansas in urging passage of the bill by the House of Representatives, and emphasized local inability and unwillingness to protect Negroes in many of the states.[146] The minority denounced the majority report as "merely a reprint of a brief filed with the committee by a society domiciled in New York which has for its sole object, not the securing of justice for negroes charged with crime, but immunity from punishment for their crimes." It further repeated the "white" version of events in Arkansas, and denounced the anti-lynching bill as unnecessary and unconstitutional.[147]

The House of Representatives passed the bill, 230–119.[148] But on the floor of the Senate, despite what Walter White called "almost literally standing on our heads" by the NAACP to get the Dyer Bill to a vote,[149] the measure was filibustered to death.[150] Thus there ended unsuccessfully the only serious effort to transform the lessons of the 1919 race riots into changes in the legal structure of the United States—changes intended to satisfy the demand for an end to violence by a federal requirement that local police act more nearly neutral between the races when confronted with racial violence. In this way there collapsed even the bare tentative beginnings of a theory of "creative disorder" and a neutral police.

* * *

Of the five major responses to the riot—demands for racial equality, hierarchy, accommodation, and "law and order," and the hint of a theory of "creative disorder" —only the goal of equality and the "non-goal" of accommodation were embodied in institutions that had direct ties to the riots. The NAACP gained strength from the riots for its insistence on equality, and the accommodationist Commission on Interracial Cooperation was born out of them. The notion of racial hierarchy was one element in the complex of nativism and anti-radicalism embodied in the revived Ku Klux Klan of the 1920s, but there is no evidence that the Klan's revival drew any of its energy from reaction to the 1919 riots.[151] Nor did the demand either for a more powerful or more neutral police system entrench itself in the national law or institutions. The Army dropped to lower levels of strength and capability than it had possessed in 1919, the training of local police to be neutral in racial clashes did not begin until the 1940s, and the anti-lynching law failed of passage. Nor did the bare hint of creative disorder become a reality until the 1950s and 1960s.

One permanent change in the American intellectual climate can, however, be traced directly to the 1919 riots. There were few Americans, of whatever race or whatever persuasion as to racial policy, who could doubt that Negroes would from 1919 on be prepared to fight back against attack. The first thaw had come in the long bleak winter of "the nadir,"[152] the "capitulation to racism."[153] And it was the Negroes themselves, turning passionately and violently against the white mobs that attacked them and against the police forces that sided with their attackers, who broke the winter. Of several generations that were to be called "new Negro," the first in American history to bear that title had now emerged.

CHAPTER X

The Role of the Police

The public responses to the 1919 riots, as well as the ways in which the riots themselves developed, make inescapable the conclusion that disagreements over the role of the police were inextricably entangled with the violence and with attempts to halt it and prevent any recurrence. Whatever other factors may have been associated with the beginning of the riots, the behavior of the local police almost universally was; whatever other factors may have helped contribute to ending each riot, a change in police behavior almost universally was; whatever other remedies were urged for preventing future riots, a major one, almost universally set forth, was reconstruction of the American system of police enforcement in one way or another.

In almost all of the riots, the behavior of the local police was closely connected with the beginnings of the riot.[1] In Longview, Washington, Chicago, and Arkansas the unneutral actions of the police on behalf of the white community had much to do with turning initial incidents into full-scale riots. In Knoxville and Omaha, the initial violence by whites was directed partly against the police themselves, in a semi-insurrectionary way. Vacillation and confusion on the part of the police then helped turn these semi-insurrectionary lynchings into pogromlike attacks on the Negro community. The absence of firm neutrality in the official possessors of legitimate violence thus provided the final spark for several different sorts of riots.

If a moderately broad view of what constitutes the "police" is taken, so as to include the armed forces of the United States as well as local policemen, then events in several of the riots provide even stronger evidence for the conclusion that unneutrality by the "police" helped to spark the outbreak of violence. In Charleston and Washington, it was soldiers and sailors in uniform who began the riots by attacking Negroes, thus seeming to involve the prestige and power of the United States Government on one side in the racial conflict. Moreover, the rumors in Arkansas and Washington that Negro ROTC units were ready to use in the riots ammunition that had been given them for military training helped keep tensions high in those cities. These rumors seem a special index to the widespread breakdown of usual beliefs in the neutral function of the official institutions of authorized violence.

The police partiality had different effects upon whites and Negroes, but in both communities encouraged violence. To whites, unneutral behavior by the police meant that it was "open season" on Negroes, and that the usual protections afforded by the law were temporarily in abeyance. To Negroes, the police one-sidedness meant that their only defense against violence was self-defense, since the law would not come to their protection. This feeling crystallized into the "fighting back" commitment. It was not only police action that contributed to the "fighting back" mood. Deep in its background seem to have been the heightened expectations of Negroes who had experienced a new level of achievement, success, and independence—in greater economic prosperity, in the wider social horizons of the northern city, and in more nearly equal treatment during service in the Army. A glimpse of the new Jerusalem had thus helped create the "new Negro" who was prepared to resist any effort to close off that prospect. But not until the police sided or seemed to side with those who were trying to shut off access to the new Jerusalem did Negroes turn political resistance into outright "fighting back."

Two specific factors in police behavior, other than simple partiality toward whites, helped contribute to the explosion of riots in 1919. The first of these was the unwillingness of police to countenance any upset of the established order, even carried on by means of pressures that were not violent. When police reacted to pressures that under the existing local rules of politics were "disorderly" as if such pressures were equivalent to outright violence, they encouraged outright violence to occur. It was the unwillingness of the authorities in Phillips County, Arkansas, to permit Negroes to press their interests by organizing a sharecroppers' union that helped force the conflict into violent channels. Such unwillingness on the part of the police was complemented by difficulties on the part of the public in creating and pressing forms of protest other than violence that could stand up under police violence. Except for James Weldon Johnson's casual and abortive suggestion of a general strike by southern Negroes, both whites and Negroes failed to invent social techniques for carrying on conflict non-violently in the face of police opposition or suppression. Violence seemed the only resort.

The second special factor in police behavior during 1919 that helped contribute to the occurrence of rioting was that the police were unready to define the use of violence by either party as absolutely illegitimate, and were therefore slow to act against rioters of either race. Thus, even after large-scale riots broke out, there was great hesitation in several cases (especially in Washington and Chicago) before the state exercised its monopoly and put enough force in the field to quell the riots. These delays in quelling the riots encouraged hesitant citizens to accept the notion that violence was probably considered legitimate by the authorities, especially since such a notion could draw upon the traditionally skeptical American attitude toward police forces, the traditionally casual American attitude toward private violence in general, and especially the traditional southern willingness to use private violence in racial conflicts. Not only among the whites and Negroes in conflict, but also among the police who might presumably have thought they possessed a monopoly of authorized violence, there were evidently strong feelings that the state should turn its head at least as long as private violence stayed at a low level.

As in their initiation, so in their conclusion the riots of 1919 were deeply affected by the behavior of the police. In almost all of the riots, a change in the power and the degree of authority of the police was necessary to bring the violence to an end. The deployment of more police power in the form of state police as in Longview, state militia as in Chicago, or federal troops as in Omaha, Washington, and Arkansas, was a major step toward bringing most of the riots under control. So was the superior neutrality of these additional police in their relations with the rioting whites and Negroes.

An examination of the five major responses to the 1919 riots shows that several of them see changes in the behavior of the police as a way of preventing future riots. Looked at in terms of their views on the role of the police, the five responses cluster into three different positions. The first of these looked toward increasing the power of the police so that they could smash opposition to the established order, whether expressed in violent riots or

disorderly protest. The second looked toward making
the police more neutral as between the parties in conflict, more single-mindedly committed to preventing or
punishing violence by whomever used, and more prepared to accept as legitimate any attempts by weaker
parties to disturb the established order by means other
than violence. The third approach tended to ignore the
police and to concentrate instead on changes in the
values and beliefs of American society.

The first view, favoring a more powerful police, was
held both by those who demanded a return to racial
hierarchy in American life and those who demanded the
re-establishment of "law and order." In the first case, hierarchists deplored what they called the "mildness" that
police in many cities had shown toward Negro rioters,
and also demanded tough federal police action against
the "radicalism" and "Bolshevism" they thought had
helped incite the Negro mobs. Among those who wanted
a return to "law and order" without specifying what sort
of established order they had in mind, the idea seems to
have been not suppression of Negroes by superior police
power, but suppression of anyone, white or black, who
disturbed the political system. The "law and order"
school seemed to hope that whenever racial conflict became disorderly or violent, government would make authoritative decisions settling the conflicts, and then enforce these decisions with a heavy hand. Despite the
difference between the two groups over the kind of
"order" to be enforced, both were prepared to enforce
order with overwhelming power.

The approach that looked toward a neutral police
force, oriented to the prevention of violence without the
suppression of conflict, was exemplified by the campaign
for a federal law against lynching and by the logic of
the Supreme Court in the Arkansas cases. In both these

instances, the argument was that the federal government could and should insist that no local mob or police force use violence on behalf of one of the parties to racial conflict. In both cases—specifically in the Arkansas cases, by clear intent in the anti-lynching campaign—this approach would have extended federal protection to such activities as the creation of Negro pressure groups and unions, no matter how "disorderly" and outrageous such activities were considered in a particular locality. But this approach would not have meant federal enforcement of a new established order of racial equality. In short, these proposals looked toward the creation of a neutral police oriented solely to the prevention of violence, not toward the increase of police power to the point where it could smash all disturbers of the established order.

The third approach to the role of the police, which tended to focus away from them and toward changing basic values in the community, was taken by those who wanted to move toward racial equality and those who supported a policy of "accommodation." Unlike supporters of racial hierarchy, supporters of racial equality did not urge the use of a powerful police force to establish and uphold their favorite version of order and to suppress their opponents. Although at first glance it may seem surprising that between believers in racial hierarchy and believers in racial equality there is so little symmetry on the question of a proper role for the police, the asymmetry seems less surprising if the facts of relative power in 1919 are taken into account. The hierarchists were entrenched in power in much of the United States (not only in the South), and could easily imagine a policy of suppression carried on by "their" police forces. The equalitarians, on the other hand, had little real power anywhere in the United States except a partial veto, and an indefinite appeal to the consciences of some of those who did hold power. It might have been hard for them to imagine, and certainly would have been absurd of them to urge, that the local and federal police power be used to uphold a new order of racial equality.

As for the "accommodationists," many of them were more cautious believers in an ultimate racial equality and many were working within the context of extremely hierarchist societies, in the South. For them the enforcement of even moderate racial change by overwhelming police action would have seemed impossible, and instead they urged the semi-official discussion and adjustment of particular issues.

Both groups therefore emphasized the need for major changes in the values held by Americans, before their values should be translated into enforceable law.

These three different approaches to the role of police —the call for a more powerful police to uphold order, the call for a more neutral police that might permit disorder without violence, and the call for a change in values before the police were asked to enforce any standard—can be developed for analytical purposes into three different basic ways of exercising political authority over a society within which there was intense political conflict carried on by powerful groups over basic issues strongly felt. These three forms of political authority might for the sake of convenience be called those of "church," of "state," and of "government."

A "church" is an institution that focuses and creates shared values by moral suasion, rather than force or coercion. Although we are used to thinking of churches as separate from the government, there are many elements of presidential and congressional authority that are symbolic rather than coercive and many aspects of court decisions on great issues that go beyond immediate, co-ercively enforceable decrees into the creation of a new consensus on basic values. In this sense some writers have spoken of the "religions" of democracy or of nationalism, and it is the institutionalization of such "religions" within some parts of the federal authority that is meant here by the word "church," rather than any particular religious body. In a society that had a single major "church," there would be no serious political conflicts; almost all the people would agree on political values and purposes. In a society where several "churches" or none existed, there might be intense political conflict, and conversely, in a society within which there was intense political conflict, it would be hard to establish a single "church" or to keep an existing one legitimate. The argument for a new "church" on racial issues was expressed in 1919 by those who hoped for racial equality or accommodation to be achieved by a change in American values.

A "state," to use—and deliberately misuse—Max Weber's definition, is an institution that has a monopoly on legitimate violence and the power to prevent or punish illegitimate violence. Weber did not mean by defining a "state" in this way to suggest that a "state" did not have other powers as well. But let us, for the sake of convenience in discussing different sorts of political authority, turn Weber's definition around and call a "state" that sort of institution which can *only* forbid private, illegitimate violence—and which can use its own legitimate violence *only* to enforce that prohibition. In a society where there were intense political conflicts, but a "state" existed, the conflicts would be likely to be fought out with no outright violence, by "disorderly" methods. In a society beset by conflicts in which there was no "state," the conflicts would be extremely likely to erupt into violence. In 1919, those who called for a neutral police system and the prohibition of violence on racial issues were demanding what we are now calling a "state."

A "government," finally, is an institution that intermixes the functions of "church" and "state." A true "government" both sets forth values and prepares to enforce them with all the legitimate violence necessary. In doing so, a "government" creates something totally new: *law* in the strict sense, which first sets forth the acts people should perform or avoid and then prescribes the use of police power to punish those who fail to obey. In a society where a strong "government" operated and true law existed on all issues, political processes would be extremely "orderly," and change might be slow and hard to bring about from the bottom, but easy to command from on high. Those who in 1919 wanted forceful police measures taken to restore "law and order" or to uphold racial hierarchy were calling for the creation of a "government" on the race question.

These "ideal types" of political authority are of course convenient ways to categorize political behavior, rather than descriptions of actual political institutions operating in the pure forms as set forth here. But a particular political institution may act much more like one than another of these ideal types. Or, on a particular issue over which there is intense conflict, a given political institution may act like one of these forms—whereas on another issue over which there is little conflict, the same political institution may act much more like another of the "ideal types." This last, on the racial issue, has been precisely the case with the United States Government in Washington. On many questions, for many decades, it has acted like a true "government"; on the race question, it has not.

Indeed, in 1919 the United States had no single "church," no "state," and no single "government" as regards the race question (though it did, on the local level, have an ill-defined and inchoate set of "governments," mostly committed to racial hierarchy). In response to the

1919 race riots, there began to grow the seeds of an American "state" on the race question—an institution, or set of institutions, that outlawed violence from either side but did not try to settle the basic conflicts that led to violence. The way in which the United States Army behaved in most of the riot situations it entered and the way in which the Supreme Court acted when the Arkansas cases reached it are the indications that the seeds had begun to grow. But they were only seeds, and not until the racial crisis of the 1960s did the notion of an American "state" on the race question begin to flower.

CHAPTER XI

Public and Private Violence: The 1960s

Between 1919 and the 1960s there were a number of explosions of racial violence, and indeed of other sorts of violence, in the United States. But the incidence of private mass violence declined throughout the period, and the *de facto* monopolization of violence by the national government increased. If one takes as a postulate growing out of European experience, Weber's assumption in 1918 that states had a monopoly of the legitimate use of physical force within their territory, then by the 1960s the United States had become much more like a European nation, with a Weberian state, than it was in 1919. In 1919 American political authorities and police had been deeply ambivalent over their role in dealing with private violence; by the 1960s that ambivalence had almost disappeared, and Americans tended much more frequently to act as if the government in Washington ought to have, and did have, a monopoly of legitimate violence.

When the 1960s began, the last instance of large-scale violence between two American social groups had been the Detroit and Harlem race riots and the Los Angeles "zoot suit" ethnic riots of 1943.[1] Through the twenties and thirties there had been a few racial clashes—at Tulsa during 1921, in Harlem during 1935—and a number of bloody labor-management riots, so that the patterns of private mass violence that had been traditional in America before 1919 had seemed to be re-established afterward.[2] But the last head-on riot between forces of labor and management occurred at the River Rouge plant of the Ford Motor Company in 1941, and from then on into the 1960s only isolated incidents of small-scale violence marked that arena of conflict which had formerly been the one most productive of violence.[3] From the Detroit, Harlem, and Los Angeles riots of 1943 until the comparatively small-scale but large-impact race riots that occurred during 1964 in Harlem, Rochester, and several New Jersey cities, no major riots of any sort disturbed the American peace.[*] That twenty-one years was the longest such era in American history, and its length is a major index of the extent to which American violence had become "Europeanized" in the Weber mode.

It was not only in the abandonment of mass private violence that the United States had by the 1960s become a more "European" state, but also in the organization and operation of public violence. The anti-military tradition of Washington's Farewell Address had given way before major changes in the international position of the United States. By the 1960s, the traditional American suspicion of standing armies had been subordinated to a belief that as a world power in the European fashion, the United States needed a large standing army. For two decades, indeed, the American armed forces had been costing about one tenth of the gross national product.[4]

It is hard to avoid making the tentative conjecture that one of these developments may have had something to do with the other: that the creation of a large and per-

---

[*] It should be remembered that we are distinguishing a riot, which is mass violence carried on between two social groups from an insurrection, which is mass violence directed against the government or the political system as a whole. The violent events of 1957 in Little Rock, Arkansas, and of 1962 in Oxford, Mississippi, though motivated by feelings that grew out of racial conflict, were not so much race riots as insurrections against federal authority.

manent standing army both symbolized the monopolization of violence by the United States Government, and
in actual practice posed a constant deterrent to using
large-scale private violence as a way of carrying on social
conflict.

Another important factor in the decline of outright
violence may conceivably have been a decline in the
prestige of violence as a way of settling conflicts. In 1919,
it looked as if war and violent revolution could "work";
that is, could advance the political goals of the victors.
But in the 1960s, there was among Americans much more
doubt as to the efficacy of violence. The most recent violent revolutions, in China and Cuba, lit almost none of
the sustained interest and enthusiasm that some Americans had given the Russian Revolution—partly because
the Russian Revolution had failed to achieve what sympathetic Americans had hoped it would, and indeed, had
created the suspicion that violent revolutions might inevitably "fail" in that sense. As for international violence,
the advent of thermonuclear weapons had seemed to
make world war a much less workable way of accom-
plishing political goals; the nation's most recent war, in
Korea, had ended not in the glorious victory of 1918 but
in frustration and stalemate that suggested even "limited," non-nuclear violence might be ineffectual; and the
most profound and prolonged international confrontation
in the nation's history was being carried on by "Cold
War" methods using non-lethal techniques of propaganda,
economic pressure, subversion, and technological competition rather than by outright warfare. Indeed, in the
1960s there appeared a spate of books that discussed
world disarmament not simply as an ethical ideal but for
almost the first time as a way of advancing the American
national interest, in effect as a special case of "military"
strategy using a non-military approach.[5] And the United

States Government committed itself to seek "general and complete disarmament" as a national goal.[6] Although this approach of the 1960s may seem little different from the widespread interest in 1919 in the League of Nations as a way of putting an end to war, two differences must be remembered: first that the United States finally rejected the League, whereas in the 1960s it accepted the nuclear test ban which symbolized the whole approach of world disarmament; and secondly, that in 1919 the rhetoric of "the war to end war" meant that war was still thought to be an effective way of achieving ends, whereas in the 1960s few if any writers expected to achieve disarmament through a successful war.

Thus there is some evidence that by the 1960s, American intellectuals and political leaders were much more dubious than they were in 1919 about the effectiveness of violence as a way of carrying on conflict. Difficult though it is to measure whether this doubt had affected the kinds of people who would have been likely to fight riots, perhaps it is important to take this general atmosphere into account.

Not only had there been a general diminution in the prestige of violence as a way of getting things done, but there had also been increasing interest in the notion that a deliberate and forceful use of "non-violence" might be an effective way of carrying on some forms of conflict. Many intellectuals had been especially impressed by Gandhi's non-violent campaigns for Indian independence, campaigns which were one major factor in finally securing British withdrawal from India. Indeed a direct connection can be traced from Gandhi to the invention of non-violent ways of carrying on racial conflict in the United States, through American Gandhians in the Fellowship of Reconciliation who helped found the Congress of Racial Equality and who helped energize Martin

Luther King in his leadership of the non-violent campaign in 1956 to end bus segregation in Montgomery, Alabama.[7]

It may seem paradoxical to suggest that the decline in private mass violence in the United States as the 1960s approached may have had one part of its origin in the creation of a large and permanent standing army as the symbol of the official monopoly over violence, and another part of its origin in an increasing disillusion with armaments and violence as a way of achieving political ends. But the two developments are by no means unconnected: it was precisely what some analysts believed to be "the hypertrophy of war,"[8] including the creation of a large permanent American military establishment, that provided the stimulus to working out means of carrying on conflict and achieving political ends that would not require war.* So far as might-be rioters were concerned, the two new developments—a strong national army and an approach toward carrying on conflict without violence—might have acted like the stick and the carrot. Warned away from rioting on the one hand, they may have been attracted toward substitute techniques, on the other hand.

Undoubtedly there were from 1940 to the 1960s many changes in American society, other than the creation of

* The connections between the two developments can be seen especially well, and can be especially appropriately compared with the world as Weber saw it in 1918, by examining the outlook of Kenneth Boulding, a social researcher and analyst of Weberian caliber. Boulding saw in the multiplication of armed forces intended only to deter each other, rather than to fight, a preface to "the separation of the armed forces from the state."[9] That concept clearly both builds upon and transforms Weber's formulation of the close connection between the state and the armed forces. Boulding also pointed to Gandhian non-violence as one new invention that might allow conflict to be carried on after the separation of state and army.[10]

a large standing army and the drop in the prestige of violence as a useful tool, which may have also had some share in reducing the amount of domestic violence. Many national ties across geographical, class, and racial lines were strengthened after 1940, partly as a result of shared experiences brought about by such newly "national" institutions as the armed forces and by improved transportation and communication; partly as a result of the blurring of conflict induced by widespread prosperity; and partly as a result of the emphasis on a national identity that grew out of an almost continuous outside threat to national security, and the actuality or possibility of war. The multiplication of these ties probably intensified feelings of shared national community in such a way as to reduce the likelihood of intense internal conflict between social groups. For this reason, there were probably fewer intense conflicts of the sort that would in the past have been likely to explode into violence; and therefore, less actual violence.

It might indeed be argued that the strengthened ties of national community are a sufficient explanation for the decline in private mass violence from 1919 to the 1960s. But there were occasions on which intense conflict occurred despite the new feelings of national community, and we must therefore look beyond the new feelings of community in order to understand why such conflicts did not explode into violence. The impact of the newly enlarged national armed forces, both in representing the state monopoly of legitimate violence and in triggering a new concern with nonviolent means of conducting conflict, may thus merit close attention as a factor in the shift from race riot to sit-in.

CHAPTER XII

The Emergence of Creative Disorder

It was not until the early 1960s that another generation of "new Negroes" forced its way to national attention. That generation invented the sit-ins, and its members were both far more vigorous and far less violent than the generation of 1919. Where the unorganized rioters of 1919 had fought back violently against violent attack, the organized sit-in movement initiated action instead of defensively responding, carried its protest against racial hierarchy into the camp of the enemy—but did so under a strict discipline of avoiding violence.*

What the new generation of Negroes was like can best be understood in the words of one of its members. Asked whom she thought of as participants in the new civil-rights movement, she smiled and answered, "Anybody who's black—and glad."[1] Millions of Negro Americans have throughout our history been black and sad; the Negro rioters of 1919 were black and bitter; many civil-

* The following chapters on racial conflict during the 1960s, and particularly during the crisis years of 1963–64, are not, like the previous discussion of racial conflict during 1919, based on the private archives of governments, organizations, or individuals. They are based instead on the public record and the author's own observations, and should be clearly seen as a tentative effort both to understand what happened in 1919 by comparison with what happened in the 1960s, and to understand what happened during the 1960s as an outgrowth of what happened in 1919. As is inevitable in trying to treat historically a period so recent, the historian takes a greater chance that facts as yet unknown to him or consequences that have not yet occurred will invalidate his interpretations.

rights workers for many decades have tried to act like angry whites. But only in the 1960s did large numbers of Negroes embrace their blackness and channel their ancient anger into joyful protest.

The new techniques of the sit-in generation brought to fruition James Weldon Johnson's bare hint of "creative disorder." Since 1919, Johnson's own NAACP had concentrated on what may be called "the politics of order" in courtroom, legislative lobby, and newspaper column —the same kind of politics that the NAACP had pursued in response to the 1919 riots.[2] What may be called "the politics of violence" had also been used in American racial conflicts since 1919—notably when race riots erupted in Detroit, Harlem, and Los Angeles during 1943[3] and when enforcement of court orders for school desegregation brought mob uprisings and military occupations to parts of the South in the 1950s.[4] But the thorough application of a third kind of politics, neither orderly nor violent, had to await the emergence of the "new Negro" generation of the 1960s.

The first act of that generation was the invention of the sit-in on February 1, 1960, in Greensboro, North Carolina.[*] Four Negro college freshmen sat down at a lunch counter where Negroes had never been served, refused to leave although they were denied service, and attracted both shouted curses and whispered support from increasing numbers of white bystanders. Their act at once reverberated in their own college, and within six weeks

[*] There had been previous "sit-ins" in a number of cities, led by the Congress of Racial Equality and youth groups of the NAACP, but none of these "caught on" nationally, and none of the Greensboro sit-inners had heard of them. The "invention" of the sit-in as a technique relevant to American society as a whole was, therefore, accomplished by the Greensboro students, with the help of a social situation that was "ready" for creative disorder in ways that it had not been in 1919 or 1943.

across the South. Two major events of the previous decade had helped bring the students to the point of action: the 1954 decision by the Supreme Court that public schools should be desegregated, and the subsequent failure of the schools they attended to be desegregated; and the 1958 boycott of segregated buses led by the Reverend Martin Luther King, Jr., in Montgomery, Alabama. The one event had bred first a major heightening of expectations and then a deep frustration and anger at the failure of those expectations to be fulfilled; the other event had offered both a hero and a basic approach —Martin Luther King and Gandhian "non-violence"—to these Negro adolescents.[5]

Out of the sit-ins that soon spread to Atlanta, Nashville, Jackson, and about sixty other southern towns, there was born the Student Nonviolent Coordinating Committee (SNCC), with an office in Atlanta. It was at first closely related to Martin Luther King's Southern Christian Leadership Conference (SCLC), which was a loose confederation built around activist Negro ministers in many southern cities. But SNCC went even further than SCLC in eschewing formal organizational patterns. Indeed, SNCC found it had a difficult task in simply trying to keep in touch with the fast-spreading student movement across the South. Within months the original sit-in notion had been generalized to wade-ins at segregated beaches, read-ins at segregated libraries, kneel-ins at segregated churches, walk-ins at segregated theaters and amusement parks. In a number of cases, the initial shock and anger of the white community was translated into mob attacks, police brutality, and jail sentences.[6]

In carrying forward the sit-in movement, SNCC organized some adolescents who in 1919 might have been found in a riot and energized them around some of the same sorts of appeals—daring, self-assertiveness, the acting out of hostility, rebellion against parental restrictions —that also characterize gangs of delinquent and violent adolescents, as well as some appeals—to "gladness," racial pride, and a sense of advancing values officially upheld by the society—that would be alien to delinquent gangs. As the sit-in movement developed, many of its members rejected any moral or religious commitment to non-violence in the Gandhian sense, and adopted instead a stance in which the choice not to use violence was based on tactical political considerations. Even on this basis, the decision to reject violence was almost universally adhered to.[7]

But even in the absence of violence, the sit-in and all its permutations were in many places taken to be clear cases of criminal trespass.[8] Not everywhere: for by September 1961, restaurants in 108 southern or border cities had ended racial segregation, as a result of the sit-ins.[9] But there were pockets of resistance—especially, though not exclusively, in the Deep South—where the sit-ins were regarded as a major challenge to what might be called the "territorial" sense of private property, the sense that along with ownership goes a defensible "boundary." As the courts began working on the problem, however, it became clear that under the force of the equal-protection clause of the Fourteenth Amendment there might be a partial restructuring of this "territorial" notion of property. The Supreme Court of Delaware held that the police could not intervene to protect an owner's "territorial" rights if he were using them to discriminate racially, since that would involve the state in racial discrimination. This left the owner free to use "self-help" —possibly including a limited amount of force—to impose racial segregation, if he wished. It also left the sit-inner free to sit-in, so far as the state was concerned. In short, it made legitimate a certain form and amount of disorder

—but probably only on the racial question, and only in places affected with a public interest.

If the exclusion were not racial, at least so far as the Delaware decision went, the owner could still call the police to enforce his territorial boundaries. Democrats, for instance, could still presumably get police help to exclude Republican sit-inners from a Democratic caucus. And if the place were not affected with a public interest, presumably the police could still enforce a racial exclusion. Thus, for example, Black Muslims could presumably still call police to keep white sit-inners out of the mosque.[10]

A view different from Delaware's—in some ways more restricted, in some ways more expansive—was set forth by the Department of Justice before the United States Supreme Court, as friend of the court in five sit-in cases in early 1964. The department was more restrictive in arguing that only when racial exclusion or segregation in public places was clearly not the mere whim of an individual owner but rather the result of a long-standing public custom having practically the force of law, were the police forbidden to intervene to arrest sit-inners. For then, the department argued, the conjunction of custom and police action would have the force of unconstitutional state action. This outlook would still leave an individual shop owner free to have a Negro sit-inner arrested, if his community had no tradition or custom of racial exclusion. But, on the other hand, the Justice Department in some ways went further than Delaware by arguing that the owner could not himself use violence to eject a sit-inner, since the permission to use private violence was also a grant from the state. In other words, the Justice Department brief would have required a non-violent confrontation between sit-inner and proprietor, each trying through calm moral suasion or angry political pressure and argument to accomplish his ends. To the degree that the Justice Department wanted the United States to enforce this state of affairs, it was calling for an American "state" on this aspect of the race question.

Both the original southern argument in these Supreme Court cases and the most developed NAACP argument were quite different from this upholding by the Justice Department of the legitimacy of disorder; and they were far more like each other in their basic theory of law and politics than either was like the Justice Department brief. Originally, the South had argued that states and localities have a right to create and defend the established order of segregation by law, if they wish; and even when that argument collapsed, the southern states continued to argue that states and localities had a right to use police power to defend a *privately* established system of segregation. As for the NAACP, it argued that any public business licensed by the state was an arm of the state and must forego segregation; in other words, that the state had an affirmative duty to create and uphold a new established order of racial integration. Both the South and the NAACP, then, were calling for "government" which could secure *order* by enforcing one set of values or another on race. The Justice Department saw the role of political authority in some aspects of the race question to be rather the prevention of outright violence, while certain kinds of *disorder* were permitted to exist because private groups were struggling over which set of values should prevail.[11]

The Supreme Court, when it ruled on the five sit-in cases, refused to accept the reasoning of Delaware or the Justice Department. The Court's opinion avoided the crucial issue, deciding some of the cases in favor of the sit-inners on trivial grounds and remanding others for re-examination in lower courts.[12] But Justice Hugo

Black, in a dissenting opinion, expressed a view that may have moved some members of the majority as well: his belief that disorder, even without violence as in the sit-in movement, would lead inevitably to outright rioting. Black argued that "Force leads to violence, violence to mob conflicts. . . . At times the rule of law seems too slow to some for the settlement of their grievances. But it is the plan our Nation has chosen."[13]

By avoiding the issue in early 1964, the Court was able to return to the problem of racially segregated restaurants after the Civil Rights Act of 1964 had been passed. By means of Title II of the new law, a new system of "law and order" had been established concerning places of public accommodation, and the Court had no difficulty in upholding both the right of Negroes who would previously have had to be sit-inners to be served in public restaurants, and the authority of federal courts and police to punish innkeepers who refused to serve Negroes.[14] In this way, the original goal of the sit-in movement was accomplished—even where voluntary desegregation under the direct pressure of the sit-ins had been refused—by legislative action that had been born out of the pressure generated by the sit-in movement.

But the generation of "new Negroes" that had awakened in 1960 with the sit-in movement had gone far beyond its original purposes by the time the Supreme Court upheld Title II of the Civil Rights Act of 1964. Indeed, many of the act's other ten titles owed much to the expanding use of "creative disorder" by the new generation of racial equalitarians.

After the wave of early sit-ins, the next focus of these newest "new Negroes" was a series of "freedom rides" in 1961. These were begun by the Congress of Racial Equality (CORE), which sent racially mixed groups of people riding on interstate buses in the South. Several of the buses were attacked by mobs, and, in the absence of police protection, many of the riders were beaten. SNCC picked up the "freedom rides" and carried them on despite continued mob violence and police arrests, often followed by brutality in prison. Finally, the federal government took action to protect some of the riders and to make effective in actuality the legal rule that interstate traffic must be desegregated.[15]

During 1962, both SNCC and the Southern Christian Leadership Conference sank deeper roots into southern soil. In the most hierarchist parts of the South—in such towns of the Black Belt as Albany, Georgia, and Mc-Comb and Greenwood, Mississippi—the drive for Negro rights began to expand beyond desegregation of public accommodations, into questions of direct political power like the right to vote and run for office. In advancing voter registration among Negroes who had previously been too cowed, too hopeless, or too ignorant of the law to try to register, the movement began more and more to use mass public marches. These were a useful technique for mobilizing Negro strength, destroying the old white images of Negro passivity, demonstrating Negro solidarity both to the Negroes themselves and to local white power structures, and attracting national attention both to their old plight and their new militance.[16]

Presumably, such public marches came under the heading of picketing or parading, and as forms of free speech were therefore perfectly legal rather than "disorderly." Nevertheless, some police departments treated such public marches as irretrievably illegal. Indeed, some police officers took this reaction so far that they exceeded any conceivable interpretation of their constitutional powers, by treating as illegal any sort of public civil rights demonstration even if it completely avoided interfering with traffic or business. Thus Chief Laurie

Pritchett of Albany, Georgia, frequently arrested single individuals as soon as they emerged on a public street carrying signs demanding integration.[17]

One of the major instances in which public marches were treated as illegal was the series of demonstrations during the spring of 1963 in what some civil rights workers called the nation's most segregated city—Birmingham, Alabama.

The Birmingham marches were held after the repeated collapse of a series of quiet negotiations that had aimed at desegregating facilities and ending racial discrimination in employment at some downtown stores. On April 3, 1963, Negro pickets and sit-inners under the leadership of the Southern Christian Leadership Conference, began to appear at a number of stores. Day after day, they were arrested and others came to take their places, until about one thousand had been jailed. Gradually the emphasis shifted from protests at particular establishments to large-scale demonstrations on the streets. During April there were also increasing demands from students of high school age and even younger that they be permitted to take part in the demonstrations. By the end of the month, the leadership had acceded to these demands and permitted the children to be trained in the tactics of non-violent protests and self-protection.

On Thursday, May 2, large numbers of students joined in the Birmingham marches. The police, who had in most cases until then been relatively restrained in making arrests, began, under orders from Police Commissioner Eugene Connor, to use dogs and high-pressure fire hoses against the children. The "black and glad" aspect of the student movement made one of its most remarkable appearances, as school children laughed and danced under the high-pressure hoses and sang their freedom songs in jazz, with a serious but not a somber note. On May 4, a notable news photograph appeared all over the world, showing a Birmingham police dog leaping at the throat of a Negro schoolboy.[18]

If there was any single event or moment at which the 1960s generation of "new Negroes" can be said to have turned into a major social force, the appearance of that photograph was it. Intense pressure upon President John F. Kennedy to initiate federal action began to be applied the moment that photograph appeared, and both financial and political support for all organizations in the civil rights movement multiplied at once.[19]

In Birmingham itself, the demonstrations continued. On May 7, thousands of students appeared on the streets, and panicky policemen and firemen began to use even more violence. Bystanders as well as demonstrators were attacked—and some onlookers who were not under SCLC discipline began to throw bricks and bottles at the police.[20] The involvement of the school children and the increase in police and private violence had several effects. It swiftly involved many more Negroes in active, vigorous support of the movement for integration—since that movement now meant not only an abstract demand for social change, but the concrete and immediate protection of their children. It also put financial pressure on the city, since the school system lost money in state and federal aid that depended in part on the number of children actually attending school. Finally, it forced the business and political leadership of the Birmingham white community to move in the direction of racial accommodation in order to end the public disorder and violence.[21]

Negotiations that had previously failed were now able to succeed, partly because a representative of the federal Justice Department took part and made clear the President's urgent wish for a settlement, and partly because the danger that further disorder would pose to Birmingham's own economy had been made clear to its business leaders. On May 10 the Negro civil rights leadership was able to announce that an agreement had been reached to move at a later date toward desegregation and non-discriminatory employment.[22]

But the leaders' accommodations had not pleased the whole of either the white or Negro community. On Saturday night, May 11, half a dozen bombs exploded in the Negro section of Birmingham; and on Sunday, angry crowds of Negroes surged out to attack the police and firemen for hours. Fifty people were hurt, several buildings destroyed, and both the Alabama State Police and federal troops had been alerted before the pleas of civil rights leaders were able to convince most of the Negroes to accept the movement's discipline and abandon violence.[23]

The Birmingham events had three major effects. First, they showed the national political leadership of the United States that civil disorder could easily descend into mass violence unless some new system of racial law and order could be made acceptable to the contending parties. We shall return to examine the way in which the President and Congress tried to create a new system of racial order, by passing the Civil Rights Act of 1964. Secondly, the events in Birmingham signaled to equalitarian whites and Negroes all over the country that there could now be no exemptions, no delay, and no retreat for them from the Southerners' climactic battle for "Freedom Now." And finally, they signaled to hierarchist whites that a new, much sharper phase of the old racial conflict had opened—a phase in which not mere outposts, but the citadels of white supremacy were themselves endangered.

In many cities in North and South, the first response of

Negroes was to demonstrate their solidarity with the Birmingham equalitarians by calling more or less "disorderly" public marches—disorderly in that frequently so many people marched that there was considerable interference with orderly traffic and business. Although most cities had laws or regulations that controlled the number and density of demonstrators, the routes that parades could take, and so on, in some northern cities in 1963 the winds of change were strong enough to blow down all the normal restraints on public protest, and to get mass marches of political anger and protest treated as if they were parades of legionnaires having fun or Irishmen honoring St. Patrick. Thus when a quarter of a million people marched down Detroit's streets to demand immediate steps toward racial equality, although they were paralyzing traffic in what might easily have been considered a disorderly act of political protest, the Mayor himself marched at their head. In the great March on Washington for Jobs and Freedom of August 28, 1963, another quarter-million people carrying a message of political protest interrupted not only the traffic but the normal flow of governmental work, yet were similarly hailed and protected, not attacked or arrested as were Coxey's Army and the bonus marchers of earlier days. At least for the moment, the mass public protest march, however disorderly, seemed to have become accepted not only as legal, but even as harmless—at least if it dealt with racial equality.[24]

The March on Washington was in many ways the high point of "gladness" in the civil rights movement of the 1960s, and also the high point of coalition between the various elements in the country, white and black, that supported the demand for racial equality. The March was led by A. Philip Randolph, the only man in the civil rights movement of the 1960s who had had an important role in the Negro leadership of 1919. In 1919 Randolph, as editor of *The Messenger,* had argued that the achievement of socialism and racial equality were mutually necessary goals, neither able to be achieved without the other. In 1963, Randolph headed the Negro American Labor Council, was still a socialist, and had a large part in urging that the March on Washington take as its goals both jobs and freedom. Indeed, the March was one of the first public manifestations of a belief that grew more and more important among civil rights workers: the belief that—both because Negroes were economically disadvantaged and because any attempt to improve their status at the expense of the white poor would endanger the Negroes themselves—an end to poverty, white or black, was a necessary prerequisite to and corollary of any achievement of actual racial equality. Around this belief the March was able to mobilize large parts of the American labor movement, the white churches and synagogues, and many intellectuals.[25]

Partly because the quarter-million marchers made themselves into the brief reality of an equalitarian society in miniature and were therefore the symbol of a more permanent and more general equalitarianism, the March released a fraternal joy among many of the marchers who had never before felt it possible to be "black and glad" and accept that others should be "white and glad," or had never before felt it possible to be "white and glad" and accept that others should be "black and glad." Partly, also, the joy remarked by almost all observers may have been due to the uncommon mixture in this march of citizenly seriousness with private humor and relaxation. Adults dozed, adolescents sang, children played, and many marchers carried on their own quiet debates over policy without disturbing their own or their neighbors' sense of high political purpose and unity.

The atmosphere was not one of centralized control and tightly imposed order, but of a gentle interior disorder, in keeping with the March's mildly disorderly challenge to the exterior political system. Thus the March felt to its participants like effective politics on a human scale: more like the Athenian Assembly meeting to discuss and decide great political issues than like an impersonal modern balloting, or a parochial and powerless local political club, or a plebiscitary crowd hailing an all-powerful Leader.[26]

But the peak of unity and gladness achieved at the March was not destined to, probably could not have, become a permanent plateau for the civil rights movement. That believers in racial hierarchy had not been converted or transformed by the March was demonstrated only two weeks later, on September 15, when a Negro church in Birmingham was bombed and four children were killed at their Sunday-school classes. Aimless bands of angry Negroes wandered Birmingham the rest of the day. The local police—once more edgy, and anti-Negro as always—killed one more Negro, and a band of white marauders killed yet another before the city quieted down.[27] Protest demonstrations in memory of the four children were held throughout the country, and this time many of the marchers were disillusioned, angry, and determined to force action to be taken.[28] From this point on, indeed, the public march was more and more discarded by the "new Negroes" as not a sufficiently forceful form of disorder. Techniques that depended more on economic and political pressure, rather than on psychological appeal, were used more and more often.

Alongside the public marches that began in 1962 and culminated in 1963, there had been an increasing use of economic boycotts by Negroes to further racial equality. Like mass public demonstrations, the economic boycott has generally been treated as if it were somewhere on the borderline between "order" and "disorder." When Negroes in some southern cities organized boycotts against companies that discriminated in hiring or serving Negroes, some officials tried to charge them with "illegal restraint of trade"; but most of these attacks came to nought, and even in most parts of Mississippi, economic pressures against segregationist businesses were increasingly treated as legal techniques. Some Negro leaders tried to sidestep legal difficulties by transforming "boycotts" against segregationist businesses into "selective buying campaigns" in favor of integrationist businesses. In the North—for example, in Philadelphia, where a well-organized "selective buying campaign" in favor of department stores that hired without regard to race was highly successful—selective buying generally came to be regarded as fully legitimate, though of course it was not especially welcomed by the "official" business and political interests.[29]

In the wake of the Birmingham crisis, metropolitan Negroes in the North not only borrowed such southern approaches as the public march and the economic boycott, but also began to invent wholly new techniques of "creative disorder" for advancing racial equality. Like the earlier means of disorder, these began to be accepted as fairly legitimate. One of them was the school boycott.

Deliberately refusing to go to school is truancy, and urging children to stay out of school has in most jurisdictions long been illegal. But no one punished 9000 Boston students in June 1963 when they invented the one-day school boycott and the substitute one-day "Freedom School."[30] Nor did anyone punish either the 250,000 Chicago and 360,000 New York students who later adopted the boycott method, or their parents and civil rights leaders who suggested and led it.[31] The aim of the school boycotts was to force an end to *de facto* school segregation, accomplished in some northern cities by gerrymandering school districts to follow racial lines and in others by failure to act affirmatively to cope with segregation based on residential discrimination. The legal status of *de facto* segregation, especially the second kind, is still under debate; but the school boycotts have done much to reduce the political viability of such patterns of official behavior. In New York, for example, the boycott stirred anguished protests from school officials and the *New York Times;* but it also forced school officials to grapple much more seriously than before with the problem of integrating big-city schools.[32]

The acceptance of such techniques was not universal. Atlanta in January, 1964, suspended several dozen students for truancy when they cut classes to demonstrate against the school board for faster integration.[33] But the emergence of the school boycott as a political weapon, which "official" figures in government, business, and the press have deplored but tolerated, points to the new openness of the political system to certain forms of disorder.

Another metropolitan form of disorder, the rent strike, also moved toward acceptability. In October and November, 1963, several groups in New York City—some of them the older civil rights groups like CORE, but especially newer organizations that looked on many Negro problems as difficulties bred more of poverty than of race, like the Community Council on Housing led by Jesse Gray—began to focus on the problem of slum housing. Where housing was utterly inadequate, as it was in hundreds of Harlem tenements that Negro families had to share with rats and bitter cold and driving rain, the tenants began to refuse to pay their rent. At least in New

York City, this form of disorder was quickly assimilated by the law. Drawing partly on New York's rent-control law, which gives tenants statutory rights to their apartments in the absence of good cause to evict them, several local courts held that landlords who provided no heat, shelter, or freedom from vermin were not really providing housing at all. Hence they were not entitled to rent, and could not claim non-payment of rent as good cause to evict the tenants. One judge ruled that the rent should be paid into a special fund under the supervision of the courts, from which withdrawals could be made only to pay for repairs of the tenements. Another judge ruled that tenants could voluntarily set up such a "repair fund" if they wished, but had no obligation to do so or to pay their rent in any other way until the landlord had put his property back in livable shape. Thus the rent strike quickly won the support of New York law, and can hardly be viewed as "disorderly" so far as New York goes.[34]

The idea at once began to be discussed in other cities, however; and in many places the housing laws and courts were by no means so likely to support the rent strike. For at least at first glance, the rent strike seems to invade the notion of private property as the right to a cash return for the owner, and to leave the decision as to what is a "fair" return to the tenant rather than to orderly determination by the courts and housing officials. Thus some landlords, even in New York, claimed that the rent strike amounted to the expropriation of property. In New York, partly because of the background and tradition of rent-control law, these landlords were immediately confronted with the argument that non-payment of rent in abominably maintained apartments was no more an expropriation of property than was the condemnation and destruction of food found to be diseased and poisonous.

But in some places, unlike New York, it was the landlord view that was written into the law; and therefore police evicted the rent strikers.[35]

The third form of disorder invented for use in northern metropolises was the job blockade. Like some of the economic boycotts, it was aimed at forcing private employers to hire more Negroes; but it used more direct and forceful tactics. As invented late in May 1963 by the Philadelphia chapters of CORE and the NAACP, the job blockade consisted of stationing dozens or hundreds of white and Negro equalitarians at the sites of allegedly discriminatory employment, in such a way as to block the entry of white workmen. The blockades were to be continued until the employer hired some Negroes. In Philadelphia, these pressures brought about a few short episodes of violence between the blockaders and white construction workers or the policemen who tried to escort them to work through the blockade lines; but after several days of the blockade, the employers did hire several Negro workmen. In San Francisco, the use of similar techniques against the local hotels and automobile dealers produced agreements to hire hundreds of Negroes, but resulted also in lengthy jail sentences for some of the blockaders. The job blockade was extended to labor unions when CORE pickets in New York blocked entrance to a plumbers' union headquarters in order to force the union to admit Negro apprentices, and won an agreement there too.[36]

Although these few efforts at using the job blockade met with considerable success, they were not widely copied. For despite its similarity to the sit-in as a physical confrontation between racial equalitarians and racial hierarchists, the job blockade was in one crucial way different from the sit-ins—and therefore less valuable. Agreeing to let Negroes eat in restaurants or attend theaters, as the sit-inners demanded, did not usually deprive white customers of their seats; but the job blockades seemed to be demanding that some whites be fired and Negroes hired in their places, in order to make employment racially equal. For this reason, the job blockades may have seemed far more likely to generate extreme opposition from the white community than the sit-in or other forms of disorder. Nor did the blockades seem likely to provide jobs for large numbers of unemployed Negroes, many of whom did not have the skills to fill the only jobs that the economy was making available. The only effective alternatives seemed to be increasing the total number of jobs, perhaps especially new kinds of jobs, or perhaps inventing new sources of income and satisfaction other than jobs. But these alternatives the blockades—directed as they were at individual employers rather than those who made basic social policy concerning the whole number of jobs—could not accomplish.

In addition to all these forms of disorder (ranging from the march and the sit-in to the rent strike and the job blockade) that in some fashion or another were partially accepted during the early 1960s as legitimate political techniques, there was one more extreme form of disorder that was only tentatively tried by the movement for racial equality, that failed a number of times and succeeded only a few, and that continued in almost all localities to be outside the pale of legitimacy. That form of disorder was the disruption of the governing process itself. The original suggestion by some integration leaders that failure to pass a civil rights bill quickly might bring sit-ins to Capitol Hill and into congressional offices brought a great outcry and a swift retreat to the much milder disorder of the March on Washington.[37] Sit-ins in mayors' and governors' offices have been

roundly condemned and so far have generally been in-
effective.[38] In Danville, Virginia, student protest groups
after suffering brutal street violence from police tried
briefly to disrupt the city government. They placed hundreds of telephone calls to City Hall, saying "Freedom!"
and hanging up when their calls were answered, and
thus interrupted the normal flow of city business as conducted by telephone. But their tactic brought no immediate results, and they abandoned it.[39]

One of the most detailed plans for general social disruption was set forth in the fall of 1963, in the days of
frustration and disillusion after the March on Washington and the Birmingham church bombing. Diane Nash
Bevel proposed that the Student Nonviolent Coordinating Committee create a non-violent army, 25,000 strong,
uniformed and militant, that would undertake such campaigns as surrounding and paralyzing southern state
capitals where governors set their faces utterly against
integration, stopping transportation by blocking airports,
highways, and railroads with their bodies, etc. This proposal never came near serious consideration by SNCC,
was bitterly attacked by the normally pro-integration
Washington Post, and was hastily dismissed by other
civil rights organizations. So far, it seems, the sort of disorder that would be involved in broad-scale social disruption has not become "legitimate" in most parts of the
country.[40]

That this sort of disorder may not remain forever forbidden may be seen, however, from the events of November 1963 in Chester, Pennsylvania. The civil rights
movement in that industrial suburb of Philadelphia began its campaign to end *de facto* segregation and to improve the quality of some abysmal schools by using the
comparatively legitimate disorder of a school boycott
and public picketing. After several days of merely pick-

eting, the demonstrators (still not using violence) blocked all entrance to one of the most overcrowded and most heavily Negro schools and forced the city to close it. Then, and over the next few days, crowds converged on Chester's City Council in numbers so huge as to force the abandonment of council sessions and, on one occasion, the flight of the councilmen. More than 100 demonstrators were arrested. But after several days of social disruption, Chester not only permanently closed the dilapidated, 95 per cent Negro school that had been the focus of the protest—but also, and more important, freed the demonstrators who had been arrested. In other words, for Chester the technique of social disruption had become at least partially legitimate, for the moment. But it is important to note that in the spring and summer of 1964 the renewal of such tactics in Chester brought vigorous (indeed, sometimes brutal) suppression from the local and state police.[41]

Perhaps the most spectacular attempts to use social disruption as a weapon for racial equality took place in New York City during the spring of 1964. A brief sit-down on the city's Triborough Bridge brought all traffic to a halt until the demonstrators could be removed.[42] Since this tactic did succeed in attracting wide public attention to some grievances of New York Negroes concerning life in the slums (though it was not successful in forcing action on these grievances), an effort was made to disrupt the city (and symbolically, "the world") by stalling all traffic to the opening ceremonies for the World's Fair on April 22, 1964. This attempt partially succeeded in that the well-publicized threat kept many drivers home, but in so doing, the threat itself helped to prevent the traffic jam that would have been necessary to disrupt the city and the Fair. Moreover, the proponents of this "stall-in" were unable to produce the large number of participants they had predicted—just as proponents of the disruption of Congress in August 1963 and proponents of a disruptive non-violent army in the South had been unable to convince large numbers of equalitarians to use such tactics.[43]

The tactic of social disruption is much more radical than the other techniques of creative disorder. It is not a more *violent* technique than the others, and there is no reason to assume that it will provoke violence any more than the others will. But it is certainly a considerable "escalation" of disorder without violence. For what disruption essentially does is challenge the entire society as a racially discriminatory *system*. The other forms of disorder challenge only a particular incident or institution that is segregated or discriminatory. In a sense, the sit-in, the rent strike, and the school boycott are, in the politics of disorder, equivalent to a riot in the politics of violence—that is, they are ways for two different social groups to carry on conflict against each other without violence, just as a riot is a way for two social groups to carry on conflict against each other by using violence. Disruption, however, is equivalent in the politics of disorder to insurrection in the politics of violence, and an insurrection is quite different from a riot. For insurrection is a way for one social group to carry on conflict not merely against another social group, but against the society as a whole, or against the government. Inventing a way to carry on an insurrection without violence may be a major act of creativity, but it is an act likely to arouse much more hostility than carrying on a "riot" without violence, as those who attempted disruption for the sake of racial equality found to be the case during 1964.

CHAPTER XIII

An Attempt at Order

From the Birmingham demonstrations on, the many and varied efforts to carry on one form or another of creative disorder put considerable pressure on the federal government to establish a new system of law and order on racial matters. In the hope that a new system of order would end the growing disorder, President John F. Kennedy on June 19, 1963, proposed a new civil rights act to Congress and asked for a moratorium on demonstrations that might lead to violence, until the bill had been passed. Discussions on the bill had been carried on within the Kennedy administration (and particularly within the Justice Department, headed by the President's brother Robert) for several weeks, in response to Birmingham and the rash of protests that followed it. First indications were that the President's bill would include only provisions for desegregating public accommodations such as restaurants, theaters, and hotels; but by the time the bill came to Capitol Hill, sections had been added that would have given the Attorney General authority to initiate suits to desegregate schools, established a Community Relations Service to accommodate local racial conflicts, prevented racial discrimination in federally supported public facilities, and improved the economic status of the white and Negro poor through federal grants for job retraining programs and vocational education.[1]

The bill received a skeptical reception from much of

the Congress. It was reported that very few party leaders on Capitol Hill believed that the public accommodations section could be passed without major restrictions
that would eliminate all but the biggest hotels and restaurants from its coverage.[2] Chairman Emanuel Celler
of the House Judiciary Committee, when he introduced
the Administration bill, added a section that would
strengthen federal enforcement of the voting rights of
Negroes, partly in the belief that voting rights would be
more likely to win congressional support than new rights
of access to public accommodations.[3] There was some
talk of adding a section ending racial discrimination in
all employment involving inter-state commerce, but several members of the Judiciary Committee thought such
a section would be only a live decoy, intended to be sac-
rificed in order to get the rest of the bill passed.[4]

But a small group of congressmen, members of the
House Judiciary subcommittee which took the first, and
crucial, look at the civil rights bill, decided to try to
strengthen it all across the board. They believed that
only a law that went further and faster than the President's bill could hope to "get the Negroes out of the
streets," as the President had put it. These men therefore rebelled against what they regarded as the Administration's watery bill, and—for the first time since the
New Deal—forced a President to move further to the
"left" than he had intended. They were denounced by
the Administration and much of the press as visionaries
or ideologues who wanted an "issue" more than a "bill."
But as one of them put it, "What we wanted was a real
bill, neither just an issue nor just anything with a pretty
title on it. We were willing to trade that fake title of the
'Civil Rights Act of 1963' for a real bill in '64. And although Bobby Kennedy publicly insisted we could not
get a tough bill passed, the President himself admitted

to us in private, at the White House, that there was a good chance we could."

The mavericks not only wrote a "tough" bill, they played "tough" politics on behalf of the bill. They put together on the Judiciary subcommittee a coalition made up of principled equalitarians of both parties; northern Democrats with large blocs of big-city Negroes in their constituencies, who could therefore, if necessary, be bludgeoned to stay in line; and angry Republicans who were not going to vote for "Bobby Kennedy's bill" and would just as soon vote for a stronger one as a weaker one. What they had to face were other Republicans who did not want to damage their conservative coalition with southern Democrats, which had for a generation normally governed Congress on economic issues, and the Administration, which feared both the loss of southern congressional support for the rest of its program and the "northern white backlash" if it did too much for civil rights.

The "tough" coalition succeeded, in part. The symbol of its initial success was that when a Chicago Democrat, Roland Libonati, made the first move to water down the tough bill that the coalition had reported from subcommittee to the full Judiciary Committee, the warnings and urgings of congressmen closer to the temper of Chicago Negroes forced him to rejoin the tough coalition. He ended up "solid as a rock," as Chicago's Mayor Richard Daley ruefully told the President. But the limit of the coalition's success was set by another big-city Democrat, Herman Toll of Philadelphia. Once the President had moved part way toward the coalition's bill, Toll left the coalition. With the bill strengthened, Toll felt White House power channeled through the arm of Representative William Green, the political boss of Philadelphia, more strongly than he felt the fear of losing Philadelphia Negro votes.

What made it possible for the "tough" coalition to succeed to the degree it did was the march of events out on the street. Because of the wide range of militant protest (jobs, restaurants, votes, schools), the Administration had been compelled to send Congress a bill which (though shallow in each section) had many sections, and was broad enough to cover almost every area from employment to voting to education to the courts. Such a bill provided an excellent starting place for section-by-section strengthening all across its broad front. Then, again because of the use of "creative disorder" across the country, the Justice Department was too busy with myriad legal problems to pay more than lackadaisical attention to the bill-drafting process in subcommittee. By the time Justice realized its own bill was being strengthened all across the board, the process had gone too far to be reversed without a struggle.

As for the congressmen themselves, it was the militant protests that kept some of them conscious of the danger of widespread violence, that brought home to others with great emotional impact (as when the Birmingham Sunday school was bombed or students were jailed in Americus, Georgia, under capital charges) the nature of the resistance to racial integration. It was the demonstrations that worked quietly on the minds and hearts of older Democrats on the subcommittee like Byron Rogers of Colorado, until suddenly they were joining with young men like Robert Kastenmeier of Wisconsin in saying it was their responsibility, as members of the majority party and as congressmen, to write as good a bill as they could—not the responsibility of the Justice Department or the Republicans or anyone else. It was the demonstrations, finally, that let Republican leader

William McCulloch tell his men that blood might be on their hands if for partisan reasons they helped Southerners block the bill and disorder followed.[5]

What did the "tough" coalition within the House Judiciary Committee accomplish? It continued the process of broadening the civil rights bill which had originally begun within the Administration. In doing this, the coalition not only guaranteed that the Administration's own proposals would be adopted substantially intact, but set a new standard for federal action so vigorous that even continuous compromise from then on during congressional debate left the Civil Rights Act when passed much more powerful than anything the Administration had asked for, or had thought possible. The coalition voted to add provisions outlawing racial discrimination in hiring, firing, and labor-union membership wherever interstate commerce was involved; to forbid the use of federal grants-in-aid in state programs that were racially discriminatory; and to provide for preventive action by the Attorney-General to protect civil rights workers and Negroes in general from police or private action to deny their constitutional rights.[6]

Once these sections had been added to the bill, they were never removed—though they, and other sections, were modified as the bill went through the House and Senate. Particularly weakened was Title III, which looked toward the concept of an American "state" on racial issues. Title III provided for advance intervention by the Attorney-General to prevent impending deprivations of constitutional rights, especially deprivations by mob violence or by the action of local policemen using locally "authorized" violence.* The reasons for the weakening of

* The basic purpose of Title III was similar to that of the federal anti-lynching statutes discussed in Congress after the 1919 race riots. Provisions directly making lynching a federal crime were pro-

this provision are particularly instructive as to official views of the nature and meaning of federal authority in the racial conflict. One congressman, Byron Rogers of Colorado, had been particularly insistent that the federal government must be given some way of protecting in advance people who had been put in such difficulties as had one of his constituents, imprisoned during a non-violent civil rights demonstration and kept in solitary confinement in Georgia for over thirty days on a capital charge of "inciting insurrection." Attorney-General Robert F. Kennedy, repeatedly met with the congressman's demand that the civil rights bill should grant the Attorney-General authority to prevent such police action, himself repeatedly replied that a "national police force" must never be created.[8]

The real issue is this quarrel was over the role of a police force: Ought it, as in the notion of a "state," only to prevent violence when two social groups come into conflict with each other, or ought it to enforce a particular "governmental" settlement of the conflict—in other words, uphold a given social order? The theory of Title III was that the rest of the civil rights bill would probably not establish so perfect a new order that civil rights workers would stop all their disorderly demonstrations, nor an order so perfect that segregationists would stop attacking civil rights workers who kept on demonstrating. What Title III tried to do was guarantee that in the spheres of conflict not ended by the Civil Rights Act, conflict could continue to be carried on, perhaps even in disorderly ways, so long as violence was not used. And the Attorney-General was to enforce this guarantee.

But Attorney-General Kennedy did not believe that

---

posed by Representative Robert Kastenmeier, one of the leaders of the "tough" coalition; but the coalition did not put them in its version of the bill.[7]

federal police action could be narrowly directed at preventing violence between believers in two different versions of justice, rather than at upholding a given view of justice. In a sense, his "governmental" view of the nature of police power agreed with that of segregationists who were wholly opposed to even those parts of the civil rights bill that Kennedy supported. For the segregationists, too, thought that a police force was intended to uphold a social order—that of white supremacy. The segregationist nightmare was that the federals would come in full force not only to enforce the particular civil rights set forth in the Act of 1964, but to establish a wholly new social order of racial equality. And the unwillingness to do this is what haunted Robert Kennedy, and prompted him to oppose a "national police force" for protecting civil rights workers. Although the FBI is a national police force against bank robbers, kidnapers, and spies, the Secret Service a national police force against counterfeiters, the T-men a national police force against drug-pushers and moonshiners, and the postal inspectors a national police force against fraud and pornography, none of these federal outlaws owns a state or local government and police force. But the segregationists owned many.

When the Attorney-General mentioned a "national police force" for civil rights, he was really imagining a conquering army—and he did not want to lead it into battle. Although he was prepared to believe that federal enforcement of a fair employment practices act, of an open accommodations act, and of school desegregation could be accomplished without conquering the South, he was not prepared to believe that the federal government could prevent local violence against (and especially police arrests of) civil rights workers, without conquering half a dozen southern states. As for the belief (expressed

in the tough coalition's support of Title III) that the use
of disorder might continue after the civil rights bill had
been passed, Kennedy hoped that the bill would encourage Negroes to use the more orderly forums of court,
polling-booth, and legislature; and for the rest, he prepared to take his chances.[9]

Like the Attorney-General, most of Congress focused
on the prevention of disorder through the establishment
of a new order, as it continued through the winter and
spring to debate and finally to pass the Civil Rights Act
of 1964. Behind and beside all the debates and all the
political persuasion brought to bear by the new President, Lyndon B. Johnson, there echoed the sounds of
"creative disorder" in the streets, as the school boycotts,
rent strikes, and attempts at social disruption went forward. It was, therefore, with an almost physical sigh of
relief that the Congress sent the act to the President to
be signed on July 2, 1964, and with an almost physical
wail of disappointment that the Congress and the Administration discovered only two weeks later that the new
act had not prevented the outbreak of the worst big-city
racial violence in twenty-one years.

CHAPTER XIV

Riots Again

The discovery that the attempt to build a new and stable system of racial order had at least temporarily failed came on July 18, 1964. On that day, a long feud between Harlem and the New York City Police Department broke into the first of a series of urban race riots, far less bloody than those of 1919 but built on many of the same frustrations and hostilities. The strongest of those hostilities, as it had often been in 1919, was the one between Negroes and the city police; and as it had often been in 1919, the precipitating incident was a direct clash between Negroes and policemen who were hostile to their protests and demands.

Two days before, a Harlem long angry over what its residents claimed was police brutality toward Negroes had been newly inflamed by the shooting to death of an adolescent boy who had attacked an off-duty policeman. Many civil rights organizations in New York City had been demanding that a civilian review board be created to sit in independent judgment on cases of alleged police brutality that were traditionally judged by the police department itself. The latest killing brought more demands for a review board; and in the context of the past year's great intensification of Negro protest activity in the city, it brought also a much greater involvement of large numbers of Negroes in active protests against the police.[1]

One of these active protests, and the police response to it, triggered the riot. During the evening of Saturday,

July 18, several New York chapters of the Congress of Racial Equality (CORE) sponsored a rally to demand creation of a review board and removal of New York's police commissioner, who had opposed such a board. CORE organizers led a crowd of about one hundred people from the rally to a police precinct station in Harlem, to present their demands. Around 8:30 P.M. they sat down in front of the precinct station and announced they would stay until some of the demands were met. The police tried to push some of the crowd back, and several scuffles began. Finally the police arrested the CORE leaders who had been controlling the crowd and dragged them into the police station. According to some reports, some of these leaders were beaten, and their cries could be heard outside. Whether or not this was true, the crowd—deprived of the only leaders who had been trained in and were committed to non-violence—began to shower bricks and bottles upon the police. Then dozens of policemen charged the crowd and forced it to move a block or so, where it began to gather adherents from the neighborhood as the noise and searchlights attracted attention. Police from other precincts joined the fray and scattered the crowd. But its members stayed on the streets, and stayed angry. Around 10:30 P.M., one youth threw a bottle of flaming gasoline at a police car, and the policeman fired back. From then on, gunfire from the police and missiles from mobs of Negroes, especially young men and late adolescents, dominated the night. By Sunday morning, one Negro had been killed by the police, twelve policemen and at least a hundred Negroes had been injured, dozens of shops had been looted, and charges of deliberate and unwarranted police brutality during the night had been made by such alleged eyewitnesses as James Farmer, national director of CORE.[2]

For the next four nights, New York City suffered from

intermittent racial violence, chiefly between white policemen and Negro youths. The violence died down considerably Monday night in Harlem, but flared up instead on Monday and Tuesday in the heavily Negro ghetto of Bedford-Stuyvesant in Brooklyn. The city's acting mayor asserted that the violence had been incited in part "by fringe groups, including the Communist Party." President Johnson issued a statement warning that there could be "no compromise . . . in the preservation of law and order," and announcing he had directed the Federal Bureau of Investigation to look into the riots. Civil rights leaders deplored the violence but insisted that police brutality and the hopeless poverty of the black ghettos were real grievances, so that only if they were ended could racial calm be guaranteed.[3]

The immediate riots in New York City petered out by Thursday, but the atmosphere of crisis took longer to disappear. On the following weekend the police obtained an injunction against a protest march planned by a few Harlem organizations accused of being dominated by Communists, stopped the march when it was called anyway, and finally vacated the injunction only on September 17. On August 6 and 14, the police department increased the number of Negro officers assigned to Harlem in an effort to ease tensions between the force and the Negro population. Any incipient feeling that the troubles were over was destroyed by the succession of race riots that followed New York's and forced New York officials to remain alert against the possibility of renewed violence.[4]

These additional riots were almost all within several hundred miles of New York,* a factor that caused fears and rumors to spread that all the riots had been incited

* All except a minor riot in Dixmoor, Chicago, an industrial suburb of Chicago.

in concert—rumors that never achieved the support of factual evidence, but that influenced some official behavior. The first of the new riots was in Rochester, a scientific-industrial city in upper New York State that had been suffering from eighteen months of racial conflict over charges of police brutality and that had finally created a civilian review board. The Rochester riot began Friday evening, July 24, when police arrested a Negro man for allegedly molesting a Negro woman at a street dance. Rumors flew among the dancers that the arrest had been carried out brutally, and the crowd turned into a mob attacking the police. More policemen poured into the area, using tear gas rather than gunfire to try to control the mobs and the individual looters who appeared; but by 3 A.M. the city authorities had decided to ask the governor to send the state police. By the time they arrived, at 8 A.M., the mobs had dispersed. But the riots were renewed on Saturday night, when one white man was killed by Negro youths and one Negro was wounded by gunfire from a white civilian, and on Sunday night, when an official helicopter trying to observe clashes between mobs and the police crashed into a home in a Negro neighborhood, killing two of the residents as well as the helicopter's pilot. Contingents of the New York unit of the National Guard were sent into Rochester on Sunday night, made a show of force in the city, but did not take up positions in the streets. By Monday, when the riot ended, 750 people had been arrested on charges of looting, riot, and unlawful possession of firearms. About three fourths of them were Negroes, the rest white youths who had begun to move into the rioting on Saturday and even more on Sunday night.[5]

Similar outbreaks, beginning in much the same fashion, occurred in three cities in New Jersey during the first two weeks of August. In Jersey City, Elizabeth, and Paterson,

particular incidents between the police and Negroes
struck fire to months and years of accumulated tinder,
and nighttime riots of two or three nights' duration struck
the cities.[6] In Paterson, according to some reports, the
riot was brought to an end only because "large numbers
of policemen were . . . [withdrawn] from the ghetto,
. . . [so that] only four patrolmen covered the area"
where there had been 200 trying to cope with the rioters
and instead simply acting as a focus for them.[7]

The last of the rash of late-summer riots occurred in
Philadelphia, and again it was much more a clash between Negroes and policemen than between two civilian
populations. As in Rochester, the riot began when a police officer, himself a Negro, tried during the evening of
Friday, August 28, to arrest a Negro who was allegedly
blocking traffic, and who allegedly resisted arrest. The
use of force in the arrest caused charges of brutality to
be hurled by angry Negroes in the weekend crowd, and
skirmishes quickly flared up between roving bands of
Negroes and squads of policemen. The riot was renewed
on Saturday night, and by its close on Sunday morning
had left two killed and several hundred injured.[8] The
Philadelphia riot contributed to rumors that a cabal of
some sort was deliberately inflaming racial violence along
the east coast, rumors which drove the mayor of Baltimore and the governor of Maryland to warn on September 1 that they had information concerning plans for a
riot in Baltimore and would take stern action to prevent
one.[9] But no violence occurred in Baltimore or elsewhere. With the Philadelphia explosion the racial violence of 1964 had run its course.

One of the major responses to this series of riots was,
as it had been in 1919, the warning that they had been
incited chiefly by subversive, and especially Communist,
agitators. Even before the riots, fears had been voiced

that the organized civil rights movement of the early 1960s had been at least partially influenced by Communists. Thus, for example, J. Edgar Hoover, who in 1919 had headed the General Investigation Division of the Federal Bureau of Investigation and in 1964 was director of the FBI itself, testified to a congressional committee in January 1964 that "Communist influence does exist in the Negro movement and it is this influence which is vitally important." He added, "It can be the means through which large masses . . . without realizing it, succumb to the party's propaganda lures."[10] When it came to the riots late in the summer of 1964, Hoover found much less evidence of radical incitement than he had found in the riots of 1919. In his report of the FBI investigation ordered by President Johnson after the Harlem riot, Hoover explained that "aside from the actions of minor [radical] organizations or irresponsible individuals there was no systematic planning or organization of any of the city riots." He did, however, list the Progressive Labor Movement, a Marxist-Leninist group condemned by the regular Communist Party as "neo-Trotskyist" and "Maoist," as one organization that had tried to "exploit Negro unrest." Hoover also mentioned, without naming, certain Negro nationalist groups and a rent-strike organizer as having tried both to capitalize on the Harlem riot after it had begun and to incite rioters to continue. But nowhere did the FBI report suggest that the riots would not have occurred without radical incitements.[11]

Indeed the FBI report specified social and economic conditions in the Negro slums, together with a general breakdown of social morale among young Americans, as the major reasons for the riots. The report did not explain why every riot began around an incident involving the police. On the contrary, it emphasized that police behavior before and during the riots was "generally re-strained . . . even in the face of continuous insults, barrages of rocks, bottles, Molotov cocktails, and fire bombs." The FBI report warned that the civilian review boards demanded by some civil rights organizations would hamper the police in their work. Rather than rec-ommend additional steps to make the police less antago-nistic toward Negroes (steps which the FBI considered unnecessary because they believed the local police were already in large part neutral on racial questions), the report recommended additional steps to strengthen the power of local police to put down riots and restore "law and order."[12]

To the major civil rights organizations themselves, the riots seemed to threaten many of their achievements of the early 1960s. Not only did they undermine the cam-paigns of creative disorder carried on during the previous few years, they threatened to become confused with those campaigns in the minds of many Americans who had already begun to entertain doubts of their agreement with the civil rights campaign. When creative disorder had expanded from the South to the North after Birming-ham, it had necessarily brought the possibility of racial change home to northern whites—some of whom had reacted with dismay. Now many equalitarians feared that the riots would complete the job of alienating a sizable part of the northern white population from the drive for racial equality. Such a reaction would be espe-cially disastrous to the equalitarians if it brought new support to candidates in the 1964 election campaign who had opposed the Civil Rights Act and other measures designed to advance racial equality.

For these reasons, leaders of the major civil rights groups met just after the Harlem riot to assess its effects and plan a strategy for the coming months. The six major groups in attendance agreed on their dismay over the riot, but disagreed over how to respond. Roy Wilkins of the NAACP, A. Philip Randolph of the Negro American Labor Council, Whitney Young of the National Urban League, and Martin Luther King of the Southern Christian Leadership Conference called for a moratorium on demonstrations—in effect, on the use of creative disorder —and for emphasis instead on getting Negroes registered to vote in the November elections. Presumably the theory here was that demonstrations (like those led by CORE in Harlem) might easily lead to riots, and so might damage the equalitarian cause. On the other hand, John Lewis of SNCC and James Farmer of CORE refused to ask for or agree to a moratorium on creative disorder— and theirs had been the two organizations most active in actually carrying on the politics of disorder. Presumably their theory was that in some cases at least, creative disorder might make riots less likely by channeling anger and discontent into organized protests under non-violent discipline, instead of leaving them to explode in unorganized violence. But SNCC and CORE also made clear that they took the election campaign of 1964 seriously and would try to bring creative disorder to bear on that election.[13] To do so, they had to turn to a new form of creative disorder that had been invented precisely to affect party politics and the elective process.

CHAPTER XV

Creative Disorder and Party Politics

Of the many different forms of creative disorder that had been carried on since the first sit-ins of February 1960, almost all had been carried on outside the elective process and party politics. Public demonstrations to demand the right to vote had been one of the major tools of the movement from 1960 on, but use of the vote itself to bring about changes in race relations by use of the power of political parties had not originally been a major interest of the movement. Instead, the elective process and party politics had been tacitly assumed to belong in the realm of "order," and the newest generation of new Negroes had tended to ignore these "orderly" techniques. Yet most "orderly" activity had been aimed at persuading judges and at lobbying legislators already in power, rather than electing new ones. So the field was still clear when the more "disorderly" equalitarians got interested.

The first important attempt to make creative disorder relevant to party politics came in the State of Mississippi. In 1962, several groups of racial equalitarians, with SNCC in the lead, had founded a Council of Federated Organizations to carry out a long-term project for achieving racial equality in the United States.* COFO, as the council was called, faced as one of its major problems the practically systematic exclusion of almost all Negroes

* The other member groups were CORE, the Southern Christian Leadership Conference, and the Mississippi State Conference of the NAACP.

from the right to vote in Mississippi. With one hand, COFO made major efforts to teach Negroes what they needed to know in order to register legally as voters; to get Negroes to try to register; and to use the orderly processes of federal law to force Mississippi officials to register them. But COFO found such efforts agonizingly slow, and few Negroes were added to the polling lists. While Mississippi prepared to hold its gubernatorial election in November 1963, COFO, therefore, with its other hand, began to invent a new form of creative disorder for use in the election campaign.

What COFO did was to open its own rolls for what it called "freedom registration." Using the principle, "One man, one vote," COFO ignored all the legal requirements for paying a poll tax, proving literacy, and demonstrating the ability to understand the state constitution. Instead it offered to register any Mississippian who wanted to vote but could not, and gave those who registered the chance to cast a "freedom ballot" for governor and lieutenant governor in which they could choose among the official Democratic and Republican candidates and a slate sponsored by COFO. About 83,000 Mississippi Negroes did "freedom register" and cast their "freedom ballots" for governor and lieutenant governor. All but about 500 of these votes went to the COFO slate of two men, one Negro and one white, who were not listed in the regular election. These "votes" would have been enough, if cast for the minority candidate in the regular gubernatorial election, to have changed its result. And so, by action outside the regular election structure but parallel to that structure, COFO both energized Negroes who had never before dreamed of participating in their state's political process, and proved how considerable their own strength might be if they were ever able to enter the regular political system.[1]

The freedom ballot, much like the sit-in and the freedom ride, simply consisted of doing outside the existing local law what could have been done legally if racial equality had already been achieved. The sit-inners sat in racially integrated groups in order to demand that restaurants be integrated; freedom voters cast ballots in order to demand that they be allowed to cast ballots.

Drawing on the experience of November 1963, COFO decided to involve civil-rights workers in a massive program of what might be called "parallel politics" for Mississippi Negroes. Students, teachers, lawyers, physicians, and ministers from the North were invited to take part in a summer project intended to teach Negroes in the state something about their own history, the state's political and economic structure, the legal regulations for voter registration and how to meet them, and the relation of the state to the national law, political system, and economy.[2] One major focus of the summer project was to be a new institution through which the political hopes of Mississippi Negroes could be expressed: the Mississippi Freedom Democratic Party.

The Freedom Party was founded in April 1964. It was declared "open to all Democrats in Mississippi of voting age, regardless of race, creed, or color,"[3] and indeed a few whites did join it; but the overwhelming body of the membership was Negro. Through the spring and summer, civil rights workers made contacts in Negro communities all over the state, explained the importance of voting and political organization in the struggle for racial equality, and tried to persuade Negroes both to attempt to register legally and to join in the Freedom Party's extra-legal campaign.[4]

Intense harassment was brought to bear against many of the workers, ranging from petty charges for alleged traffic offenses, through beatings and church bombings, to the murder on June 20 of three men who were working in a Philadelphia, Mississippi, "freedom community center." This group of three in Philadelphia was made up of one native Negro Mississippian who had been working on COFO projects, one white Northern civil rights worker who had also been working in Mississippi for COFO, and another white Northerner who was a student volunteer in the 1964 summer project and had just arrived in the state. The three men disappeared after presumably being released late at night from a Mississippi jail where they had been brought on minor charges. The presumption that they had been kidnaped and killed brought intense national attention to the summer project. Considerable pressure for federal protection of the summer volunteers had already been exerted on the White House by some northern congressmen like William Fitts Ryan of New York and Donlon Edwards of California, some of whose constituents were among the volunteers; and after the Philadelphia case occurred, the pressure increased until President Johnson ordered a considerable increase in the number of FBI men assigned to investigate violence used against voter-registration and similar efforts among Negro Mississippians. The bodies of the three Philadelphia workers were found by the FBI on August 4, but the strengthened federal presence continued, and many COFO workers believed it had a restraining effect on white Mississippians who might otherwise have used more violence than they did against the civil rights movement.[5]

During the summer, efforts at registering Negroes to vote legally went slowly, but "freedom schools" to educate Negroes in the political and social problems of Mississippi and the nation enrolled more students than had been expected, and the work of organizing the Freedom Party went forward. In July, precinct meetings of the

Freedom Party were held across the state, to choose delegates to county conventions, which then chose delegates to a state-wide convention held on August 6. The state convention then took steps to win recognition for the Freedom Democrats as the only true Democratic Party in the state of Mississippi, by sending a state delegation to the Democratic National Convention in Atlantic City and demanding to be seated in place of the regular delegation from Mississippi.[6]

When the Freedom Party delegates arrived in Atlantic City late in August, the stage had been set for a major confrontation between "orderly" politics and the politics of "creative disorder." Despite previous warnings of the seriousness of the Freedom Party challenge, the general support to be given it by the national civil rights movement, and the wave of sympathy accorded it by a number of Democratic delegations to the convention from northern states, the leadership of the Democrats assumed that the Mississippi challenge would constitute no major impediment to the smooth operation of a carefully planned convention. So far as President Johnson and the national leadership of the party were concerned, orderliness was to be the keynote to the convention. As the delegations began to arrive in Atlantic City, "the word" began to seep out that the Freedom Party would be offered places as "honored observers," and the regular delegation from Mississippi would be seated.[7] The bearer of this Administration offer to those who had espoused the Freedom Party's cause was Senator Hubert Humphrey. In 1948 he had himself led a rebellion at the Democratic Convention in support of civil rights, against the wishes of the White House and the party leadership; but in 1964 he was anxious to keep in close accord with the White House. He had been quietly informed that the President feared loss of the South in the election if the

Freedom Party were seated, and therefore intended to prevent such a decision by the convention. Precisely because Humphrey's greatest strength was among the most vigorous racial equalitarians in the convention, he was expected to prevent the equalitarians from disturbing the equilibrium of the convention and the party by voting to seat the Freedom delegation.

The first major obstacle to plans for an orderly convention was created by the testimony of the Freedom Party before the convention's Credentials Committee on the Saturday before the convention itself began. A passionately equalitarian lawyer, Joseph L. Rauh of Washington, D.C., had marshaled legal arguments for the Freedom Party on two lines: since the regular Mississippi delegation and its party had repeatedly abandoned the Democratic Party's national ticket and platform, they were not legally entitled to claim seats at the Democratic National Convention any more than a Mississippi Republican delegation could have; and since the Freedom Democrats were the only political group in Mississippi committed to supporting the party's national ticket and platform, they were legally entitled to recognition as the only Democratic delegation from the state. The regular Democrats rested their case chiefly on their long-standing acceptance as legitimate Democrats and their ability to deliver real, legal, and countable votes—as against the Freedom Party's "freedom votes" outside the legal election system. But the legal arguments turned vague and empty before the anguished tales of repression told by Negro Mississippians like Mrs. Fannie Lou Hamer and by white civil rights workers like the widow of one of the three men murdered at Philadelphia. Their testimony swayed many members of the Credentials Committee, and "disorderly" politics thus had its first victory at the convention.

That night, the Freedom Party and its allies moved to convert sympathy into political support. They did so by bringing together in alliance one of the leading spokesmen for creative disorder and an imaginative member of that orderly institution, the House of Representatives. Martin Luther King, who had offered his help to the Freedom Party challenge, met with Representative Robert W. Kastenmeier, who had been a leader of the "tough coalition" on civil rights in the House Judiciary Committee and who was now a member of the Credentials Committee himself. Together they talked with a dozen other members of the Credentials Committee, and by noon the day before the convention was to open officially had organized a sizable minority of the Credentials Committee behind a compromise proposal. This compromise had been shaped by Representative Edith Green of Oregon, who suggested that an oath of loyalty to the Democratic nominees and platform be administered publicly to each delegate from the regular and from the Freedom Party delegation; that each delegate who assented to the oath be seated and all others sent home; and that all the acceptable delegates share the total vote to which Mississippi was entitled.

Agreement on this compromise was not easy. It was the continuous presence in these private conferences of Mrs. Hamer and others of the Freedom delegation who had suffered beatings and bombings for their disorderly politics that made it possible to keep "orderly" politicians stirred to the depths necessary to make them support the Green Compromise against pressures from the Administration. As for the practitioners of disorder themselves, it was not easy to persuade them that any seats in a Democratic Convention should go to representatives of the political system that had had them beaten, their churches burned, and their homes bombed. But when they were appealed to simultaneously on the grounds of political necessity and on the grounds of offering a Gandhian reconciliation to their enemies, enough of them agreed.

From Sunday noon until Tuesday noon, this Green Compromise proposal blocked the smooth and orderly progress of the convention machinery. The Freedom Party's supporters remained a minority for those two days, but under the rules were a sufficiently large one to force the issue to the floor. And there, if a public roll-call vote of the states could be obtained, it was believed likely that the Freedom Party could win as Senator Humphrey had won in 1948. In fear of such a public debacle, the Administration delayed taking a vote on the Credentials Committee and tried through a combination of cajolery, threats of political reprisals upon those who held out in favor of the Freedom Party, and warnings of political disaster for the Democratic Party in the election if the South were alienated, to end the blockage of its plans. But the Freedom Party and its supporters held firm, and by Tuesday noon many members of the Credentials Committee thought a floor fight would take place that night.

Faced with the imminent threat of a collapse in its orderly plans and with a highly visible and growing public vigil and demonstration outside the convention building,* the Administration decided to retreat. Early Tuesday afternoon, it proposed to the Credentials Committee that a loyalty oath be administered to the regular Mississippi Democrats, those who refused it being barred from the convention; that two members of the Freedom Party delegation, whom the Credentials Committee itself would name, be offered seats as "delegates at large" with full voting rights, but no recognition as representa-

---

* This public demonstration was run chiefly by CORE, in close cooperation with SNCC.

tives of the people of Mississippi; and that provision be made for seeing that all delegations to future Democratic conventions be chosen without any racial exclusion or discrimination. This new offer by the Administration won the grudging acceptance of most of the South, although most of the Mississippi regulars refused to take the oath. To most of the supporters of the Green Compromise on the Credentials Committee, the new offer seemed a reasonable solution. It would end any danger of embarrassment to Senator Humphrey, it would end any danger that the whole South might bolt the convention and so hurt the party's chances in November, and it would end the danger of an open fight and possible defeat for President Johnson on the floor of the convention. Enough of the Freedom Party's allies on the Credentials Committee accepted the proposal to make it impossible under the rules for the fight to be carried to the floor.

The fact that the Administration had been forced to make this offer, after several days of inability to put across its original formula, was a major victory for the politics of disorder. Again creative disorder had shown —as in the debates over the civil rights bill—a capacity for making the politics of order bend and change. But the limits of the change had been set by what some of those on the far frontier of "order" had been willing to accept. When the world of order had bent a bit, enough members of the Credentials Committee had left the minority to make it unable to hold out any longer.

Among the practitioners of creative disorder themselves, the Administration plan occasioned an intense debate. There were three parties to this debate, two of whom came to it with well-worked out theoretical positions. These two were the national civil rights leadership and the full-time field staff of COFO, SNCC, and the Freedom Party. The third group was made up of the Freedom Party delegation itself—mostly Negro Mississippians from nineteenth-century-type towns and farms. It was they who would have to make the final decision whether to let two of their number, named by the Credentials Committee, accept seats as delegates-at-large.

Both among the national civil rights leadership and the field staff, there were strong currents of opinion based on the belief that orderly and disorderly politics could not mix. To many of the national leaders, this belief meant that when "protest" movements entered party politics they must and should give up their "protest" style and their purity of conviction, and must be prepared to compromise. Those national leaders who felt this way urged the Freedom Party to accept the Administration's offer. To many of the field staff, on the other hand, the same belief that politics and protest were incompatible meant that protest movements ought to stay out of party politics, ought to preserve their purity and the protest style, and ought not to get mixed up in compromise at all.

But among some members of both groups there was a contrary view: the belief that the style and tone of creative disorder could conceivably be made to soak through and into the machinery of party politics, until that machinery itself had changed and grown. Those who held this view believed that in all sorts of politics some kinds of compromise were necessary, but that effective politics, even in the political-party arena, required a refusal to destroy or abandon for the sake of compromise the minimum moral basis upon which one's own constituency had been built. And they argued that acceptance of the Administration offer would have been seen among Negro Mississippians as precisely such an abandonment. Thus those who believed in transforming orderly politics through infusions of disorderly politics believed that the offer should be rejected, but that the fact it had been made proved that efforts to bring disorderly politics to bear on the party system worked, and should be kept up.

It was this last view—that disorderly politics should neither lightly compromise with nor lightly withdraw from the arena of party politics—that carried the day. The Freedom Party delegation itself thought in no such abstract terms, but decided on the basis of more vivid responses to the concrete situation. Many members of the delegation were shocked and angered that if two seats were to be offered them, they had not been given the right to choose which of their members should sit in those seats. To these Mississippians, the Administration offer seemed reminiscent of the old southern etiquette of race relations, in which it was whites who decided whom to recognize as Negro leaders. To some, the offer of two seats rather than a full complement seemed reminiscent of token desegregation, in which a few "well-scrubbed" Negroes were allowed into southern schools and conferences so long as the much larger number of poor, awkward, and unsophisticated Negroes stayed out. It also seemed to some delegates that accepting seats assigned "at large" and in limbo, rather than as part of the Mississippi delegation, would mean an abandonment of the claim that the Freedom Party spoke for the people of Mississippi. For all these reasons, an overwhelming majority of the Freedom delegation felt that accepting the offer would mean attempting to please the national leadership of the Democratic Party and of the civil rights movement at the expense of betraying and alienating their constituents in Mississippi. On political as well as moral grounds, the delegation therefore voted on two separate occasions to reject the offer.

Now the politics of creative disorder became directly

relevant to the convention. Instead of mobilizing only the memories of disorder in Mississippi, the Freedom Party decided to carry on creative disorder in Atlantic City. The leadership in this decision came from Robert P. Moses, director of SNCC's Mississippi projects and a major figure in the creation of COFO and the Freedom Party. Moses acted partly in response to feelings of deep bitterness and frustration that had gripped large numbers of the SNCC, COFO, and Freedom Party staffs as well as some members of the Freedom Party delegation. Many of them had originally said they expected little from the Democratic Party but nevertheless felt betrayed when the party, which at some deeper level they had regarded as "part of the family," refused to surrender to the Freedom Party's combination of moral appeal and political pressure. The bitterness with which they greeted this "betrayal" might well have exploded into attempts at disrupting the convention, had not Moses proposed the alternative of a controlled form of creative disorder.

What he proposed was a sit-in, in many ways the very acme and pitch of all sit-ins: that the Mississippi Freedom Democratic Party should enter the convention hall, work its way to the seats of the Mississippi delegation, and publicly lay claim to those seats by simply sitting in them. And that is what the Freedom delegates did, on both Tuesday and Wednesday nights of the convention, August 25 and 26. With the help of supporters from Michigan, Oregon, Wisconsin, California, and other states who got them onto the floor itself by clandestine means, the Negro Mississippians walked to and took possession of their state's space on the floor, which had been abandoned by the regulars. For twenty minutes the convention authorities tried to have them removed by force, but ultimately left the Freedom delegation in possession of Mississippi's seats. There at the Mississippi standard, with television bringing the event to millions of Americans, the Freedom Party argued by their deeds the case for bringing a major infusion of creative disorder not merely to peripheral institutions like restaurants and schools, but to the heart of political power in the United States, to the party system itself. Their act brought disapproval from the Democratic leadership, from many supporters of civil rights in the party, and from parts of the national leadership of the civil rights movement.[8] But it afforded the Freedom delegation and its staff an opportunity to say that creative disorder would continue and that the established order must be prepared to continue coping with it, continue opening to include it, and continue changing the rules to meet at least some of its demands.

CHAPTER XVI

The Meaning of Creative Disorder

American society in the 1960s had such difficulty in coping with the concept of a whole range of politics lying between order and violence that it could find no single separate word for this sort of politics, and instead fell back on a negative definition by calling it "disorder" or "non-violence." We have here preferred the term "disorder" because much of the creative disorder in racial conflict of the 1960s was not "non-violent" in the pure Gandhian sense with which that word was often used. As we have used the term "disorder" here, it describes only behavior that is not violent in deed. But "non-violence," as exemplified in the racial crisis of the 1960s by the work of Martin Luther King, came to mean specifically the Gandhian politics of love, the confrontation of conscience, and conversion through example and dignity.[1]

Much of the civil rights movement of the 1960s was carried on according to King's and Gandhi's standards, but by no means all. Much of the politics of racial disorder had little to do with love or the confrontation of conscience—but equally little to do with outright violence. By Gandhi's standards, one should hate the oppressive system but love the oppressor himself as a human being; in a great deal of disorderly politics, young Negroes expressed intense anger and hatred not only for the segregation system but for the segregationists themselves or even for all whites.[2] And yet this hatred was expressed by pursuing change, not by attacking the enemy; it was often pursued with no outright act of violence, though often with a "violent" heart and mind. What might be called the "not-quite-violent" and the "non-violent" approaches both, therefore, make up what we have here called the politics of disorder.

But there is a still deeper problem in the assessment of "disorder" as a form of politics: the difficulty in distinguishing it, in actual practice, from the politics of order and violence. For example, the efforts by SNCC to get Negro voters registered in Albany, Georgia—seemingly a thoroughly "orderly" notion that fit into traditional election politics—were closely connected with street marches for equal access to public accommodations and economic boycotts against discriminatory employers—and these marches and boycotts were unconventional and sometimes "disorderly" techniques. In such a case, it may not be easy to disentangle the politics of disorder from the politics of order. Again, after some mass public demonstrations by Negroes in some southern cities met with brutal violence from white mobs, some Negroes outside the official civil rights movement responded with street violence of their own. In such a case, it is not easy to disentangle the politics of disorder from the politics of violence.

Yet there seem to be some crucial differences, which perhaps can be expressed this way: All three forms of politics as used by the civil rights movement were concerned with bringing about change. But there was a difference in the extent to which people using the different forms tended to focus on the changes to be achieved, to the exclusion of focusing on the rules of the system that was to be changed or on those who defended that system. In the politics of order, people divide their attention between the changes to be accomplished and the accepted rules of society about the "legitimate" ways of bringing about change. In the politics of violence, people divide their attention between the changes to be accomplished and those powerful people who get in the way of change —the enemy. In the politics of disorder, people tend to reduce greatly their interest in both the given rules and the enemy; instead they focus very strongly on the changes to be accomplished. To oversimplify a bit: in the politics of order, men follow the rules; in the politics of violence, they attack their enemies; in the politics of disorder, they pursue change.

It can be argued that the civil rights movement of the 1960s actually accomplished more change in race relations than did either the politics of violence in 1919, 1943, and since, or the politics of order in 1866 and 1875 (the years of the first civil rights acts) and 1954 (the year of the Supreme Court's school desegregation decision). If so, the reason may well be that in focusing on the achievement of change rather than on the rules or the enemy, "disorder" in the racial struggle has actually brought about more change.

To the degree that the politics of disorder is aimed at bringing about change, it is generally invented by people who are "outside" a particular system of political order, and want to bring change about so that they can enter. In doing so, they tend to use new techniques that make sense to themselves out of their own experience, but that look disorderly to people who are thinking and acting inside the system. The Negroes were by no means the first to initiate this process. For example, in the seventeenth and eighteenth centuries, urban lawyers and merchants who could not get the entrenched politicians to pay attention to their grievances (and who were scarcely represented in Parliament) used the illegal and disorderly device of political pamphleteering against the established order.[3] In the same way, nineteenth-century workers who could not get their employers or the elected legislators to pay attention to their demands used unionization and the strike—which at first were illegal—to call attention to their grievances.[4] In both these cases, using the politics of disorder not only got the users accepted into the political order and got their immediate grievances looked after, but also got the new techniques accepted into the array of authorized and approved political methods. In short, the system of "order" was itself changed. Thus the "criminal libel" of political pamphleteering was enshrined as freedom of the press, and the "criminal conspiracy" of striking was enshrined in the system of free labor unions. One century's disorder became the next century's liberty under ordered law. Whether this will occur with the forms of creative disorder used by Negro Americans in their movement for racial equality has yet to be decided; but there are many indications that the process has begun.

Although we have focused upon the invention and use of "disorderly" techniques by racial equalitarians in the 1960s, these techniques have also been used by supporters of racial hierarchy and segregation. When the segregationists believed themselves to be the "outsiders," they turned to techniques not usually considered legitimate in the normal political order. For example, when segregationist Mississippians feared that federal marshals might try to arrest Governor Ross Barnett for contempt of a court order desegregating the University of Mississippi, thousands of them sat down around the governor's mansion to interpose their bodies—perhaps intending a "not-quite-violent" resistance—between him and the forces of law and order.[5] Similarly, in parts of the South segregationists have used pressures analogous to the Negroes' economic boycott, as when they cut off bank credit or refused to sell tools and evicted tenants who tried to register to vote.[6] In some northern cities, white parents have picketed school boards that tried to end *de facto* segregation in the schools, and in New York City especially, parents who opposed measures taken to desegregate "neighborhood" schools imitated the whole system of short-term boycotts of the public schools and the creation of short-term private protest schools that the Negroes had previously used.[7]

The seeming paradox that both racial equalitarians and racial hierarchists could on occasion believe themselves "outside" the legitimate political order and therefore forced to use "disorderly" forms of politics is in reality no paradox at all. During the 1960s one of these groups which had long been securely within the political order—the hierarchists and segregationists—was slowly being pushed outside it. At the same time, the equalitarians and integrationists, or at least the bulk of the Negroes among them, who had long been excluded from the political order, were slowly being included for the first time. During the transition period, both groups had reason to feel like "outsiders" and to use the methods of disorder.

During this period of sustained disorder from both sides in the racial conflict, the federal government moved further than it had during the brief period of violence in 1919 toward acting like a "state." Because both of those groups using the politics of disorder were so powerful and because opinion in the society at large remained so deeply divided over the values of racial hierarchy as against racial equality, during the early 1960s there was strong pressure on practically all American political institutions to tolerate disorder when used by either side on the racial question, so long as violence was avoided; to prevent, halt, and punish violence by either side; and to draw back from what would have been a truly "governmental" act, the police enforcement of either side's view of the race question. Even then, there was difficulty in bringing an American "state" on the race question to full fruition. Attorney-General Kennedy's difficulty in distinguishing a "state" from a "government," as when he opposed the original Title III of the civil rights bill for fear that a "national police force" could not simply prevent violence but would have to conquer the South, was one measure of the difficulty. But the growing strength of the "state" position can be seen from the desire of congressmen to enact Title III and from the position taken by the Justice Department in its *amicus* brief for the Supreme Court on the sit-in cases.

In both of these instances, unlikely organs of government were defending the notion that federal power should be exerted to protect disorder without violence. Obviously, neither the Justice Department nor members of Congress came easily to the position that the protection of disorder was more desirable than the establishment of a new order; their institutional roles require both of them to fear disorder and insist on the value of order. But because of the depth and intensity of the conflict over racial equality or hierarchy, both came to believe that an attempt to impose order might result instead in violence, and disorder should therefore be permitted and protected so long as it did not become violence. The transformation of disorder into order would have to await the creation of a much broader agreement on which "order" should be upheld.

As for the "church" aspects of federal authority, it could be argued that the 1954 Supreme Court decision on school segregation was the crucial event in beginning to establish official values based on racial equality. Although in several instances direct violations of court or-

ders for school desegregation were confronted by federal
enforcement of the orders, the court decision had far
more impact in the realm of values and morality—for
example, in raising the expectations of young Negroes
that finally erupted in the sit-ins—than it did in establishing directly enforceable law. And it is important to note
that despite its high permanent prestige as an American
"church," the Supreme Court from almost the moment of
its decision began to suffer vigorous attacks, which demonstrated the absence of any real national consensus and
the resistance to any single national "church" on the race
question.

It was not really until the Civil Rights Act of 1964 was
passed that the aspects of the "state" on racial issues that
the Federal government had begun to take on in response to the 1919 riots and the aspects of the "church"
on racial issues that it had begun to take on in 1954 were
merged effectively into new law. Thus not until 1964 can
there be said to have emerged the beginnings of an
American "government" on the race question.*

What is likely to happen to that "government," barely
born in 1964, and what may happen to the politics of
order, disorder, and violence as they have been used in
the racial conflict? To the extent that the Civil Rights
Act of 1964 created a "government" on the race question,
it is only a weak and tentative government. As the Negroes of Mississippi and Harlem—more generally speaking, the Deep South, most rural and most repressive, and
the Deep North, most urban and most desperate—made
clear as soon as the act was passed, it did not meet their
problems. It would take new acts of "government" to
bring Harlem and Mississippi fully into the American
political system. And if the past is any indication of the

---

* An abortive effort at creating a true federal "government" on the
race question was made during Reconstruction, but soon failed.

future, such acts of new "government" are more likely to occur if they have been demanded by those who are still outside the political system, through acts of creative disorder.

What then is likely to be the future of the politics of disorder within the movement for racial equality? Will the new political forms wither away if equalitarians win more and more victories, or will the techniques outlive the particular issues? Which of the techniques are likely to prove most effective and creative? Is disorder often likely to escalate from the boycott or the sit-in to full-scale social disruption, or will the hostility to this form of attack prevent its being often used?

The answers to these questions will depend mostly upon two factors: the response of political authorities to the use of controlled forms of disorder as ways of attracting public attention to and bringing about a resolution of particular conflicts; and the degree of inventiveness and self-discipline in the Negro community as it tries to create new techniques to cope with whatever failures may occur in the use of controlled disorder.

As to the political authorities: if the local police try to smash equivalents of a "riot" that use no violence, they are much more likely to find real riots blossoming before them, or perhaps efforts at general social disruption. Even if the police attack not the organized, deliberate equalitarian movements that are using creative disorder (as the police more frequently do in the South) but instead a number of unorganized, individual, "troublesome" Negroes (as they more frequently do in the North), they may find the Negro community ready to boil over into riots. If, on the other hand, all the governments concerned, local and national, step back and allow sit-ins, boycotts, and rent strikes to be "fought out" just as most labor strikes and lock-outs are, so long as neither side uses violence, and if local and national authorities act to punish violence used by either side in the racial conflict, then it is unlikely that efforts at creative disorder will degenerate into rioting. But a movement in this direction would require from the federal government the imagination necessary to build the kind of federal police force that could check and prevent particular acts of violence against Negroes, even violence by local police, without taking over entire cities or states.

It is not only deliberate police action to smash controlled creative disorder that may result in its degeneration into violence or disruption. If political authorities simply ignore attempts to use controlled disorder, its users may try the more threatening techniques. Limited forms of disorder seem less able to attract attention and disturb the authorities in a great and complex northern metropolis than in a middle-sized southern town or the rural Black Belt. Frustrated protestants in the northern cities who see their efforts at controlled disorder going for nought might well keep on trying such generally disruptive techniques as the World's Fair stall-in or blocking New York's Triborough Bridge, especially since the greater complexity of metropolitan society is likely to make it more vulnerable to small but carefully chosen acts of social disruption. Or if the failure of controlled creative disorder disillusions and discourages large numbers of urban Negroes, they may become ready tinder for a spark of riot. On the other hand, forms of limited disorder might become accepted throughout the United States as reasonable methods for persuading legislators and officials to change their minds—akin to free speech, in other words. If this is the direction of change—if the Congress and local governments fully accept sit-ins, marches, boycotts, and rent strikes as legitimate expressions of public desires and change their behavior accordingly—then it is rather unlikely that disorder will escalate into efforts at social disruption, or into rioting.

As to the degree of inventiveness in the Negro community: The question will be whether there is in existence a leadership that is committed to avoiding violence, that is capable of creating new forms of disorder without violence, and that can keep in close touch with its constituents in the Negro population. If so, the chances for riot would decrease, as compared to the chances of new forms of disorder. So far, Negro leaders in the North seem to have had difficulty in inventing new forms of disorder that would appeal to one specific and extremely important group: adolescent youths and young men without jobs or education. The southern sit-ins and marches have evidently appealed to some of the same qualities of masculinity and physical courage that make many young men good soldiers. But the northern rent strike and economic boycott seem to appeal to or be activities more easily carried out by quieter, older people. Although school boycotts and job blockades may appeal to the young, they cannot easily involve those who have already quit school or those who do not have the skills necessary to hold existing jobs; and it is exactly these men who are most likely to resort to violence. In the absence of new inventions in creative disorder that appeal to young men in the North, therefore, riots there may become more likely.*

* These words were written before, and seem partially confirmed by, the Los Angeles race riot of September 12–16, 1965. In the area of heaviest rioting, unemployment levels among young men were especially high, action under the official poverty program had been stymied by the refusal of local authorities to accept major involvement of the poor in determination of their own needs and goals, and unofficial institutions that might have energized the poor into non-violent action and protest (such as SNCC or CORE) had made few efforts to activate the area, partly for lack of ideas as to how to focus non-violent action around the real needs of people

Such new inventions would not only have to appeal to the young, but show hope of dealing with the deeper diseases of life in the great northern metropolises. Thus they would have to be directed at increasing the total number of jobs, and perhaps at getting new sorts of activity that did not utilize presently recognized skills accepted into the arena of paid employment—rather than at merely getting more Negroes into the present jobs. They would have to be aimed at improving the schools and perhaps at changing the kinds of schools made available—rather than at merely trying to integrate the present schools. Similarly with housing, the welfare system,

---

in the area. As for the indigenous invention of non-violent protest by residents of the riot area, the only evidence of indigenous organization is the report that a "War Council" of young men formed after the first day of the riot to manage continued attacks and distribute assignments. Its focus at that time was clearly on the politics of violence, not of creative disorder; but its emergence may offer a starting point for future efforts to encourage the development of creative-disorder protests in Los Angeles.

In light of the theory of riots that has been sketched above, particularly in Chapter X, it is interesting to note that the riot was triggered by an incident involving the arrest of a Negro by a white policeman, and fed upon the belief, widely and strongly held by Negroes in the area, that the Los Angeles police were bitterly anti-Negro in deed as well as word. This belief may well have been reinforced during the riot itself by the tenor of the statements made by Chief of Police William H. Parker in constantly repeated television appearances. There is some slight evidence that the intervention of the California National Guard may have helped reduce the violence because the Guard did not have an established anti-Negro reputation. But the anti-police aspects of the riot, especially when added to those apparent in the Harlem, Philadelphia, and Rochester riots of 1964, suggest that measures to ensure the neutrality of the police on racial questions may have to go beyond the creation of civilian review boards and similar devices. For example, the legitimacy of the police might conceivably be strengthened in large cities by making subdivisions of the police force in some measure responsible to neighborhoods or large sections of the city—through area-wide election of division police chiefs, for example, or even of policemen on the beat, on the same principle as the election of sheriffs in rural America.[8]

and other aspects of metropolitan life. Since most of these issues are decided not by private interests chiefly but by the local and federal governments, such new forms of disorder might have to confront particular agencies of government without posing a disruptive or "insurrectionary" threat to the social system or government as a whole.*

The two sets of changes that from the discussion above seem to be necessary if violence and social disruption are to be avoided can be summed up as, first, the bringing to fruition of an American "state" on racial questions; and second, the invention and legitimation of a number of new techniques of controlled creative disorder. The first of these means that some form of federal police force must be created to prevent violence from being used by either side in the racial conflict, including violence that takes on the color of legitimacy because it is carried on by local police who are in fact merely acting on behalf of one side or the other. Such a force would have to be carefully aimed at the protection of creative disorder used by either side in the racial conflict, and would have to be carefully restricted from itself defending one view or the other of racial justice. Indeed, it would probably be wise to set up a separate force for this purpose, so as to avoid involving those enforcement officers who carry out "governmental" mandates to the degree that they

* One proposed form of creative disorder that might meet these criteria is that of Paul Jacobs for a "work-in," in which unemployed whites and Negroes might learn the medium-level skills necessary for jobs that need doing but are unfilled or do not exist (such as assistant nurses and assistant teachers), and simply show up to do such jobs, risking arrest if necessary in order to persevere at the work-in until their new jobs were recognized and paid for. This would reverse the symbolism of the job blockade, which tries to prevent others from working.[8A]

exist on the racial issue—for example, the public accommodations provisions of the Civil Rights Act of 1964.*

Conceivably, such a force might be most effective if there were also created a system for managing and coping with particular disorderly techniques used in racial conflict, just as the Wagner Labor Relations Act created ways of recognizing certain agents of labor and management as legitimate conflict organizations, approving some forms of labor-management disorder, ruling others out of bounds, and encouraging bargaining between the parties. If American society were to achieve new levels of consensus on new aspects of the race question, through the clash of ideas and power involved in creative disorder, then new enforceable "law" would presumably be created and the responsibility for dealing with the areas covered by the new laws would shift from agencies behaving like a "state" to agencies behaving like a "government."

The second of what seem to be the crucial prerequisites to avoiding racial violence—the invention and legitimation of new forms of controlled creative disorder that would be applicable to new areas of racial conflict—may have some implications and effects that go beyond the racial arena. As in the extension of the legitimacy of the free press beyond the issues and social groups for which it was first espoused to new issues and other social groups, so it is possible that some forms of creative disorder invented by Negroes in the movement for racial equality will become legitimate for other social groups as well. For example, it is not impossible to imagine some

* Such a new and specialized federal police force might become especially necessary if major changes in international relations—such as world disarmament—were to cause major reductions or abolition of the large American military establishment, if the suggestion made in Chapter XI is correct—that the creation of this large military force after 1940 helped reduce mass private violence.

of the white miners of eastern Kentucky, many of whom have been without jobs for many years, sitting-in on federal unemployment compensation offices. It is not impossible to imagine school boycotts by students protesting the firing of a professor, or protesting against their schools being put on a split-shift schedule. In other words, if the new forms of disorder become legitimate there is no reason to expect that only Negroes will find them useful and necessary.*

The new techniques are also likely to revivify the practice of that kind of democracy in which all the citizens participate directly, in which each man has an active share in the shaping of his own destiny and that of his society. For it is in the nature of the new forms of disorder that they are creative in two ways. Not only do they help to reshape the society, they reshape those who carry on the disorder. It takes a much deeper commitment on the part of much larger numbers of people to carry on a school boycott or a rent strike or a mass public march than it does to pursue a more orderly politics. The new forms of disorder involve large numbers of people in the process of politics, they make that process immediate and relevant and productive for people who before were outside of politics and fearful or destructive of it. In this sense those who carried the signs that called for "Freedom Now" during the racial conflict of the early 1960s may have been more accurate than many of them knew. They were thinking about racial "freedom," which they soon discovered would take time to achieve and would come only "tomorrow," not "now." But to the extent that the very act of protest and the creation of new sorts of politics activated those who had been politically apa-

---

* These words were written before, and seem to be partially confirmed by, the use of sit-ins by students in the Free Speech Movement at the University of California in December 1964.[9]

thetic, it freed men who had been unfree. Thus the very process of creating disorder in the hope of racial "freedom tomorrow" was helpful in bringing individual "Freedom Now." Just as the disorderly pamphleteering press focused the energies of the urban middle class and the disorderly labor movement focused the energies of working men, so the new forms of disorder have already indicated they have the power to create a politically alive citizenry out of the Negro Americans who have been one of the last of America's excluded groups.

CHAPTER XVII

The Control of Conflict

To this point, we have examined the 1919 race riots and the racial disorder of the 1960s chiefly for their illumination of two particular historical developments: changes in American patterns of race relations and changes in American ways of coping with official and private violence. But the riots and the movement for creative disorder can be looked at not only as events in a specifically American history, but also as special cases in a historical process that has occurred, and may occur, more generally: the process by which the means of carrying on intense conflict is transformed from violent to non-violent.

From 1919 to the 1960s there was a major decline in the level of violence used in American racial conflict. This decline in violence is especially striking if we take into account the considerable increase from 1919 to the 1960s in the intensity and urgency of the conflict between racial equalitarians and racial hierarchists. A study of the process by which this decline in violence occurred might conceivably, along with other, similar studies in other areas of conflict, contribute to the creation of a general theory of the connections between conflict and violence.

Aside from the sheer intellectual pleasure involved in building such a theory of conflict, there might emerge from it some new ideas for policy: that is, for the actual carrying into practice of theory in order to solve problems in the real political world. The control of conflict so that it does not explode into violence is no minor problem

facing those in and out of governments who are trying
to shape policy. Indeed, the special question of how to
keep international conflicts from exploding into thermonuclear war has exercised statesmen and citizens of many
countries for many years.

There has been a special difficulty for shapers of policy
in attempting to think about a world in which international conflict could be carried on by means other than
the use or threat of war. The difficulty is that such a future world seems to be unprecedented, and therefore
study of the past seems not to be useful as a way of understanding how to construct or operate such a world.
But human beings in general and statesmen in particular
have tended to depend on history, the collective memory
of mankind, for guides to new action. What has worked
before has been tried again. Sometimes there has been
misunderstanding of what element in the old solution
was crucial to its success, sometimes old lessons have
been misapplied—and sometimes it has been the mis-
takes in understanding or application that have worked
in the new situation. But however imperfectly, men have
turned to the past for solutions. There have been a few
attempts at imagining a transcendently new world and
then moving toward it, but even these utopian and revolutionary movements have soon discovered they had to
rely on lessons from the human past for ways of accom-
plishing their ends.

For these reasons, it may be necessary to discover new
ways of looking at the past so that, in what appears to
be a past without precedents for carrying on international
conflict without war, there can be found events and processes that are sufficiently comparable to international
conflict without war that a policy for moving in that direction can be founded on the comparison. This requires
developing a general theory of conflict by which some

conflicts can be said to be comparable with others. No such general theory is as yet available, although attempts to build such a theory have begun. Chiefly in response to the belief that traditional ways of settling international conflict were becoming extremely dangerous, there did begin to emerge in the late 1950s a scholarship drawing upon history, sociology, economics, mathematics, psychology, and other disciplines and directed to the study of conflict as a general phenomenon.[1]

Scholars in the nascent profession of conflict research have paid little attention to the history of interracial violence and of efforts at its control as possible special cases in the kind of conflict that also includes international violence and efforts at *its* control. Nor have citizens or officials concerned with shaping policy toward international violence frequently examined the means of controlling conflict that have been used to cope with interracial violence.

It would certainly be unwise to make easy and dogmatic generalizations from the field of interracial conflict and violence to that of international conflict and violence. There may be differences in the way violence is carried on in the two cases that may make the comparison difficult. For example, wars are fought by very large agglomerations of people mobilized over long periods of time and commanded by well-organized small groups of men operating within well-defined institutions. Race riots are more likely to be fought by casual crowds of comparatively small size, gathered hastily around an immediate focus and often quickly dispersed, to form again only in new combinations. When race riots are fought in part by organized gangs, as occurred on one side in the Chicago riot of 1919, or in large part by the police, as occurred on one side in the Harlem riot of 1964, there may be a higher level of organization and discipline on at least one side of the violence, thus making it more similar perhaps to an international war. It may be true that the policies necessary to make casual rioters refrain from violence in order to carry on their conflict by other means would not work with organized national governments. But it may not be true that this is an important difference. We can make a judgment only if we first try to build a generalized theory of the control of violence, try to apply it to occasions in the past on which international violence has been controlled, and see how effective such comparisons can be.

If we look at the process of change in the conduct of racial conflict from 1919 to the 1960s, what seems to emerge is a spiral in which Negro protest and pressure, together with changes in the "official" value system of America, provide the motive power for forcing the spiral to move from violence to disorder without violence. We begin in 1919 with a fairly vague and inchoate system of local established orders—"governments"—based on the assumption of racial hierarchy. But two new forces were emerging in 1919: an uneasy and tentative commitment by some elements in American society to a value system tied to "making the world safe for democracy" and therefore to racial equality; and increasing feelings of power, prosperity, and dignity among Negroes. These two emergent facts helped energize a series of unorganized pressures and organized protests by Negroes against the system of racial hierarchy. These protests met opposition from the existing local systems of racially hierarchical "governments," and this opposition was focused in and through unneutral police behavior, in opposition to the Negroes. From this behavior, and the unwillingness of Negroes to retreat, came the riots in which Negroes fought back. The riots spawned a fear of violence in the society at large which had the effect of giving form to

early seeds of the American "state" on race relations—
that is, to neutral police behavior.

At this point the cycle began again, but on the different level caused by the emergence of bare beginnings of
a "state." Again there was an increasing acceptance in
the society at large of the moral value and legitimacy of
racial equality: in other words, a strengthening of the
embryonic "church" of equality. Again there was an improvement in the lives and therefore an increase in the
expectations of Negroes. Again the increased power of
Negroes was channeled into protest activity, but this time
the protest was met not by an absolutely anti-Negro police reaction but by a more nearly neutral form of police
behavior. The protests therefore were more often carried
on by means of creative disorder, rather than rioting. The
fear that violence might erupt out of disorder further
strengthened the flowering notion of the "state." The increasing legitimacy of the new "church" of equalitarianism, the increasing power of the Negroes as their use of
disorder succeeded, and the increasing fear of disorder
as well as of violence all worked together to energize the
political authorities to move (through the Civil Rights
Act) toward the creation of a new system of order, a
new "government" more oriented to racial equality.

The summary above might be useful as a model of the
way in which a group which stands outside a political
system may simultaneously move into the system and
stretch the system to encompass new forms of politics. It
may also suggest ways in which this process of entry by
outsiders may give new form, detail, and definition to a
political system that existed only in hazy and undefined
form previously, as in this case the pressure of Negroes
to enter the political order transformed a vague set of
local "governments" based on racial hierarchy into a more
carefully and consciously defined, though embryonic

"government" on the federal level, oriented to racial equality. The model also suggests several points at which research might throw valuable light on the means by which violent ways of carrying on conflict can be replaced by ways that avoid violence.

The first of these strategic points for research is the process of change in police techniques that makes rioting less likely and disorder more workable. In the particular case of American racial conflict during the last half-century, two aspects of change in the American police system are worthy of research. The process of strengthening police power, including both the creation of a permanently large United States Army and the increasing professionalization of local police forces, should be closely studied. When, how, and under what conditions has the Army been used to quell domestic violence since 1919? Have major changes occurred since 1919 in the relative weaponry available to urban police forces and the urban citizenry? Have private groups that once might have used violence testified to any deterrent effect that the Army or police had upon them? The second aspect of police work that should be examined is the process of training local policemen to be more nearly neutral as between racial groups. Who has ordered such training and for what reasons? Has recruitment of police from different ethnic groups or economic levels changed the behavior of the police toward these or other groups? Have Negro policemen, in particular, behaved differently from their white colleagues in dealing with Negro civilians? Have increases in the local political power of minorities, particularly Negroes, had an effect on local police behavior? Have institutional changes like the creation of civilian review boards or close supervision by an independent federal or state body affected local police?

Research is also needed into the conditions under

which new forms of creative disorder, like the sit-ins, freedom rides, and rent strikes of the 1960s have been invented, publicized, and adopted. Have different sorts of people initiated disorder in urban and in rural areas, in the North and South? How important to the continuation of disorder has been the immediate local success of an action, as against its acceptance into the mass media as a major focus of attention? How important to the success of creative disorder has been the careful specification of demands for particular changes, as against holistic demands for global change; and how important has been the use of disorderly pressures upon specific institutions, as against their use upon the whole of society? Comparisons should be made of situations in which disorderly techniques have been used without violence, as against situations in which these non-violent techniques were known and were available but were not used, and violence occurred instead. An examination should be made of efforts to disarm conflicting groups by prohibiting the sale or possession of weapons to them, with particular attention to the question whether such efforts at disarmament went along with the use of non-violent techniques. What of self-discipline within "disorderly" groups to disarm those who might have been expected to participate in rioting?

The third special area of research is that of the role played by changing feelings of legitimate social values, the growth of a new "church" on racial questions, in encouraging the use of creative disorder by groups whose goals were formerly "officially" felt to be illegitimate. It seems clear that the more legitimate the ends of an "outsider" group are felt to be, the more likely that it will be permitted and encouraged to use techniques (like disorder) about which there might otherwise have been doubt and distaste. Once the means have been accepted as legitimate, their use may be permitted even when new groups borrow them whose ends are not considered so legitimate. Although this study has focused upon the role of the emerging "state" in the changing patterns of racial conflict, there are many questions to be answered concerning the role of the "church." For example, what is the relationship between the "church" form of political authority (as exemplified by presidential speeches and proclamations, congressional speeches and resolutions, and *obiter dicta* from the Supreme Court) and private expressions of morality from the churches or collections of scholarly information and recommendations like that of the Chicago Commission on Race Relations? What effects do major "church" proclamations on social conflicts, like the Supreme Court school desegregation decision of 1954, have on those who have some sort of commitment to but are mostly apathetic about one or another side of the conflict? What occurs when the protesting group fails to gain support from the organs of "church" authority; is suppression likely?

For all three of these specific areas of research, there are analogous problems outside the racial arena that also ought to be examined. Periods of religious and ethnic violence in American cities during the first half of the nineteenth century, the transformation of labor-management violence in many countries into economic "warfare" without violence, and periods during which international conflict has been carried on by deliberate substitutes for war (such as the "Commercial War" between Britain and America from 1805 to 1812) ought to be carefully examined. In each such case, it should be possible to see what "police" institutions were imagined or invented for preventing resorts to violence; how new forms of carrying on intense conflict were invented; and how the structure of value systems and legitimacy as regards the conflicting ends affected the means being used by the parties in conflict. To the degree that such studies are done in a conscious effort to advance the new discipline of conflict research, hypotheses on conflict and violence as general categories of human history might be revised and improved.

One of the most important areas for such research may be the exploration of presumably transitory stages in the process of social conflict—particularly that stage in which there is still intense conflict but the level of outright violence is low. If the model of social change through conflict that has been sketched out above has any general application, one may think of four successive stages: a period of established, but rather hazy, order; a period of violence as that order is challenged; a period of disorder without much violence; and finally a period in which a new and more carefully defined system of order is agreed upon and established, incorporating as new liberties the forms of disorder used to challenge the old order and incorporating (at least in part) the social group that had been carrying on the challenge. The period of disorder may be of particular interest for purposes of coping with international violence in the last third of the twentieth century, when intense conflicts between nations and coalitions of nations can be expected to continue, but there is widespread interest in avoiding outright war as a means of resolving those conflicts.

In the international arena, the transition period of high conflict along with low violence may at first seem difficult to place in a sequence that does not begin with any clearly defined world "government" in favor of any established order. There have clearly been conflicting elements, and there has clearly been violence, in the international arena; but it may seem hard to identify an established international order against which the violence was being used. It must be remembered, however, that it was only in a vague, inchoate way that the United States had in 1919 a series of local systems of order based on racial hierarchy. In the international arena there has probably been even less of an established order than in the American racial arena of 1919, so that internationally there have been violent "riots" between shifting coalitions of competing nations, but there could hardly have been a world "insurrection" against the established order because the established order was itself so amorphous.

Not only has there been no definable "government" of the world, there has been no "state" or "church" either—no institution able to monopolize violence and prevent others' use of it, no institution able to focus and articulate widespread hopes and dreams. Whereas in the United States in 1919 there was no "church," no "state," and no "government" on the race question but on other issues there was one or another of these political authorities, for the world at large in the twentieth century there has been no such authority on any issue. There has, however, been an institution that has seemed to bear the seeds of any or all of these three forms of political authority—the United Nations.

Those who have called the United Nations a "great debating society" or the "grand forum of mankind" have hoped that it would develop into a "church," able to focus the values of all mankind on such issues as colonialism, human rights, and economic justice. Those who have concentrated on its peace-keeping functions have seen it as a possible future "state," able to prohibit any resort to war. Those who have talked of revising the UN charter to provide an independent income for the organization, of channeling funds for economic development of the hungry nations through the UN, of using UN power to end *apartheid* in South Africa have seen it as a future

world "government." But there has been little serious analysis of the process of social change that could, for example, encourage the development of a world "state" in
or through the UN. Such an analysis might well draw on
historical studies of the emergence of police forces neutral as between conflicting parties but committed to prevent the use of violence by any of them, or historical
studies of the ways in which the emergence of a "state"
and the emergence of creative disorder have marched,
side by side. It might suggest ways in which the invention of non-lethal equivalents of war might be encouraged, out of analogies from the invention of disorderly
equivalents of rioting; and ways in which such non-lethal
equivalents of war could be made "legitimate" in the international arena.[2]

In order to be of value in helping to shape policy concerning international conflict, a scholarly study of the
control of conflict would have to confront the problem
of how scholarly analyses and recommendations can be
used in a conflict situation. For one of the crucial problems for policy-makers and -shapers who are trying to
prevent future violence is the difficulty of acting, or getting others to act, out of a dimly perceived possible future. In 1919, the first steps toward making the police
more nearly neutral were taken only after the riots had
begun, in the hope of stopping them—rather than beforehand, in the hope of preventing them. Other such measures were taken immediately after the riots in the hope
of preventing new riots. The sense of urgency often declined fairly soon afterward, so that even after the vivid
experience of a riot, preventive measures that were
talked over at leisure were less likely to be put into effect.
But of all the possible stages at which action might conceivably have been taken, the one least used in actuality
was the period before a riot. It was evidently most diffi-

cult for officials to act if they had not had any chance to
"learn" from past events what the actuality of violence
meant to the lives, fortunes, and equanimity of those involved. Imagining the future was less potent than learning from the past. It would almost seem that riots had to
be experienced before the alternative of creative disorder
could be explored.

This intellectual and political problem may become
even more troublesome in cases in which the violence to
be prevented has no precedent and can therefore only be
imagined, as is the case with thermonuclear war. For
that reason, we need to examine the ways in which research on past conflict could be made to substitute for an
actual experience of war as a stimulus to and support of
ways of controlling conflict. In trying to examine the uses
of scholarship for such purposes, scholars might well find
it important to examine self-reflectively the social origins
and impacts of scholarship concerning conflict. Why the
Chicago Commission's scholarly response to the Chicago
riot? Why the scholarly response of the "conflict researchers" to the threat of thermonuclear war? Which segments
of the scholarly world have tended to respond to violence by wanting to study it, and how have their analyses differed from those of politicians and journalists?
What has been the impact of such scholarship on the
conflicts studied? Have scholars had more effect upon
the conflicts they studied when they not only made recommendations for new policy out of their analyses of the
past but also suggested how the political forces involved
could be energized to put their recommendations into
effect? The answers to such questions might suggest
whether scholarship of the sort attempted in this study of
racial conflict in 1919 and the 1960s can be of value in the
making of policy and the analysis of social change.

Until such a history or sociology of the knowledge of

conflict can be attempted, we cannot know for certain the effects of conflict research. But in the meantime, perhaps we can surmise that scholarly examination of the history of conflict might replace vague images of the future as a guide to policy. Where the future seems unprecedented, as it does in contemplation of thermonuclear war or of a disarmed world, it may be that an adequate and sophisticated scholarship of conflict can point to analogous situations in the past. Thus perhaps a study of the 1919 race riots can suggest some of the problems to be faced by those who would like to control international conflict; and perhaps a study of the change from riot to sit-in as a means of conducting racial conflict can suggest some of the opportunities to be seized by those who wish to prevent international violence.

Minor Racial Violence in 1919

The following list of "pogroms," minor riots, and similar affrays that took place in 1919 is taken from the file on "Mob Violence, 1919," NAACP MSS. The attached descriptions are brief summaries of the NAACP's own notes on these incidents, and quotations are from the NAACP's notes. The incidents are listed in chronological order.

Berkeley, Georgia. Reported *Columbia Statesman*, February 28. Attempted lynching, resulted in death of several white would-be lynchers. One Negro killed, four whites.

Millen, Georgia. Reported *Memphis Commercial Appeal*, April 15. On April 14 seven deaths reported as result of race riots begun April 13 at Buckhead Church. Two white men, four Negroes killed, one Negro lynched. Whites killed were W. C. Brown, policeman, T. H. Stephens, marshall.

New London, Connecticut. Reported *St. Louis Argus*, June 13. Street battle between white and Negro sailors. Police and firemen unable to stop riot. Detachment of Marines called out and did so. Beginnings of riot seemed to be sailor highjinks in Hotel Bristol.

Bisbee, Arizona. Reported New York papers, July 5. Clash between Negro cavalrymen and white policemen resulting in five wounded, three Negroes and two whites. Fourteen Negroes arrested and turned over to military authorities.

Dublin, Georgia. Reported *Dublin Courier Herald*,

July 6; *Brooklyn Times,* July 12; *Atlanta Constitution,* July 12. Attempted lynching of one Negro ended in killing of white by another Negro. To protect the latter, company of eighty guards called into service. "Savannah Home Guard and Savannah troops ordered by Governor Service to hold themselves in readiness."

Coatesville, Pennsylvania. Reported *Philadelphia Public Ledger,* July 8. "Race riots narrowly averted, Negro reported to have attacked white girl, fifteen, was said to have been captured; was to be taken from jail and lynched. More than 500 Negroes voiced protest against any attempted lynching. Later nine Negroes on their way to City Hall with baseball bats were arrested."

Philadelphia, Pennsylvania. Reported *Philadelphia Public Ledger,* July 8. Small racial incident started free-for-all fight. "Whites, finding themselves outnumbered, retreated, but returned with reinforcements. General riot call sent out and 100 police stopped the trouble. Eight colored men arrested."

Port Arthur, Texas. Reported *Shreveport Times,* July 15, 1919. "Clarence Paxton and J. B. Pierre, Negroes, are in hospitals seriously injured; several others less seriously hurt as a result of clash between 20 whites and 14 Negroes."

Norfolk, Virginia. Reported New York papers, July 22. Clash between Negroes and white policemen started "when policemen tried to arrest Negroes fighting among themselves." Report continues, "Norfolk was quiet and orderly. City officials decided to end the celebration of home-coming of Negro troops. Double force of patrolmen on duty in the Negro district." From *Baltimore Daily Herald,* July 23.

New Orleans, Louisiana. Reported Associated Press, July 23. "Timely reference by a squad of traffic policemen going on duty at one of the RR stations here last night broke up a threatened free-for-all fight between whites and Negroes. A mob of Negroes had attacked a white chauffeur. The police arrested the leader of the Negroes and held at bay white men who were going to the rescue. The whites demanded that the Negro under arrest be delivered to them, but the police landed him safely in jail." From *Shreveport Journal*, July 23.

Syracuse, New York. Reported *New York Evening Sun*, July 31. "Rioting broke out between striking moulders and Negro strikebreakers at the plant of the Globe Malleable Iron Co. The rioters were subdued by the police and four men were arrested."

Montreal, Canada. Reported *New York Times*, August 20. "A race riot in which whites and Negroes battled freely was quelled only after police reserves were rushed to the Negro quarter, where the disturbance took place." Report says riot followed attack by three Negroes on white watchmen in hotel near the Negro section.

Ocmulgee, Georgia. Reported New York papers, August 29. "Eli Cooper, Negro, shot to death by mob in a church, which then burned the church, other Negro churches and a lodge room in the vicinity, after reports had been circulated that the Negroes were 'planning to rise up' and wipe out the white people. Cooper, alleged to have been leader among Negroes, was taken from Caldwell, Laurens County, to Ocmulgee by the mob. It is said many whites in Laurens are planning to raise funds to rebuild the destroyed churches."

Baltimore, Maryland. Reported *New York Evening Sun*, October 2. "Trouble between several hundred soldiers and Negroes, in which shots were fired and sticks and stones hurled, were checked by police after six arrests had been made. The trouble started when a bottle was thrown by someone at four infantrymen who had gathered a crowd of two hundred soldiers and tried to terrorize the neighborhood. The six men arrested (all soldiers) were: Thomas Michael, Harry Lubni, Donald McMonagal, Laurence Collins, Hurley Brown, John A. Critzer."

Wilmington, Delaware. Reported *New York Tribune*, November 14. "Rioting between whites and Negroes followed by killing of one policeman and the wounding of another by Negroes whom they were questioning regarding a recent robbery. Ballnel Field, Negro, was wounded in the head, when 300 whites came upon 4 Negroes, 3 Negroes were saved by the prompt arrival of 15 policemen. The Negroes alleged to have been implicated in the shooting were taken from the jail and sent to Philadelphia because it was feared that an attempt might be made to lynch them. (Lemmuel and John Price.) Policemen killed: Tom M. Zebley." Further report summarized from *New York Call*, November 15, "Police patrols took precautions to prevent renewal of fight of last night. Aroused by the removal of the two Negroes to Philadelphia, crowds collected on the streets. Buck Hayes, a Negro, opened fire on a group of white men. The whites returned the fire, wounding one Negro. The mob then stormed the Negro quarter. Order was finally restored and a guard placed over the jail. The Price brothers were held for a special session of the Grand Jury, November 17."

Bogalusa, Louisiana. Reported Northern and Southern papers, November 23 to 25, *New Orleans Vindicator*, November 29, and *New York Sun*, December 8. Situation growing out of labor difficulty. Three white men, all labor unionists, killed while protecting a Negro, Saul Dechus, or Sol Dakus, from members of the Loyal Legion, "which has been conducting a campaign against racial adjutators. The Negro was alleged to have been stirring up members of his own race."

Posters in Negro Areas of Chicago during the 1919 Riot

The following are verbatim reproductions of posters, notices, and throwaways published in the Chicago Negro community during the 1919 riot, and discussed above in Chapter V. Only one is dated, a one-page extra edition of the *Chicago Whip,* a Negro newspaper. The others are given here in approximate order of their appearance, as indicated from internal evidence that they appeared during the worst of the riot, as the violence was reduced, and as the riot ended. All are from NAACP MSS.

NOTICE! *To the Citizens of Chicago*

We the Colored Citizens of Chicago, appeal to all the White Citizens for prompt cooperation and a final adjustment of the present lawless conditions which now prevail in parts of our city. By virtue of misunderstandings and misrepresentations, induced by improper publicity, without the absolute facts being known, the people of both races have been misled.

The cause of this deplorable situation was the unfortunate circumstance which occurred at the 29th Street Bathing Beach where an innocent colored boy was stoned and drowned. Is this a good and valid reason why the city should be turned over to the prejudices, and violent assaults, that have caused so much sorrow and grief, to both races and in most cases those, the least to blame?

The present state of affairs should be stopped at once, as it is a grave menace to the welfare of the community and an undying disgrace to Chicago. The white people that know us best and have direct dealings with us are doing business as usual, without molestation to them or their families. Outside deliveries are being made without difficulty and these people are sorely grieved because of the present situation.

Let the cause of this trouble be forgotten, and to this end, let every individual do all in his power, to restore peace and harmony. COMMITTEE OF 100

Listen to Me Fellows!

You all know Eugene F. Manns, and you know he is the only man in the Black Belt who Really Does Big Things for You and Your Family. Now fellows let's all of us go home and don't stand around the corners. As I am now in consultation behind closed doors with the mayor and chief of police fighting for you and your family's rights and arranging that all guilty persons who molested you be punished.

> Yours for Good Luck
> Eugene F. Manns
> 5003 S. State Street—Te. Kenwood 8742

FOR NEEDY RIOT VICTIMS

FREE MEALS
At Olivet Bapt. Church
31st and South Park Avenue, Beginning
Saturday, Aug. 2, '19
After 10 O'clock A.M.
DR. L. K. WILLIAMS, Pastor
Northwestern Book Co., Printers, 12 W. 27th St.

TO THE NEGRO OF CHICAGO

We welcome the fast approach of normal conditions in Chicago once more, and urge the colored man to do all in his power to speed such coming.

Since last Sunday we have experienced conditions deplorable, such, we hope never to see again.

While the state and city authorities, backed up by Chicago's best thinking white people are doing all they can to establish the peace that this great city has heretofore enjoyed, let it not be said that a single Negro would do anything to thwart the effort.

Do not pay any attention to such statements as were said to be made by Mr. B. F. Mosley, at the Idlewild Hotel Wednesday evening to the effect, that "This is a white man's country," for we know that the Negro is a part of this great government, and no charge of un-american has ever been preferred against him.

The Chicago Daily News printed Mr. Mosleys statement which may be found on the third page of the News, July 31st. Such utterances of would-be leaders, does more to hurt, than help conditions.

The pastors, who fill the pulpits of this country, are, first of all, the real leaders of the people, and would never think of making such statements, for they know that the Holy Bible teach us that God has made of one blood, all nations to dwell upon the face of the earth, and if we are anything at all to the white man, we are his brother, and brothers should feel each others care.

F. A. McCOO, Pastor St. John Baptist Church,
3434 Wabash Avenue

TO MY PEOPLE!

Fellow Workers:

I have to report the following. I attended the Conference at the Stock Yards this morning. Present at the meeting were:

S. C. FRAZEE, Superintendent Wilson and Co.,

J. P. DOWDING, Assistant Superintendent Armour and Co.

W. B. FARRIS, Superintendent Morris and Co.

R. M. JACKSON, Swift and Co.

JOHN M. FELDHAKE, Supt. South Side Elevated R.R.

JOS. BURNS, Swift and Co.

P. A. TWISS, Swift and Co.

HENRY W. KRUGER LIBBY, McNEIL & LIBBY

E. C. HALL, Armour and Co.

MYRICK D. HARDING, Armour and Co.

ASST. CHIEF OF POLICE ALCOCK

CAPT. HOGAN, Halsted Street Station

AND YOUR HUMBLE SERVANT

Your jobs are open and ready for you. THE ABOVE SUPERINTENDENTS WANT YOU TO REPORT FOR WORK MONDAY MORNING 7:00 O'CLOCK SHARP. They guarantee proper police protection. The entire Stock Yards will be policed inside and out. Use the Elevated Railroad and go to work orderly. No man or woman white or colored will be admitted to the Yards who had fire arms on his or her person. Keep good order on the Elevated trains.

Sincerely your humble servant MAJOR R. R. JACKSON
                                    Alderman 2nd Ward

ATTENTION!
ALL LAW-ABIDING CITIZENS:

THE RIOTING IS OVER SO GO ON BACK TO WORK
AND

Help the Police Keep the Situation in Hand by Not Congregating on the Streets, Car Lines, or Corners, Holding Conversation.

Avoid all Inflammatory Remarks. Obey all Police Orders.

COMMITTEE OF COLORED CITIZENS

HARVEY B. SAUNDERS	R. M. LEACH
GEO. W. HOLT	EUGENE F. MANNS
DR. R. FINN	WM. B. LYLES
W. L. HARRISON	GEO. M. PORTER
GEO. W. HOLT,	EUGENE F. MANNS,
Chairman	Secretary.

FELLOW WORKERS

We go back to work Monday 7:00 a.m. Sharp. Use the
Elevated Road. Keep Cool and use your heads. Remember
loud talk never gets much else but trouble. The riot is over.
LETS FORGET IT. We need food and work for our families
so do you.

STEADY AND COOL IS THE WATCHWORD.

Signed
ARMOUR EFFICIENCY CLUB
MORRIS INDUSTRIAL CLUB
WILSON CO-OPERATIVE CLUB OF THE WABASH
AVENUE Y.M.C.A.

ATTENTION

The Chicago Urban League advises all men and women
to return to their jobs today, as our investigations convince
us that there is no further trouble. This applies to the workers
in all places as well as those in the Stockyards.

If you do not get your job, report to us immediately and
we will go at once to your employer.

CHICAGO URBAN LEAGUE
T. ARNOLD HILL
3032 S. Wabash Avenue
Telephone Calumet 4919

THE RIOT IS OVER

1000 New Depositors
Two Thousand Stock Yard Employee's Checks Were
Cashed in the Last Two Days, Totalling more than $20,000.00
at the WOODFOLK BANK 32nd & State Streets

We had the money. Men out of work during the fierce riot needed money and we gave it to them. This Bank's doors stood open with the strength of the Rock of Gibralter in the time of need. We had money to cash all of these checks amounting to thousands of dollars and we can handle your money. DO BUSINESS WITH YOUR OWN PEOPLE who live with you, eat with you, sleep with you, and are willing and able to help you.

Keep cool heads. Don't gather on the corners. Stop all loud talking. Respect the Soldiers and visit Woodfolk's Bank when you need money or want to deposit your money. Put all of your money as close to you and your people as possible. Young Colored Men and Women Cashiers, Tellers, Receivers, Investors, Bank Messengers, Stenographers, and Real Estate Assistants can handle your business in your own community. LET US GET TOGETHER NOW.

We are cashing all checks from 9 a.m. to 6 p.m. A BANK BEHIND YOUR BOOK. $8000 Vaults and Safety Deposit BOXES. Bring in your valuables. Every Business Man and Bank recognizes Woodfolk's Bank Checks—WHY? We PAY them when presented. $1.00 Opens A Savings Account.

WOODFOLK BANK
3201 South State Street
Phone: Douglas 4541

Chicago Whip, EXTRA, August 2, 1919, one-page sheet

PEACE ON EARTH, GOOD WILL TOWARD MEN.

The Riot is over. Let us go back to our work and forget that it ever happened. Your jobs await you; your safety is guaranteed.

But Dont forget the State and City of Authorities who have labored untiringly to give equal protection to all peaceful citizens both white and black . . .

Special credit should be given to Chief John J. Garrity, 1st Deputy Alcock, and the entire police force . . .

On account of labor shortage, we are not able to get out our normal supply of papers this week. Therefore we reprint at the request of several civic organizations our front page editorial of this week's issue:

THE RIOT AND THE HIDDEN HAND . . . We admit that there has been a laxity on the part of authorities which in all probability served as an incubator for the growth of the trouble.

But the hand which contrived with criminal cleverness to originate the Ku Klux Klan, Jim Crow car and other unwholesome organizations and conveyances is ninety per cent responsible for this horrible state of affairs . . .

The Whips Dont's for avoiding trouble: Dont forget that interests of white and colored people are so intertangled you cannot harm one to any extent without damage to the other. Dont congregate on corners. Dont carry a chip on your shoulder. Dont allow your sentiment to overcome best judgment . . . Dont forget that the good name of Chicago is at stake.

NOTES

NOTES TO CHAPTER I

1. The second volume of the trilogy is simply titled, *Nineteen Nineteen*. John dos Passos, *U.S.A.*, p. i.
2. Hannah Arendt, *On Revolution*, p. 9.
3. Hans Gerth and C. Wright Mills, *From Max Weber: Essays in Sociology*, p. 78. This remark was made by Weber in a speech given in 1918 and published as "Politik als Beruf" in 1919. *Ibid.*, n. p. 77.
4. Ray A. Billington, *The Protestant Crusade*.
5. John W. Caughey, *Their Majesties the Mob*.
6. Samuel Yellen, *American Labor Struggles*; John A. Fitch, *The Causes of Industrial Unrest*; Louis Adamic, *Dynamite*; Robert V. Bruce, *1877: Year of Violence*.
7. Arthur Raper, *The Tragedy of Lynching*.
8. Henry S. Commager, ed., *Documents of American History*, p. 171.
9. John R. Commons *et al.*, *History of Labor in the United States, 1896–1932*, Vol. IV, *Labor Movements*, by Selig Perlman and Philip Taft, p. 433.
10. Wilfrid H. Crook, *Communism and the General Strike*, p. 21.
11. *Ibid.*, p. 52.
12. *Ibid.*, pp. 56–57.
13. *Ibid.*, pp. 57–58.
14. William Preston Jr., *Aliens and Dissenters*, pp. 198–206.
15. *Ibid.*, pp. 207–220; Zechariah Chafee, *Free Speech in the United States*, pp. 196–240.
16. Commons *et al.*, IV, 427–28; Adamic, pp. 298–305.
17. Louis Brownlow, *A Passion for Anonymity*, pp. 83–89.
18. Commons *et al.*, pp. 446–47.
19. Brownlow, p. 88.
20. George Soule, *Prosperity Decade*, p. 194; Adamic, pp. 288–90; Fitch, pp. 195–96.
21. Commons *et al.*, IV, 466–67.
22. Soule, 195–96.
23. Memo, Office of Army Chief of Staff to Adjutant-General, November 8, 1920, War Department MSS., National Archives.

24. Commons *et al.*, IV, 473.
25. Gunnar Myrdal, *An American Dilemma*, pp. 558–66.
26. *Ibid.*, p. 566.
27. *Ibid.*
28. John Hope Franklin, *From Slavery to Freedom*, p. 275; Samuel E. Morison and Henry S. Commager, *Growth of the American Republic*, I, 706.
29. Franklin, p. 433; Myrdal, p. 567.

NOTES TO CHAPTER II

1. James Weldon Johnson, *Along This Way*, p. 341.
2. John Hope Franklin, *From Slavery to Freedom*, p. 472.
3. File on "Mob Violence, 1919," NAACP MSS.
4. In Appendix A there is a list of "pogroms," minor riots, and similar affrays not further discussed in this study.
5. *Charleston News and Courier*, May 11, 12, and 16, 1919, NAACP MSS.; United States Bureau of the Census, *Fourteenth Census of the United States*, 1920, III, 2.
6. *Ibid.*, May 12 and 16, 1919, NAACP MSS.
7. *Ibid.*, May 12 and 16, 1919, NAACP MSS.
8. *Ibid.*, May 16, 1919, *Springfield Republican*, July 31, 1919, NAACP MSS.
9. Richard H. Mickey to John R. Shillady, May 29, 1919, NAACP MSS.
10. F. W. Morton to Josephus Daniels, June 21, 1919, NAACP MSS.
11. Memoes from Morton to Shillady, June 9 and 14, 1919, Morton to Mickey, June 23, 1919, NAACP MSS.
12. Daniels to Shillady, June 23, 1919, NAACP MSS.
13. Memo by Secretary of the Navy, July 22, 1919, memo from Secretary of the Navy to Chief, Bureau of Navigation, Aug. 28, 1919, Judge Advocate General to Sen. Kenneth McKellar, Sept. 24, 1919, Navy Dept. MSS., National Archives.
14. Morton to Mickey, June 23, 1919, NAACP MSS.
15. E. F. Smith to Secretary of Sixth Naval District, Oct. 29, 1919, Franklin D. Roosevelt to Smith, Nov. 6, 1919, Mayor John P. Grace to Mrs. Emma Dawson, July 23, 1920, Dawson to Secretary of the Navy, Sept. 18, 1920, memo from Gordon Woodberry to Commandant, Sixth Naval District, Oct. 7, 1920, Navy Dept. MSS.
16. Affidavit by Cyril Burton, May 14, 1919, Navy Dept. MSS.
17. R. L. Craggy to Secretary of State, Feb. 11, 1921, Navy Dept. MSS.

18. Norman H. Davis to Secretary of the Navy, March 2, 1921, Navy Dept. MSS.
19. Theodore Roosevelt to Secretary of State, March 18, 1921, Navy Dept. MSS.
20. Henry P. Fletcher to Secretary of the Navy, April 1, 1921, Navy Dept. MSS.
21. Theodore Roosevelt to Speaker Frederick H. Gillett, June 1, 1921, Navy Dept. MSS.
22. Affidavit by Cyril Burton, June 4, 1921, memo from C. G. Mayo to the Solicitor, Navy Disbursing Office, June 14, 1921, Navy Dept. MSS.
23. *Shreveport Times*, July 12, 1919, *Wichita Protest*, July 25, 1919, NAACP MSS.; United States Bureau of the Census, *Fourteenth Census of the United States*, 1920, III, 25.
24. Chicago Commission on Race Relations, *The Negro in Chicago*, pp. 87–92.
25. *Shreveport Times*, July 12, 1919, NAACP MSS.
26. *Ibid.*
27. *Ibid.; Marshall Sentinel* (Texas), July 11, 1919, *Baltimore Herald*, July 12, 1919, NAACP MSS.
28. *Shreveport Times*, July 12, 1919, *Shreveport Journal*, July 11, 1919, NAACP MSS.
29. *Shreveport Times*, July 12, 1919, NAACP MSS.
30. *Shreveport Journal*, July 11 and 12, 1919, *Shreveport Times*, July 15, 1919, NAACP MSS.
31. *Shreveport Times*, July 12, 1919, NAACP MSS.
32. *Ibid.*, July 13, 1919, NAACP MSS.
33. *Ibid.*, July 15, 1919, NAACP MSS.
34. *Shreveport Journal*, July 12, 1919, *Shreveport Times*, July 13, 1919, NAACP MSS.
35. *Ibid.*
36. *Ibid.*
37. *Ibid.*, July 15 and 17, 1919, *Pittsburgh Courier*, July 26, 1919, NAACP MSS.
38. Unnamed paper, July 26, 1919, NAACP MSS.
39. *Shreveport Times*, July 27, 1919, NAACP MSS.
40. P. A. Williams to NAACP, Aug. 19, 1919, NAACP MSS.
41. John R. Shillady to Robert R. Church, July 18, 1919, NAACP MSS.
42. Williams to Shillady, Aug. 11, 1919, NAACP MSS.
43. Mary White Ovington to Williams, Aug. 21, 1919, Shillady to Church, July 18, 1919, NAACP MSS.

NOTES TO CHAPTER III

1. John Hope Franklin, *From Slavery to Freedom*, pp. 445–46; Constance McLaughlin Green, *Washington: Capital City*, pp. 218–26.
2. *New York World*, Aug. 10, 1919, NAACP MSS.
3. *New York Call*, July 26, 1919, NAACP MSS.
4. *Amsterdam News*, Aug. 6, 1919, NAACP MSS.
5. Author's interview with Rayford W. Logan, 1959.
6. Louis Brownlow, *A Passion for Anonymity*, p. 84; author's interview with Brownlow, 1959; Herbert J. Seligmann, *The Negro Faces America*, pp. 120–22; *New York Call*, July 26, 1919, *Baltimore Herald*, July 8, 1919, NAACP MSS.
7. *Philadelphia Public Ledger*, July 28, 1919, NAACP MSS.
8. *Washington Times*, July 10, 1919, NAACP MSS.
9. *Washington Post*, July 19, 1919, NAACP MSS.
10. *Ibid.*
11. *Washington Times*, July 20, 1919, NAACP MSS.
12. *Ibid.*
13. *Philadelphia Public Ledger*, July 28, 1919, NAACP MSS.
14. E. David Cronon, *The Cabinet Diaries of Josephus Daniels, 1913–1921*, p. 427.
15. *Washington Post*, July 21, 1919, *Washington Times*, July 21, 1919, NAACP MSS.
16. *Ibid.*, *Washington Post*, July 21, 1919, NAACP MSS.; *Washington Star*, July 21, 1919, *Washington Bee*, July 26, 1919.
17. *Ibid.*
18. Author's interviews with Brownlow, Campbell Johnson, and West A. Hamilton, 1959; Edward H. Lawson, "Teaching How to Riot," in *The American Teacher*, Oct. 1919, NAACP MSS.
19. *Washington Post*, July 22, 1919, NAACP MSS.
20. *Philadelphia Public Ledger*, July 28, 1919, NAACP MSS.
21. *Washington Post*, July 22, 1919, NAACP MSS.; *Washington Star*, July 22, 1919.
22. *Washington Times*, July 21, 1919, NAACP MSS.; *Washington Star*, July 22, 1919.
23. *Washington Times*, July 21, 1919, NAACP MSS.
24. Lawson, *loc. cit.*; memo from Seligmann to NAACP staff, NAACP MSS.
25. Author's interview with Campbell Johnson, 1959.
26. *Washington Times*, July 21, 1919, NAACP MSS.
27. *Washington Post*, July 22, 1919, NAACP MSS.; *Washington Star*, July 22, 1919.

28. *Ibid.*
29. *Ibid.*
30. *Washington Post,* July 22, 1919, *Washington Star,* July 22, 1919, *Washington Times,* July 22, 1919, NAACP MSS.
31. *Ibid.*
32. *Washington Post,* July 23, 1919, NAACP MSS.; Cronon, *Cabinet Diaries of Josephus Daniels,* pp. 427–28; *Washington Times,* July 23, 1919, *Washington Star,* July 23, 1919.
33. *Ibid.*
34. William G. Haan to Major Gen. Thomas H. Barry, July 30, 1919, Haan MSS., Wisconsin State Historical Society.
35. *Ibid.*
36. *Philadelphia Public Ledger,* July 28, 1919, NAACP MSS.
37. *Washington Post,* July 23, 1919, NAACP MSS. See also *Washington Bee,* July 26, 1919, and Aug. 2, 1919, on Negroes' suspicion of the police.
38. E. W. Libby to C. E. Stewart, July 22, 1919, Justice Dept. MSS., National Archives.
39. Karl G. Phillips to George E. Haynes, July 22, 1919, Labor Dept. MSS., National Archives.
40. *Washington Post,* July 23, 1919, NAACP MSS. See also *Washington Star,* July 23, 1919, Wilson MSS., Library of Congress.
41. Newton D. Baker to Woodrow Wilson, July 23, 1919, Wilson MSS., Library of Congress.
42. Memo from Seligmann to NAACP staff, NAACP MSS.
43. *Washington Post,* July 25, 1919, NAACP MSS.; *Washington Star,* July 24, 1919.
44. *Washington Post,* July 25, 1919, NAACP MSS.
45. *Ibid.; Washington Star,* July 30, 1919.
46. Edgar M. Grey, *The Washington Riot,* in Schomburg Collection, New York Public Library.
47. *Washington Star,* July 27, 1919, NAACP MSS.
48. John R. Shillady to A. Mitchell Palmer, July 25, 1919, Robert P. Stewart to Shillady, July 29, 1919, Justice Dept. MSS.
49. J. Milton Waldron to Palmer, Aug. 1, 1919, Palmer to Waldron, Aug. 8, 1919, Palmer to John E. Laskey, Aug. 8, 1919, Laskey to Palmer, Aug. 12, 1919, Justice Dept. MSS.
50. Isaac Siegel to Palmer, July 30, 1919, Stewart to Siegel, Aug. 1, 1919, Stewart to Laskey, Aug. 1, 1919, Laskey to Palmer, Aug. 4, 1919, Justice Dept. MSS.
51. *Washington Herald,* Sept. 2 and 9, 1919, NAACP MSS.; NAACP *Branch Bulletin,* October, 1919, in files of Senate Judiciary Committee, Legislative MSS., National Archives.
52. Rochester newspaper, no name, July 26, 1919, *Minneapolis National Advocate,* Aug. 2, 1919, NAACP MSS.

53. Senators James Phelan and Arthur Capper, quoted in *Washington Post*, July 22, 1919, NAACP MSS.
54. *New York Herald*, July 26, 1919, NAACP MSS.
55. *Utica Press*, July 25, 1919, NAACP MSS.
56. *New York Globe*, July 23, 1919, NAACP MSS.
57. *New York Tribune*, July 23, 1919, NAACP MSS.
58. *Amsterdam News*, Aug. 6, 1919, NAACP MSS.
59. *New York Commoner*, July 23, 1919, NAACP MSS.
60. *Washington Post*, July 25, 1919, NAACP MSS.
61. *New York Call*, July 25, 1919, *New York Globe*, July 29, 1919, NAACP MSS.
62. *Pittsburgh Courier*, July 26, 1919, NAACP MSS. See also United Civic League Press Service release, July 30, 1919, NAACP MSS.
63. *New York World*, July 23, 1919, *Des Moines Evening Tribune*, July 22, 1919, *New York Tribune*, July 23, 1919, *New York Call*, July 25, 1919, NAACP MSS.
64. *New York Globe*, July 29, 1919, *New York World*, July 29, 1919, NAACP MSS.
65. J. G. Robinson to Woodrow Wilson, July 26, 1919, Justice Dept. MSS.
66. *New York Post*, July 23, 1919, *Survey*, Aug. 2, 1919, NAACP MSS.
67. Edward H. Lawson, "Teaching How to Riot," *The American Teacher*, Oct. 1919, NAACP MSS.
68. *Young Democracy*, Aug. 1, 1919, *L'Homme Libre* and *L'Avenir* quoted in *Chicago Tribune*, July 25, 1919, NAACP MSS.
69. *New York Times*, July 23, 1919, NAACP MSS.
70. *Brooklyn Eagle*, July 27, 1919, NAACP MSS.
71. *Syracuse Herald*, July 24, 1919, *Albany Argus*, July 24, 1919, NAACP MSS.
72. *Nashville Banner*, July 22, 1919, Memphis Press, July 24, 1919, NAACP MSS.
73. Montgomery, Alabama, newspaper, no name, no date, NAACP MSS.
74. Author's interviews with Campbell Johnson, West A. Hamilton, and Rayford W. Logan, 1959.

NOTES TO CHAPTER IV

1. Chicago Commission on Race Relations, *The Negro in Chicago*, pp. 4–5. (Hereafter referred to as *Negro in Chicago*). This work includes an excellent history of the Chicago riot,

and much of the first ten pages of this chapter is based upon it, except where other sources are specified.

2. *Negro in Chicago*, p. 79; William S. Rossiter, *Increase of Population in the United States, 1910–1920*, pp. 127–28.

3. *Negro in Chicago*, pp. 124–30; Charles S. Duke, *The Housing Situation and the Colored People of Chicago*.

4. Author's interviews with Joseph D. Lohman and V. K. Brown, 1959; *Negro in Chicago*, pp. 272–80.

5. *Ibid.*, pp. 385–431; Carl Sandburg, *The Chicago Race Riots*; Joel E. Spingarn, "Hasty Notes in Chicago," July 30, 1919, NAACP MSS.

6. *City Club Bulletin*, Aug. 18, 1919, in Chicago Municipal Reference Library.

7. Chicago Urban League, *Second Annual Report for the Fiscal Year Ended October 31, 1918*.

8. William T. Hutchinson, *Lowden of Illinois*, I, 339–40.

9. Lloyd Wendt and Herman Kogan, *Big Bill of Chicago*, pp. 133–34, 168–70, 173–74.

10. John G. Oglesby, Acting Governor, to Adjutant-General of Illinois, July 28, 1919, Chicago Commission on Race Relations MSS., Illinois Archives (hereafter referred to as CCRR MSS.); *Negro in Chicago*, p. 40; Wendt and Kogan, *op. cit.*, p. 174.

11. Edward Osgood Brown *et al.* to Chief of Police of Chicago, July 28, 1919, Rosenwald MSS., University of Chicago.

12. *Chicago Tribune*, July 31, 1919, NAACP MSS.

13. Field Orders Number One and Two by Colonel James Ronayne, Chief of Staff, Mobilized State Force, July 30, 1919, CCRR MSS.

14. *Chicago Daily News*, Aug. 2, 1919, NAACP MSS.

15. *Chicago Herald-Examiner*, Sept. 13, 1919, NAACP MSS.; Ronayne, Special Order Number Four, Aug. 6, 1919, CCRR MSS.; *Negro in Chicago*, p. 663.

16. Wendt and Kogan, *op. cit.*, pp. 143–46; Walter F. White to John R. Shillady, Aug. 26, 1919, NAACP MSS.

17. *Chicago Post*, Aug. 7, 1919, NAACP MSS.

18. *Ibid.*, *Christian Science Monitor*, Aug. 15, 1919, NAACP MSS.

19. Shillady to Mary White Ovington, Aug. 4, 1919, NAACP MSS.

20. *Ibid.*; White to Ovington, Aug. 7, 1919, NAACP MSS.

21. Joel E. Spingarn to Ovington, July 30, 1919, White to Ovington, Aug. 8, 1919, Shillady to Ovington, Aug. 4, 1919, NAACP MSS.

22. *Ibid.*

23. *Ibid.*, White to Ovington, Aug. 7, 1919, NAACP MSS.

24. Ovington to Shillady, Aug. 11, 1919, NAACP MSS.

25. Ovington to Shillady, Aug. 12, 1919, NAACP MSS.

26. *Ibid.*

27. *Ibid.*
28. Press release to *Chicago Defender et al.*, Aug. 16, 1919, NAACP MSS.
29. Author's interviews with Augustus L. Williams and former City Councilman John Lyle, 1959.
30. Shillady to Ovington, Aug. 20, 1919, White to Ovington, Aug. 21, 1919, NAACP MSS.
31. Shillady to Ovington, Aug. 20, 1919, White to Ovington, Aug. 21, 1919, A. Clement MacNeal to White, Sept. 5 and 16, 1919, Memo by White to NAACP, Sept. 9, 1919, MacNeal to Shillady, Oct. 21 and November 18, 1919, NAACP MSS.
32. Edward O. Brown to Robert McMurdy, Aug. 15, 1919, NAACP MSS.
33. MacNeal to White, Sept. 5, 1919, NAACP MSS.
34. Public statement of NAACP "Regarding defense of Chicago Riot Victims," no date, NAACP MSS.
35. Minutes of Joint Emergency Committee, Sept. 22, 1919, NAACP MSS.
36. White to NAACP, Sept. 8, 1919, NAACP MSS.
37. M. A. Hirschl to MacNeal, Aug. 29, 1919, NAACP MSS.
38. MacNeal to NAACP, Dec. 31, 1919, NAACP MSS.
39. Hirschl to MacNeal, Aug. 29, 1919, memo from White to NAACP, Sept. 8, 1919, NAACP MSS.
40. MacNeal to Shillady, Oct. 21, 1919, NAACP MSS.
41. Shillady to MacNeal, Nov. 21, 1919, NAACP MSS.
42. Ovington to Edward O. Brown, Jan. 12, 1920, Shillady to Brown, Jan. 13, 1920, NAACP MSS.
43. MacNeal to NAACP, Dec. 31, 1919, NAACP MSS.
44. Shillady to Brown, Jan. 13, 1920, NAACP MSS.
45. MacNeal to NAACP, Dec. 31, 1919, and Jan. 26, 1920, NAACP MSS.
46. White to Ovington, Aug. 21, 1919, affidavit of Count J. Jeffner, Aug. 22, 1919, White to August Grand Jury of Cook County, Aug. 24, 1919, White to Shillady, Aug. 26, 1919, White to Maclay Hoyne, Aug. 30, 1919, George F. Kenney to White, Sept. 2, 1919, Louis B. Anderson to White, Sept. 31, 1919, NAACP MSS.
47. MacNeal to NAACP, Dec. 31, 1919, NAACP MSS.
48. *Chicago Herald-Examiner*, Sept. 12, 1919, NAACP MSS.; Frederic M. Thrasher, *The Gang*, pp. 19, 67, 209.
49. *Negro in Chicago*, pp. 49–52; Peter M. Hoffman, Coroner of Cook County, *The Race Riots: Biennial Report of Coroner*, pp. 3–7.
50. *Chicago Herald-Examiner*, July 31, 1919, NAACP MSS.
51. *Chicago Tribune*, July 31, 1919, *Chicago Journal*, July 31,

1919, *Chicago Daily News,* July 31, 1919, *Chicago American,* Aug. 2, 1919, NAACP MSS.

52. *Chicago Daily News,* Sept. 1, 1919, NAACP MSS.

53. *Chicago Defender,* Aug. 9, 1919, NAACP MSS.

54. Rev. I. D. Stone to Woodrow Wilson, Oct. 29, 1919, Labor Dept. MSS., National Archives.

55. *Chicago Herald-Examiner,* Aug. 4, 1919, NAACP MSS.

56. *The New Majority,* Aug. 9, 1919, *Chicago Tribune,* Aug. 18, 1919, NAACP MSS.

57. Harrison George, *Chicago Race Riots.*

58. *Ibid.*

59. *Chicago Defender,* Aug. 9, 1919, NAACP MSS.

60. *Chicago Daily News,* Aug. 13, 1919, NAACP MSS.

61. George R. Arthur to Stock Yards Community Clearing House Committee, Dec. 21, 1921, Wabash Ave. YMCA MSS.

62. *New York American,* July 30, 1919, NAACP MSS.

63. *Chicago Post,* July 31, 1919, NAACP MSS.

64. *Chicago Tribune,* Aug. 3, 1919, NAACP MSS.

65. *Ibid.,* Aug. 2 and 31, 1919, NAACP MSS.

66. *Ibid.,* Aug. 7, 1919, NAACP MSS., author's interview with Lyle, 1959.

67. *Chicago Daily News,* Aug. 7, 1919, NAACP MSS.

68. Graham Taylor to James F. Basiger, Aug. 8, 1919, Taylor MSS., Newberry Library.

69. Memo by Shillady on "Interview with Mrs. Meta Harvey on Kenwood and Hyde Park Improvement Association meetings on June 20 and June 27, 1919," Aug. 3, 1919, NAACP MSS.

70. Charles E. Fox to Mayor William H. Thompson, in Kenwood and Hyde Park Property Owners Association, *Your Rights and Mine: A Short Symposium on Current Events as applied to and affecting Realty Values* (pamphlet in NAACP MSS.).

71. Kenwood and Hyde Park Property Owners Association October 1919 poster, "Dear Sir" public letter [no date], *Chicago Tribune,* Oct. 21, 1919, *Chicago Daily News,* Oct. 21, 1919, NAACP MSS.

72. Charles E. Bentley to Shillady, Oct. 23, 1919, NAACP MSS.; *Negro in Chicago,* 117–35.

73. Howard R. Gold and Byron K. Armstrong, *A Preliminary Study of Inter-Racial Conditions in Chicago,* pp. 2–3.

74. Frank O. Lowden to Francis W. Shepardson, Feb. 2, 1920, Shepardson to Lowden, Feb. 2, 1920, Graham Romeyn Taylor to Shepardson, June 19, 1920, CCRR MSS.; *Baltimore Afro-American,* March 12, 1920, *Chicago Daily News,* April 15, 1920, NAACP MSS.

75. *Negro in Chicago,* pp. 59–67.

76. Author's interviews with Joseph D. Lohman, Roi Ottley, and Augustus L. Williams, 1959.
77. Memo from Herbert J. Seligmann to NAACP, ca. Aug. 30, 1919, *The Survey*, Aug. 2 and 9, 1919, in NAACP MSS.
78. William Griffith to Seligmann, Aug. 15, 1919, NAACP MSS.; George Foster Peabody to Newton D. Baker, Sept. 29, 1919, Baker MSS., Library of Congress.
79. *New York Journal*, Aug. 2, 1919, NAACP MSS.
80. Chicago Urban League, [*Third*] *Annual Report . . . 1919*.
81. *Birmingham News*, July 30, 1919, NAACP MSS.
82. *Chicago Tribune*, Aug. 31, 1919, *Chicago Herald-Examiner*, Aug. 8, 1919, NAACP MSS.
83. *New Orleans Vindicator*, Sept. 20, 1919, NAACP MSS.
84. *New York American*, Oct. 4, 1919, NAACP MSS.
85. *St. Louis Argus*, Aug. 30, 1919, NAACP MSS.
86. *New York Mail*, July 30, 1919, *New York Tribune*, Sept. 1, 1919, NAACP MSS.
87. *New York Times*, Aug. 3, 1919, NAACP MSS.
88. *New York World*, July 30, 1919, NAACP MSS.
89. *Reconstruction*, October 1919, NAACP MSS.
90. Peabody to Baker, Sept. 29, 1919, Baker MSS.
91. Ovington to Sophonisba Breckinridge, Aug. 18, 1919, Ovington to Judge William M. Dunn, Aug. 16, 1919, NAACP MSS. Reports from Gary, Indiana, and Savannah, Georgia, that the sale of guns to Negroes had been halted, but not to whites, were among the reasons for Mrs. Ovington's concern. Elizabeth E. Lyttle to Ovington, Aug. 5, 1919, *Atlanta Constitution*, Aug. 4, 1919, NAACP MSS.
92. *New York Times*, July 28, 1919, NAACP MSS.
93. *Baltimore News*, July 30, 1919, *Brooklyn Eagle*, Aug. 2, 1919, NAACP MSS.
94. *Ibid*.
95. *New York Globe*, July 30, 1919, NAACP MSS.

NOTES TO CHAPTER V

1. Joel E. Spingarn, "Hasty Notes in Chicago," July 30, 1919, NAACP MSS.
2. Chicago Commission on Race Relations, *The Negro in Chicago*, p. xv. (Hereafter cited as *Negro in Chicago*.)
3. Herbert J. Seligmann to Spingarn, telegram, July 28, 1919, Spingarn to Mary White Ovington, telegram, July 30, 1919, Spingarn, "Hasty Notes," NAACP MSS.
4. *Negro in Chicago*, p. xv; also see "Memorandum on meeting

at Union League Club," Chicago Commission on Race Relations MSS., Illinois Archives. (Hereafter cited as CCRR MSS.)

5. Abraham Bowers to Francis W. Shepardson, Aug. 27, 1919 and Graham Taylor to _____ [multiple letter], July 31, 1919, CCRR MSS.: Graham Taylor, "Diary," July 31 and Aug. 1, 1919, Taylor MSS., Newberry Library.

6. *Negro in Chicago,* p. xv.

7. Shepardson to John Cummings, April 15, 1919, CCRR MSS.

8. CCRR Minutes, Oct. 9, 1919, CCRR MSS.

9. Ivan O. Ackley to Shepardson, Aug. 4, 1919, Harve Budgerow to Shepardson and Shepardson to Budgerow, Aug. 5, 1919, L. Brackett to Shepardson, Aug. 5, 1919, Shepardson to James P. Hall, Aug. 9, 1919, William H. Huff to Everett C. Dodds, Aug. 1, 1919, Shepardson to Huff, Aug. 11, 1919, W. H. Riley to Frank O. Lowden, Aug. 15, 1919, CCRR MSS.; Hugh Reed to George E. Haynes, Aug. 8, 1919, Labor Dept. MSS., National Archives.

10. Alice H. Wood to Shepardson, Aug. 14, 1919, and Shepardson to Wood, Aug. 16, 1919, A. L. Jackson to Shepardson, telegram, Aug. 15, 1919, Shepardson to Julius Rosenwald, Aug. 21, 1919, Sophonisba P. Breckinridge to Shepardson, Aug. 19, 1919, and Shepardson to Breckinridge, Aug. 21, 1919, E. A. Kelly to Shepardson, Aug. 18, 1919, and Shepardson to E. A. Kelly, Aug. 18, 1919, CCRR MSS.

11. Shepardson to Wood, Aug. 16, 1919, CCRR MSS.

12. Undated memorandum in Shepardson's hand, CCRR MSS.

13. *Negro in Chicago,* pp. xvi and 652–53.

14. *Ibid.,* p. xvi.

15. CCRR Minutes, Oct. 9, 1919, CCRR MSS.

16. William C. Graves to Shepardson, Sept. 5, 1919, CCRR MSS.

17. Shepardson to Graves, Sept. 15, 1919, CCRR MSS.

18. Graham Romeyn Taylor to Shepardson, Aug. 26, 1920, CCRR MSS. (Graham Romeyn Taylor, son of Graham Taylor, will hereafter be referred to as G. R. Taylor.)

19. CCRR Minutes, Oct. 9 and Oct. 20, 1919, CCRR MSS.

20. CCRR Minutes, Nov. 13 and Dec. 18, 1919, Shepardson to Charles W. Folds, Nov. 15 and Nov. 22, 1919, Folds to Shepardson, Nov. 20, 1919, Shepardson to Harry Eugene Kelly, Nov. 21, 1919, CCRR MSS.

21. CCRR Minutes, June 16 and Nov. 23, 1920, G. R. Taylor to Shepardson, July 8 and Aug. 10, 1920, Charles S. Johnson to Shepardson, Sept. 10, 1920, undated multigraphed letter "sent to 300 negroes," CCRR MSS.

22. CCRR Minutes, Oct. 20, 1919, Shepardson to Folds, Nov. 15, 1919, CCRR Minutes, March 19, 1920, CCRR Financial

Statement, Nov. 1, 1920, Edgar A. Bancroft to James B. Forgan, Dec. 22, 1920, CCRR MSS.

23. Graves to G. R. Taylor, Dec. 31, 1919, and Jan. 30, 1920, G. R. Taylor to Rosenwald, Jan. 29, 1920, CCRR MSS.

24. CCRR Minutes, April 21 and June 16, 1920, Shepardson to G. R. Taylor, March 26 and July 28, 1920, CCRR MSS.

25. G. R. Taylor to Shepardson, Aug. 26, 1920, CCRR MSS.

26. M. E. Filer to Kelly, Oct. 4, 1920, G. R. Taylor to Shepardson, Nov. 11, 15, and 20, 1920, CCRR MSS.

27. CCRR Minutes, Nov. 23, 1920, CCRR MSS.

28. G. R. Taylor to Shepardson, Dec. 1, 3, and 16, 1920, Gen. Abel Davis to Shepardson, Dec. 8, 1920, CCRR Minutes, Dec. 28, 1920, CCRR MSS.

29. Rosenwald to Victor F. Lawson, April 7, 1921, and Graves to Davis, May 9, 1921, Rosenwald MSS., University of Chicago; Lowden to Folds, April 14, 1921, and Davis to Lowden [ca. April 30, 1921], Lowden MSS., University of Chicago.

30. CCRR Minutes, Oct. 9, 1919, CCRR MSS.

31. Paul V. Kellogg to Graves, Oct. 23, 1919, Rosenwald MSS.; CCRR Minutes, Oct. 9 and Oct. 20, 1919, CCRR MSS.; *Negro in Chicago*, p. 653; author's interview with Mrs. G. R. Taylor, 1959.

32. CCRR Minutes, Nov. 5, 13, 20, and 28, 1919, Graves to Rosenwald, Nov. 4, 1919, Shepardson to Johnson, Dec. 6, 1919, CCRR MSS.

33. Graves to Rosenwald, Dec. 12, 1919, Rosenwald MSS.

34. Author's interview with Mrs. G. R. Taylor, 1959; memo by Johnson to Shepardson, Oct. 5, 1919, memo by G. R. Taylor and Johnson to CCRR, Dec. 12, 1919, CCRR MSS.

35. CCRR Minutes, Oct. 8 and 20 (third meeting missing), Nov. 5, 13, 20, and 28, Dec. 4, 11, and 18, 1919 (eleventh meeting missing), Jan. 23, Feb. 6, March 12, April 21, June 16, Nov. 23, Dec. 28, 1920, CCRR MSS.

36. CCRR Minutes, Dec. 11, 1919, CCRR MSS.

37. CCRR Minutes, Dec. 4, 1919, CCRR MSS.

38. *Chicago Tribune,* Oct. 30, 1919, NAACP MSS.; CCRR Minutes, Nov. 5, 1919, CCRR MSS.

39. CCRR Minutes, Dec. 4, 11, and 18, 1919, CCRR MSS.

40. Lowden to Shepardson, Feb. 2, 1920, Shepardson to Lowden, Feb. 2, 1920, CCRR Executive Committee Minutes, Feb. 20, 1920, CCRR MSS.

41. *Chicago Daily News,* Feb. 25, 1920, NAACP MSS.

42. Johnson to Shepardson, Sept. 10, 1920, CCRR MSS.

43. *Negro in Chicago,* pp. 59–64; Shepardson to G. R. Taylor, June 21, 1920, G. R. Taylor to Shepardson, June 21, 1920, CCRR MSS.

44. G. R. Taylor to Shepardson, June 21, 1920, Shepardson to G. R. Taylor, June 23, 1920, Shepardson to Lowden, June 23, 1920, CCRR MSS.

45. CCRR Minutes, March 12, 1920, CCRR MSS.

46. *Chicago Daily News*, Nov. 5, 1919, CCRR MSS.

47. Graves to David Lawrence, Nov. 5, 1919, Lawrence to Graves, Nov. 10, 1919, CCRR MSS.

48. Shepardson to Francis Garvan, Nov. 14, 1919, Castle M. Brown to Shepardson, Nov. 29, 1919, CCRR MSS.

49. CCRR Minutes, Dec. 4, 1919, CCRR MSS.

50. *Ibid.; Negro in Chicago*, p. 574; Shepardson to C. M. Brown, Dec. 8, 1919, CCRR MSS.

51. Shepardson to Lowden, June 4, 1920, CCRR MSS.

52. G. R. Taylor to Shepardson, Aug. 10, 1920, Shepardson to G. R. Taylor, Dec. 10, 1920, CCRR MSS.; Lowden to Runnells, telegram, Feb. 25, 1921, Lowden MSS.

53. CCRR Progress Report, Dec. 21, 1920, CCRR MSS.

54. Memo by G. R. Taylor and Johnson to CCRR, Dec. 12, 1919, CCRR MSS.

55. *Negro in Chicago*, pp. 653–55; undated memorandum of G. R. Taylor and Johnson to CCRR, CCRR MSS.

56. Memo by G. R. Taylor and Johnson, Sept. 15, 1920, CCRR MSS.; Chicago League on Urban Conditions among Negroes, *First Annual Report* (1917) and *Second Annual Report* (1918), pamphlets, University of Chicago. Park makes a special point in his introduction to these reports of Rosenwald's generosity to the Chicago Urban League. See also author's interview in 1959 with Esther Fulks Scott, former research worker for CCRR, for evidence of Park's constant help with research and analysis.

57. Author's interview with Esther Fulks Scott and Mrs. G. R. Taylor, 1959; CCRR Minutes, Jan. 23, 1920, Progress Reports, Dec. 21, 1920, CCRR MSS.

58. Undated memo by G. R. Taylor and Johnson to CCRR, CCRR Minutes, March 12, 1920, CCRR MSS.

59. Author's interview with Chicago Urban League officials, 1959. G. R. Taylor and Shepardson debated in 1921 where these files should be kept, both of them agreeing that the University of Chicago Library or the Crerar Library would be both safer and more accessible to scholars than the Urban League, which had requested them. Yet the Urban League got them. The correspondence files (out of which, Taylor reported, the confidential material had been destroyed) were sent to the Illinois State Archives. G. R. Taylor to Shepardson, Sept. 12, 1921, Shepardson to G. R. Taylor, Sept. 20, 1921, Rosenwald MSS.

60. G. R. Taylor to Shepardson, Oct. 7, 1920, CCRR MSS.
61. Shepardson to G. R. Taylor, July 28, 1920, CCRR MSS.
62. CCRR Minutes, Jan. 23 and Feb. 6, 1920, CCRR MSS., *Negro in Chicago,* p. 152.
63. Undated memo from G. R. Taylor and Johnson to CCRR [*ca.* March 1, 1920], CCRR MSS.
64. Undated staff memo on "Suggested Questions for Conference on Negro Housing," CCRR MSS.
65. *Negro in Chicago,* pp. 360–61, 385; CCRR Minutes, Feb. 6, 1920, Executive Committee minutes, Sept. 15, 1920, G. R. Taylor to CCRR, Aug. 12, 1920, CCRR MSS., Report of CCRR Conference on the Negro in Industry, April 23, 1920, Rosenwald MSS.
66. CCRR Minutes, Feb. 6, 1920, undated staff memo, "Selected Questions for Persons in Industrial Conferences," CCRR MSS.
67. Questionnaire on "Intensive Court Study," CCRR MSS.
68. *Negro in Chicago,* pp. 327–56.
69. Undated staff memo on "Lines of Inquiry for Persons called into Conference on the Negro in the Courts," CCRR MSS.
70. Minutes of CCRR Committee on Racial Contact. March 11, 1920, CCRR MSS.; *Negro in Chicago,* p. 255.
71. Memo from G. R. Taylor to CCRR, Dec. 15, 1920, CCRR MSS.
72. *Negro in Chicago,* pp. 436–594.
73. G. R. Taylor to Rosenwald, Feb. 18, 1920, Rosenwald MSS.
74. Undated staff memo [*ca.* Dec. 1, 1920], CCRR MSS.
75. Undated memo from G. R. Taylor to CCRR [*ca.* Dec. 1, 1920], CCRR MSS.
76. Memo of CCRR executive committee meeting, Sept. 15, 1920. Progress Report, Dec. 21, 1920, CCRR MSS.
77. Progress Report, Dec. 21, 1920, CCRR MSS.
78. Memo of CCRR executive committee meeting, Sept. 15, 1920, CCRR MSS.
79. CCRR Minutes, Dec. 28, 1920, CCRR MSS.
80. Bancroft to Rosenwald, Jan. 10, 1922, Rosenwald MSS.
81. Lowden to Bancroft, Aug. 16, 1922, Lowden MSS.
82. Bancroft to Lowden, undated, Lowden MSS.
83. *Negro in Chicago,* p. 449.
84. Bancroft to Lowden, Aug. 7, 1922, Lowden MSS.
85. *Negro in Chicago,* p. xviii.
86. Bancroft to Joseph T. Ryerson, MS. letter pasted in author's copy of *Negro in Chicago.*
87. *Negro in Chicago,* p. 258.
88. *Ibid.,* 258–61, 267.
89. *Ibid.,* p. 329.
90. *Ibid.,* p. 330.

91. *Ibid.*, pp. 323, 355-56, 622.
92. *Ibid.*, p. 342.
93. *Ibid.*, pp. 373-74.
94. *Ibid.*, p. 390.
95. *Ibid.*, p. 431.
96. *Ibid.*, pp. 414-15.
97. *Ibid.*, pp. 303-4.
98. *Ibid.*, pp. 393-96.
99. *Ibid.*, pp. 415.
100. *Ibid.*, p. 340.
101. *Ibid.*, pp. 248-51, 253.
102. *Ibid.*, p. 292.
103. *Ibid.*, pp. 248-51, 397.
104. *Ibid.*, pp. 113-21.
105. *Ibid.*, p. xxii-xxiv.
106. *Ibid.*, p. 493, 540.
107. *Ibid.*, p. 539.
108. *Ibid.*, p. 646.
109. *Ibid.*, p. 647.
110. *Ibid.*, p. 649.
111. Herbert J. Seligmann, *The Negro Faces America*, pp. 279-80, 290; G. R. Taylor to Shepardson, Oct. 30, 1920, CCRR MSS.
112. *Negro in Chicago*, pp. 324-26.
113. *Ibid.*, p. 649.
114. *Ibid.*, pp. 647-49.
115. *Ibid.*, pp. 587-89.
116. *Ibid.*, 476, 489-90; Seligmann, *op. cit.*, p. 291-94.
117. *Negro in Chicago*, pp. 220, 229.
118. *Ibid.*, pp. 35-39, 122-32, 199, 203, 344.
119. *Ibid.*, pp. 12, 16-17, 55.
120. See above, p. 91.
121. *Negro in Chicago*, p. xiv.
122. *Ibid.*, xv, 2, 595, 602, 640.
123. Walter F. White to Ovington, Aug. 21, 1919, NAACP MSS.
124. *Chicago Broad Axe*, Jan. 24, 1920, CCRR MSS.
125. CCRR Minutes, Dec. 18, 1919, and Feb. 6, 1920, CCRR MSS.
126. G. R. Taylor to Shepardson, July 8 and Aug. 10, 1920, CCRR MSS.
127. Johnson to Shepardson, Sept. 10, 1920, CCRR MSS.
128. CCRR Minutes, Nov. 23, 1920.
129. *Negro in Chicago*, p. 518-19, quoting *The Crisis* of January 1921.
130. Quoted in *Literary Digest*, Oct. 28, 1922, NAACP MSS.
131. Alexander R. Lawton, *The Negro in the South and Else-*

where (Annual Address to University of Georgia Alumni, 1923: no publisher).

132. St. Clair Drake and Horace R. Cayton, *Black Metropolis*, pp. 78–83, 212.

133. *Negro in Chicago*, p. 645; Drake and Cayton, *op. cit.*, p. 92.

134. Author's interviews with Joseph D. Lohman, Roi Ottley, Esther Fulks Scott, Joseph D. Bibb, and Augustus L. Williams, 1959.

135. See, e.g., Hans H. Gerth and C. Wright Mills, *Character and Social Structure*, pp. 432–37; Robert E. L. Faris, *Social Disorganization*, pp. 393–97; Ralph Turner and Lewis M. Killan, *Collective Behavior*, pp. 83–161.

136. John Hope Franklin, *From Slavery to Freedom*, p. 616.

137. Frederic M. Thrasher, *The Gang*, pp. 54, 202, 453, 472.

138. Drake and Cayton, *op. cit.*, pp. 69–73, 99, 102, 212.

139. Gunnar Myrdal, *An American Dilemma*, pp. 567, 1126–27.

NOTES TO CHAPTER VI

1. United States Bureau of the Census, *Fourteenth Census of the United States, 1920*, p. 2; Herbert J. Seligmann, *The Negro Faces America*, pp. 177–79.

2. *New York Times*, Aug. 31, 1919, *New York Sun*, Sept. 5, 1919, NAACP MSS.

3. *New York Times*, Aug. 31, 1919, *New York Telegram*, Aug. 31, 1919, *New York Tribune*, Aug. 31, 1919, NAACP MSS.

4. *New York Telegram*, Aug. 31, 1919, NAACP MSS.

5. *New York Tribune*, Sept. 1, 1919, NAACP MSS.

6. *Ibid.*, *New York Telegram*, Aug. 31, 1919, NAACP MSS.

7. *Chicago Daily News*, Sept. 1, 1919, *New York Tribune*, Sept. 1, 1919, NAACP MSS.

8. NAACP press release, Sept. 24, 1919, *Shreveport Times*, Sept. 2 and 3, 1919, NAACP MSS.

9. *Ibid.*, Sept. 2 and 3, 1919, *New York Sun*, Sept. 4, 1919, NAACP MSS.

10. *New York World*, Sept. 9, 1919, NAACP MSS.

11. *Knoxville Sentinel*, Oct. 4, 1919, *Nashville Banner*, Oct. 4, 1919, NAACP MSS.

12. *Knoxville Sentinel*, Oct. 25, 1919, NAACP MSS.

13. *Ibid.*, Oct. 27, 1919, NAACP MSS.

14. *East Tennessee News*, Nov. 13, 1919, *New York Globe*, Nov. 4, 1919, NAACP MSS.

15. *East Tennessee News*, Nov. 13, 1919, NAACP MSS.

16. *New York World*, Sept. 2, 1919, NAACP MSS.

17. *New York Evening Post*, Sept. 1, 1919, *Scranton Times*, Sept. 1, 1919, *Brooklyn Standard Union*, Sept. 1, 1919, NAACP MSS.
18. *Ibid.*
19. *Knoxville Sentinel*, Sept. 1, 1919, NAACP MSS.
20. *Greensboro Daily News*, Sept. 2, 1919, NAACP MSS.
21. *New York Age*, Sept. 6, 1919, quoted in Robert T. Kerlin, *The Voice of the Negro, 1919*, pp. 84–85; *Philadelphia Public Ledger*, Sept. 2, 1919, NAACP MSS.
22. United States Bureau of the Census, *Fourteenth Census of the United States, 1920*, III, 2; Seligmann, *op. cit.*, pp. 170–71; *New York Times*, Oct. 2, 1919, Dec. 28, 1919.
23. Unnamed Omaha newspaper, *ca.* April 13, 1919, NAACP MSS.; notes from *NAACP Branch Bulletin*, October 1919, in files of Senate Judiciary Committee, Legislative MSS., National Archives.
24. *Ibid.*; *Omaha Bee*, Sept. 26, 1919, Jessie Hale-Moss to John R. Shillady, Sept. 28, 1919, NAACP MSS.
25. *Omaha World-Herald*, Oct. 1, 1919, NAACP MSS.
26. *New York Call*, Sept. 29, 1919, *New York Age*, Oct. 4, 1919, NAACP MSS.
27. *Omaha Bee*, Sept. 26, 1919, NAACP MSS.
28. *New York Call*, Sept. 29, 1919, NAACP MSS.
29. *Wichita Protest*, quoted in Kerlin, *op. cit.*, pp. 85–86; *Omaha World-Herald*, Oct. 1, 1919, *New York Tribune*, Sept. 29, 1919, *New York World*, Sept. 30, 1919, NAACP MSS.
30. *New York Tribune*, Sept. 29, 1919, *Brooklyn Times*, Sept. 29, 1919, *New York World*, Sept. 30, 1919, *Omaha Bee*, Oct. 2, 1919, NAACP MSS.
31. Telegram from Jacob Wuest to Adjutant General, Central Dept., Chicago, 2:04 A.M., Sept. 29, 1919, War Dept. MSS.
32. Telegram from J. M. Petty, General Staff, Washington, to Leonard Wood, Sept. 29, 1919, War Dept. MSS., National Archives.
33. Telegram from Chief of Staff to Wood, Sept. 29, 1919, War Dept. MSS.
34. Telegram from Humphrey to Wood, Sept. 29, 1919, War Dept. MSS.
35. *New York World*, Sept. 30, 1919, NAACP MSS.
36. *Ibid.*, *New York Times*, Sept. 30, 1919, NAACP MSS.
37. *Ibid.*
38. *New York World*, Sept. 30, 1919, NAACP MSS.
39. Telegram from John E. Morris, Commanding, Omaha, to Wood, 6:09 P.M., Sept. 29, 1919, War Dept. MSS.
40. Telegram from Morris to Wood, 8:32 P.M. and 11:30 P.M., Sept. 29, 1919, War Dept. MSS.

41. *New York Times*, Sept. 30, 1919, NAACP MSS.
42. Wood to Adjutant General, U. S. Army, Sept. 30, 1919, War Dept. MSS.
43. *New York Times*, Oct. 1, 1919, NAACP MSS.
44. *Omaha Bee*, Oct. 1, 1919, NAACP MSS.
45. Wood to Adjutant General, Oct. 1, 1919, War Dept. MSS.
46. *Arkansas Gazette*, Oct. 1, 1919, NAACP MSS.; Seligmann, *op. cit.*, pp. 166–67.
47. *Omaha Bee*, Oct. 2, 1919, NAACP MSS.
48. *Ibid., Omaha World Herald*, Oct. 1, 1919, NAACP MSS.
49. Telegrams, Wood to Adjutant General, Oct. 2 and 3, 1919, War Dept. MSS.
50. *New York Tribune*, Oct. 3, 1919, NAACP MSS.; telegrams from Alexander Dade, Omaha, to Wood, Chicago, Oct. 6, 1919, and Wood to Dade, Oct. 6, 1919, War Dept. MSS.
51. Telegrams, Morris to Wood, Oct. 11, 1919, W. G. Ure to Wood, Oct. 11, 1919, War Dept. MSS.
52. Wood to Samuel R. McKelvie, Oct. 14, 1919, McKelvie to Wood, Oct. 15, 1919, Wood to Morris, Oct. 15, 1919, War Dept. MSS.
53. Morris to Wood, Oct. 16, 1919, Wood to Morris, Oct. 16, 1919, War Dept. MSS.
54. Thomas H. Christian to Michael Clark, Oct. 16, 1919, Morris to Wood, Oct. 20, 1919, War Dept. MSS.
55. Eli A. Helmick to Commanding Officer, Fort Crook, Neb., Oct. 27, 1919, Edwin A. Saunders to Chief of Staff, Oct. 27, 1919, War Dept. MSS.
56. *Omaha World Herald*, Oct. 22, 1919, NAACP MSS.
57. *New York Call*, Nov. 13, 1919, H. J. Pinkett to Seligmann, Nov. 26, 1919, NAACP MSS.
58. Helmick to U. S. Army Balloon School, Fort Omaha, Oct. 23, 1919, Wood to Humphrey, Oct. 31, 1919, War Dept. MSS.
59. *Omaha Bee*, Nov. 19, 1919, *Omaha News*, Nov. 20, 1919, NAACP MSS.
60. Seligmann, *op. cit.*, pp. 167–68.
61. Telegrams from John Albert Williams to John R. Shillady, Sept. 29, 1919, NAACP MSS.
62. James Weldon Johnson to Charles Curtis, Sept. 29, 1919, NAACP MSS.
63. Shillady to A. Mitchell Palmer [multiple letter], Sept. 30, 1919, Justice Dept. MSS., National Archives.
64. Telegram from Shillady to E. P. Smith, Sept. 29, 1919, NAACP MSS.
65. Telegrams from Johnson to Williams, Sept. 29, 1919, Shillady to Mrs. Jennie Hale-Moss, undated, NAACP MSS.

66. *New York Tribune,* Oct. 1, 1919, Seligmann to the Editor, *New York Sun,* Sept. 30, 1919, NAACP MSS.
67. Walter F. White to H. J. Pinkett, Oct. 8, 1919, NAACP MSS.; Seligmann, *op. cit.,* pp. 162–64.
68. Mary White Ovington to Pinkett, Oct. 10, 1919, Pinkett to Ovington, Oct. 13, 1919, Pinkett to W.E.B. Du Bois, Oct. 15, 1919, memo from Ovington to Seligmann, Oct. 27, 1919, NAACP press release, Oct. 30, 1919, NAACP MSS.
69. *New Orleans States,* Sept. 30, 1919, *Utica Globe,* Oct. 4, 1919, *New York Call,* Oct. 1, 1919, *Omaha Bee,* Oct. 1, 1919, NAACP MSS.
70. *Jacksonville Times-Union,* Sept. 30, 1919, *Boston Post,* Sept. 30, 1919, *New York Telegraph,* Oct. 1919, *Indianapolis News,* Oct. 1, 1919, NAACP MSS.
71. *Omaha World-Herald,* Oct. 1, 1919, NAACP MSS.
72. *Lincoln State Journal,* Oct. 4, 1919, NAACP MSS.
73. *Memphis Press,* Oct. 3, 1919, NAACP MSS.
74. *New York Day,* Sept. 30, 1919, *New York Jewish News,* Sept. 30, 1919, NAACP MSS.

NOTES TO CHAPTER VII

1. *Arkansas Gazette,* Oct. 1, 1919, NAACP MSS.; *Arkansas Democrat,* Oct. 1, 1919, Charles Brough Scrapbooks, Arkansas History Commission.
2. *Ibid.;* Petition and Complaint in the District Court of the United States, *Ex parte* Frank Moore, NAACP MSS.
3. This estimate of the situation is based chiefly on the evidence set forth hereafter in the chapter. But there is additional support in the views expressed in an interview with the author in 1965 by Federal District Judge John E. Miller, who in 1919 was Prosecuting Attorney in the Phillips County cases. He doubts that there was a long-standing insurrectionary conspiracy among the Negroes of Phillips County, although he believes that they were highly excited about alleged grievances, that they were ready to and did use arms to protect the privacy of the Progressive Union, and that he was correct in prosecuting for murder those who were convicted.
4. "Memoranda on Tenancy in the Southwestern States (Extracts from the Final Report of the United States Commission Industrial Relations, 1916)," NAACP MSS.
5. *Arkansas Gazette,* Oct. 10, 1919, *Chicago Daily News,* Oct. 18, 1919, NAACP MSS.
6. O. S. Bratton to U. S. Bratton, Nov. 5, 1919, U. S. Bratton to

Frank Burke, Nov. 6, 1919, Robert L. Hill to U. S. Bratton, Dec. 4, 1919, anonymous statement [by U. S. Bratton] called "The Story of a Southern White Man," statements by E. C. Reed of Pine Bluff, Ark., Jan. 5, 1920, Mrs. Mary Moore of Little Rock to NAACP, no date, enclosing loose pages from pamphlet "The Arkansas Rioters," Arthur Henderson of Gould, Ark., to U. S. Bratton, Aug. 30, 1919, NAACP MSS.; U. S. Bratton to David Y. Thomas, Sept. 15, 1921, Thomas MSS., University of Arkansas.

7. Petition, *Ex parte* Moore, *op. cit.*
8. *New York Times*, Oct. 6, 1919, NAACP MSS.
9. Thomas to A. C. Millar, Dec. 21, 1919, Millar to Thomas, Dec. 23, 1919, Thomas to E. M. Allen, Jan. 1, 1920, Allen to Thomas, Jan. 4 and 21, 1920, Thomas to Greenfield Quarles, Jan. 1, 1920, Quarles to Thomas, Jan. 5, 1920, Thomas to the editor of the *New York Times*, March 9, 1920, Thomas MSS.
10. *Arkansas Gazette*, Oct. 1, 1919, *New York Times*, Oct. 6, 1919, *New York World*, Nov. 16, 1919, NAACP MSS.
11. *Arkansas Gazette* and *New York Times*, Oct. 4, 1919, NAACP MSS.
12. *New York Times*, Feb. 8, 1920, Thomas to U. S. Bratton, Feb. 17, 1920, Bratton to Thomas, March 1, 1920, Thomas to the editor of the *New York Times*, March 9, 1920, Thomas MSS.
13. Petition in *Ex parte* Moore, *op. cit.*
14. H. F. Smiddy and T. K. Jones, affidavits in support of NAACP brief in Moore *et al. vs.* Dempsey, in United States Supreme Court, *Transcript of Records*, XLVI, docket no. 199, October term 1922, incorporating no. 995, pp. 87–97. (Hereafter referred to as Supreme Court *Transcript*, XLVI.)
15. *Ibid.*, pp. 87–88.
16. *Ibid.*, pp. 87–88.
17. *New York World*, Nov. 16, 1919, petition in *Ex parte* Moore, *op. cit.*, *Arkansas Gazette*, Oct. 1, 1919, John E. Miller, Prosecuting Attorney in Phillips County, to Thomas C. McRae, Governor of Arkansas, June 6, 1921, NAACP MSS.
18. O. S. Bratton to U. S. Bratton, Nov. 5, 1919, NAACP MSS.
19. *Arkansas Democrat*, Oct. 2 and 4, 1919, NAACP MSS. and Brough Scrapbooks.
20. *Arkansas Gazette*, Oct. 4, 1919, NAACP MSS. and Brough Scrapbooks.
21. *Little Rock Daily News*, Oct. 2, 1919, Brough Scrapbooks.
22. *Ibid.*, petition in *Ex parte* Moore, *op. cit.*, NAACP MSS.
23. Statement by George Washington Davis, Nov. 30, 1920, Walter F. White to Thomas Mufson, Dec. 9, 1921, NAACP MSS.

24. *Memphis Press,* Oct. 2, 1919, notes for anonymous report in *The Crisis* [by Walter F. White], NAACP MSS.
25. *Memphis Press,* Oct. 4, 1919, NAACP MSS.
26. *Arkansas Gazette,* Oct. 4, 1919, NAACP MSS. and Brough Scrapbooks.
27. *Ibid.,* Oct. 2, 1919, NAACP MSS. and Brough Scrapbooks.
28. Harris, War Dept., to Commanding General, Camp Pike, Ark., Oct. 1, 1919, War Dept. MSS., National Archives.
29. *Arkansas Gazette,* Oct. 2, 1919, NAACP MSS. and Brough Scrapbooks.
30. Col. F. H. Trainor, by order of Col. Isaac Jenks, to the Division, Camp Pike, Oct. 1, 1919, Special Orders 264 by Col. John B. Schoessel, Oct. 1, 1919, War Dept. MSS.
31. W. S. Kirby to Army Chief of Staff, telegram, Oct. 2, 1919, penciled memos in Office of Chief of Staff, Oct. 2, 1919, Brig. Gen. E. D. Anderson to the Adjutant-General, Oct. 2, 1919, War Dept. MSS.
32. Memo from Major General Henry Jervey to Adjutant-General, Oct. 3, 1919, War Dept. MSS.
33. Memo from Jenks to Commanding General, Camp Pike, Oct. 14, 1919, War Dept. MSS.
34. *Ibid.*
35. *Arkansas Gazette,* Oct. 6, 1919, War Dept. MSS.
36. Jenks to CG, Camp Pike, Oct. 14, 1919, War Dept. MSS.
37. *Arkansas Gazette,* Oct. 6, 1919, War Dept. MSS.
38. Notes for anonymous report to *The Crisis* [prob. by Walter F. White], NAACP MSS.
39. Jenks to CG, Camp Pike, Oct. 14, 1919, War Dept. MSS.
40. E. M. Allen to Thomas, Jan. 4, 1920, Thomas MSS.
41. Allen to Thomas, Jan. 21, 1920, Thomas MSS.
42. U. S. Bratton to Mary White Ovington, Dec. 6, 1919, NAACP MSS.
43. Petition in *Ex parte* Moore, *op. cit.;* statement of case of Frank Moore, Ed Hicks, J. E. Knox, *et al.,* before United States Supreme Court, October term 1922, no. 199.
44. Supreme Court *Transcript,* XLVI, pp. 89, 95.
45. Major General S. D. Sturgis, Commanding Camp Pike, to Adjutant-General, Oct. 28, 1919; Lt. Col. Jesse Gaston to CG, Camp Pike, Oct. 5, 1919, War Dept. MSS.
46. *Arkansas Gazette,* Oct. 6, 1919, War Dept. MSS.
47. Sturgis to Adjutant-General, Oct. 28, 1919, War Dept. MSS.
48. Poster in War Dept. MSS.
49. Memo from Capt. David E. Lane to CG, Camp Pike, Oct. 27, 1919, War Dept. MSS.
50. O. S. Bratton to U. S. Bratton, Nov. 5, 1919, affidavits by

James H. Guy, A. M. Thomas, Elisha Scott, and Hugh T. Fisher, May 18, 1920, NAACP MSS.

51. Guy G. Bratton to U. S. Bratton, Nov. 9, 1919, NAACP MSS.

52. John R. Shillady to U. S. Bratton, Feb. 9, 1920, U. S. Bratton to Shillady, May 11, 1920, U. S. Bratton to Walter F. White, Nov. 28, 1922, NAACP MSS.; U. S. Bratton to Sen. William P. Dillingham, Feb. 21, 1920, Legislative MSS., National Archives.

53. *Arkansas Gazette*, Oct. 4, 1919, Walter F. White to James W. Johnson, Oct. 10, 1919, Arthur Hoskins to William Anthony Aery, Oct. 20, 1919, Allen to Aery, Nov. 20, 1919, NAACP MSS.

54. Hoskins to Aery, Oct. 20, 1919, NAACP MSS.

55. John E. Miller to Gov. Thomas C. McRae, June 6, 1921, *New York Times*, Oct. 4 and 6, 1919, statement of the case of Frank Moore *et al.* before Supreme Court, *op. cit.*, NAACP MSS.; Supreme Court *Transcript*, XLVI, pp. 89, 95.

56. Committee of Seven to Governor of Arkansas, Nov. 14, 1920, NAACP MSS.

57. *Arkansas Gazette*, Oct. 30 and Nov. 4, 1919; statement of the case of Frank Moore *et al.* before Supreme Court, *op. cit.*, NAACP MSS.

58. *Ibid.*

59. *Arkansas Gazette*, Nov. 4, 1919, NAACP MSS.

60. *Ibid.*, Nov. 6, 7, and 18, 1919, NAACP MSS.

61. *Ibid.*, Nov. 12 and 20, 1919, NAACP MSS.

62. A. C. Millar, editor, *Arkansas Methodist*, to Thomas, Dec. 23, 1919, Thomas MSS.

63. *Arkansas Gazette*, Oct. 12, 1919, War Dept. MSS.

64. *Shreveport Weekly Caucasian*, Oct. 9, 1919, NAACP MSS.

65. *New York Sun*, Oct. 7 and 8, 1919, NAACP MSS. See also *Nashville Banner*, Oct. 4, 1919, *St. Louis Post-Dispatch*, Oct. 12, 1919, NAACP MSS.

66. *Memphis Commercial Appeal*, Oct. 3, 1919, NAACP MSS.

67. *Boston Evening Transcript*, Oct. 2, 1919, NAACP MSS.

68. *Arkansas Gazette*, Oct. 4, 1919, NAACP MSS.

69. *Chicago Plaindealer*, Nov. 8, 1919, NAACP MSS.

70. *St. Louis Argus*, Nov. 7, 1919, NAACP MSS.

71. *Baltimore Herald*, Nov. 8, 1919, NAACP MSS.

72. Helen A. Holman to _____ [multiple letter], Nov. 27, 1919, John E. Milholland to Ovington, Dec. 4, 1919, Ovington to Milholland, Dec. 17, 1919, Ovington to Darwin J. Meserole, Dec. 11, 1919, NAACP MSS.

73. A. Slayton and B. Mandel, resolution of Socialist Party sent to House Judiciary Committee, Jan. 19, 1920, Legislative MSS., National Archives; George H. Bell to James Weldon Johnson,

Nov. 26, 1919, Bruno Lasker to White, Dec. 13, 1919, Sen. David Walsh to White, Dec. 16, 1919, NAACP MSS. See also *Pittsburgh Courier*, Nov. 8, 1919, NAACP MSS.

74. *New York World*, Oct. 8, 1919, *Portland Oregonian*, Oct. 8, 1919, NAACP MSS.
75. *New York Call*, March 30, 1923, NAACP MSS.
76. *Springfield Republican*, Oct. 21, 1919, NAACP MSS.; H. Paul Douglass to Shillady, Dec. 10, 1919, NAACP MSS.
77. *Boston Chronicle*, Nov. 1, 1919, NAACP MSS.
78. *Ibid.*, *Baltimore Herald*, Oct. 9, 1919, NAACP MSS.

NOTES TO CHAPTER VIII

1. Walter F. White to Harry H. Pace, Oct. 3, 1919, Pace to White, Oct. 3, 1919, Robert R. Church, Jr., to White, Oct. 6, 1919, NAACP MSS.
2. White to John R. Shillady, Oct. 7, 1919, NAACP MSS.
3. White to Charles H. Dennis, Oct. 9, 1919, NAACP MSS.
4. White to Pace, Oct. 7, 1919, White to Robert T. Scott, Oct. 9, 1919, Scott to White, Oct. 10, 1919, NAACP MSS.
5. White to James Weldon Johnson, Oct. 10, 1919, NAACP MSS.
6. *Ibid.*, White to Johnson, Oct. 13, 1919, White to Scott, Oct. 17, 1919, White to Charles E. Bentley, Oct. 24, 1919, NAACP MSS.; Walter F. White, *A Man Called White* (New York: Viking, 1948), pp. 49–51.
7. White to Dennis, Oct. 9, 17, and 19, 1919, *Chicago Daily News* to White, Oct. 17, 1919, Dennis to White, Oct. 18, 1919, NAACP MSS.
8. White, "Statement on Race Disturbances in Arkansas," NAACP MSS.
9. *Pittsburgh Dispatch*, Oct. 24, 1919, *Boston Chronicle*, Nov. 1, 1919, and *Buffalo Express*, Oct. 14, 1919, NAACP MSS.
10. *Montgomery Journal*, Oct. 23, 1919, *Little Rock Gazette*, Oct. 14, 1919, NAACP MSS.
11. William Anthony Aery to Arthur C. Hoskins, Nov. 10, 1919, Aery to E. M. Allen, Nov. 11, 1919, Allen to Aery, Nov. 20, 1919, NAACP MSS. Allen wrote the NAACP office in Washington, asking whether White had visited Helena and if so what Negroes he had seen. The Washington office acknowledged the letter, but there is no evidence that Allen got his questions answered. Allen to NAACP, Nov. 22, 1919, S. M. Kendrick to Allen, Nov. 25, 1919, Kendrick to White, Nov. 25, 1919, White to Kendrick, Nov. 28, 1919, NAACP MSS.

12. E. C. Morris to Robert R. Moton, Dec. 22, 1919, quoted in Monroe N. Work, "A Report on the Elaine Riots, Not to be Published," NAACP MSS.

13. White to Aery, Nov. 28 and Dec. 4, 1919, Aery to White, Dec. 2, 1919, NAACP MSS.

14. White to Scott, Oct. 17, 1919, White to John T. Creighton, Oct. 31, 1919, White to Aery, Dec. 4, 1919, NAACP MSS.

15. Memo by Ethel G. Stone on conference between John R. Shillady and U. S. Bratton, Oct. 31, 1919, memo by White, Nov. 1, 1919, NAACP MSS.

16. *Ibid.*

17. Mary White Ovington to Mrs. Fannie Crowell, Oct. 21, 1919, NAACP MSS.

18. Thomas J. Price to White, Oct. 27, 1919, White to Price, Oct. 31, 1919, NAACP MSS.

19. White to Scipio A. Jones, Nov. 3, 1919, NAACP MSS.

20. U. S. Bratton to Morris, Nov. 19, 1919, NAACP MSS.

21. Joseph A. Booker to William Pickens, *ca.* Feb. 20, 1920, NAACP MSS.

22. U. S. Bratton to Ovington, Dec. 5 and 6, 1919, Ovington to Edith Wharton Dallas, Nov. 11, 1919, office memorandum on "Arkansas Riots Cases," NAACP MSS.

23. Monroe N. Work, "Report on the Elaine Riots," received April 8, 1920, Shillady to Work, April 10, 1920, White to Work, April 30, 1920, NAACP MSS.

24. Shillady to George W. Wickersham, Nov. 6, 1919, Legislative MSS., National Archives.

25. Wickersham to Frank P. Kellogg, Nov. 7, 1919, Wickersham to Shillady, Nov. 7, 1919, Legislative MSS.

26. Press release, Nov. 6, 1919, NAACP MSS.

27. Press release, Nov. 15, 1919, NAACP MSS.; James Weldon Johnson to Woodrow Wilson, Nov. 14, 1919, Johnson to A. Mitchell Palmer, Nov. 14, 1919, Justice Dept. MSS., National Archives.

28. R. P. Stewart to Johnson, Nov. 21, 1919, NAACP MSS.

29. White to William King, Nov. 29, 1919, NAACP MSS.

30. Shillady to J. E. Mitchell, Nov. 12, 1919, NAACP MSS.

31. J. Edgar Hoover to Stewart, Nov. 7, 1919, Agent Fred S. Dunn to Hoover, June 10, 1921, Justice Dept. MSS.

32. U. S. House of Representatives Committee on Judiciary, *Hearings on . . . HR 259, 4123, and 11873* (January 15 and 29, 1920, 66 Cong., 2 Sess. [Government Printing Office: Washington, 1920]), pp. 64–65.

33. U. S. Bratton to Shillady, Nov. 22, 1919, *Arkansas Gazette,* Jan. 18, 1920, NAACP MSS.

34. W.E.B. Du Bois to Editor, *New York World,* Nov. 23, 1919, NAACP MSS.
35. White to Herbert Croly, Oct. 31, 1919, White to H. R. Mussey, Nov. 13 and 29, 1919, White to Arthur F. Requa, Dec. 3, 1919, White to Henry L. Mencken, Dec. 20, 1919, NAACP MSS.
36. White to Requa, Dec. 3, 1919, NAACP MSS.
37. Shillady to Gov. Henry J. Allen, Jan. 23, 1920, NAACP MSS.
38. NAACP to Hugh Fisher, Jan. 23, 1920, Shillady to Fisher, Jan. 23, 1920, NAACP MSS.
39. *Ibid.,* Fisher to Shillady, Jan. 26, 1920, NAACP MSS.
40. Fisher to George W. Murphy, Jan. 27, 1920, Fisher to Shillady, Jan. 27, 1920, Fisher to White, Jan. 31, 1920, NAACP MSS.
41. Fisher to Shillady, Jan. 30, 1920, NAACP MSS.
42. Fisher to Shillady, Feb. 13, 1920, Shillady to Johnson, Feb. 13, 1920, NAACP MSS.
43. Shillady to Fisher, Feb. 16, 1920, Johnson to Shillady, Feb. 16, 1920, NAACP MSS.
44. *Ibid.,* Pickens to Booker, Feb. 24, 1920, Fisher to Shillady, Feb. 25, 1920, Shillady to Fisher, March 1, 1920, NAACP MSS.
45. Telegram from Executive Committee of Commission on Race Relations (J. H. Reynolds, John L. Hunter, Louis Altheimer, J. M. Conner, J. M. Cox, and Joseph A. Booker) to Governor Henry Allen, Feb. 2, 1920, Brough Scrapbooks, Ark. History Commission; "Chronology of Arkansas Riot Cases," p. 2, *Topeka Daily Capital,* Feb. 2, 1920, Fisher to Shillady, Feb. 3, 1920, Fisher to White, Feb. 3, 1920, NAACP MSS.
46. *Conway County Union* (Ark.), no date, *Arkansas Democrat,* Nov. 19, 1919, *Little Rock Daily News,* Nov. 25, 1919, Brough Scrapbooks; author's interviews with John E. Miller, T. W. Coggs, and Joseph Wergis, 1965.
47. Pickens to J. M. Conner, James M. Cox, and Booker, Feb. 6, 1920, Cox to Pickens, Feb. 13, 1920, Booker to Pickens, *ca.* Feb. 2, 1920, NAACP MSS.
48. Pickens to Cox, Feb. 24, 1920, NAACP MSS.
49. Shillady to NAACP branches, Feb. 6, 1920, Shillady to Fisher, Feb. 6, 1920, NAACP MSS.
50. Fisher to Shillady, March 23 and 24, 1920, Shillady to Fisher, March 23, 1920, NAACP MSS.
51. Fisher to Shillady, March 24, 1920, NAACP MSS.
52. Shillady to Fisher, March 20, 1920, NAACP MSS.
53. Fisher to Shillady, April 10, 1920, NAACP MSS.
54. *Ibid.,* Fisher to Shillady, April 13 and 14, 1920, NAACP MSS.
55. Fisher to Shillady, May 6, 1920, NAACP MSS.

56. Shillady to Bratton, May 7, 1920, NAACP MSS.
57. Bratton to Shillady, May 11, 1920, Shillady to Fisher, May 11, 1920, NAACP MSS.
58. Affidavits by Fisher, James H. Guy, and A. M. Thomas, May 18, 1920, NAACP MSS.
59. Shillady to Fisher, May 21, 1920, White to Johnson, May 24, 1920, NAACP MSS.
60. Johnson to White, Oct. 11, 1920, Fisher to Johnson, Oct. 18, 1920, White to Arthur B. Spingarn, Oct. 28 and 30, 1920, NAACP MSS.
61. Ovington to _____ [multiple letter], Nov. 26, 1919, Johnson to Church, Dec. 2, 1919, NAACP MSS.
62. J. E. Mitchell to Shillady, Nov. 17, 1919, Shillady to Mitchell, Nov. 22, 1919, NAACP MSS.
63. Ovington to William F. Fuerst, Dec. 11, 1919, NAACP MSS.
64. Shillady to A. Clement MacNeal, Nov. 21, 1919, NAACP MSS.
65. "Memorandum Re Proposed Agreement . . ." Nov. 21, 1919, Shillady to Bratton, Nov. 24, 1919, "Chronology of Arkansas Riots Cases," NAACP MSS.
66. Shillady to Work, April 10, 1920, White to Scipio A. Jones, March 8, 1921, NAACP MSS.
67. Ovington to _____ [multiple letter], Nov. 26, NAACP MSS.
68. Ovington to Fuerst, Dec. 15, 1919, Ovington to Dallas, Dec. 9, 1919, NAACP MSS.
69. "Chronology of Arkansas Riots Cases," p. 2, Cox to Pickens, Feb. 13, 1920, Ovington to John E. Milholland, Dec. 17, 1919, NAACP MSS.
70. "Report on Citizens Defense Fund, April 7, 1920," enclosed in J. H. McConico to Shillady, April 30, 1920, "Statement on Citizens Defense Fund," enclosed in McConico to Editor, The Crisis, March 2, 1921, Monroe N. Work, "Report on the Elaine Riots," April 8, 1920, NAACP MSS.
71. "Report on Citizens Defense Fund, April 7, 1920," Work, "Report on the Elaine Riots," NAACP MSS.
72. U. S. Bratton to NAACP, no date, Thomas J. Price to White, Nov. 26, 1919, White to Price, Dec. 1, 1919, NAACP MSS.
73. Johnson to Church, Dec. 2, 1919, NAACP MSS.
74. "Report of Citizens Defense Fund Commission," NAACP MSS.
75. McConico to Shillady, June 10, 1920, McConico to Ovington, July 31, 1920, NAACP MSS.
76. White to Johnson, Oct. 17, 1920, White to McConico, Oct. 26, 1920, McConico to White, Nov. 4, 1920, White to Arthur B. Spingarn, Nov. 12, 1920, NAACP MSS.

77. White to Jones, March 8, 1921, NAACP MSS.
78. Johnson to McHaney, Sept. 15 and 17, 1921, and Murphy, McHaney, and Dunaway to NAACP, Sept. 16, 1921, NAACP MSS.
79. J. M. Cox to Pickens, Feb. 13, 1920, NAACP MSS.
80. "Chronology," p. 2, White to Bruno Lasker, Dec. 15, 1919, NAACP MSS.
81. "Chronology," p. 4, NAACP MSS.
82. *Ibid.*, p. 12, NAACP MSS.
83. United States Supreme Court, *Transcript of Records*, XLVI, Docket no. 199, October term 1922, incorporating no. 995, p. 42.
84. Murphy to Bratton, Aug. 10, 1920, Bratton to White, Oct. 15, 1920, NAACP MSS.
85. "Chronology," p. 22, NAACP MSS.
86. Murphy to Bratton, Aug. 10, 1920, NAACP MSS.
87. *New York World*, Nov. 9, 1920, NAACP MSS.
88. Sheriff D. R. Dalzell to Gov. Charles A. Brough, Nov. 10, 1920, Resolutions of Helena American Legion, Civitan Club, Rotary Club, and Committee of Seven to Brough, filed with NAACP by Scipio A. Jones, Nov. 1920, NAACP MSS.
89. *Little Rock Democrat*, Nov. 17, 1920, NAACP MSS.
90. Committee of Seven to the Governor, Nov. 14, 1920, NAACP MSS.
91. *Arkansas Gazette*, Nov. 16, 1920, Brough Scrapbooks.
92. Jones, "Statement Made to Evening Paper Today," Dec. 1, 1920, NAACP MSS.
93. *Arkansas Democrat*, Dec. 6, 1920, Jones to Johnson, Dec. 6, 1920, NAACP MSS.
94. *Arkansas Democrat*, Dec. 6, 1920, NAACP MSS.
95. Oliver Wendell Holmes, opinion for United States Supreme Court in Moore *et al. vs.* Dempsey, p. 5; Robert T. Kerlin to Thomas C. McRae, May 25, 1921, NAACP MSS.
96. Kerlin to Johnson, May 8, 1921, NAACP MSS.
97. White to Kerlin, May 11 and 21, 1921, NAACP MSS.
98. Kerlin to McRae, May 25, 1921, NAACP MSS.
99. Miller to McRae, June 6, 1921, NAACP MSS.
100. Kerlin to White, June 17, 1921, White to Kerlin, June 20, 1921, White to Jones, June 20, 1921, Thomas Mufson to Herbert J. Seligmann, Dec. 7, 1921, NAACP MSS.
101. Holmes for the Supreme Court in Moore *et al. vs.* Dempsey, p. 5; McReynolds, dissenting, pp. 5–6.
102. Petition in *Ex parte* Moore, NAACP MSS.; Supreme Court, *Transcript*, XLVI, 15–18, 87–97.
103. *Ibid.*, 99–121.

104. Johnson to Moorfield Storey, Nov. 2, 1921, memo on conference of Johnson with Jones, Sept. 14, 1922, NAACP MSS.
105. Storey to Ovington, Nov. 13, 1922, White to Storey, Nov. 15, 1922, NAACP MSS.
106. Storey to White, Nov. 16, 1922, NAACP MSS.
107. *Ibid.*, Bratton to White, Nov. 28, 1922, Jones to White, Nov. 25 and Dec. 6 and 21, 1922, White to Bratton, Dec. 7, 1922, White to Jones, Dec. 4 and 26, 1922, NAACP MSS.
108. Johnson to Shelby Davidson, Jan. 6, 1923, NAACP MSS.
109. Galley proofs of Storey's brief in Moore *et al. vs.* Dempsey, NAACP MSS.
110. Bratton to White, Jan. 11, 1923, NAACP MSS.
111. *Ibid.*, White to Jones, Jan. 12, 1923, NAACP MSS.
112. Jones to White, Jan. 16, 1923, NAACP MSS.
113. *Helena World,* Feb. 2, 1923, NAACP MSS.
114. Ed Ware to Sipio [*sic*] Jones, Feb. 12, 1923, NAACP MSS.
115. Davidson to Johnson, telegram, Feb. 19, 1923, NAACP MSS.
116. Holmes for the Court in Moore *et al. vs.* Dempsey, pp. 4–5.
117. McReynolds, dissenting in Moore *et al. vs.* Dempsey, pp. 2, 8.
118. *Arkansas Gazette,* Feb. 21, 1923, NAACP MSS.
119. *Toledo Times,* Feb. 22, 1923, NAACP MSS.
120. *St. Louis Post-Dispatch,* Feb. 25, 1923, NAACP MSS.
121. *Boston Chronicle,* March 10, 1923, *Dallas Express,* March 10, 1923, NAACP MSS.
122. American Civil Liberties Union, *Law and Freedom Bulletin,* March 23, 1923, NAACP MSS.
123. White to Bratton, Feb. 23 and March 1, 1923, NAACP MSS.
124. Bratton to White, Feb. 26, 1923, NAACP MSS.
125. John E. Miller to Jones, March 24, 1923, NAACP MSS.
126. Jones to White, April 2, 1923, NAACP MSS.
127. Robert W. Bagnall to Jones, April 11, 1923, NAACP MSS.
128. Storey to Ovington, April 14, 1923, NAACP MSS.
129. Bagnall to Jones, April 19, 1923, NAACP MSS.
130. Storey to White, May 16, 1923, NAACP MSS.
131. White to Storey, May 17, 1923, Johnson to Storey, May 28, 1923, NAACP MSS.
132. Storey to George B. Rose, May 28, 1923, NAACP MSS.
133. Motion for discharge in Lee Circuit Court of defendants, and response to motion, April 19, 1923, NAACP MSS.
134. *Arkansas Democrat,* May 22, 1923, Justice Wood speaking for the Supreme Court of Arkansas in Ware *et al. vs.* State, June 25, 1923, Jones to Ovington, June 25, 1923, NAACP MSS.
135. *St. Louis Argus,* June 29, 1923, NAACP MSS.
136. Author's interview with Joseph Wergis. 1965.
137. White to *Chicago Defender,* June 25, 1923, NAACP MSS.
138. Bratton to NAACP, June 26, 1923, NAACP MSS.

139. *Arkansas Sentinel-Record, ca.* July 1, 1923, *Arkansas Gazette, ca.* July 1, 1923, NAACP MSS.
140. Rose to Miller, July 2, 1923. NAACP MSS.
141. Miller to Rose, July 3, 1923, NAACP MSS.
142. C. E. Yingling to Rose, July 3, 1923, NAACP MSS.
143. Jones to White, Sept. 14, 1923, NAACP MSS.
144. Jones to White, Nov. 3, 1923, NAACP MSS.
145. Jones to White, Nov. 6, 1923, NAACP MSS.
146. Jones to White, Nov. 3, 1923, memo by Johnson, Nov. 3, 1923, NAACP MSS.
147. *Arkansas Survey,* Nov. 10, 1923, NAACP MSS.
148. NAACP press release, Nov. 16, 1923, NAACP MSS.

NOTES TO CHAPTER IX

1. Robert T. Kerlin, *The Voice of the Negro, 1919,* p. 186; Memorial to the Congress of the United States by the Commission on After-War Problems of the African Methodist Episcopal Church, Sept. 22, 1919, Legislative MSS., National Archives.
2. Press release from United Civic League, July 30, 1919, NAACP MSS. See also *Syracuse Post-Standard,* July 29, 1919, NAACP MSS.
3. William H. Wilson before House Committee on Judiciary, *Segregation* (U. S. House Docs., Jan. 15, 1920, 66 Cong., 2 Sess., ser. no. 14), p. 11.
4. *Cleveland Gazette,* Aug. 30, 1919, *Pittsburgh Courier,* July 26, 1919, NAACP MSS.
5. *New York Times,* Oct. 5, 1919, NAACP MSS.
6. *New York Call,* July 25, 1919, NAACP MSS.
7. *Ibid.,* July 28, 1919, *New York Times,* July 29, 1919, NAACP MSS.
8. *New York Globe,* July 29, 1919, NAACP MSS.
9. *New York Commoner,* July 23, 1919, *Washington Post,* July 25, 1919, *New York Age,* July 26, 1919, *Cleveland Gazette,* Aug. 30, 1919, *Boston Chronicle,* Nov. 1, 1919, NAACP MSS.
10. *New York World,* Aug. 3, 1919, NAACP MSS.
11. *New York Evening Mail,* July 30, 1919, NAACP MSS.
12. John Haynes Holmes, "The Race Riots," in *Unity,* Aug. 21, 1919, NAACP MSS.
13. Eugene Kinckle Jones to George E. Haynes, Aug. 8, 1919, Labor Dept. MSS., National Archives.
14. *Chicago Herald-Examiner,* Aug. 4, 1919, NAACP MSS. See

also *The Public,* Aug. 9, 1919, *New York Tribune,* July 23, 1919, NAACP MSS.

15. *Baltimore Herald,* Aug. 30, 1919, NAACP MSS.
16. *Independent,* Aug. 9, 1919, NAACP MSS.
17. *New York Call,* July 29, 1919, NAACP MSS.
18. Walter Lippmann, "Introductory Note," in Carl Sandburg, *The Chicago Race Riots.*
19. Edmund David Cronon, *Black Moses,* p. 189.
20. *Ibid.,* p. 50.
21. *Ibid.,* p. 75–76.
22. Chicago Commission on Race Relations, *The Negro in Chicago,* pp. 60, 493.
23. F. W. Morton to Richard H. Mickey, June 23, 1919, John Albert Williams to John R. Shillady, Sept. 29, 1919, NAACP MSS.
24. Notes on "Major Riots," Shillady to Robert R. Church, July 18, 1919, NAACP MSS.
25. S. H. Tarbet to NAACP, July 4, 1920, J. W. Ross to James Weldon Johnson, Feb. 14, 1921, H. J. Pinkett to Mary White Ovington, Oct. 13, 1919, NAACP MSS.
26. A. Clement MacNeal to Shillady, July 17, 1919, NAACP MSS.
27. Gilbert Seldes to Shillady, July 21, 1919, Herbert J. Seligmann to Seldes, July 25, 1919, E. L. Bernays to Seligmann, Aug. 5, 1919, NAACP MSS.
28. *Washington Post,* July 25, 1919, NAACP MSS.
29. Seligmann to Walter Lippmann, July 30, 1919, Herbert Croly to Seligmann, Aug. 1, 1919, Seligmann to William Griffith, Aug. 7, 1919, Griffith to Seligmann, Aug. 15, 1919, W. D. Heydecker to Ovington, Sept. 12, 1919, Seligmann to A. Philip Randolph, Oct. 8, 1919, Walter F. White to Walter A. May, Dec. 19, 1919, Bruno Lasker to White, Dec. 13, 1919, Seligmann to Harry W. Laidler, Nov. 19, 1919, Seligmann to Lippmann, Oct. 23, 1919, White to C. H. Dennis, Oct. 19, 1919, NAACP MSS.
30. Shillady to *Albany Journal,* Oct. 30, 1919, W.E.B. Du Bois to *New York World,* Nov. 23, 1919, Seligmann to *New York Sun,* Sept. 30, 1919, Seligmann to *Current Opinion,* Aug. 29, 1919, Seligmann to *Survey,* Sept. 15, 1919, NAACP MSS.
31. Herbert J. Seligmann, *The Negro Faces America* (New York: Harper, 1920); Seligmann to William H. Briggs, Nov. 29, 1919, Shillady to U. S. Bratton, March 13, 1920, NAACP MSS.
32. *Memphis Press,* July 24, 1919, NAACP MSS.
33. *Atlanta Constitution,* Aug. 4, 1919, NAACP MSS.
34. P. A. Williams to Shillady, Aug. 11, 1919, NAACP MSS.

35. *Utica Globe*, Oct. 4, 1919, NAACP MSS. See also *New Orleans State*, Sept. 30, 1919, NAACP MSS.
36. *Tampa Tribune*, undated, NAACP MSS.
37. *Ibid.*
38. Anonymous letter to Attorney-General from Erie, Pennsylvania, Oct. 6, 1919, Justice Dept. MSS., National Archives; *Baltimore Herald*, July 8, 1919, *Shreveport News-American*, July 24, 1919, *Brooklyn Eagle*, July 27, 1919, NAACP MSS.
39. *Ibid., Cincinnati Commercial Tribune*, July 25, 1919, NAACP MSS.
40. *Shreveport Journal*, Aug. 4, 1919, *Syracuse Herald*, July 24, 1919, *New York Times*, July 23, 1919, *Baltimore Star*, July 30, 1919, NAACP MSS.
41. *Seattle Times*, Oct. 6, 1919, NAACP MSS. See also *Shreveport Weekly Caucasian*, Oct. 9, 1919, *Little Rock Gazette*, Oct. 8, 1919, *New York Sun*, Oct. 8, 1919, *New York World*, Nov. 16, 1919, NAACP MSS.
42. *Philadelphia Inquirer*, July 31, 1919, *Albany Argus*, July 24, 1919, *New York Times*, Aug. 3, 1919, *Brooklyn Eagle*, Aug. 2, 1919, *Baltimore Star*, July 30, 1919, *Minneapolis National Advocate*, Aug. 2, 1919, *Brooklyn Eagle*, July 27, 1919, *Shreveport Times*, Aug. 3, 1919, *New York Times*, July 23, 1919, NAACP MSS.
43. *Wheeling Intelligencer*, Sept. 3, 1919, NAACP MSS.
44. *Springfield Republican*, July 31, 1919, NAACP MSS.
45. *New York Times*, July 23, 1919, *Brooklyn Eagle*, July 27, 1919, *Atlanta Constitution*, July 30, 1919, unnamed paper, *ca.* Aug. 2, 1919, *Birmingham News*, July 30, 1919, NAACP MSS.
46. Bolton Smith to Attorney-General, Aug. 1, 1919, Justice Dept. MSS.
47. *Salt Lake City Herald*, Aug. 24, 1919, NAACP MSS.
48. *Birmingham News*, July 30, 1919, NAACP MSS. See also *Buffalo Enquirer*, July 29, 1919, *Chicago Post*, July 31, 1919, *Knoxville Sentinel*, Sept. 1, 1919, *Chicago Tribune*, Aug. 3 and 7, 1919, NAACP MSS.
49. John Higham, *Strangers in the Land*, pp. 254-60; William Preston, Jr., *Aliens and Dissenters*, pp. 191-205.
50. *New York Times*, July 28, 1919, NAACP MSS.
51. *Boston Herald*, July 30, 1919, NAACP MSS.
52. *Baltimore News*, July 30, 1919, NAACP MSS.
53. *New York World*, Aug. 4, 1919, NAACP MSS.
54. *Brooklyn Eagle*, Aug. 2, 1919, NAACP MSS. See also *ibid.*, Aug. 22, 1919, *Minneapolis National Advocate*, Aug. 2, 1919, NAACP MSS.
55. *New York Times*, Oct. 5, 1919, NAACP MSS.

56. *Syracuse Post-Standard,* July 29, 1919, NAACP MSS.
57. *Philadelphia Inquirer,* July 31, 1919, NAACP MSS. See also *The Independent,* Aug. 9, 1919, NAACP MSS.
58. *New York World,* Aug. 3, 1919, NAACP MSS.
59. *Shreveport Journal,* Aug. 4, 1919, NAACP MSS.
60. Seligmann to *New York Sun,* Sept. 30, 1919, NAACP MSS. See also "an American Citizen" to Attorney-General, Sept. 29, 1919, Justice Department MSS.
61. *Nashville Banner,* Oct. 4, 1919, *Seattle Times,* Oct. 6, 1919, *New York Sun,* Oct. 7, 1919, NAACP MSS.
62. *New York Journal,* Oct. 7, 1919, NAACP MSS.
63. Robert T. Scott to Walter F. White, Oct. 10, 1919, Justice Dept. MSS.; United States Attorney-General, *Annual Report for the Year 1919,* pp. 15–16.
64. *New York World,* Oct. 16, 1919, NAACP MSS.
65. *Chicago Daily News,* Nov. 5, 1919, David Lawrence to William C. Graves, Nov. 10, 1919, Chicago Commission on Race Relations MSS.
66. Robert P. Stewart to Hon. Carl Hayden, Nov. 8, 1919, Justice Dept. MSS.
67. Memo from J. Edgar Hoover to Stewart, Nov. 7, 1919, Justice Dept. MSS.
68. United States Attorney-General, *Investigation Activities of the Department of Justice* (U. S. Senate Docs., Nov. 17, 1919, 66 Cong., 1 Sess., doc. no. 153, ser. no. 7607), pp. 162, 187. Hereafter cited as Investigation Activities.
69. *Ibid.,* pp. 162–87.
70. *Ibid.,* p. 13.
71. *Ibid.,* p. 162.
72. *Ibid.,* pp. 9 and 14.
73. *Ibid.,* p. 162.
74. *Ibid.*
75. *Ibid.,* pp. 162–63.
76. *Ibid.,* pp. 165–67, 169–70, 179, 181.
77. *Ibid.,* p. 173.
78. *Ibid.,* pp. 183–84.
79. *Ibid.,* p. 187.
80. *Ibid.,* pp. 172–84.
81. United States Congress, House of Representatives, *Sedition, Syndicalism, Sabotage and Anarchy: Hearings before the Committee on Judiciary* (December 11 and 16, 1919, 66 Cong., 2 Sess., ser. no. 10), p. 7.
82. *Ibid.,* p. 12.
83. *Shreveport Times,* Jan. 15, 1920, Summary of headlines and lead paragraphs in newspaper stories, Jan. 15, 1920, NAACP MSS.

84. United States Congress, House of Representatives, *Sedition: Hearings before the Committee on Judiciary* (Feb. 4, 1920, 66 Cong., 2 Sess., ser. no. 16), pp. 15–16.
85. Moorfield Storey to A. Mitchell Palmer, Feb. 5, 1920, Justice Dept. MSS.
86. Palmer to Storey, Feb. 23, 1920, Justice Dept. MSS.
87. W. H. Hurley to Hoover, June 2, 1921, Justice Dept. MSS.
88. Report by Fred S. Dunn to Federal Bureau of Investigation, June 10, 1921, Justice Dept. MSS.
89. Neval H. Thomas to Palmer, Nov. 19, 1919, NAACP MSS.
90. *Shreveport Times*, Jan. 15, 1920, *Survey*, Jan. 24, 1920, NAACP MSS. See also United States Congress, House of Representatives, *Segregation and Anti-Lynching: Hearings before the Committee on Judiciary* (Jan. 15 and 29, 1920, 66 Cong., 2 Sess., ser. no. 14), p. 11. Hereafter cited as *Segregation and Anti-Lynching*.
91. Kelly Miller, *Radicalism and the Negro* (Washington: Published by the Author, n.d.).
92. *Baltimore Evening Sun*, Jan. 22, 1920, *Baltimore American*, Jan. 23, 1920, NAACP MSS.
93. *New York Globe*, Sept. 3, 1919, NAACP MSS.
94. *New York World*, Aug. 11, 1919, NAACP MSS.
95. *New York Times*, Oct. 5, 1919, NAACP MSS.
96. *Philadelphia Inquirer*, July 31, 1919, NAACP MSS.
97. Haynes to Secretary of Labor, May 17, 1919, Labor Dept. MSS., National Archives.
98. *New York Times*, Oct. 5, 1919, NAACP MSS.
99. *East Tennessee News*, Dec. 11, 1919, NAACP MSS.
100. Edward Flud Burrows, "The Commission on Interracial Cooperation, 1919–1944" (Ph.D. Thesis, University of Wisconsin, 1954), p. 51.
101. *Ibid.*, p. 73.
102. *Wheeling News*, Oct. 7, 1919, NAACP MSS.
103. John Hope Franklin, *From Slavery to Freedom*, p. 480.
104. George E. Haynes, "Race Riots in Relation to Democracy," *Survey*, Aug. 9, 1919, NAACP MSS.
105. *New York Post*, July 23, 1919, NAACP MSS.
106. *Chicago Tribune*, Sept. 30, 1919, NAACP MSS. See also *New York Globe*, July 30, 1919, NAACP MSS.
107. *New York World*, July 22, 1919, NAACP MSS.
108. *Albany Argus*, Oct. 1, 1919, NAACP MSS.
109. *New York Globe*, July 23, 1919, NAACP MSS.
110. *Scranton Times*, Sept. 1, 1919, NAACP MSS.
111. *New York Herald*, July 1919, unnamed Rochester paper, July 1919, *Cincinnati Commercial Tribune*, July 25, 1919, NAACP MSS.

112. *New York World,* Sept. 2, 1919, *Washington Star,* July 22, 1919, *Washington Times,* July 22, 1919, NAACP MSS.
113. *Washington Post,* July 23, 1919, NAACP MSS.
114. *Ibid.*
115. *Memphis Press,* Oct. 3, 1919, NAACP MSS.
116. *Utica Press,* July 25, 1919, *Washington Post,* July 25, 1919, NAACP MSS. See also *Shreveport Times,* July 17, 1919, NAACP MSS.
117. *New York Times,* July 23, 1919, NAACP MSS.
118. C.W.W., Lieutenant, U.S. Army, to Editor, *New York Times,* July 29, 1919, in *New York Times,* July 31, 1919, NAACP MSS.
119. Henry A. Bellows, *A Treatise on Riot Duty for the National Guard,* pp. 7–16, 22–25, 129.
120. Edward S. Farrow, *Riots and Riot Duty.*
121. *New York Post,* Sept. 1, 1919, NAACP MSS.
122. Maj. Gen. Henry Jervey to Adjutant General, Oct. 3, 1919, Gen. P. C. Harris to George Huddleston, Oct. 4, 1919, War Dept. MSS., National Archives; *New York World,* Sept. 30, 1919, *Boston Evening Transcript,* Oct. 2, 1919, NAACP MSS.
123. *New York World,* Oct. 16, 1919, NAACP MSS.
124. *New York Times,* Dec. 1, 1919, NAACP MSS.
125. Eugene Kinckle Jones to Haynes, Aug. 8, 1919, Labor Dept. MSS.
126. *New York Tribune,* July 23, 1919, NAACP MSS.
127. *Survey,* Aug. 9, 1919, NAACP MSS.
128. *Buffalo Express,* July 24, 1919, Philadelphia Press, July 30, 1919. *Brooklyn Standard Union,* Sept. 1, 1919, NAACP MSS.
129. Senate Resolution 189, 66 Congress, Sept. 22, 1919, James Weldon Johnson to Charles Curtis, Sept. 29, 1919, John R. Shillady to E. P. Smith, Sept. 29, 1919, Mary White Ovington to Pinkett, Sept. 29, 1919, Memo from White to NAACP, Oct. 1, 1919, Shillady to Charles Evans Hughes, William Howard Taft, Elihu Root, Will Hays, George W. Wickersham (identical letters), Nov. 6, 1919, NAACP MSS.
130. Petitions, Senate Judiciary, 66 Cong., Legislative MSS., National Archives.
131. Hugh M. Dorsey to Knute Nelson, Oct. 6, 1919, George P. Crothers to Nelson, Oct. 15, 1919, Earl Cranston to Nelson, Oct. 9, 1919, Legislative MSS.
132. Wickersham to Shillady, Nov. 7, 1919, Taft to Shillady, Nov. 8 and 16, 1919, NAACP MSS.; Wickersham to Sen. Frank P. Kellogg, Nov. 7, 1919, Legislative MSS.
133. William Phillips to Sen. William P. Dillingham, Oct. 18, 1919, Legislative MSS.
134. Curtis to Johnson, Jan. 6, 1920, NAACP MSS.
135. Storey to Johnson, Jan. 9, 1920, NAACP MSS.

136. Sen. William P. Dillingham to Storey, Feb. 24, 1920, NAACP MSS.

137. Shillady to G. H. Edmunds, May 11, 1920, Johnson to Curtis, Nov. 11, 1920, NAACP MSS.

138. *New York Sun*, Jan. 15, 1920, Shillady to Bolton Smith, Jan. 20, 1920, NAACP MSS.

139. Leonidas C. Dyer to Johnson, Jan. 13, 1920, NAACP MSS.

140. Shillady to Esther Morton Smith, Jan. 21, 1920, Johnson to Archibald H. Grimke, Jan. 16, 1920, NAACP MSS.

141. *Segregation and Anti-Lynching*, pp. 32, 37, 45, 62, 68.

142. *Ibid.*, pp. 19, 64-65.

143. Minutes of House Judiciary Committee, Jan. 29, 1920, Legislative MSS.

144. *Ibid.*, May 20, 1920, Legislative MSS.

145. *Ibid.*, May 27, 1920, Legislative MSS.

146. United States Congress, House of Representatives, Committee on Judiciary Report No. 1027, 66 Cong., 2 Sess., Legislative MSS.

147. *Ibid.*

148. Franklin, *From Slavery to Freedom*, pp. 478-79.

149. White to Scipio A. Jones, Dec. 4, 1922, NAACP MSS.

150. White to Bratton, Dec. 7, 1922, NAACP MSS.; Franklin, *op. cit.*, p. 479.

151. John Moffat Mecklin, *The Ku Klux Klan*, pp. 4-10.

152. Rayford W. Logan, *The Negro in American Life and Thought: The Nadir, 1877-1901*, p. 52.

153. C. Vann Woodward, *The Strange Career of Jim Crow*, p. 49.

NOTES TO CHAPTER X

1. Writers on other race riots have also emphasized the involvement of the police in the origins of the riot. See Elliott M. Rudwick, *Race Riot at East St. Louis, July 2, 1917*, pp. 217-33, and Allen D. Grimshaw, "A Study in Social Violence: Urban Race Riots in the United States," *passim*.

NOTES TO CHAPTER XI

1. Alfred McClung Lee and Norman D. Humphrey, *Race Riot*, pp. 20-104; Robert Shogan and Tom Craig, *The Detroit Race Riot*.

2. *New York Times,* June 2, 3, 4, 5, 8 and 26, 1921, March 21, 22, 23, 24, 25, 26, 28, 29, 30, 31, 1935.
3. Irving Howe and B. J. Widick, *The UAW and Walter Reuther,* pp. 100–6.
4. *Statistical Abstract of the United States, 1962,* Table #327; *Economic Report of the President, January 1964,* p. 207.
5. See, for example, Donald Brennan, ed., *Arms Control, Disarmament, and National Security;* Amitai Etzioni, *The Hard Way to Peace;* James Roosevelt, ed., *The Liberal Papers;* Charles Osgood, *An Alternative to War and Surrender;* Seymour Melman, *The Peace Race;* Walter Millis, *The Abolition of War;* and Arthur I. Waskow, *The Limits of Defense.* For an analysis of this new approach to disarmament, see Waskow, "Disarmament as a Special Case in Military Strategy," *World Politics XVI* (Jan. 1964), pp. 322–27.
6. John F. Kennedy, "A Truce to Terror," address to the General Assembly of the United Nations, September 25, 1961.
7. William Robert Miller, *Nonviolence: A Christian Interpretation,* pp. 298–306; Martin Luther King, *Stride Toward Freedom,* pp. 90–107.
8. Walter Millis, *Arms and Men,* pp. 272–307.
9. Kenneth Boulding, *Conflict and Defense,* p. 339.
10. *Ibid.,* pp. 337–38.

NOTES TO CHAPTER XII

1. Author's interview with Miss Jean Wheeler at Howard University Conference on Youth and Social Action, 1963.
2. Langston Hughes, *Fight for Freedom,* pp. 12–13, 122–27.
3. Alfred McClung Lee and Norman D. Humphrey, *Race Riot,* pp. 20–104.
4. Wallace Westfeldt, "Communities in Strife," in Don Shoemaker, ed., *With All Deliberate Speed,* pp. 36–55.
5. Fredric Solomon and Jacob R. Fishman, "Youth and Social Action: II. Action and Identity Formation in the First Student Sit-in Demonstration," *Journal of Social Issues,* XX (April 1964), No. 2, pp. 36–45; Southern Regional Council, "Direct Action in the South," *New South* XVIII (Oct.–Nov. 1963), No. 10–11, p. 3.
6. Howard Zinn, *SNCC: The New Abolitionists,* pp. 16–39.
7. Jacob R. Fishman and Fredric Solomon, "Youth and Social Action: I. Perspectives on the Student Sit-in Movement," *American Journal of Orthopsychiatry* XXXIII (Oct. 1963), pp. 878–80; Solomon and Fishman, "The Psychosocial Mean-

ing of Nonviolence in Student Civil Rights Activities," *Psychiatry* XXVII (May 1964), No. 2, pp. 94–96.

8. Southern Regional Council, *loc. cit.*, p. 25.

9. *Ibid.*, p. 5.

10. *New York Times*, Nov. 8, 1963.

11. United States Department of Justice, "Supplemental Brief for the United States as *Amicus Curiae*," Cases 6, 9, 10, 12, and 60, United States Supreme Court, October term, 1963; "Brief for Petitioners," Cases 9, 10, and 12, *ibid.*, pp. 33–48; "Brief for the Appellants," Case 60, *ibid.*, pp. 19–27; "Reply of the City of Columbia to the Supplemental Brief of the United States," Cases 9 and 10, *ibid.*, pp. 12–14, 24–27.

12. Bell *et al.* *vs.* Maryland, June 22, 1964.

13. Black, dissenting, in Bell *et al.* *vs.* Maryland, p. 29.

14. *New York Times*, Dec. 15, 1964.

15. Zinn, *op. cit.*, pp. 40–61; James Peck, *Freedom Ride.*

16. Tom Haydon, "Just a Matter of Timing?" *Liberation* VII (Oct. 1962), No. 8, pp. 24–26.

17. Author's interview with Charles Sherrod, 1964.

18. Vincent Harding, "Beginning in Birmingham," *The Reporter* XXVIII (June 6, 1963), No. 12, pp. 13–19; Dave Dellinger, "The Negroes of Birmingham," *Liberation* VIII (Summer 1963), No. 5–6, pp. 17–21; *Washington Post*, May 4, 1963; *New York Times*, May 4, 1963.

19. *New York Times*, May 12, 1963, May 19, 1963.

20. Harding, *loc. cit.*, p. 16.

21. Dellinger, *loc. cit.*, p. 21.

22. Harding, *loc. cit.*, p. 15.

23. *Ibid.*, pp. 18–19; *New York Times*, May 13, 1963.

24. José Rames, "Racial Anatomy of a City," *New University Thought* III (September–October 1963), No. 2, p. 20.

25. *New York Times*, Aug. 27, 28, and 29, 1963.

26. Author's observations, 1963; Murray Kempton, "The March on Washington," *New Republic* CXLIX (September 14, 1963), No. 11, pp. 19–20.

27. *New York Times*, Sept. 16 and 17, 1963.

28. Author's observations; *New York Times*, Sept. 23, 1963.

29. *New York Times*, Nov. 25, 1962.

30. *Ibid.*, June 18, 1963; author's interview with Noel Day, 1963.

31. *Washington Afro-American*, March 3, 1964.

32. *New York Times*, Feb. 3 and 4, 1964.

33. *Ibid.*, Jan. 8, 1964.

34. *Ibid.*, Jan. 7, 1964 and Feb. 11, 1964.

35. *Washington Afro-American*, May 5, 1964; *Washington Post*, May 5, 1964; author's interview with Stokely Carmichael, 1963.

36. *New York Times*, May 25, 26, 29, and 31, June 1, 4, 9, 18, 20,

and 21, 1963, and May 13, 14, and 15, 1964; *The Liberal Democrat*, May 1964 and Aug. 1964.
37. *New York Times*, June 12 and 23, 1963.
38. *New York Times*, Aug. 7, 23, 27, and 28, 1963, and Oct. 8, 1963.
39. Interview with Leonard Holt, 1964. The phone-in took place between Aug. 5 and 8, 1963, in Danville.
40. *Washington Post*, Sept. 23 and 24, 1963.
41. Students for a Democratic Society, "Community Organization in the Other America: Chester, Pennsylvania"; *New York Times*, April 23, 24, 25, 26, and May 5, 1964.
42. *New York Times*, March 7, 1964.
43. *Ibid.*, April 23, 1964.

NOTES TO CHAPTER XIII

1. *New York Times*, June 1, 2, 3, and 20, 1963.
2. *Ibid.*, June 20, 1963.
3. HR 7152, introduced in the House of Representatives by Emanuel Celler, June 20, 1963.
4. The following discussion of the Civil Rights Act of 1964 is based on the author's confidential interviews with several congressmen and lobbyists, 1963.
5. *Ibid.*
6. HR 7152, Committee Print of October 2, 1963; HR 7152, Committee Print No. 2 of October 30, 1963; HR 7152, as passed by the Senate, June 19, 1964, and showing version passed by the House of Representatives.
7. HR 7702, introduced in the House of Representatives by Robert W. Kastenmeier, July 23, 1963.
8. Author's confidential interviews with several congressmen and lobbyists, 1963.
9. *Ibid.*

NOTES TO CHAPTER XIV

1. *New York Times*, July 17, 18, 19, and 20, 1964.
2. *Ibid.*, July 20, 1964; *New York Herald Tribune*, July 20, 1964; *Washington Afro-American*, July 21, 1964; *Washington Post*, July 26, 1964; *I. F. Stone's Weekly*, Aug. 10, 1964; author's interview with Val Coleman, 1964; Lez Edmond, "Harlem Diary," *Ramparts* III (Oct. 1964), No. 2, pp. 18–28; Murray

Kempton, "How Cops Behave in Harlem," *New Republic* CLI (Aug. 22, 1964), Nos. 8-9, pp. 7-8.

3. *New York Times,* July 21, 22, 23, 24, 25, and 26, 1964.
4. *Ibid.,* July 27, Aug. 7 and 15, and Sept. 18, 1964.
5. *Ibid.,* July 26, 27, and 28, 1964.
6. *Ibid.,* Aug. 3, 4, 13, 14, and 15, 1964.
7. *Ibid.,* Aug. 15, 1964.
8. *Ibid.,* Aug. 29 and 30, 1964; *Washington Afro-American,* Sept. 12, 1964.
9. *Baltimore Sun,* Sept. 2, 1964.
10. "Testimony of John Edgar Hoover, Director, Federal Bureau of Investigation, before the House Subcommittee on Appropriations, on Jan. 29, 1964," available from the FBI.
11. *New York Times,* Sept. 27, 1964.
12. *Ibid.*
13. *Ibid.,* Sept. 30 and Oct. 1, 1964; *The Student Voice,* Aug. 5, 1964.

NOTES TO CHAPTER XV

1. Howard Zinn, *SNCC: The New Abolitionists,* pp. 99-100; *The Student Voice,* Nov. 11, 1963.
2. "Prospectus for the Summer Project," in Aaron Henry, Robert Moses, and David Dennis to Arthur I. Waskow [multiple letter to northern college faculties], April 8, 1964.
3. Joseph Rauh, *et al.,* "Brief Submitted by the Mississippi Freedom Democratic Party . . . to the Democratic National Convention," p. 15.
4. *Wall Street Journal,* May 25, 1964; *New York Times,* May 30, June 29, and July 8, 1964; *Washington Post,* Oct. 4, 1964.
5. *New York Times,* June 21, 22, and 23, 1964, Aug. 5, 6, and 8, 1964; author's interviews with Aaron Henry, Robert Moses, and Walter Tillow, 1964.
6. Rauh *et al., op. cit.,* pp. 16-20.
7. This and the following material about the convention challenge is based chiefly on the author's direct observation of events in Atlantic City. See also *New York Times,* Aug. 21, 22, 23, 24, 25, and 26, 1964; and Stanley L. Newman, "Atlantic City—Case Study in the New Politics," MS. paper.
8. *Washington Post,* Sept. 3 and 5, 1964.

NOTES TO CHAPTER XVI

1. Martin Luther King, *Stride Toward Freedom*, pp. 90–107.
2. Jacob R. Fishman and Fredric Solomon, "Youth and Social Action I: Perspectives on the Student Sit-in Movement," *American Journal of Ortho-Psychiatry* XXXIII (Oct. 1963), 879–80.
3. James M. Landis, "Freedom of Speech and the Press," *Encyclopedia of the Social Sciences*, VI, 455–58; John Milton, *Areopagitica*.
4. John R. Commons, *et al.*, *History of Labor in the United States*, pp. 138–46; 401–12.
5. *New York Times*, Oct. 1, 1963.
6. Testimony of Mrs. Vera Pigee, reprinted in the *Congressional Record*, June 16, 1964, p. 13512; testimony of Mrs. Fannie Lou Hamer, reprinted in the *Congressional Record*, June 16, 1964, p. 13513; testimony of Mr. Hartman Turnbow, reprinted in the *Congressional Record*, June 16, 1964, p. 13520; *Delta Democrat-Times*, May 10, 1964.
7. *New York Times*, Oct. 5, 6, and 7, 1964.
8. *New York Times*, Aug. 13–27, 1965; *Los Angeles Times*, Aug. 13–27, 1965; *Washington Post*, Aug. 13–27, 1965; *Washington Afro-American*, Aug. 17 and 21, 1965; *The Economist* (London), Aug. 21, 1965, pp. 692–93; author's interviews with James A. Roosevelt, Esther Jackson, Paul Albert, and Mike Miller, 1965; Columbia Broadcasting System, "The Los Angeles Riots, Who Is to Blame?" as broadcast Aug. 15, 1965 (mimeographed).
8A. Paul Jacobs, "Shadows of Freedom," MS. paper available from the Center for Study of Democratic Institutions.
9. *Ibid.*, Dec. 3, 4, 5, 6, 7, and 8, 1964.

NOTES TO CHAPTER XVII

1. See the *Journal of Conflict Resolution*, founded in 1957; Kenneth E. Boulding, *Conflict and Defense;* and Roger Fisher, ed., *International Conflict and Behavioral Science.*
2. See Arthur I. Waskow, "Nonlethal Equivalents of War," in Fisher, *op. cit.*

BIBLIOGRAPHY

BOOKS AND PAMPHLETS

Adamic, Louis. *Dynamite*. Gloucester, Mass.: Peter Smith, 1960.

Allport, Gordon W. *The Nature of Prejudice*. Cambridge, Mass.: Addison-Wesley, 1954.

Arendt, Hannah. *On Revolution*. New York: Viking Press, 1963.

Armstrong Association of Philadelphia: Eleventh Annual Report, 1919.

Babcock, Louis L. *Manual for the Use of Troops in Aid of the Civil Authority*. New York: George H. Doran Co., 1918.

Baker, Paul E. *Negro-White Adjustment: An Investigation and Analysis of Methods in the Interracial Movement in the United States*. Pittsfield, Mass.: Sun Printing Co., 1934.

Baker, Ray Stannard. *Following the Color Line*. New York: Doubleday, Page, 1908.

Beale, Howard K. *The Critical Year*. New York: Ungar, 1958.

Bellows, Henry A. *Manual for Local Defense*. New York: Macmillan, 1918.

Beloff, Max. *Public Order and Popular Disturbances, 1660–1714*. London: Oxford University Press, 1938.

Berry, Brewton. *Race and Ethnic Relations*. Boston: Houghton Mifflin, 1958.

Billington, Ray A. *The Protestant Crusade*. New York: Rinehart, 1952.

Binder, Carroll. *Chicago and the New Negro*. Chicago: Chicago Daily News, 1927.

Bond, Horace Mann. *The Education of the Negro in the American Social Order*. New York: Prentice-Hall, 1934.

Boulding, Kenneth. *Conflict and Defense: A General Theory*. New York: Harper, 1962.

Bowen, Louise de Koven. *The Colored People of Chicago: An Investigation Made for the Juvenile Protection Association*. Chicago: Juvenile Protection Association, 1913.

Broderick, Francis L. *W.E.B. Du Bois*. Stanford, Cal.: Stanford University Press, 1959.

Brown, Warren. *Check List of Negro Newspapers in the United States*. (Lincoln University Journalism Series 2.) Jefferson City, Mo., 1946.

Brownlow, Louis. *A Passion for Anonymity: The Autobiography of Louis Brownlow,* Second Half. Chicago: University of Chicago Press, 1958.

Bruce, Robert V. *1877: Year of Violence.* Indianapolis: Bobbs-Merrill, 1959.

Callaway, J. E. *"The Road to Righteous Judgment": A Brief on the Negro Question.* Arkadelphia, Ark.: Siftings Herald Printing Co., 1922.

Cannon, Poppy. *A Gentle Knight: My Husband Walter White.* N.p., n. pub., 1956.

Catalogue of Books in the Moorland Foundation ("United States Works Progress Administration Projects 271 and 328"). Washington, D.C.: Howard University, 1939.

Caughey, John W. *Their Majesties the Mob.* Chicago: University of Chicago Press, 1960.

Chafee, Zechariah. *Free Speech in the United States.* Cambridge: Harvard University Press, 1948.

Chicago Commission on Race Relations. *The Negro in Chicago: A Study of Race Relations and a Race Riot.* Chicago: University of Chicago Press, 1922.

Chicago Urban League. First Annual Report, for the Fiscal Year Ended October 31st, 1917. Chicago: Chicago Urban League, n.d.

————. Second Annual Report . . . 1918. Chicago: Chicago Urban League, n.d.

————. [Third] Annual Report . . . 1919. Chicago: Chicago Urban League, n.d.

————. Fourth Annual Report . . . 1920. Chicago: Chicago Urban League, n.d.

————. Seventh Annual Report . . . 1923. Chicago: Chicago Urban League, n.d.

————. Tenth Annual Report . . . 1926. Chicago: Chicago Urban League, n.d.

————. Two Decades of Service, 1916–1936. Chicago: Chicago Urban League, n.d.

City Club of Chicago. Eleventh Year Book. Chicago: n. pub., 1917.

Coleman, James. *Community Conflict.* Glencoe, Ill.: Free Press, 1957.

Commager, Henry S., ed. *Documents of American History.* New York: Appleton-Century-Crofts, 1958.

Commission on Interracial Cooperation. *Justice in Race Relations.* Atlanta: n. pub., n.d.

————. *Progress in Race Relations, 1924–25.* Atlanta: Commission on Interracial Cooperation, n.d.

————. *Progress in Race Relations, 1926.* N.p.: Commission on Interracial Cooperation, n.d.

_____. *Race Relations in 1927*. Atlanta: Commission on Inter-racial Cooperation, n.d.

_____. *Southern Women and Race Cooperation: A Story of the Memphis Conference, 1920*. N.p.: *ca.* 1921.

Commons, John R. *et al. History of Labor in the United States, 1896–1932*. New York: Macmillan, 1935. Vol. IV, Labor Movements, by Selig Perlman and Philip Taft.

Confessions of a Negro Preacher. Chicago: Canterbury Press, 1928.

Cronon, Edmund David. *Black Moses: The Story of Marcus Garvey and the Universal Negro Improvement Association*. Madison: University of Wisconsin, 1955.

_____. *The Cabinet Diaries of Josephus Daniels*. Lincoln: University of Nebraska Press, 1963.

Crook, Wilfrid H. *Communism and the General Strike*. Hampden, Conn.: Shoe String Press, 1960.

Dabney, Lillian G. *History of Schools for Negroes in the District of Columbia, 1807–1947*. N.p.: n. pub., 1949.

Darvall, Frank Ongley. *Popular Disturbances and Public Order in Regency England*. London: Oxford University Press, 1934.

Davis, Allison, and Dollard, John. *Children of Bondage: The Personality Development of Negro Youth in the Urban South*. Washington, D.C.: American Council on Education, 1940.

Davis, Allison, Gardner, Burleigh B., and Gardner, Mary R. (directed by W. Lloyd Warner). *Deep South: A Social Anthropological Study of Caste and Class*. Chicago: University of Chicago Press, 1941.

Detweiler, Frederick G. *The Negro Press in the United States*. Chicago: University of Chicago Press, 1922.

Dollard, John. *Caste and Class in a Southern Town*. New Haven: Yale University Press for the Institute of Human Relations, 1937.

Dos Passos, John. *U.S.A.* New York: Modern Library, 1937.

Dowd, Jerome. *The Negro in American Life*. New York: Century, 1926.

Drake, St. Clair and Cayton, Horace R. *Black Metropolis: A Study of Negro Life in a Northern City*. New York: Harcourt, Brace, 1945.

Du Bois, W. E. Burghardt. *Darkwater*. New York: Harcourt, Brace & Howe, 1920.

_____. *Dusk of Dawn*. New York: Harcourt, Brace, 1940.

Duke, Charles S. *The Housing Situation and the Colored People of Chicago*. Chicago: n. pub., April, 1919.

Duncan, Hannibal Gerald. *The Changing Race Relationship in the Border and Northern States*. Philadelphia: University of Pennsylvania, 1922.

Duncan, Otis Dudley, and Duncan, Beverly. *The Negro Population of Chicago*. Chicago: University of Chicago Press, 1937.

Dutcher, Dean. *The Negro in Modern Industrial Society: An Analysis of Changes in the Occupations of Negro Workers 1910–1920.* Lancaster, Pa.: Science Press Printing Co., 1930.

Eleazer, Robert B. *An Adventure in Faith.* Atlanta: Commission on Interracial Cooperation, 1929.

―――. *An Adventure in Good Will.* Atlanta: Commission on Interracial Cooperation, n.d.

Faris, Robert E. L. *Social Disorganization.* New York: Ronald, 1948.

Farley, John W. *Statistics and Politics.* N.p.: n. pub., 1920.

Farrow, Edward S. *Riots and Riot Duty.* Asbury Park, N.J.: Military-Naval Book Corporation, 1919.

Fitch, John A. *The Causes of Industrial Unrest.* New York: Harper, 1924.

Franklin, John Hope. *From Slavery to Freedom: A History of American Negroes.* New York: Knopf, 1952.

Frazier, E. Franklin. *Negro Youth at the Crossways: Their Personality Development in the Middle States.* Washington, D.C.: American Council on Education, 1940.

―――. *The Negro Family in Chicago.* Chicago: University of Chicago Press, 1932.

―――. *The Negro in the United States.* New York: Macmillan, 1957. Rev. ed.

George, Harrison. *Chicago Race Riots.* Chicago: Great Western, 1919.

Gerth, Hans, and Mills, C. Wright. *Character and Social Structure.* New York: Harcourt, Brace, 1953.

―――. *From Max Weber: Essays in Sociology.* New York: Oxford University Press, 1946.

Gold, Howard R., and Armstrong, Byron K. *A Preliminary Study of Interracial Conditions in Chicago:* Made under the Survey Division, Industrial Relations Department, Interchurch World Movement of North America. New York: Home Missions Council, c. 1920.

Gosnell, Harold F. *Negro Politicians: The Rise of Negro Politics in Chicago.* Chicago: University of Chicago Press, 1935.

Green, Constance McLaughlin. *Washington: Capital City, 1879–1950.* Princeton: Princeton University Press, 1963.

Grey, Edgar M. *The Washington Riot: Its Cause and Effect.* New York: Self-published (?) 1919.

Grimke, Francis J. *A Phase of the Race Problem, Looked at from Within the Race Itself.* N.p.: n. pub., n.d.

Haynes, George E. *Negro Migration and its Implications North and South:* Speech to 77th Annual Meeting of American Medical Association, October 23, 1923. New York City: n. pub., n.d.

―――. *The Trend of the Races.* New York: Council of Women for

Home Missions and Missionary Education Movement of the United States and Canada, 1922.

Headley, J. T. *The Great Riots of New York*. New York: Treat, 1873.

Hoffman, Peter Michael, Coroner of Cook County. *The Race Riots*. Biennial Report of Coroner. N.p.: n. pub., n.d.

Howe, Irving, and Widick, B. J. *The UAW and Walter Reuther*. New York: Random House, 1949.

Hughes Everett Cherrington, and Hughes, Helen MacGill. *Where Peoples Meet*. Glencoe, Ill.: Free Press, 1952.

Hughes, Langston. *Fight for Freedom*. New York: Norton, 1962.

Hutchinson, William T. *Lowden of Illinois*. Chicago: University of Chicago Press, 1957.

Illinois. *Third Administrative Report of the Directors of Departments . . . together with the Adjutant-General's Report for the Year, July 1, 1919, to June 30, 1920*. Springfield: Illinois State Journal Co., 1921.

Interchurch World Movement. Survey Division, Industrial Relations Department. *The Inter-Racial Situation in Chicago, Bulletin No. 1*. Chicago: Interchurch World Movement, *ca.* 1920.

Jackson, Alexander L. *The Race Problem in Chicago—Whose Responsibility?* Chicago: City Club of Chicago, April 1919.

Johnsen, Julia E. (compiler) *Selected Articles on the Negro Problem*. New York: H. W. Wilson, 1921.

Johnson, James Weldon. *Along This Way*. New York: Viking, 1935.
_____. *Black Manhattan*. New York: Knopf, 1930.

Jones, William H. *Recreation and Amusement among Negroes in Washington, D.C.* Washington, D.C.: Howard University Press, 1927.

Kennedy, Louise Venable. *The Negro Peasant Turns Cityward*. New York: Columbia University Press, 1930.

Kerlin, Robert T. *The Voice of the Negro, 1919*. New York: Dutton, 1920.

King, Martin Luther. *Stride Toward Freedom*. New York: Harper, 1958.

Kirksey, T[homas], and Hewlett, J. Henry. *Who Stopped the Race Riots in Washington: Real Causes and Effects of Race Clashes in the District of Columbia*. N.p.: Murray Bros., n.d.

Lawton, Alexander R. *The Negro in the South and Elsewhere*. Athens: (?) University of Georgia, 1923.

Lee, Alfred McClung, and Humphrey, Norman Daymond. *Race Riot*. New York: Dryden Press, 1943.

Logan, Rayford W. *The Negro in American Life and Thought: The Nadir 1877–1901*. New York: Dial Press, 1954.

Lohman, Joseph D. *The Police and Minority Groups*. Chicago: Chicago Park District, 1947.

360   FROM RACE RIOT TO SIT-IN

Mangum, Charles S. *The Legal Status of the Negro.* Chapel Hill: University of North Carolina Press, 1940.

Mebane, L. H. *To a Member of Our Oppressed Race.* N.p.: n. pub., 1919.

Mecklin, John Moffat. *The Ku Klux Klan: A Study of the American Mind.* New York: Russell and Russell, 1963.

Meier, August. *Negro Thought in America, 1900–1915.* Ann Arbor: University of Michigan Press, 1963.

Melden, Charles M. *From Slave to Citizen.* New York: Methodist Book Concern, 1921.

Miller, Kelly. *Radicalism and the Negro.* Washington, D.C.: pub. by self, Murray Bros. printers, 1920.

_____. *The Everlasting Stain.* Washington, D.C.: Associated Publishers, 1924.

Miller, William Robert. *Nonviolence: A Christian Interpretation.* New York: Association Press, 1964.

Millis, Walter. *Arms and Men.* New York: New American Library, 1958.

Morison, Samuel E., and Commager, Henry S. *Growth of the American Republic.* New York: Oxford University Press, 1950.

Myrdal, Gunnar, with the assistance of Sterner, Richard, and Rose, Arnold. *An American Dilemma: The Negro Problem and Modern Democracy.* 1 vol. edition. New York: Harper, 1944.

National Association for the Advancement of Colored People. *Mobbing of John R. Shillady, Secretary of the National Association for the Advancement of Colored People, at Austin, Texas, August 22, 1919.* New York: National Association for the Advancement of Colored People, 1919.

National Urban League. *Source Materials on the Urban Negro in the United States, 1910–1938.* 2nd edition. New York City: Urban League, May 1939.

Ottley, Roi. *The Lonely Warrior: The Life and Times of Robert S. Abbott.* Chicago: Regnery, 1955.

Ovington, Mary White. *Portraits in Color.* New York: Viking, 1927.

Park, Robert Ezra. *Race and Culture.* Glencoe, Ill.: Free Press, 1950.

Parrish, Mary E. Jones. *Events of the Tulsa Disaster.* N.p.: n. pub., n.d.

Peck, James. *Freedom Ride.* New York: Grove Press, 1962.

Powell, A. Clayton, Sr. *Riots and Ruins.* New York: R. R. Smith, 1945.

Preston, William, Jr. *Aliens and Dissenters.* Cambridge: Harvard University Press, 1963.

Pride, Armistead S. *Negro Newspapers on Microfilm.* Washington, D.C.: Library of Congress, 1953.

Proctor, Henry Hugh. *Between Black and White: Autobiographical Sketches.* Boston: Chicago: Pilgrim Press, 1925.

Quarles, Benjamin. *The Negro in the Civil War.* Boston: Little, Brown, 1953.

Raper, Arthur. *The Tragedy of Lynching.* Chapel Hill: University of North Carolina Press, 1936.

Rice, Arnold S. *The Ku Klux Klan in American Politics.* Washington: Public Affairs Press, 1962.

Rich, Bennett Milton. *The Presidents and Civil Disorder.* Washington, D.C.: Brookings Institute, 1941.

Richardson, Clement (ed.) *National Cyclopedia of the Colored Race.* Montgomery, Ala.: National Publishing Co., 1919.

Robinson, Rev. J. G. *Why I Am an Exile.* N.p.: self-published, 1919.

Rudwick, Elliott M. *Race Riot at East St. Louis, July 2, 1917.* Carbondale: Southern Illinois University Press, 1964.

Sandburg, Carl. *The Chicago Race Riots.* New York: Harcourt, Brace & Howe, 1919.

Scott, Emmett. *Demobilization and the Negro Soldier.* N.p.: Ethical Bureau, National War Work Council of Young Men's Christian Association, February 1919.

_____. *Negro Migration During the War.* (Carnegie Endowment for International Peace: Preliminary Economic Studies of the War, No. 16.) New York: Oxford University Press, 1920.

_____. *The American Negro in the World War,* N.p.: n. pub., 1919.

Scott, Estelle Hill. Occupational Changes Among Negroes in Chicago. (Works Progress Administration Project 665–54–3–336.) Chicago: Works Progress Administration, District 3, 1939.

Seligmann, Herbert J. *The Negro Faces America.* New York: Harper & Bros., 1920.

Shoemaker, Don (ed.) *With All Deliberate Speed.* New York: Harper, 1957.

Shogan, Robert, and Craig, Tom. *The Detroit Race Riot: A Study in Violence.* Philadelphia: Chitton, 1964.

Signers of the Call for the National Conference on Lynching to be held in New York City May Fifth and Sixth, Nineteen Hundred and Nineteen. N.p.: n. pub. [Actually National Association for the Advancement of Colored People], n.d.

Smith, Charles Spencer. *The First Race Riot Recorded in History.* Detroit: n. pub., 1920.

Soule, George. *Prosperity Decade.* New York: Rinehart, 1947.

Southern Sociological Congress. Provisional Program of the Ninth Annual Convention. N.p.: n. pub., 1920.

_____. *Purpose* [etc.: Prospectus.] Nashville: pub. by Author, n.d.

_____. *The Reconstruction Conference.* [J. E. McCulloch (?)

Secretary.] McLachlen Building, Washington, D.C.: n.pub., n.d.

_____. *You Are Invited to the Reconstruction Congress of Southern Leaders at Knoxville, Tennessee, May 11 to 14, 1919.* N.p.: Congress of Southern Leaders, n.d.

Stockton, Richard, Jr., and Dickinson, Sackett M. *Troops on Riot Duty: a Manual for the Use of the Armed Forces of the United States.* 3rd ed. rev. Menasha, Wisconsin: Collegiate Press, 1918.

Storey, Moorfield. *Problems of Today.* Boston: Houghton Mifflin, 1920.

Thompson, Edgar T. (ed.) *Race Relations and the Race Problem.* Durham, N.C.: Duke University Press, 1939.

Thrasher, Frederic M. *The Gang: A Study of 1,313 Gangs in Chicago.* Chicago: University of Chicago Press, 1927.

Torrence, Ridgely. *The Story of John Hope.* New York: Macmillan, 1948.

Turner, Ralph H., and Killian, Lewis M. *Collective Behavior.* Englewood Cliffs, N.J.: Prentice-Hall, 1957.

Union League Club of Chicago. *Chicago Civic Agencies . . . 1927.* Chicago: University of Chicago Press, 1927.

United States Army Service Schools, Fort Leavenworth. *Military Aid to the Civil Power.* Fort Leavenworth, Kans.: General Service Schools Press, 1925.

Warner, W. Lloyd, Junker, Buford H., and Adams, Walter A. *Color and Human Nature: Negro Personality Development in a Northern City.* Washington, D.C.: American Council on Education, 1941.

Weaver, Robert C. *The Negro Ghetto.* New York: Harcourt, Brace, 1948.

Weckler, J. E. and Hall, Theodore E. *The Police and Minority Groups.* N.p.: n. pub., n.d.

Wells-Barnet, Ida B. *The Arkansas Race Riot.* Chicago: pub. by Author, n.d.

Wendt, Lloyd and Kogan, Herman. *Big Bill of Chicago.* Indianapolis: Bobbs-Merrill, 1953.

White, Walter. *A Man Called White.* New York: Viking, 1948.

_____. *Rope and Faggot.* New York: Knopf, 1929.

Williams, Jr., Robin M. *The Reduction of Intergroup Tensions: A Survey of Research on Problems of Ethnic, Racial, and Religious Group Relations.* Bulletin #57. New York City: Social Science Research Council, 1947.

Wood, Junius B. *The Negro in Chicago.* N.p.: Chicago Daily News, 1916.

Woodson, Carter G. *A Century of Negro Migration.* Washington, D.C.: Association for Study of Negro Life and History, 1918.

Woodward, C. Vann. *The Strange Career of Jim Crow.* Rev. ed. New York: Oxford University Press, 1957.

Woofter, T. J., Jr. *Negro Problems in Cities.* Garden City, New York: Doubleday, Doran, 1928.

Work, Monroe N. (ed.) *Negro Year Book, 1918–1919; 1921–1922.* Tuskegee Institute, Alabama: Negro Year Book Publishing Co., 1919, 1922.

————. *A Bibliography of the Negro in Africa and America.* New York: H. W. Wilson, 1928.

Works Progress Administration Writers' Project. *Arkansas.* (American Guide Series) New York: Hastings House, 1941.

Yellen, Samuel. *American Labor Struggles.* New York: Russell, 1956.

Zinn, Howard. *SNCC: The New Abolitionists.* Boston: Beacon Press, 1964.

ARTICLES

Barnett, Claude A. "A Southern Statesman," 187–206 in William Hardin Hughes and Frederick D. Patterson, eds., *Robert Russa Moton of Hampton and Tuskegee.* Chapel Hill: University of North Carolina Press, 1956.

Bond, Horace M. "Negro Leadership Since Washington," *South Atlantic Quarterly,* XXIV (1925), 115–30.

Butts, J. W. and James, Dorothy. "The Underlying Causes of the Elaine Riot of 1919," *Arkansas Historical Quarterly,* XX (Spring 1961), 95–104.

City Club [of Chicago] *Bulletin,* IX (January 10, 1916), 1–11, "The Police in Strikes"; XII (March 17, 1919), 75, "Chicago's Negro Problem"; XII (August 18, 1919), 169–70, "The Housing of Colored People."

Dahlke, H. Otto. (Race and Minority Riots–a Study in the Typology of Violence," *Social Forces,* XXX (May 1952), 419–25.

Edmond, Lez. "Harlem Diary," *Ramparts* III (October 1964), no. 2, pp. 18–28.

Fishman, Jacob R. and Solomon, Fredric. "Youth and Social Action, I: Perspectives on the Student Sit-in Movement," *American Journal of Orthopsychiatry* XXXIII (October 1963), 872–82.

Gordon, Eugene. "The Negro Press," *The Annals,* American Academy of Political and Social Sciences, CXXXX (November 1928), 248–56.

Grimshaw, Allen D. "Lawlessness and Violence in America and Their Special Manifestations in Changing Negro-White Relationships," *Journal of Negro History*, XLIV (January 1959), 52–72.

Harris, Abram L. "The Negro Problem as Viewed by Negro Leaders," *Current History* XVIII (1923), 410–18.

Holmes, Jack D. L. "The Effects of the Memphis Race Riot of 1866," *West Tennessee Historical Society Papers*, XII (1958), 58–79.

_____. "The Underlying Causes of the Memphis Race Riot of 1866," *Tennessee Historical Quarterly*, XVII (September 1958), 195–221.

Kempton, Murray. "How Cops Behave in Harlem," *New Republic* CLI (August 22, 1964), No. 8–9, pp. 7–8.

_____. "The March on Washington," *New Republic* CXLIX (September 14, 1963), No. 11, pp. 19–20.

Landis, James M. "Freedom of Speech and the Press," *Encyclopedia of the Social Sciences* (New York: Macmillan, 1930), VI, 455–58.

Rames, José. "Racial Anatomy of a City," *New University Thought* III (Sept.-Oct. 1963), No. 2, pp. 20–33.

Solomon, Fredric and Fishman, Jacob R. "Youth and Social Action: II. Action and Identity Formation in the First Student Sit-in Demonstration," *Journal of Social Issues*, XX (April 1964), No. 2, 36–45.

_____. "The Psychosocial Meaning of Nonviolence in Student Civil Rights Activities, *Psychiatry* XXVII (May 1964), No. 2, 91–99.

Southern Regional Council. "Direct Action in the South," in *New South* XVIII (Oct.-Nov. 1963), Nos. 10–11, pp. 1–32.

UNPUBLISHED THESES

Bontemps, Arna. "Special Collections of Negroana." Unpublished master's thesis, University of Chicago, 1943.

Burrows, Edward Flud. "The Commission on Interracial Cooperation, 1919–1944." Unpublished Ph.D. dissertation, University of Wisconsin, 1954.

Davis, Charles Twitchell. "Prose Literature of Racial Defense, 1917–1924." Unpublished master's thesis, University of Chicago, 1942.

Davis, Ralph Nelson. "The Negro Newspaper in Chicago." Unpublished master's thesis, University of Chicago, 1939.

Dobbert, Guido A. "A History of the Chicago Race Riot of 1919." Unpublished master's thesis, University of Chicago, 1957.

Graham, Irene Jeannette. "Negroes in Chicago, 1920: An Analysis of United States Census Data." Unpublished master's thesis, University of Chicago, 1929.

Green, Loraine Richardson. "The Rise of Race and Consciousness in the American Negro." Unpublished master's thesis, University of Chicago, 1919.

Grimshaw, Allen D. "A Study in Social Violence: Urban Race Riots in the United States." Unpublished Ph.D. dissertation, University of Pennsylvania, 1959.

Reichley, Martin S. "Federal Military Intervention in Civil Disturbances." Unpublished Ph.D. dissertation, Georgetown University, 1939.

Spackman, Barbara Spencer. "The Woman's City Club of Chicago. A Civic Pressure Group." Unpublished master's thesis, University of Chicago, 1930.

Young, Damon Palma. "Negro-White Contacts in Washington, D.C." Unpublished Ph.D. dissertation, Howard University, 1926.

GOVERNMENT DOCUMENTS

Bellows, Henry A. A Treatise on Riot Duty for the National Guard. Washington, D.C.: Government Printing Office, 1920.

Commissioners of the District of Columbia. Report for the Year Ended June 30, 1920. Washington, D.C.: Government Printing Office, 1920.

District of Columbia Commissioners. Annual Report Year Ended June 30, 1920. (Miscellaneous Reports, Vol. I.) Washington, D.C.: Government Printing Office, 1921.

District of Columbia National Guard. Manual on Guard Duty. Washington, D.C.: Government Printing Office, n.d.

Drake, St. Clair. Churches and Voluntary Associations in the Chicago Negro Community. Report of Works Progress Administration Project 465-54-3-386. Chicago: Works Progress Administration, District 3, December, 1940.

Michigan Governor's Committee to Investigate Detroit Race Riot. "Factual Report." (Mimeographed; Appends. photostatted, n.p. 1943).

Palmer, A. Mitchell. (comp.) Red Radicalism as Described by its own Leaders. Washington, D.C.: Government Printing Office, 1920.

Rossiter, William S. Increase of Population in the United States, 1910-1920. (Department of Commerce, Census Bureau, Census Monographs, I.) Washington, D.C.: Government Printing Office, 1922.

United States Attorney-General. Annual Report, 1919; 1920; 1921.

Washington, D.C.: Government Printing Office, 1919, 1920, 1921.

————. Investigation Activities of the Department of Justice. (66th Cong., 1st Sess.; Sen. Doc. 153, Serial #7607.) Washington, D.C.: Government Printing Office, n.d.

United States Bureau of the Census. Fourteenth Census of the United States, 1920. Washington, D.C.: Government Printing Office, 1920.

United States Congress, House of Representatives. [39th Cong., 1st Sess., Report #101]. Memphis Riots and Massacres. Washington, D.C.: Government Printing Office, 1867.

United States Congress, House of Representatives, Select Committee on New Orleans Riots. Report . . . on the New Orleans Riots. Washington, D.C.: Government Printing Office, 1867.

United States Congress, House of Representatives. Committee on Judiciary, Sedition, Syndicalism, Sabotage, and Anarchy. (Hearings on H.R. 10210, 10379, 10614, 10616, 10650, 11039.) [December 11 and 16, 1919.] Serial 10. Washington, D.C.: Government Printing Office, 1919.

United States Department of Labor, Division of Negro Economics. Negro Migration in 1916–17. Washington, D.C.: Government Printing Office, 1919.

————. The Negro at Work during the World War and during Reconstruction. N.p.: n. pub., n.d.

United States War Department, War Plans Division. Military Protection, United States Guards: The Use of Organized Bodies in the Protection and Defense of Property during Riots, Strikes, and Civil Disturbances, Corrected to July 15, 1919. (War Department Doc. 882, Office of Adjutant-General.) Washington, D.C.: Government Printing Office, 1919.

Works Progress Administration. Washington, City and Capital. (Federal Writers' Project. American Guide Series.) Washington, D.C.: Government Printing Office, 1937.

————. A Classified Catalogue of the Negro Collection in the Collis P. Huntington Library, Hampton Institute. (Compiled by Works Progress Administration Writers Program in Virginia, under Roscoe E. Lewis.) Hampton, Va.: Hampton Institute, 1940.

ARCHIVAL NOTE

The locations of manuscript collections consulted or used in this study are listed below, in approximate order of their usefulness in this particular study. I am deeply grateful to the many librarians and custodians of these collections, of three important libraries of Negro history—the Schomburg Collection of the New York Public Library, the Moorland Collection of Howard University, and the George Cleveland Hall Branch of the Chicago Public Library—and of the Arkansas Supreme Court Library and the United States Supreme Court Library.

NAACP MSS., in the possession of the national office of the National Association for the Advancement of Colored People, in New York City.

Chicago Commission on Race Relations MSS. (CCRR MSS.), in Illinois State Archives, Springfield.

War Department MSS., National Archives, Washington, D.C.

Justice Department MSS., National Archives, Washington, D.C.

Navy Department MSS., National Archives, Washington, D.C.

Legislative MSS. (House and Senate Judiciary Committees), National Archives, Washington, D.C.

Labor Department MSS. (Division of Negro Economics), National Archives, Washington, D.C.

Frank O. Lowden MSS., University of Chicago.

Julius Rosenwald MSS., University of Chicago.

Graham Taylor MSS., Newberry Library, Chicago.

David Y. Thomas MSS., University of Arkansas, Fayetteville.

Charles A. Brough Scrapbooks, Arkansas History Commission, Little Rock.

William G. Haan MSS., Wisconsin State Historical Society, Madison.

Woodrow Wilson MSS., Library of Congress, Washington, D.C.

Newton D. Baker MSS., Library of Congress, Washington, D.C.

Charles A. Brough MSS., University of Arkansas, Fayetteville.

Victor Lawson MSS., Newberry Library, Chicago.

Mary McDowell MSS., Chicago Historical Society.
Robert E. Park MSS., University of Chicago.
Cyrus H. McCormick MSS., Wisconsin State Historical Society, Madison.
Wabash Avenue YMCA MSS., in possession of Wabash Avenue Branch of Young Men's Christian Association of Metropolitan Chicago.
District of Columbia Archives, Washington, D.C.
American Civil Liberties Union MSS., New York Public Library.
Will W. Alexander Oral History, Columbia University.

INDEX